The New Jewish Leaders

BRANDEIS SERIES IN AMERICAN JEWISH HISTORY, CULTURE, AND LIFE

Jonathan D. Sarna, Editor
Sylvia Barack Fishman, Associate Editor

For a complete list of books that are available in the series, visit www.upne.com

Jack Wertheimer, editor
  The New Jewish Leaders: Reshaping the American Jewish Landscape
Jonathan B. Krasner
  The Benderly Boys and American Jewish Education
Derek Rubin, editor
  Promised Lands: New Jewish American Fiction on Longing and Belonging
Susan G. Solomon
  Louis I. Kahn's Jewish Architecture: Mikveh Israel and the Midcentury American Synagogue
Amy Neustein, editor
  Tempest in the Temple: Jewish Communities and Child Sex Scandals
Jack Wertheimer, editor
  Learning and Community: Jewish Supplementary Schools in the Twenty-first Century
Carole S. Kessner
  Marie Syrkin: Values Beyond the Self
Leonard Saxe and Barry Chazan
  Ten Days of Birthright Israel: A Journey in Young Adult Identity
Jack Wertheimer, editor
  Imagining the American Jewish Community
Murray Zimiles
  Gilded Lions and Jeweled Horses: The Synagogue to the Carousel
Marianne R. Sanua
  Be of Good Courage: The American Jewish Committee, 1945–2006
Hollace Ava Weiner and Kenneth D. Roseman, editors
  Lone Stars of David: The Jews of Texas
Jack Wertheimer, editor
  Jewish Education in an Age of Choice

Edward S. Shapiro
  Crown Heights: Blacks, Jews, and the 1991 Brooklyn Riot
Marcie Cohen Ferris and Mark I. Greenberg, editors
  Jewish Roots in Southern Soil: A New History
Kirsten Fermaglich
  American Dreams and Nazi Nightmares: Early Holocaust Consciousness and Liberal America, 1957–1965
Andrea Greenbaum, editor
  Jews of South Florida
Sylvia Barack Fishman
  Double or Nothing? Jewish Families and Mixed Marriage
George M. Goodwin and Ellen Smith, editors
  The Jews of Rhode Island
Shulamit Reinharz and Mark A. Raider, editors
  American Jewish Women and the Zionist Enterprise
Michael E. Staub, editor
  The Jewish 1960s: An American Sourcebook
Judah M. Cohen
  Through the Sands of Time: A History of the Jewish Community of St. Thomas, U.S. Virgin Islands
Naomi W. Cohen
  The Americanization of Zionism, 1897–1948
Seth Farber
  An American Orthodox Dreamer: Rabbi Joseph B. Soloveitchik and Boston's Maimonides School
Ava F. Kahn and Marc Dollinger, editors
  California Jews

The New Jewish Leaders

Reshaping the American Jewish Landscape

Edited by JACK WERTHEIMER

Brandeis University Press   *Waltham, Massachusetts*

Research for this project was conducted under the auspices of the AVI CHAI Foundation, which in North America seeks to nurture Jews who are Jewishly literate, view their lives through the lens of the Jewish religion and feel a deep connection to the world-wide Jewish people, with its center in Israel.

BRANDEIS UNIVERSITY PRESS
An imprint of University Press of New England
www.upne.com
© 2011 Brandeis University
All rights reserved
Manufactured in the United States of America
Designed by Katherine B. Kimball
Typeset in Sabon by Integrated Publishing Solutions

University Press of New England is a member of the Green Press Initiative. The paper used in this book meets their minimum requirement for recycled paper.

For permission to reproduce any of the material in this book, contact Permissions, University Press of New England, One Court Street, Suite 250, Lebanon NH 03766; or visit www.upne .com

Library of Congress Cataloging-in-Publication Data

The new Jewish leaders : reshaping the American Jewish landscape / edited by Jack Wertheimer.
    p.   cm. — (Brandeis series in American Jewish history, culture, and life)
Includes bibliographical references and index.
ISBN 978-1-61168-183-3 (pbk. : alk. paper) — ISBN 978-1-61168-184-0 (ebook)
1. Jewish leadership—United States. 2. Jews—United States—Social conditions. 3. Young adults—United States—Attitudes. 4. Judaism—United States—History—21st century.
5. United States—Ethnic relations. I. Wertheimer, Jack.
E184.36.S65N49   2011
305.892'4073—dc23   2011037158

5 4 3 2 1

Contents

Preface

By the closing years of the twentieth century, new patterns of affiliation were palpably transforming organized Jewish activity in the United States. National organizations that had been dominant since the middle decades of the twentieth century saw their membership rolls shrink due to the passing of an older generation and a failure to attract enough young Jews to replace them. More generally, institutions of national prominence could no longer rally forces and mobilize ever-larger sums of money as they had in their heyday during the half century after World War II.[1] Two economic recessions in the first decade of the new century have only worsened an already difficult situation, necessitating deep budgets cuts and the attendant dismissal of personnel vital to organizational missions. Simultaneously, institutional life has been weakened by an onslaught upon the fundamental assumptions undergirding policies: the belief that Jews have responsibilities to one another; Israel must be central to Jewish collective activity; the maintenance of some boundaries between Jews and non-Jews and between Judaism and other belief systems is vital for group survival; and some balance must be struck by Jews between their support for universal—i.e., nonsectarian—causes, on the one hand, and their maintenance of specifically particularistic institutions designed to perpetuate and enrich the lives of Jews, on the other. All these long-standing assumptions have come under intense scrutiny, and often have been subjected to withering criticism. Indeed, given the decline in formal affiliation and the breakdown of consensus, some observers have come to wonder whether it is useful any longer to speak of *an* American Jewish community.

Even as the established institutions have contracted, a countervailing trend has become evident: a host of new initiatives has been launched to reach into every corner of the community in order to make place for as many Jews as possible. New initiatives aim to attract those Jews who may have felt marginalized in the past—new immigrants and their offspring, religious seekers, the disabled, the gay, lesbian, bisexual, and transgender population, poor Jews, the intermarried, those who eschew denominational labels, the socially and environmentally conscious, and many others who previously may have had only limited options to participate in Jewish activities. Particularly on the local level, entrepreneurial leaders have been busy launching new programs and institutions to address what they consider unmet needs and underserved niche populations. These multifarious efforts highlight and also celebrate the sheer diversity of American Jewish life, perhaps as never before.

In short, a new American Jewish community is forming before our eyes, with contours that are not yet fully defined. It is premature to write off the large organizations despite their weakened condition, for they continue to remake themselves in a bid to recapture a larger share of the Jewish market. And it is also too early to judge the staying power of new initiatives, which continue to evolve in new directions—and form partnerships with each other and with established institutions and funders. At least in the short term, it appears that the old and the new will coexist and influence one another, in some localities uneasily and in others quite comfortably. But even if we cannot foretell the long-term outcome, the dynamism of the moment warrants attention.

Driving many of these changes is a new generation of Jews in their twenties and thirties whose choices and commitments are shaping the new contours of American Jewish life. Just as the so-called GI generation, with its predilection for joining and group association, propelled the massive growth of local agencies and a national Jewish infrastructure, and just as the baby boomers, with their suspicion of formal organizations, heralded the retreat from Jewish associationalism, it appears that the current generation of younger Jewish adults is shaping a new landscape of Jewish organizational life based upon its particular outlook on Jewish collective action.[2]

Though much of the change remains subterranean, evidence of new thinking and organizing periodically rises to the surface, suggesting that fundamental changes are afoot. The activities of Mechon Hadar and more than sixty additional independent minyanim, religious quorums unaffiliated with any of the denominations, for example, have served notice about the alienation of some highly literate young Jews from conventional synagogue life—and their willingness to create their own settings for prayer and study. Similarly, the rapid growth of service programs and environmental causes under Jewish auspices are emblematic of a new emphasis on social action directed to the world at large, rather than parochial Jewish needs.[3] A much remarked upon article by Peter Beinart in the *New York Review of Books* provided evidence of internal tensions some younger Jews feel between their liberal politics and their ties to Israel, and perhaps more broadly between their universal and Jewish allegiances. The article's title, moreover, "The Failure of the American Jewish Establishment,"[4] highlighted the connection Beinart makes between new ways of thinking about Israel and the disenchantment of some younger Jews with the established organizations. And then there are the growing numbers of young people experimenting with new initiatives, some of which have garnered support from Jewish foundations.[5] These and other manifestations point to a spirit of innovation and critique evident among some sectors of young leaders.

The New Jewish Leaders sets out to examine the far-reaching changes in outlook and patterns of affiliation among younger Jews by looking at its leadership cadre. Conceived as a team research effort, this book is the first to examine in a systematic and rounded fashion the attitudes,[6] background, and activities of young women and men between the ages of twenty-two and forty who serve as leaders of Jewish endeavors. The most basic questions we asked about these leaders were: What have been their formative educational and socializing experiences? How do they define Jewish identity today and how do they relate to the Jewish people, Israel, Judaism, and Jewish culture? What do they have to say about the current structure and orientation of the established Jewish institutions? And what is their vision of the American Jewish future?

As with leadership research generally, the term "Jewish leader" encompasses figures with a range of activities and roles: some are leaders because they have spearheaded new initiatives, while others direct the activities of existing groups; some are professionals, and others are volunteers; some are culture shapers, exercising influence through their ideas, their writing, or their performances; others make things happen through their contacts, communications skills, and energy. A broad range of Jewish leaders is represented in this book, including activists who eschew the term "leadership" to describe their own enterprising efforts. We deliberately cast our net widely to include all kinds of individuals who are assuming positions of influence among their peers.

The book opens with my own effort to map the scene by offering a typology of organizations and initiatives available for Jews in their postcollege years to join. The chapter addresses these questions: What is the range of programs, organizations, and initiatives that are being headed by the leaders we studied? How does geographic location and community size affect the range of options? And how well coordinated are programs for twenty- and thirtysomethings?

From here we move to two analyses of quantitative data by Steven M. Cohen. The first compares views and educational backgrounds along two axes, age and type of institutions—e.g., those leaders younger than age forty versus those older than forty, and those involved with an establishment organization compared with those involved with a nonestablishment one. In the course of this analysis, Cohen identifies a number of sharp differences in the way older establishment leaders and younger nonestablishment leaders view the Jewish agenda, a shift that has enormous implications for the future of organized Jewish life. Cohen's second chapter asks, in essence, the following question: what are the major commitments of participants in one organization as compared with another? His answer is straightforward: not all "innovative" groups are alike. They differ considerably in the extent to which their supporters are engaged with Jewish issues.

Sarah Bunin Benor's chapter then invites readers to join her in visiting events for young Jews held in one city, Los Angeles, so that we can experience firsthand the distinctive cultures of those organizations and listen to the way young leaders explain their own efforts. Her essay demonstrates just how much fluidity of movement there is between different types of Jewish organizations. Neither the leaders nor the followers necessarily opt only for establishment institutions or nonestablishment ones, deciding instead to seek benefits from programs that best match their personal inclinations.

The remaining chapters offer thematic perspectives. Sylvia Barack Fishman presents a portrait of influential cultural figures who give voice to the aspirations and worldview of their peers. Jews in their twenties and thirties, reports Fishman, maintain a strong attachment to Jewish ethnicity but define Jewish music, food, books, comedy, cultural performances, family styles, and religious rituals as the *primary* expressions of their ethnicity. Their vision is universalistic rather than tribal or even national. Global social justice is for many a burning passion that they take personally. Ari Y. Kelman examines the ways in which young people are utilizing the Internet for Jewish purposes and identifies the linkages between sites visited by younger Jews. Among the study's key findings are the significance of information-sharing sites, the prominence of sites that cater to diverse audiences of religious and nonreligious Jews, the importance of blogs in leveling the online communications landscape, and the preponderance of sites targeting younger audiences and presenting a more youthful editorial voice. And Shaul Kelner traces the historical evolution of training programs central to the recruitment and nurturing of future Jewish leaders. Kelner's essay illuminates the role of private philanthropic foundations, which collectively have shaped communal discourse and policies on the subject of young leaders. Finally, a concluding chapter highlights some of this study's key findings about young Jewish leaders and points toward implications.

This book is based on a great deal of shared information. The contributors benefited not only from the generous leads and advice offered by fellow team members and outside consultants but also from the gracious help extended by thousands of leaders who agreed to speak with us and/or completed questionnaires. Collectively, members of the research team interviewed more than 250 leaders across the country situated in all kinds and sizes of organizations. This interviewing work was augmented by and informed surveys that elicited responses from nearly 4,500 Jewish leaders of all ages, providing a basis to compare younger with older Jewish leaders, as well as younger leaders in different types of organizations.

For reasons explained in the appendix on the research design, our study does not claim respondents to the survey are precisely representative of the entire population of Jewish leaders. The absence of up-to-date demographic data on trends in American Jewish life makes it impossible to know for sure. In this study, we can report on the Jewish leaders we encountered but cannot know with certainty how many others there are. We therefore limit our quantitative analysis to comparisons of subpopulations—i.e., how leaders in one category differ from those in another. Our extensive interviews have served as a further source of data and a means of checking the validity of our quantitative data.

The data vacuum faced by researchers on the American Jewish community is made plain by the absence of up-to-date estimates on the size of the American Jewish population between ages twenty-two and forty. Relying upon figures from the 2000–2001 National Jewish Population Study (NJPS), we estimate that the United States is home to one to one-and-a-quarter million Jews between ages twenty-two to forty. (Because we will not have a new NJPS any time in the near future, we lack more up-to-date estimates.) It is impossible to know what percentage of this population actively identifies as Jewish or what proportion participates in any of the activities we have studied. Interviews with leaders of many types of organizations yield the same overall conclusion: vast numbers of young Jews, perhaps the majority, do not participate and certainly do not engage in a sustained fashion with any of these groups, but significant minorities do participate. The more that is asked of them, the fewer participate. A Chabad rabbi working with younger Jews employs the metaphor of a funnel to describe people in this age group who enter into some form of Jewish group engagement: the largest mass of participants attends events requiring the lowest threshold of investment, most commonly a "happy hour" or another social gathering. Gradually, smaller numbers move on to educational or social action programs, until the population shrinks to a fraction of its initial size for sustained activism, regular study, or religious participation. As noted, though, we lack data on the numbers who even enter the funnel.

A word about nomenclature: the research team wrestled with the best language to use to describe the leaders we have studied, settling on the term younger Jewish leaders to denote those between the ages of twenty-two and forty. We are not alone in struggling to find the best terminology. The psychologist Jeffrey Jensen Arnett coined the term "emerging adulthood" to denote "the age period from the late teens to the mid-twenties."[7] But he emphatically rejected the use of this term to refer to individuals in their thirties, who are no longer emerging but have attained adulthood. Thirty-year-olds are very much part of the populations studied in this book. Others use the term young adults, but as employed colloquially, this refers to teen-agers. We also decided to reject terms such as Millennials or Gen Yers because of their imprecision. Though no offense to the over-forty crowd is intended, we opted to delimit a divide at forty, referring to young or younger versus older leaders on that basis.

A second linguistic issue we faced was how to describe the initiatives, programs, and agencies led by our younger Jewish leaders. We chose to de-scribe the long-standing ones as establishment organizations. Those founded by younger people, we identify as nonestablishment both because they do not have the longevity and because they often, though not always, operate with some sense of distance from the establishment. Some writers, especially those drawn from the nonestablishment sectors, seem to favor the terms in-novative or nonconventional, but these are heavily value-laden terms. Not all new organizations are particularly innovative nor are they necessarily nonconventional. With the passage of time since the 1960s, when "establish-ment" carried a pejorative connotation, we concluded that the term has be-come sufficiently neutral to serve our purposes.

Two further caveats are in order. One concerns Orthodox leaders in their twenties and thirties. Though Orthodox Jews who play leadership roles are well represented in our survey data and interviews, this study does not pur-port to describe the world of younger Orthodox leaders in all its variety and complexity. To begin with, few Haredi or Hasidic leaders participated in our study, thereby eliminating as much as 60 percent of the Orthodox world from consideration. Those Orthodox Jews who did complete our survey instru-ment tend to work with non-Orthodox populations—i.e., they are a select and more open group within the larger world of Orthodoxy. Still Orthodox Jews are over-represented in our sample, constituting 20 percent of young establishment leaders self-identify as Orthodox. The research team intention-ally decided against including more insular Orthodox leaders—those not involved with their non-Orthodox peers—on the assumption that their lives and preoccupations are so dramatically different that we would be compar-ing apples and oranges. Jews in the more traditional sectors of Orthodoxy tend to marry and bear children in their early twenties, a time when most of their non-Orthodox peers are still living out their odyssey years, experiment-ing with employment and living as singles.

We note, as well, that research for this project was initiated before the Great Recession struck. Though fieldwork continued through the summer of 2009, the full impact of the economic downturn was not accounted for by the time all research ceased. Like the larger American not-for-profit sector, Jewish organizations of all sizes and missions have been forced to tighten their belts, eliminate programs and personnel, and, in a few cases, close their doors. (Indeed, while this book was in production JDub Records folded and several nonestablishment organizations merged in order to streamline their operations—for example, Jewish Mosaic and Keshet merged, as did the Progressive Jewish Alliance and the Jewish Funds for Justice.) Younger Jews in leadership positions have been affected by these developments, although no evidence as yet suggests that the broad contours of the institutional life described in these pages have been altered significantly. Establishment and nonestablishment organizations and initiatives continue their work.

The chapters that follow trace patterns of dramatic change in the ways younger Jews organize and relate to collective Jewish efforts. Indeed, they dramatize how some younger leaders are reenvisioning American Jewish communal arrangements. Such a process of reimagining ought not to surprise us. Writing about the late nineteenth century, historian Jonathan Sarna has described the ways young Jewish men and women pioneered new organizational structures to build a vibrant American Jewish culture.[8] Focusing on the 1970s, a number of scholars have highlighted the agenda and outlook promoted by the Havurah movement and the Jewish political counterculture, which in their separate ways presaged new ways of thinking about community, participation, decorum, aesthetics within worship services, and, not least, politics and policy.[9] Today's younger Jewish leaders are engaged in a similar, and perhaps even more far-reaching, reconsideration. Their ways of viewing Jewish issues, their efforts to remake existing institutions and found new ones, and their particular blending of Jewish and universal concerns set them apart from earlier generations. Our collective volume provides the first systematic study of this creative generation of Jewish leaders, and offers a tantalizing glimpse of the American Jewish future.

NOTES

1. For an overview, see "The Fragmentation of American Jewry and Its Leadership: An Interview with Jack Wertheimer," Jerusalem Center for Public Affairs, February 2008, www.jcpa.org. The declining fortunes of the organized Jewish community are also discussed by Steven M. Cohen in chapter 4 of this book. On the declining fortunes of the Federation movement, see Gerald Bubis and Steven Windmueller, *From Predictability to Chaos?? How Jewish Leaders Reinvented Their National Communal System* (Baltimore: Center for Jewish Communities Studies), 2005.

2. On the associationalism of the GI generation, see, for example, Marshall Sklare and Joseph Greenblum, *Jewish Identity on the Suburban Frontier: A Study of Group Survival in the Open Society* (New York: Basic Books, 1967). On the moderately affiliated baby boomers who viewed institutional engagement with deep suspicion, see Steven M. Cohen and Arnold Eisen, *The Jew Within: Self, Family and Community* (Bloomington: Indiana University Press, 2000).

3. Enough such programs exist to warrant the funding of an umbrella agency named Repair the World whose self-proclaimed goal is to "make service a defining part of American Jewish life." See http://werepair.org.

4. Peter Beinart, "The Failure of the American Jewish Establishment," *New York Review of Books*, May 12, 2010, www.nybooks.com.

5. This system has been studied and celebrated in a report sponsored by Jumpstart, the Natan Fund, and the Samuel Bronfman Foundation: *The Innovative Ecosystem: Emergence of a New Jewish Landscape* (April 2009), www.jewishjumpstart.org.

6. For earlier studies, see Steven M. Cohen and Ari Y. Kelman, *Beyond Distancing: Young Adult American Jews and Their Alienation from Israel* (Jewish Identity Project of Reboot, 2007); Barbara Kirshenblatt-Gimblett, *The "New Jews": Reflections on Emerging Cultural Practices*, http://www.nyu.edu/classes/bkg/web/yeshiva.pdf; Steven M. Cohen, Elie Kaunfer, J. Shawn Landres, and Michelle Shain, *Emergent Jewish Communities and Their Participants: Preliminary Findings from the 2007 National Spiritual Communities Study* (Mechon Hadar, November 2007).

7. Jeffrey Jensen Arnett, "Emerging Adulthood: A Theory of Development from the Late Teens through the Twenties," *American Psychologist* 55 (5) (May 2000): 469–80. See also, by the same author, *Emerging Adulthood: The Winding Road from Late Teens through the Twenties* (New York: Oxford University Press, 2004).

8. Jonathan Sarna, *A Great Awakening: The Transformation That Shaped Twentieth Century American Judaism and Its Implications for Today* (Cleveland: Mandel Foundation, 2008), www.mandelfoundation.org.

9. Chava Weisler, *Making Judaism Meaningful: Ambivalence and Tradition in a Havurah Community* (New York: AMS Press, 1989); Riv-Ellen Prell, *Prayer and Community: The Havurah in American Judaism* (Detroit: Wayne State University Press, 1989); Michael E. Staub, *Torn at the Roots: The Crisis of Jewish Liberalism in Postwar America* (New York: Columbia University Press, 2002).

Contributors

SARAH BUNIN BENOR is an associate professor of contemporary Jewish studies at Hebrew Union College–Jewish Institute of Religion (Los Angeles). She received her PhD in linguistics from Stanford University in 2004. She teaches about American Jewish language, culture, and community, and she has published several articles on Jewish languages, Orthodox Jews, and Yiddish and Hebrew influences on the English of American Jews. She is founder and editor of the Jewish Language Research Website and is writing a book titled *Becoming Frum: How Newcomers Learn the Language and Culture of Orthodox Judaism*.

STEVEN M. COHEN, a sociologist of American Jewry, is research professor of Jewish Social Policy at Hebrew Union College–Jewish Institute of Religion, and director of the Berman Jewish Policy Archive at New York University's Wagner School. In 1992 he made aliyah, and taught for fourteen years at the Hebrew University of Jerusalem. Previously, he taught at Queens College, with visiting appointments at Yale, Brandeis, and the Jewish Theological Seminary. With Arnold Eisen, he wrote *The Jew Within* and with Charles Liebman, *Two Worlds of Judaism: The Israeli and American Experiences*. His current research interests focus on the emerging patterns of Jewish identity and community among Jews in their twenties and thirties. He also serves as research director of Synagogue 3000, an organization dedicated to synagogue renewal, and director of the Florence G. Heller/JCCA Research Center.

SYLVIA BARACK FISHMAN is chair of the Department of Near Eastern and Judaic Studies and professor of contemporary Jewish life at Brandeis University, as well as codirector of the Hadassah Brandeis Institute. She is the author of seven books and numerous articles. Two recent works, *Choosing Jewish: Conversations about Conversion* and *Double or Nothing? Jewish Families and Mixed Marriage*, have created lively scholarly and communal discussion. Her latest book, *The Way into the Varieties of Jewishness*, explores changing understandings of Jewish peoplehood and faith from biblical times to the present day.

ARI Y. KELMAN is an associate professor of American studies at the University of California at Davis. He is the author of *Station Identification: A Cultural History of Yiddish Radio in the United States* and editor of *Is Diss a System? A Milt Gross Comic Reader*. He is also coauthor of a number of influential studies of contemporary Jewish life and culture, including studies of cultural activities attracting young Jews, the impact of deferred marriage on Jewish social patterns, and the weakening bonds between American Jews and Israel.

SHAUL KELNER is an assistant professor of sociology and Jewish studies at Vanderbilt University. He is the author of *Tours That Bind: Diaspora, Pilgrimage and Israeli Birthright Tourism* (NYU Press, 2010). Professor Kelner received his PhD from the City University of New York, which he attended as a Wexner Graduate Fellow. He has been a fellow of the Hebrew University of Jerusalem's Institute for Advanced Studies and a visiting scholar in Tel Aviv University's Department of Sociology and Anthropology.

JACK WERTHEIMER is a professor of American Jewish history at the Jewish Theological Seminary and director of the Center for Research and Policy at the AVI CHAI Foundation in New York. Most recently, he has directed projects for the foundation on trends in American Jewish education and Jewish supplementary schools; the former culminated in an edited volume titled *Family Matters: Jewish Education in an Age of Choice*, and the latter resulted in *Learning and Community: Jewish Supplementary Schools in the Twenty-first Century*, both published by Brandeis University Press.

1 Mapping the Scene

How Younger Jewish Adults Engage with Jewish Community

FIFTY YEARS AGO, observers of American Jewish life were struck by the frenetic engagement of Jews in organizational activity. "What distinguishes the Jew from the non-Jew," wrote Harold Weisberg, dean of the graduate school of Brandeis University, in 1964, "is, increasingly, not a specific ethic, religious discipline, or language, but the intensity and pervasiveness of his organizational commitments and activities. . . . At present, Jewish culture in the United States is predominantly what Jews do under the auspices of Jewish organizations."[1] Other midcentury observers joined Weisberg in marveling at the extent to which theirs was a time of joining, especially for newly transplanted urban Jews who had settled in suburbia after World War II. American Jews in record numbers became members of synagogues, Jewish Community Centers, and national organizations; they contributed to the campaigns of local federations of Jewish philanthropy; and in other ways they enacted their Jewishness through association. Noting these patterns, a major sociological study of the time commented on the "overwhelming" variety of Jewish organizations on the local level, which, in turn, played a "critical role . . . to help mediate the crisis in Jewish identity" and maintain "Jewish group survival."[2]

By the end of the twentieth century, in marked contrast, one of the most influential analyses of Jewish identity and community began with the premise that a vast swathe of "moderately affiliated" Jews, mainly of the baby boom generation, served as bellwethers of a massive shift within the American Jewish community. Writing of the *privatized* nature of Jewish identification, Steven M. Cohen and Arnold Eisen determined that for many of these Jews, "the public sphere [of Jewish life] bears the burden of demonstrating its importance to Jewish loyalties nurtured and focused elsewhere." More than 40 percent of respondents to the authors' survey concurred with the statement "I find Jewish organizations remote and irrelevant to me." Rather than regarding Jewish organizations as a potential "locus for friendship, a place where they could socialize with other Jews in an easy and relaxed atmosphere," many American Jews perceived Jewish organizational life as exploitative, expecting much and giving little in return.[3] Hence, like the contemporaneous research on broader trends in American society conducted by Robert Putnam,[4] the authors of *The Jew Within* found a baby boomer population characterized by *loose connections* and comparatively *low rates of affiliation.*

If the generation that came of age after World War II was characterized by joining formal Jewish institutions, and if the baby boomers associated with Jewish organizations far more episodically and, perhaps, suspiciously, what can be said about the participation in organized Jewish activities by the succeeding generation of American Jews—the population now in their twenties and thirties that has been shaped by cultural and social trends at the end of the twentieth century and the beginning of the current one? Unfortunately, this question is not amenable to quantitative answers in the absence of an up-to-date national Jewish population study. We simply do not know how large a percentage of the roughly million-and-a-quarter younger Jewish adults attend any programs with Jewish content;[5] nor can we pin down how frequently attendees participate in various types of Jewish programming.

What seems beyond dispute is that the range of options created by and for this population is extraordinarily wide. Those who are inclined to engage with other Jews can choose from a broad array of new programs organized by their peers and also from more conventional types of activities held under the auspices of long-established organizations. Undoubtedly, social gatherings draw the largest turnout, as do concerts, film festivals, and other cultural events. Smaller numbers attend Shabbat and holiday celebrations, retreats, and recreational programs such as outdoor treks. Depending on their interests, young Jewish adults participate in peer-led minyanim, Orthodox outreach programs, or religious services sponsored by local synagogues of various denominational hues—all directed exclusively *to* younger Jews. They also elect to engage with other Jewish peers in social action projects for nonsectarian or Jewish causes. Some attend demonstrations and programs advocating for Israel or criticizing its policies, while some participate in programs offered specifically for peers of their age by national Jewish organizations. Those who identify with a specific subpopulation, such as an immigrant group, the gay, lesbian, bisexual, and transgender (GLBT) community, or Jews who share a specific Jewish religious outlook, are able to join affinity groups.

The present essay maps the range of options available to young adults who are open to partaking in some form of Jewish group activity. Based upon some eighty-five interviews with young Jewish leaders in fourteen different communities around the United States, and written material available either in print or online, it surveys the spectrum of organizations that attract Jews in their twenties and thirties.[6] As already noted, some of these organizations and programs were created at the initiative of established Jewish organizations; others arose through the efforts of young adults as so-called start-ups; and still others have come about and are supported by a mix of establishment and nonestablishment institutions. (Moreover, not all draw participants *exclusively* from the population of Jews in their twenties and thirties. Programs and organizations aimed primarily at this age group and/ or led by younger Jewish leaders have been included in this survey.) After presenting examples of programs run by both established institutions and nonestablishment ones around the country, the analysis will explore how new agencies have sprung up to address the special interests of subgroups within the population of Jewish young adults and how local history and culture shape the options available in a particular community.

Two important qualifications: first, though it casts a wide net to include communities in different regions of the country and of varying sizes, this essay does not purport to offer a comprehensive listing of all programs and institutions available to young Jewish adults; rather, it presents illustrative examples of the various *types* of groupings.

Second, the roughly eighteen-year age span of participants in these programs (from twenty-two to forty) seems fairly compact but in fact masks large variations in career paths, status, and life-cycle stages. There are major differences between recent college graduates who are only beginning to set a life course as compared to men and women in their late thirties who have embarked on careers and perhaps attained professional credentials. Marital status is also a critical marker: vast distances separate those who are single from those who are married, and individuals who have become parents have their own transformed life experience.[7] Within this population, key dividing lines also exist between those who identify strongly with Jewish life in some form and those who are quite distant, if not alienated. And finally, a constellation of subpopulations identify far more strongly with others who share their own history, experiences, or interests than they do with an amorphous mass of people roughly the same age. We will need to be attuned to these distinctions rather than lump all younger Jewish adults together.

What Establishment Institutions Offer to Young Jewish Adults

It is no secret that federations of Jewish philanthropy, Jewish Community Centers (JCCs), synagogues, and the major national organizations have been hard-pressed to recruit significant numbers of young Jewish adults. When asked to explain the lack of appeal, professionals in these organizations cite young adults' limited financial resources; they lack the discretionary dollars to make charitable contributions and pay dues that are expected—and needed—by synagogues, federation campaigns, and large membership organizations. People preoccupied with the life-defining tasks of establishing a career also have time constraints associated with deciding where to live, finding a spouse, and starting a family. Faced with these weighty challenges, how many young adults will set aside time to participate in programs with any regularity? Young adults also may find it difficult to relate to the establishment organizations on other grounds: they may associate them with a previous generation's Jewish self-expression, not with cutting-edge programs for today's young adult population. "Why would my peers support all the same institutions that our parents and grandparents once funded?" asks Sharna Goldseker, an organizer of programs for peers her age and a philanthropist in her own right.[8]

Moreover, as quite a few report firsthand, the culture of many establishment institutions creates numerous barriers to involvement. One frequently heard complaint is that establishment Jewish organizations are exclusive. "What is off-putting to young people are organizations that feel restrictive and events where non-Jews and same-sex partners are not welcome," a young funder named Jos Thalheimer complains. For those who are single, moreover, the focus of many institutions such as synagogues on family units with children leaves them feeling "demographically disenfranchised," as one study reports.[9] And when they join, young adults quickly learn that they are expected to bide their time before assuming positions of real leadership—this in marked contrast to the many opportunities young adults have today to advance rapidly in their professional lives and in many nonestablishment endeavors. Why deal with the frustration if other outlets for social and philanthropic action exist outside the establishment communal channels in the wider nonsectarian world?[10] And then there is the question of whether establishment groups speak to young Jews' sensibilities about the world and Jewish life—or even take them into account. Describing his demoralizing experience at a Jewish fundraiser, one young philanthropist explained why he fled the scene: "We couldn't even relate to it; . . . no one talked about how young people can add value." Another young observer of Jewish philanthropy contrasted the style of organizations supported by previous generations to those that appeal to her: "They're so huge and amalgamous [sic], and they don't hit the niche interests that a lot of people my age have."[11] All these factors serve as serious deterrents to participation in programs organized by establishment groups.

Long-established synagogues and federations of Jewish philanthropy seem to be struggling most in addressing this population, albeit for different reasons. The former are largely geared to engage family units and have long relied upon Jews to join once they have children of school age. This emphasis on pediatric Judaism, however, will not do for singles or even newly married young couples, particularly at a time of deferred family formation in all sectors of the American Jewish community except the Orthodox one.[12] How then to draw them into synagogue involvement? A limited number of congregations have actively taken up this challenge. Among them is Temple Israel, the oldest Reform congregation in Boston, which under the leadership of Rabbi Jeremy Morrison organizes Kabbalat Shabbat services and dinners on Friday evenings, Havdala on Saturday evenings, and study circles all held in private homes in several Boston neighborhoods.[13] Programs are also held at Temple Israel to integrate these people into the synagogue. Of the 1,500 attendees at programs, several hundred have joined the congregation, Morrison reports.[14] Another Reform temple, Congregation Beth Elohim (CBE) in the Park Slope section of Brooklyn, has become the home of several outreach programs to the thousands of young Jews of "Brownstone Brooklyn." The largest of these was founded by CBE's rabbi, Andy Bachman, before he assumed the congregation's pulpit. Called Brooklyn Jews, the program runs its own services in CBE on the High Holidays using a Conservative *mahzor* (High Holiday prayer book) and also runs Shabbat programs throughout the year.[15] A second program called Altshul offers a traditional egalitarian service and attracts a fair number of formerly Orthodox Jews, as well as products of the Conservative movement. And a third program is directed to adult education, particularly for intermarried Jews. A portion of the participants in all three groups have become members of CBE, notwithstanding its affiliation with the Reform movement.

Among the best known and successful programs organized by Conservative synagogues is Friday Night Live, sponsored by Sinai Temple in Los Angeles, which attracts more than a thousand people once a month and has developed a range of other programs, concerts, married couples' events, and lectures specifically for the twenty-five- to forty-year-old population.[16] Whereas Friday Night Live features a band and congregational singing led by Craig Taubman, a professional musician, Adas Israel of Washington, D.C., another large Conservative congregation, runs a young professionals group, which features a once monthly "lay-led" Kabbalat Shabbat service. It also hosts various social programs throughout the year for younger adults in the Washington area.[17]

Rounding out this small sampling of denominational synagogues that have done well in attracting younger adults as members and participants, we cite Kol Tzedek in Philadelphia, a Reconstructionist congregation, which has the distinction of having been led throughout its brief history by a series of presidents all under age thirty. According to its rabbi, Lauren Grabelle Hermann, 70 percent of its four to five hundred participants are younger than age forty. Most who attend come from nontraditional Jewish backgrounds, and the congregation, which does not meet every week, offers ample time for public discussions designed to explore Jewish spirituality and the meaning of rituals and prayers; it also strives to build community by encouraging members to gather and pray in each other's homes on those Sabbath days when services are not held in the synagogue.[18]

What accounts for the relative success of these congregations in attracting young adults? Congregations situated in neighborhoods with large numbers of young Jewish adults have a major advantage over suburban synagogues far removed from such populations. The five congregations just cited all fall into the former category. But population density alone is not sufficient: for the most part, a synagogue functionary, usually a rabbi, must be prepared to invest personally in building and guiding programs for this age demographic. Many establishment congregations cannot woo this crowd because they lack the staff resources and the commitment to invest congregational funds in programs for individuals who may never join the synagogue. Why, some congregations ask, expend limited budgetary dollars on programs for young adults, especially singles, who are not apt to pay membership dues or, if they do, will ask for steep discounts? From the perspective of the congregation, this is a risky expenditure. Only more far-sighted synagogues seem to grasp how vital it is to keep young adults connected to Jewish life—even if there is no immediate payoff for the congregation in the form of young, new members.

Federations face a different set of challenges in attracting young Jewish adults. Despite their central roles in many communities, federations seem distant and their mission opaque, perhaps because they serve as an umbrella cause in an age of targeted giving. As quite a few younger leaders note, an organization must demonstrate its relevance to the concerns of twenty- and thirty-year-olds in order to win their support. "If [younger Jews] cannot make the personal connection [with a philanthropy's mission]," comments one observer, "the automatic support won't come." The financial needs of a senior citizens' residence or family services agency seem remote to most young Jews, and the heavy focus on fundraising may be off-putting. Moreover, young adults who are used to taking an activist role in their professions have little patience for the glacial pace of advancement within the federation system and the bureaucratic obstacles. All these factors have led some young

Jewish adults who are involved with their federations to comment that "the system is broken."

Nevertheless, federations do attract young adults through a variety of programs. The most common of these involve social events designed to attract hundreds of singles and young couples at a time. For the most part, little effort is devoted at such events to any formal discussion about the mission of the federation or other organizations or even to more substantive challenges facing the Jewish community. Instead, the focus is on drawing singles and young couples eager to meet their Jewish peers. The opportunity to network with other young professionals is attractive, as is the possibility of meeting new people.

Organizers of these events are quite candid about what draws crowds: the chance to socialize and the relaxed mood brought on by drink. As one federation organizer has put it, "What attracts them is alcohol!" In fact, many of the large-scale events are held at bars and advertised explicitly as "happy hour" gatherings. Although none can compete in scale with the Matzo Ball phenomenon sponsored by a private business venture, which claims to draw as many as four thousand people on Christmas eve to an event in Manhattan alone and now plans to hold similar events all around the country,[19] personnel at federations and national organizations claim they attract several hundred people at a time to their bar events.

If the attraction for attendees is straightforward, what is the motivation of the sponsors? Why would federations, the American Jewish Committee (AJC), and Chabad, to name a few Jewish organizations, bother? After all, critics have described such alcohol-fueled gatherings as the "last vestiges of organized Jewish groups." But the organizations offer a rationale: these events serve as the best opportunity to draw in young Jews who are otherwise unaffiliated. "It's hard to find them," laments a young staff person at a Jewish foundation. The drinking parties bring people out of the woodwork. At that point, organizations strive to identify individuals who are prepared to engage in weightier forms of Jewish interaction. The commonly expressed perception is that young Jewish adults are skittish about programs with serious Jewish content. In the words of more than one organizational staffer, "Young Jews fear that Jewish things will hit them over the head." Organizations therefore sponsor social gatherings with little or no official program attached as a means to meet potential recruits. A staff person at the Atlanta Federation describes how she, as well as representatives of the major organizations in town—the JCC, the AJC's Access Program, even Chabad—fan out during these social events, talking to young adults and identifying any who may become more active. In some communities, such as Atlanta and

Philadelphia, the key personnel staffing local Jewish organizations that seek to attract younger adults meet monthly to coordinate and jointly publicize their programs.

Depending on their size, federations may also offer a range of additional programs through their Young Leadership Divisions, including Krav Maga self-defense classes, Israeli wine-tasting evenings, lectures and panel discussions, classes, film screenings, missions to Israel, retreats, and outdoor activities—in addition to various types of socials. At least once a year, federations organize service days for the benefit of nonsectarian or Jewish agencies. Most federations also encourage attendees to pledge a gift to their annual campaign, with the minimum price tag of $54 for Jews in their twenties and larger gifts for those in their thirties; though small in size, the gifts initiate younger people into the ethos of communal giving. Staff personnel who work with young adults stress the centrality of federations in the life of the community, the indispensability of federations in getting things done, and the neutral setting they provide for Jews who may feel put off by religiously or ideologically oriented programs. Federations, they contend, serve as a safe space.

Through the Jewish Federations of North America (JFNA), formerly known as the United Jewish Communities, the umbrella agency for federations, local federations can channel young adults to participate in programs outside their communities. The JFNA sponsors missions to Israel, which offer a more in-depth exposure to Israeli society than does Birthright Israel. It also coordinates service programs in places such as New Orleans and organizes national conferences on large policy issues, such as energy. Here the combination of local federations linked to a national entity extends the reach of federations.

A number of federations in recent years, often in partnership with their local JCCs and Hillel chapters, have sponsored an agency called GesherCity as still another avenue to provide service to and connection with younger Jewish adults. Originally founded in Boston with the support of the Combined Jewish Philanthropies, Gesher City now operates in twenty communities, with plans to expand to at least fifteen more.[20] The goal of Gesher City is to serve in those communities as "the hub" for connecting young Jewish adults. In cities such as St. Louis and Denver, Gesher City organizes clusters of small organic groups based on common interests, encompassing everything from poker clubs to people who enjoy going to new restaurants together, from "Bark Mitzvah" dog-lover groups to Shabbat dinner groups. The idea is to decentralize activities so that small clusters of younger Jews meet in private homes or in business establishments, but not necessarily in Jewish institutions. Building upon the popularity of start-ups, the Gesher model tries to be innovative and flexible, even as it is funded by establishment institutions. At least in some communities, Gesher City has become *the* address for newcomers who wish to connect with their Jewish peers or, as GesherCity Boston describes itself, as "a comprehensive one-stop shop for all things Jewish for twenties and thirties in Boston."[21]

Most of the major national Jewish organizations have developed programs on the local level to draw young adults into their work. Among the most successful is the Access Program of the AJC. The first Access was organized in Atlanta twenty years ago, and that program is still seen by locals as one of the more popular and vibrant options for this age population. In the past few years, Access groups have been founded in other cities. Like so many other organizations, Access utilizes happy hour socials to bring in large numbers of people who are then informed about the nature of Access and recruited as potential activists. The program tries to interest young adults in the key foci of AJC work—interreligious programs, interethnic partnership, Jewish identity and Israel, and foreign affairs—by sponsoring lectures and panel discussions. Access staff report on efforts to connect young Jews with their counterparts from other American ethnic groups, such as the Indian-American and African-American communities. Access programs also feature various forms of interreligious conversation—or, in one case, comedy, as when Jewish, black, and Catholic comedians shared a program designed to explore how far humor can be pushed before it veers into stereotyping.

The trademark initiative of Access programs may well be the opportunities it creates to meet with foreign consuls stationed in the United States, particularly young diplomats. The idea is to educate these future foreign leaders about matters of Jewish concern and develop connections between them and up-and-coming young Jewish adults. In this realm, the programs in Washington, D.C., and New York have unparalleled access to foreign diplomats, but even in places such as Atlanta, the local Access provides opportunities to meet with consular officials. The capstone of such efforts is an annual two-day trip to Washington, where Access leaders from around the country have the opportunity to meet with foreign ambassadors. Given the AJC's international reach, Access programs also send participants to Israel, Germany, and Switzerland, both to inform participants about broader issues and give them experience in advocating on behalf of Jews.

The Anti-Defamation League (ADL) also runs programs for young adults in twenty-three regions around the country. These tend to focus on a limited number of people—between ten and thirty per region—who participate in the Glass Leadership Institute, an intensive educational program that meets monthly to provide education about the issues of concern to the ADL. The focus of these locally developed programs tends to be civil rights issues, discrimination, and, of course, antisemitism. Participants also meet with local law enforcement officials and engage in joint programs with young leaders drawn from other minority groups. An annual Washington event brings together participants from local programs for lobbying on Capitol Hill and networking with one another. As with Access, part of the allure of the Glass Institute is its effort to bring together young professionals—mainly attorneys, teachers, and social workers—to meet one another and form professional networks.

Both the ADL and Access programs place serious emphasis on explaining their organizations' respective positions on Israel and playing a role in advocating on behalf of the Jewish state. We shall see that some nonestablishment groups take a different stance on Israel or avoid any political questions, but when queried, leaders of establishment organizations do not duck controversial questions or soft-pedal their commitment to the welfare of Israel. They are joined in local communities by regional chapters of AIPAC, some of which have separate staff working with populations in their twenties and thirties, while others work primarily with students on campuses. In some locales, the American Zionist Movement runs educational programs on many aspects of Israeli life beyond politics—such as gays in Israel and Israeli environmental issues—and claims to attract people who do not necessarily come to other Jewish events. Friends of the Israel Defense Forces has created Young Leadership Divisions in a handful of the largest Jewish population centers. Their programs include casino nights, Shabbat dinners, concerts, parades, and cocktail parties, all of which have an element of informing attendees of needs within the Israel Defense Forces and providing ways to raise funds to help combat soldiers continue their education or to renovate mobile facilities used by the troops.[22] The Jewish National Fund, one of the oldest establishment philanthropies, dating back to 1901, has worked intensively in a half dozen larger Jewish communities to attract younger Jews interested in environmental questions and community development in Israel, thus yoking together the Zionist dream with contemporary ecological preoccupations.[23]

Establishment organizations have also embraced service as a means to connect with and stimulate young adults. Perhaps the best known of these is the American Jewish World Service, which organizes college students as well as older volunteers to work in Africa, Asia, and Latin America, mainly with impoverished and illiterate local populations who are not Jewish. By contrast, the American Jewish Joint Distribution Committee (JDC) sends Jewish adults, ranging from college students to older volunteers, on seven- to ten-day trips to work in Jewish communities in need—in Israel, Eastern Europe, and the former Soviet Union and other locations. Through a recently created Next Generation and Service Initiatives division, the JDC engages young adults through three types of programs: (1) international service trips; (2) leadership training programs with serious content; and (3) local awareness programs for those who cannot travel abroad but wish to address domestic Jewish needs. Since 2004, three thousand young Jewish adults have participated in these programs, coming from communities as far flung as Kansas City, New Orleans, Houston, and Denver. Like other national organizations, the JDC has invested in programs for young adults with an eye to recruiting future leaders. But it also is motivated by a desire to inform younger Jews about Jewish poverty and educational deficiencies. The head of its Next Generation initiative notes the dearth of information about Jews in need around the world, and some participants have told her such needs were unknown to them until they saw them firsthand.

As we conclude this brief overview of programs sponsored by establishment Jewish institutions, we might pause to assess the widely reported indifference of young Jewish adults to the Jewish establishment. Drastic declines in donors to federation campaigns and in the membership rolls of Jewish organizations as well as synagogues suggest that these institutions are failing to attract Jews in their twenties and thirties in large numbers. Interviews with federation staff in a dozen communities also suggest that only small minorities of Jews in these age groups are on the radar screens of federations— or on their Facebook pages and email lists. One staffer in Chicago estimates that of some 70,000 young Jewish adults in the greater metropolitan area, only 20,000 appear on federation mailing lists; of these, merely 3,000 engage actively in federation-sponsored programs—this in a community with one of the nation's strongest and most encompassing federations. Based upon its most recent demographic study, the Atlanta Jewish community, which is also well organized, seems to have a population of some 40,000 Jews in their twenties and thirties. But like in Chicago, only a fraction of these young adults attend federation programs. To cite two other communities: a staff member in Dallas estimates a young adult Jewish population of 1,200, but the largest events sponsored by the federation attract only 100 to 150 individuals. And in Cleveland, a powerful federation city of roughly 80,000 Jews, the Young Leadership Division has a mailing list of 3,000; only 1,300 of these contribute to the campaign. The general estimates offered by federation staff people is that between 10 and 20 percent of young adults seem to engage with federations *in any way*.[24] As to local chapters of the national organizations and synagogues, they attract considerably smaller numbers because they are oriented toward cultivating individuals who are ideologically committed to their programs.

From a quantitative perspective, then, the establishment institutions have little to boast about. But they hardly concede this population to other groups.

To begin with, they attribute their limited success to the particular challenges all programs face in attracting single and newly married twenty and thirtysomethings, a population distracted by career-building, a surfeit of opportunities to volunteer and socialize outside the Jewish community, and the stresses of forging a life path, which eventually may include family formation. It is a population, moreover, that hardly feels obligated to join Jewish organizations or synagogues.

In marketing themselves to young adults, the establishment organizations try to capitalize on their history, culture, prestige, and experience. They provide entrée for young Jewish adults to meet establishment Jewish leaders in their own communities and to national figures.[25] Such connections may serve as important sources of professional and social networking and also, under the best of circumstances, may lead to a young person finding a mentor. Participants also learn how the Jewish community has addressed certain perennial issues—building community relations, forging alliances with other American groups, engaging in civil rights work, combating antisemitism, and lobbying elected officials, whether local, state, or national. For some young adults, this engagement can be a heady experience and certainly one they find compelling. There is something powerful, too, about learning "how things are done" in the face of particular communal challenges; within established organizations experience and expertise are transmitted from one generation to the next. While the work of start-ups is often touted as the nonestablishment cutting edge of Jewish life, let us not underestimate the attractiveness of institutions with a long history of achievement, a network of men and women of professional and social stature, and the opportunity to learn from seasoned communal leaders. The long-established organizations know of these attractions and try to woo young adults with them.

Establishment organizations also are striving to overcome institutional handicaps. Across the spectrum, staff members concede that their organizations have been slow to adapt to the new social media. But they are consciously working to catch up, amassing email lists, sponsoring blogs (such as Oy!Chicago, which is headed up by a staff person at the Jewish United Fund), and developing Facebook pages to keep people informed of events.[26] The ADL has placed videos of lectures and programs, as well as archival footage, on YouTube, even as a staff member tweets updates during public events. The technological and communications backwardness of some establishment organizations has put them at a disadvantage in competing for younger members, but they are scrambling to make up for lost time. It is reasonable to assume that as establishment organizations hire more staff members in this age group, they will receive a further push toward more up-to-date recruitment methods. Most important, some of the more forward-looking professionals in establishment organizations reject the notion that they are in a zero-sum game: they regard other Jewish institutions, including the non-establishment initiatives, as potential partners rather than as competitors.

Programs and Initiatives of the Nonestablishment Sector

We have begun our survey with an examination of some establishment organizations, if only because they are often written off as unviable contenders for the allegiance of younger Jewish adults. Our discussion suggests a more complicated story. By contrast, observers of the scene have lavished far more attention on nonestablishment programs founded by and for individuals in their twenties and thirties—and understandably so, since such individuals have poured their creative energies into getting new initiatives off the ground. The nonestablishment groups provide tangible evidence, in short, of serious commitment to some aspect of Jewish life. Equally important, such efforts have unquestionably captured a market of young adults who seem to be otherwise disconnected from organized Jewish life.

The start-ups may be divided into six different categories, based upon their primary programmatic focus.

Independent Minyanim

Since the late 1990s, approximately seventy independent prayer groups have been formed by and for younger Jews. Perhaps the best known of these is Mechon Hadar, on the Upper West Side of Manhattan, which has evolved into a purveyor of practical guidance and Jewish learning to independent minyanim. Though most of the early independent minyanim were established in large urban centers with relatively dense populations of younger Jews—cities such as New York, Los Angeles, Boston, and Washington, D.C.— the phenomenon has spread to places with smaller Jewish concentrations, such as Charlottesville, Virginia, Princeton, New Jersey, Palo Alto, California, Kansas City, and Minneapolis, as well as medium-size Jewish communities— in Atlanta, San Francisco, and Philadelphia, among others. Elie Kaunfer, one of the driving forces behind Hadar, has noted some of the distinguishing features of this movement: it connects with people virally, grows rapidly, does not have uniform standards for ritual practices, and generally does not consist of breakaways from existing congregations. The last point is especially significant for this discussion: these minyanim are not inhabited by people who wanted to reform existing congregations but by those who sought an entirely different model of community, prayer, and learning.[27] Much speculation has surrounded the ultimate home minyan members will find when they no longer live in areas mainly attracting singles: Will they found min-yanim in the suburbs? Will they stay in central city locations in order to maintain membership in a minyan? Or will they join conventional syna-gogues as they raise families? For the meantime anyhow, the independent minyanim are a powerful expression of the search for quality, participation, and spirituality in prayer settings.[28]

Cultural Activities

In a number of cities, Jewish innovators have founded start-ups that offer cultural programming for young adults. To cite one prominent example, three Jewish men whose names all happened to begin with "E" founded E-3 in Denver. Self-consciously modeling their program on Makor, a cultural center in Manhattan founded by philanthropist Michael Steinhardt, they conceived of E-3 "as a bridge between popular culture and Jewish culture," reports cofounder Ezra Shanken. The Chai Life Series promoted by E-3 of-fers programs in four areas of artistic expression, with a strong emphasis on the work of young artists. To be sure, some activities are heavily social, such as E-3's Hanukkah parties, which are held on Christmas Eve and attract five hundred people, and its "Jews and Brews Bus Tours."

When interviewed, the "three Es" cite the goal of their start-up as offering young Jewish adults "cultural gatherings in safe and nonthreatening"[29] set-tings. Moreover, they conceive of programs as "gateway events for those escaping the bonds of the Jewish East [Coast] or Jewish West [Coast], so they won't feel threatened if they don't want to join the Jewish community." By making it possible for hundreds of young adults to "hang out" together (events usually draw between two and four hundred participants), the found-ers hope to connect them with other Jews and thereby convey that being Jewish is not solely a private matter but also an identification with a larger group. They do this by deliberately circulating at events and introducing people to one another.

The founders are not alone in working the room. A number of Jewish professionals attend E-3 events to scout for potential recruits for their own organizations. These include federation professionals as well as professionals in organizations such as the Jewish National Fund (JNF), the AJC, the ADL, and synagogues.[30]

Chicago offers a stark contrast, where establishment organizations seem to hold the programs of Kfar at arm's length. Kfar is led by entrepreneur Adam Davis, who has slowly and with minimal funding sponsored cultural events. Initially, Kfar sponsored a series of performances, including a Jewish punk band, a Hurray for Hanukkah gala, and several other events that have drawn between one and two hundred people. The project is now envisioned as increasingly ambitious, with a core of artists at the center, an outer circle of art lovers, and a still wider circle of consumers. Kfar is intended not only as a producer of events, but as a community, a *village* of creative artists (*kfar* means "village" in Hebrew). More recent events have included Lag Bonfire (on the Jewish holiday of Lag B'Omer) and a Purim celebration. It hopes to sponsor cross-cultural events—featuring Ladino songs, black and Jewish musicians, and other hybrid musical programs. Kfar also places an emphasis on the visual arts, sponsoring gallery openings. In the view of its founder, Kfar events tend to attract young adults who otherwise are anti-institutional, and whose connections are episodic.

An annual highlight of cultural activities held on the West Coast is the Dawn Festival, which has been celebrated since 2004 in San Francisco. Sponsored by Reboot, a national effort based in New York and with branches in Los Angeles and San Francisco, *Tablet Magazine*, an online journal funded by a Jewish philanthropy, and several local groups, Dawn is an overnight extravaganza of culture and study held each year on the first night of the Jewish holiday of Shavuot, a night when Jews traditionally have engaged in Torah study until dawn. Its promotional material in May 2010, Dawn was described as follows:

> DAWN 2010 will feature a packed, late-night evening of headlining performances and events including live bands, theatrical and spoken word performances, premiere film screenings, visual arts, dancing, DJs, lectures, comedy, readings and open-space discussion forums.[31]

It is noteworthy that Dawn grew out of partnerships between national and local organizations, and is supported by a mix of Jewish foundation money and local Jewish philanthropy.[32]

Collectives Offering Jewish Programming

In a small, recent movement, collectives buy or rent a number of houses clustered in one part of town to house younger Jewish adults. These homes then become the locus of activities for a larger community of younger adults. The best known of these is the chain of Moishe Houses, numbering twenty in the United States alone, with thirteen more in countries such as Argentina, Austria, China, Great Britain, and Poland. Begun in 2006, Moishe Houses offer rent subsidies to young Jewish adults who are prepared to use their house as a neighborhood center for Jewish programs—everything from Shabbat dinners to Purim parties, social action activities, and Jewish study circles. As part of their contract, housemates agree to post pictures and written descriptions of their events on the Moishe House blog, as well as to start a blog of their own. The stated goal of the effort is to use the house as a base to have "more Jewish adults actively live vibrant Jewish lives in their homes and communities."[33]

Situated in the section of Seattle after which it is named, the Ravenna Kibbutz began as a Moishe House but now encompasses activities beyond the norm. For one thing, the kibbutz takes in adults older than thirty, the cutoff for Moishe Houses. For another, the kibbutz offers more opportunities for Jewish exploration than does the average Moishe House. The kibbutz offers study groups on Hasidism and Jewish mysticism, as well as the opportunity to explore Jewish identity questions in depth. One animating leader of the kibbutz, Ilana Mantell, even likens it to a Chabad House because some two hundred individuals operate in its orbit and join its activities; it also has the feel of Chabad because of its study groups and because it draws Jewish seekers. "Jewish identity in America is the over-arching question. It comes out as a question for people who come here," Mantell observes. Unlike Chabad, though, the kibbutz is completely pluralistic: kitchens have kosher and non-kosher dishes, and tolerance for all forms of Jewish expression is a requirement. Like so many other programs directed at this age group, Ravenna relies heavily on Facebook as a means of communication. "This community could not have existed before the Internet," declares Mantell, and Facebook is the preferred means of communication.[34]

Both the Ravenna Kibbutz and the Moishe Houses draw inspiration from the cohousing movement begun in the early 1980s by American architects under the influence of the Danish "living community" model.[35] In the main, Jewish versions of the cohousing model subscribe to the fundamental principles of this movement: (1) Participatory process. Residents participate in the design of the community so that it meets their needs. (2) Neighborhood design. The physical layout and orientation of the buildings (the site plan) encourage a sense of community. (3) Common facilities. Common facilities are designed for daily use, are an integral part of the community, and are always supplemental to the private residences. (4) Resident management. Residents manage their own cohousing communities, and also perform much of the work required to maintain the property. (5) Nonhierarchical structure and decision-making. Leadership roles naturally exist in cohousing communities, but no one person (or persons) has authority over others. (6) No shared community economy. The community is not a source of income for its members.[36] Like the cohousing movement generally and the original kibbutz movement, the Jewish collectives tend to attract people on the left wing of the social and political spectrum. Perhaps for this reason, and despite its name, the Ravenna Kibbutz tends to stay away from Israel-related themes.

Near Ravenna a different kind of Jewish collective is growing, called the Kavanah Cooperative. The cooperative does not conform to the principles of the cohousing movement but rather draws inspiration from Hillel campus organizations. "It has a co-op structure and a Hillel approach but for adults and families, meaning that it is pluralistic and aims to help people who are looking for meaningful Jewish experiences," reports Kavanah founder Rabbi Rachel Nussbaum. Though it sponsors a minyan, Kavanah is far more likely to attract people who want to engage in serious textual study and in social justice events. And despite its being headed by a personally observant rabbi ordained by the Jewish Theological Seminary, Kavanah's approach to Jewish observance is that "there is no one right way." Its goal is to increase levels of knowledge and awareness, not to develop a particular form of religious practice or discipline. As to Israel, the founding rabbi has strong connections to the country and tries to push programs, but the participants feel more ambivalence than anything else, which leads to little public attention devoted to Israel. The business model is based on contributions from local benefactors, relatives who live out-of-town but are thrilled their children and grandchildren have found a Jewish place, and grants.[37] There are no dues. True to its cooperative commitments, Kavanah seeks to "empower partners to become 'producers' rather than 'consumers' of their Jewish life."[38]

What these and other experiments in communal arrangements point to is a quest for a community that is more cooperative in its decision-making style than most Jewish institutions, a collective that reaches out to a wider population rather than confining its programs only to members. These experiments also employ business models different from those commonly associated with Jewish organizational life. Rather than base their budgets on membership fees and fundraising, these collectives rely upon volunteering, grants, and other forms of payments to help them function. They also rely heavily on the participation of all members. Here is how Kavanah describes its expectations: In "our cooperative model . . . each partner commits to taking an active role, to being a 'producer,' rather than just a 'consumer,' of Jewish life. There are no bystanders." In their decision-making structures, business models, community outreach, and programming, these experimental communities self-consciously offer alternatives to the practices of established Jewish institutions.

Social Action

Young entrepreneurs have also organized programs to engage their peers in social action. One of the most successful is J Corps, a New York City–based entity that targets college students and people in their twenties who wish to volunteer for service. According to its website, J Corps was designed to address two concerns: "Young Jewish adults found it difficult to extend their social circles after college, and organizations in New York were facing a shortage of reliable volunteers. J Corps has enabled thousands of Jewish college students and young adults to connect while helping to improve their cities."[39] Defining itself as a "social volunteering organization," J Corps has grown explosively over just a few years, and now has franchises in four countries and is poised to spread to half a dozen U.S. cities.

The J Corps formula is simple: volunteers must be Jewish, between ages eighteen and twenty-eight, and single. To create a clear identity for the initiative, every volunteer wears the same J Corps t-shirt. Individuals register and then receive email alerts about upcoming volunteering opportunities; if they do not sign up quickly, they may find themselves without a reservation because programs are oversubscribed. Among the places served are soup kitchens, children's hospitals, old-age homes, schools, parks, and urban revitalization projects.[40]

J Corps prides itself on its nondenominational Jewish orientation but eschews programming on the Jewish Sabbath and holidays. Lest one imagine that activities only include volunteering, the J Corps website makes clear that social get-togethers and fundraisers are very much part of the attraction. Indeed, the organizational slogan captures its dual agenda: "Make friends, and make a difference."[41]

A very different type of program is run by the Jewish Funds for Justice, a twenty-year-old former "start-up" that now receives funding from major foundations. The Atlanta office of the organization has received a grant from the Marcus Foundation to send volunteers on four- to six-day trips all over the South. In partnership with neighborhood groups, the Sierra Club, and other organizations, the Jewish Service Corps, as the program is called, sends young Jewish volunteers to work with impoverished Americans, mainly minorities. Volunteers have primed and painted a hurricane-damaged home, planted trees as part of a reforestation project, engaged in door-to-door canvassing to help create resources for youth in a low-income neighborhood, and worked on an organic farm. The Jewish Service Corps also has a study component, through which volunteers learn about local conditions prevailing at service sites and study Jewish texts. Aside from reunions by alumni at their own initiative, no follow-up programming occurs once volunteers return from their service work.[42]

A far more sustained version of this program is AVODAH: The Jewish Service Corps. Founded in 1998, it combines elements of a collective with a focus on local needs and the study of Jewish texts. AVODAH volunteers serve for an entire year in inner-city areas of Chicago, New Orleans, New York, or Washington D.C. The primary focus of work is on helping alleviate poverty and provide housing for inner-city dwellers.[43]

On the West Coast, the Progressive Jewish Alliance (PJA) fills a similar niche, albeit with very different kinds of programming. Since 1999, the Alliance has worked in Los Angeles and the San Francisco Bay Area to educate younger Jews both about social needs in their communities and the tradition of Jewish social action. In its own formulation, the Alliance engages in the following efforts:

> PJA is a new kind of Jewish organization, one that serves as a vehicle connecting Jews to the critical social justice issues of the day, to the life of the cities in which they live, and to the Jewish tradition of working for *tikkun olam*. We believe that to *kvetch* is human, to act . . . divine. We fight for economic justice by educating Jews about our obligation to stand with the working poor, and then we organize the Jewish community to join in campaigns to improve working conditions and secure a living wage for low-wage workers. We work to reform the criminal justice system and to promote a more just and humane system of restorative, rather than retributive, justice through a groundbreaking program that trains volunteers to mediate between non-violent juvenile offenders and their victims throughout Los Angeles. We work to promote understanding and tolerance by facilitating several tracks of Muslim-Jewish dialogue.[44]

These start-ups often work cooperatively with service programs sponsored by establishment Jewish organizations.[45]

Israel-Oriented Programs

Ever since the Six Day War of 1967, if not before, virtually every national Jewish organization has fielded an Israel affairs department. To the present day, most establishment organizations continue to engage with Israel through some mixture of philanthropy, advocacy, lobbying, sponsored trips (or missions, as they are often called), cultural programming, and investment. Nonestablishment organizations, by contrast, deliberately tend to avoid public discussions about the conflict between Israel and its neighbors. During the course of numerous interviews, nonestablishment leaders across the country shared a similar approach to the conflict: we do not speak openly about Israel because the relationship between Israel and the Palestinians evokes powerful responses on both extremes. For the sake of *shalom bayit*, maintaining a modicum of calm and civility, we avoid rocking the boat. At the independent minyanim, speakers delivering *divrei* Torah, an explication of the weekly portion, are strongly discouraged from commenting upon current events in Israel. Study programs cover all manner of subjects but generally fail to address the history or contemporary condition of the Israel-Arab conflict. And cultural programs sponsored by nonestablishment groups tend to focus on aspects of Israeli culture not connected to the conflict—music, art, environmental issues, and so on—if they refer to Israel at all.

A few significant exceptions, among the nonestablishment organizations, confront the conflict head-on. One is Encounter, a program designed to create a space for public conversation about the relationship between Israelis—and, by extension, American Jews—and Palestinians. Encounter defines itself as "an educational organization dedicated to providing global diaspora leaders from across the religious and political spectrum with exposure to Palestinian life." It brings such leaders to Palestinian areas and offers educational programs in the United States, led by speakers who address thousands of Jews in congregations, JCCs, educational institutions, and other settings where American Jews congregate.

Though it claims not to advocate any particular solution to the conflict, Encounter sets forth a very direct analysis of the impact of the conflict upon American Jewish life:

> The way we talk about Israel within the Jewish community is often toxic and demagogic. Sometimes we avoid the Israel conversation altogether, many times we antagonize those who disagree with us and, more often than not, we end up congregating with and preaching to our small choir. As a result, relationships in families, synagogues and local and national institutional Jewish communities are unraveling.

Moreover, in the view of Encounter, the way this conversation is held is harming younger Jews in particular:

> Heavy-handed, simplistic advocacy and education on Israel are, according to research, inadvertently driving young Jews standing at the gates of the Jewish community to say "not for me" and walk away. We are responding inappropriately to a generation that wants to ask hard questions, imbibe multiple and complex perspectives and decide for themselves what they think.

Founded by Rabbi Melissa Weintraub in 2005, Encounter has won acclaim, particularly among younger Jews, for its innovative programming.[46]

On the other end of the spectrum are two organizations engaged in Israel advocacy efforts, particularly in educating people about Israel's official point of view—the David Project[47] and Stand With Us.[48] The former is based in Boston, with offices in New York and elsewhere along the East Coast; the latter was founded in Los Angeles, and has offices in nine cities, especially concentrated on the West Coast, as well as in Israel and Australia. Both organizations are heavily involved in recruiting and training campus advocates for Israel. Stand With Us defines itself as "an international education organization that ensures that Israel's side of the story is told in communities, campuses, libraries, the media and churches through brochures, speakers, conferences, missions to Israel, and thousands of pages of Internet resources." The David Project is active in middle and high schools, and particularly on college campuses across the country. Both are nonestablishment and of fairly recent origin—with the David Project founded in 2002 and Stand With Us established a year earlier—and both have mainly young staff members. The groups' funding and impetus, however, came from Jews older than forty who were concerned about engaging younger Jews in the battle of ideas about Israel. And neither of these groups limits its work solely to the twenty- and thirty-year-old population.

We shall yet see that many other organizations sponsor programs about Israeli culture—cinema, music, dance, literature, and current events. What sets apart Encounter, the David Project, and Stand With Us are their national scope and, most important, their explicit mandate to encourage study and discourse on the Israel-Arab conflict.

Philanthropic Efforts

Young Jewish adults are also assuming leadership roles in the philanthropic community by developing new ways to pool resources, train up-and-coming donors, and ferret out worthy but largely unsupported new Jewish ventures.[49] Usually, these ventures come about through partnerships between young philanthropists and foundations. For example, the Rose Foundation in Denver trains twenty-five- to forty-year-olds in philanthropy by entrusting them to allocate between $50,000 and $90,000 of the foundation's largess. The goal is to engage young adults in the act of philanthropy, rather than solicitation. The effort is also designed "to create a safe, warm place where people don't feel hijacked by other people's agenda," notes Shawna Friedman of the foundation. In New York, Grand Street, which is under the auspices of the Andrea and Charles Bronfman Philanthropies, serves a similar function,[50] although the money allocated comes from young donors entirely. These programs are part of a larger trend toward creating "givers' circles."[51]

Even as young funders are mobilizing, networks of innovators have also formed, often with the help of funders. Among them is Reboot, mentioned earlier, which bills itself as "a catalyst to catalysts." Its annual gatherings—called "summits"—are premised on the assumption that "there are no easy ways to understand generational changes in identity, community and meaning." The summits convene "an eclectic and creative mix of people from the realms of literature, entertainment, media, technology, politics, social action and the academy, and give them room to question . . . with no preconceived outcomes, to see what, if anything, emerges. We use a conference methodology called Open Space, where the questions of the participants create the agenda. Participants for each year's summit are nominated by past participants."[52] The expectation is that these conversations will spur collaborations leading to creative explorations of Jewish life and Judaism.

In the social justice sphere, the Progressive Jewish Alliance in partnership with Jews United for Justice in Washington, D.C., runs training programs for Jeremiah Fellows eager to engage in local work on behalf of the poor. One goal is to bring together socially conscious young people and nurture them as community organizers and future leaders.[53] And in the realm of Jewish religion and culture, the Wexner Foundation fosters promising younger people displaying leadership potential through its graduate fellows gatherings.[54] Now boasting some 290 alumni, the fellows program primarily targets professionals working in the Jewish community, linking them to networks. Quite a few combine their professional activities with active leadership of nonestablishment types of endeavors.

Stepping back from our discussion of nonestablishment programs, we note that the examples offered serve as but a small sampling of some three hundred programs created by and for younger Jewish adults since the late 1990s.[55] The role of foundations in supporting programs opens a larger question: do start-ups operate in isolation from other Jewish institutions, whether foundations or establishment organizations? Some, to be sure, seem to function on an entirely different plane, as by the fact that federation Young Leadership personnel in some cities had little or no knowledge of nonestablishment organizations operating in their own communities. We have also seen that some start-ups attract young adults who have no other connections to Jewish life.

To be sure, foundations, as independent operators, are free to pick and choose partners as they see fit. The Rose Foundation in Denver frequently has made grants of up to $10,000 to grassroots organizations such as Limmud Colorado, prayer groups, E-3, and others, through its Roots and Branches program. The Marcus Foundation, as we have seen, funds the Jewish Service Corps in Atlanta and New York, and the Andrea and Charles Bronfman Philanthropies work with a number of start-ups. In some cases, federations join in as cosponsors of nonestablishment programs designed by young adults.

The UJA–Federation of Greater New York works in partnership with start-ups such as J-Dub Records, Avoda Arts, and the long-established Foundation for Jewish Culture to support the Six Points Fellowship for Emerging Jewish Artists.[56]

A different model of collaboration between a family foundation and the local federation led to the formation of The Collaborative in Philadelphia, a joint venture cosponsored by the Lindy Foundation and the Philadelphia Federation. The Collaborative functions in some ways as a start-up, providing seed funds for small group encounters such as holiday get-togethers, social opportunities for couples, and programs for the GLBT community. These gatherings are sometimes social events, and other times offer cultural programs. Initiatives of The Collaborative are not tied to a particular denominational group: some programs include nonkosher fare, while others are held on Friday evenings as Shabbat gatherings. Thus, this instance shows that launching new initiatives may involve smudged lines between start-ups, foundations, and the establishment community.

The same is true about pioneers of other nonestablishment programs. Take, for example, Club 1948, a group in Chicago dedicated to offering cultural programs about Israel. The club, which attracts Israelis and American Jews, runs "Shabbat on the Beach," as in Tel Aviv; a Purim party that attracted 450 people; a Maimouna celebration; Rosh Hashana wine and cheese; and for Hanukkah an Israeli band. It also sponsors Israeli performers and features Israeli films as well as educational programs about contemporary Israel. Among its cofounders is a staff person of the American Zionist Movement who sees no incompatibility between her volunteer work for the club and her professional work with young adults on behalf of a national organization.

E-3, discussed earlier, is one of the most interesting and lively start-ups, and it remains independent of other organizations even as it works closely with quite a few. Two of the cofounders first met on a federation-sponsored mission to Budapest, where they conceived of the idea. "The federation mission made a huge impact when I realized that what they support is all for Jews. And the Budapest model gave us the idea of doing something to connect Jews through cultural events. Now E-3 is a concierge into other Jewish experiences; it is a start," explains cofounder Eric Elkins. The third cofounder headed the Young Leadership Division of the Denver Federation. Representatives from all the major Jewish organizations attend E-3's events, implicitly vouching for its credentials as a portal to Jewish life. These representatives all pitch their own programs—and find some recruits. In many instances, young leaders move easily between establishment organizations and start-ups, often having a hand in both. For this reason, some establishment organizations find ways to cooperate with the nonestablishment groups. One model is that of the Boston Federation, which circulates a list of some forty-five programs available in the metropolitan area for young Jewish adults, featuring establishment organizations and start-ups—with no distinction between federation programs and those of any other group.[57] We will shortly see that the lines are blurred for participants too.

Affinity Groups: Between Establishment and Nonestablishment Organizations

Young leaders of establishment and nonestablishment organizations report that programs must appeal directly to the interests of individuals to attract participants, rather than rely upon appeals to a general Jewish solidarity or nostalgia. Many of the programs already described seek to draw people in by offering them content and opportunities for active participation. This task is simplified when attendees share a specific common characteristic or experience, as is the case with participants in affinity groups. Among these are programs that target individuals who have a shared immigrant experience, religious seekers, or individuals who share a common sense of marginalization. Affinity groups operate at the intersection of establishment and nonestablishment programs; depending on their origin and leadership, they have characteristics of one or the other or both.

New Americans

The largest affinity groups work with Jewish immigrant populations. According to the National Jewish Population Survey of 2000–2001, close to a half million U.S. residents were living in households with a Jewish immigrant or immigrants at the turn of the millennium, with at least 20 percent of these classified as children.[58] A decade later, many of these children have reached their twenties. Specifically, the largest immigrant population by far to arrive since 1980 hails from the former Soviet Union (FSU), so we can assume that the great majority of younger onetime Jewish immigrants also come from Russia, perhaps numbering 100,000 souls.

Though data are hard to come by regarding how many of these Russian immigrants were U.S. born and how many immigrated as children, professionals who work with this population conventionally distinguish between so-called Seventy-niners, who arrived at the tail end of the Communist era in response to the partial lifting of the Iron Curtain, and those who migrated in the 1990s after the collapse of the Communist dictatorship. This distinction is important in planning programs because those who arrived earlier tend to have mainly negative feelings about Russia, are quite alienated from Russian culture, and prefer to speak English when they socialize; those who arrived after the Communist era feel a certain nostalgia for the Russia they left, often were exposed to Jewish experiences while still in the FSU, and are more comfortable conversing in Russian.

We can get some sense of the multilayered society these Jews of Russian origin constitute by comparing the mission statements of two organizations. We begin with R Jeneration, begun in San Francisco with an active branch in Manhattan, which proudly describes its population as follows:

> We came to America as kids, brought by our parents. Some were born en route, and some were born here. We are a generation of Americans with a second culture and language, a Russian heritage, Jewish roots, and a defining immigrant experience. We've juggled our "hybrid" Russian-Jewish-American identity throughout our lives.
>
> We speak English without an accent. Many of us went to the top high schools and colleges in the country. We speak Russian . . . well, kinda. Some better than others. Runglish is more our style. We're Jewish, despite yeshiva traumas. We're in our 20s and 30s, busy building successful careers in every imaginable field. Some of us are already household names—Sergey Brin, Gary Shteyngart, Regina Spektor, David Bezmozgis, Lenny Krayzelberg and Mila Kunis. Many others are sure to follow and make their mark.[59]

The emphasis here is on adaptation to America while maintaining traces of a Russian Jewish cultural heritage. R Jeneration is directed to upwardly mobile, highly educated young adults who may or may not speak Russian but still maintain some connection to their parents' culture.

In contrast, EzraUSA, with branches in New York and Boston, sets forth a far more Jewish survivalist agenda—and a greater sense of urgency:

> As our primary concern we see the strengthening of the Jewish identity of the young Russian Jews living in the U.S. For them the link to the past has been lost or is weak and insufficient. Russian-speaking Jews have never become part of the American Jewish community and are currently on their way to complete assimilation. They require a very special approach for the time-being in order for them to eventually become an integral part of a larger Jewish community and to internalize the sense of belonging to the entire Jewish nation (*Klal Israel*).[60]

Other layers of this large population consist of those who actively practiced Judaism in the FSU, such as the Bukharians, and those who were assimilated into the large cities of Moscow and Leningrad. And then there is the distinction between those who maintain strong family ties to relatives in

Israel and those who do not. Programming must take all these features into account if it is to attract young adults.

In the greater New York City area, with its huge concentration of Jews from the FSU, numerous programs are hosted by establishment institutions that recognize the needs of this population and also the potential for recruiting new members. The JCC of the West Side runs Generation R for a Manhattan audience, while its counterpart the Shorefront Y in Brighton Beach sponsors programs for Brooklyn Jews. Then there is the Young Russian Leaders Division of the UJA–Federation of Greater New York, which tends to attract more Americanized and upwardly mobile young adults, in contrast with the Russian American Jewish Experience (RAJE), which features Russian-language events and communicates in Russian on its website.[61]

Event planners at these programs take into account the cultural predisposition of their audience. Religion tends to be a subject many avoid or soft-pedal because the population they seek to attract regards religion with suspicion or hostility. And yet both EzraUSA and RAJE are under Orthodox auspices; the former includes religious rituals with a light touch, the latter with a more explicit emphasis on Torah study. Many programs offer Shabbat meals and small doses of religious rituals in order to educate those individuals who have had little exposure to Judaism. As compared to many organizations directed at American-born younger adult Jews, the ambience of programs for Russian Jews tends to be hawkish on Israeli topics, in line with the general orientation of Jews from the FSU (although this, too, seems to be changing for the youngest population, which has been exposed to American campus life). A connection with Israel, along with a strong sense of Jewish ethnic identity, forms the backbone of Jewish identification for young Russian Jewish adults, providing all the more reason for programs to feature Birthright and other trips to Israel to nurture these connections.

Without exception, program leaders of Russian Jewish origin point to the challenge of educating their peers about the virtues of voluntarism and philanthropy. "Volunteering, *tzedaka*, and *tikkun olam* are not part of the vocabulary at home," laments Anna Rachmansky, a thirty-five-year-old lay leader who serves as president of the Shorefront Y in Brooklyn. "The idea of giving back to the Jewish community is hard to relate to," observes Inna Goryachkovskaya, a twenty-five-year-old staffer at EzraUSA. "There [in Russia] it was the survival of the fittest." And yet leaders of this population point out that almost all immigrant families from the FSU were beneficiaries of communal organizations—the JDC, the Hebrew Immigrant Aid Society (HIAS), and the federations. They stress this point in order to encourage younger adults from the FSU to link their fortunes to the larger American Jewish community—which provided their families with support and services in their time of need. EzraUSA sponsors trips to Newport, Rhode Island, to expose young adults to the Touro Synagogue (the nation's oldest synagogue structure), and thereby to the early American Jewish experience, and to Washington, D.C., for a tour of the U.S. Holocaust Memorial, as a reminder of the common fate of all European Jewry. The organization sponsors Hebrew-language classes, works with the JNF on environmental issues in Israel, and also works with the David Project (the Israel advocacy group mentioned earlier) and Limmud, which sponsors an annual festival of study and the arts.

Outside New York, organizing events specifically for Jews from the FSU is harder since a critical mass is needed. In fact, a common lament of some who work with this population in places with relatively sparse numbers is that they identify first with others of Russian Jewish origin, then with other Russians, and only last with American Jews (most of whom, ironically, are also of Russian origin, albeit as fourth- and fifth-generation Americans). All this adds to the sense of urgency of groups that wish to connect these Jews to the larger Jewish community before they assimilate into the larger American population. Among the more ambitious efforts are the placement of *shlichim* (emissaries) in San Francisco and Chicago by the Jewish Agency for Israel to work with young adults of Russian Jewish origin. A consortium of philanthropists of Russian origin called the Genesis Foundation is also planning initiatives for their *landsleit* in the Bay Area and Boston. And nationally, the Council of Jewish Émigré Community Organizations (COJECO) is working to create an organization that will unify young adults of Russian origin across the country. The Genesis Foundation and the COJECO initiative are especially important because they are examples of leadership coming from within the Russian Jewish population rather than from outside, which has been far more common to date.

If American Jews have been behind much of the initiative for programming addressed to Jews of Russian origin, Syrian and Persian Jews, by contrast, seem far more invested in addressing their own communal needs. Both communities tend to be insular, officially Orthodox, and work hard to keep younger adults under a tight rein. Nothing exemplifies this more than the emphasis on marriage within the respective groups. Toward that end, SephardicLink serves as an online dating service, albeit one under close rabbinic scrutiny.

Another key immigrant group consists of young Israelis in cities such as New York and Los Angeles, and in Silicon Valley. These may be divided into two groups: individuals who came as adults and are enrolled in graduate programs or are pursuing their careers, and so-called hybrids—adults born in the United States to Israeli parents who settled in the United States. Until the recent establishment of Dor Chadash, an organization originally begun in

New York and now with a branch in Los Angeles, few resources existed for Israeli young adults.

Dor Chadash is designed to bridge the worlds of Israelis in the United States with their American Jewish peers. It bills itself as a "community of thousands of Israeli and American Jews who share a passion for Israel."[62] The American Jews who attend have all experienced Israel firsthand, either through Birthright trips or on more substantial stays. They also have picked up enough Hebrew to converse in the language of discourse at Dor Chadash events—"Hebrish," a mix of Hebrew and English.

Events include a huge Yom Ha'Atzmaut celebration drawing thousands and held on the USS *Intrepid*, Purim celebrations, and other parties. A social action committee plans various volunteering events, such as run-walks to raise money. Perhaps most critically, Dor Chadash features on its menu performances by Israeli musicians and talks by prominent Israelis and American Jews about Israel-related themes. The organization claims to have attracted 30,000 attendees over its first six years. Dor Chadash represents a partnership of innovators, establishment organizations (such as the New York Federation), and foundations.

Rounding out the picture of organizations for young Jewish immigrants,[63] we cite a start-up called Jewish International Connection New York (JICNY). Based in Manhattan, this Orthodox outreach organization created by volunteers offers "an international Shabbat dinner" once a month, as well as a monthly movie, cooking classes, and courses on various topics in Judaica offered in English, French, Russian, and Spanish. JICNY attracts Jews who emigrated from twenty-five different countries—including Turkey, France, Argentina, and New Zealand—and is aimed specifically at the twenty-five- to forty-year-old population, with an estimated attendance of nearly 11,000 people in 2008.

Innovators who started this organization aim to fill a special niche. Jews from smaller communities, they contend, have particular needs in that they usually lack family connections in New York, come from foreign cultures, and are used to different styles of Jewish worship. The leaders of JICNY are Orthodox, with some connections to Aish HaTorah, an outreach organization of the Haredi sector, but independent of any particular organization and open to Jews of all outlooks. Their programs depart from the usual approach of immigrant aid societies, which have tended historically to work with newcomers from a single country; here the emphasis is upon bringing together immigrants from many different lands who share the common challenges posed by emigration and adapting to the American environment, along with a common affinity for traditional Judaism.

Orthodox Outreach Programs

JICNY is but one example amid an extensive network of programs maintained by Orthodox Jews to reach the unaffiliated, including twenty- and thirty-year-olds who are disconnected from Jewish life. The best known of these so-called outreach programs are Chabad Houses located on college campuses and in communities around the country. Many Chabad Houses work with younger adults. To take one example, a Chabad House in center city Atlanta runs events year round specifically for singles and young married couples to celebrate Shabbat and Jewish holidays. The focus, reports the Chabad rabbi, Ari Solish, is not on restrictions Judaism places upon adherents but on showing how "Judaism can be exciting." Sabbath evenings offer "great food, elaborate dinners, and an escape from material demands," says Solish. On Simchat Torah the emphasis is on "martinis and mitzvahs," as individuals commit to taking on a new practice, such as "calling grandma more often, observing one Shabbat, or eating kosher-only for a day."

Were he to operate in a Christian context, Rabbi Zvi Drizin would be identified with "young adult ministry." The Dallas-based Chabad rabbi specializes in working solely with this age population. He explains that his two most important tools are Facebook and his own friendly face. Regarding the former, he notes proudly that at the last gathering of *shlichim* Chabad emissaries), his presentation on how Chabad can utilize Facebook was the best-attended session. As to his own approach, he says, "Most people look at me as their friend." "If you are open," he adds, "people will gravitate to you." Drizin meets young Jews where they tend to gather—at bars. (When asked what he himself does there, he replies, "I drink.") He encourages young adults to try his study programs and to visit the special hangout he has created in a former bookstore. Between 80 and 90 percent of the rent is paid through donations, he reports, by Jews under the age of thirty-five whom he has attracted.

A very different type of outreach program called the Manhattan Jewish Experience presents itself as a Modern Orthodox organization for "uninitiated Jews in Manhattan"—that is, for people who are not part of a Jewish community. At its three Manhattan sites, it offers a mix of programs: social gatherings—such as a Green Party with an ecology motif—summer parties, and other introductory experiences for large numbers. Some programs have drawn more than a thousand people. Perhaps as many as one quarter of participants in these programs take the next step by attending Jewish educational programs and abridged Friday-evening services. For the most interested recruits of all, staff members offer far more personalized attention, which connects people to one another, a particular rabbi or educators, families, and even a potential spouse.[64]

The Manhattan Jewish Experience claims to have attracted some 7,000 individuals to its events over its first decade. To cultivate the right ambience and avoid alienating individuals who attend social gatherings, the program is emphatic about excluding people older than forty and will not admit Orthodox people, only those not yet engaged with Jewish life. A bouncer enforces these rules.

Is the Manhattan Jewish Experience a start-up? It originated as a beginners' service at the Modern Orthodox synagogue Kehilath Jeshurun, and with the support of donors expanded to include a staff of Modern Orthodox rabbis and women educators, all of whom had previous experience in outreach work. And yet the Manhattan Jewish Experience is not owned by any particular institution. In brief, here again we see the blurring of boundaries among innovators, funders, and establishment institutions.

Two other forms of Orthodox outreach merit mention. A growing number of community *kollelim*, institutes of advanced Jewish study, numbering fifty at present, are appearing across the United States to offer some service to the local Jewish population, including younger adults. The primary activity of the *kollelim* is to offer educational opportunities, mainly in the form of classes, small group study, and even one-on-one sessions. What is noteworthy about these *kollelim* is that the leadership is drawn from the Haredi sector that formerly eschewed contact with non-Orthodox Jews. Now *kollel* rabbis who continue their studies beyond ordination, are reaching beyond the confines of their insular communities.

As one speaks with people in different communities, it also becomes apparent that freelancers unconnected to any official organization are engaging in Orthodox outreach. In Philadelphia, for example, the Chevra announces itself as "a group for Jewish professionals in their twenties and thirties that provides a unique blend of social, cultural, educational, spiritual, and volunteer experiences." Like many local programs for younger adults, the Chevra offers film screenings and follow-up discussion, billing itself as a place where "the social meets substance." A number of times each year, the Chevra arranges for up to two hundred people to be housed in Lower Bala Cynwyd for Shabbat so that they can spend the day together. These events draw mainly singles and exclude Orthodox Jews.

At first blush, Orthodox outreach programs aimed at minimally engaged younger adults seem to be the creations of establishment institutions and leaders. But the many private entrepreneurs active in these efforts suggest that outreach is a more complex and decentralized phenomenon, perhaps more akin to the nonestablishment sector in funding, methods of recruitment, and style. Moreover, Orthodox outreach workers tend to be far more tech-savvy than those of most establishment groups, using the Internet and Twitter to communicate and build networks. Finally, while some programs compete directly with one another, others are linked and work cooperatively.[65]

GLBT Programs

To date, only a limited number of start-ups serve the Jewish GLBT population in a capacity other than to promote inclusion. Mosaic, for example, a national organization based in Denver and the Bay Area and founded by young adults, works with other groupings and religious movements to promote the acceptance of gays through endeavors such as diversity training. But that agenda is different from offering a setting for Jews in the GLBT population to build a community. On campuses the National Union of Jewish GLBT Students runs local chapters, and Nehirim, based in New York, offers spirituality retreats for GLBT Jews of all ages. In addition, fourteen U.S. synagogues identify as GLBT outreach congregations. Many of these have significant numbers of heterosexual participants, and as growing numbers of Reform, Reconstructionist, and Conservative synagogues have become more open to GLBT Jews, the need to segregate has lessened.

Some exceptions do exist, including JQ International in Los Angeles, which offers social programs specifically for gay Jewish young adults. (It is partially funded by the Los Angeles Jewish Federations.) Hebro plays a similar role for gay men in New York, as do other groups such as JPride in San Diego. In New York and Boston, Orthodox groups for gay men offer Shabbat and holiday programs. For a variety of reasons, gay and lesbian Jews tend to gravitate to social activities sponsored by the larger local GLBT organizations, such as film festivals, rather than to socialize mainly with other Jews. Indeed, a recent survey by Caryn Aviv, Steven M. Cohen, and Judith Veinstein found that only 11 percent of young GLBT Jews were in romantic relationships with another Jew.[66] And according to Gregg Drinkwater of Mosaic, because interdating is the norm in the Jewish GLBT population, few organizations explicitly try to discourage it.

As a prototype of a local GLBT start-up, we may cite the example of Keshet (Rainbow) in Boston. Keshet offers special programs for those in their twenties and thirties.[67] These may include Shabbat meals, bar events, and other socializing opportunities. Educational events focus on training programs to teach others in the Jewish community about the needs of GLBT Jews. And there are also gay pride events. In the words of one of the organizers, "Keshet is the first place for some where their Jewish and GLBT identities come together." For those who seek additional connections, several of the Reform and Conservative synagogues in the area are considered "GLBT friendly," as are some minyanim and Kavod House, a social justice house. These latter entities are not the same, though, as affinity groups solely for GLBT Jews.[68]

Young Adults with Intermarried Parents

As the numbers of children being raised in interfaith families soar, one would expect a corresponding growth of organizations to address the population of young adults who are struggling to define their relationship with Judaism. To date, however, outreach programs have not proliferated in this area. Groups such as Interfaithfamily.com and the Jewish Outreach Institute are mainly concerned with offering support to adults who are in interfaith relationships and marriages, and in serving as advocates for including the intermarried in Jewish communal planning and institutions. The absence of programming for adult children raised by intermarried parents is duly noted on the website of the Half-Jewish Network:

> Astonishingly, at the present time—despite the fact that there are thousands of us living in countries all over the world, including Israel—there are almost no resources for us of any kind.
>
> We have very few opportunities to network—to meet, socialize, share stories and information, and form friendships and relationships.
>
> There is very little known about us. There are very few research studies on us, or brochures and literature for us, or groups engaged in outreach to us.
>
> We also have almost no public "voices" or organizational spokespersons to give feedback or comments when decisions are made about us in the Jewish world and in other faith-based and secular communities.
>
> This is in glaring contrast to the huge amount of research on—and numerous organizations and spokespersons for—interfaith couples (our parents)—and the related support groups for the parents of interfaith couples (our grandparents)—within both Judaism and Christianity.[69]

The Half-Jewish Network strives to bridge these gaps by serving as an advocate and online resource. One start-up trying to create face-to-face meeting opportunities for young adults who were raised by intermarried parents is Interfaithways. An initial conference titled *Jews in ALL Hues: A Gathering for Adult Children of Interfaith Families*, held in Philadelphia in the spring of 2009, brought together thirty people to develop a plan for further gatherings.[70] It next plans to convene individuals who work as professionals at Jewish communal agencies to offer the participants a chance to "share their common discomfort at disclosing their upbringing," notes Mira Colflesh, an associate at Interfaithways.

Our overview of affinity groups makes plain that they address many targeted populations and stem from multiple sources. Some affinity groups are clearly start-ups founded by insiders, whereas others have been created by funders and other outsiders who wish to reach underserved populations. The latter characterization is especially true of Orthodox outreach programs and many of the agencies serving Russian Jews and other immigrants; the former is more evident in groups for the GLBT population and the nascent organizations for children of intermarriage.

Variations by Community and Region

When we shift the terms of analysis from types of programs and their founders to the offerings available in particular communities, we find that programs for younger adults are not distributed randomly across the United States but rather reflect local culture. To begin with the most basic question, what is the relationship between population density and the availability of program options? The largest concentrations of Jews in their twenties and thirties are served by the highest numbers and greatest variety of programs. Not surprisingly given their critical mass of Jews, New York City and greater Los Angeles have more programs than anywhere else in the country, including the largest number of nonestablishment programs. Other communities with comparably modest Jewish populations, however, also support quite a range of initiatives. This is especially so of Boston and Washington, D.C., in the East and the Bay Area in the West. Each of these cities serves as a magnet for younger adults from other origins—to Washington by the allure of government and policy work, to Boston by the plethora of universities and research opportunities, to San Francisco by Silicon Valley and, for some, the large gay and lesbian populations. The size of specific subpopulations also helps explain the creation of affinity groups. Consider, for instance, the large concentrations of Iranian Jews in Los Angeles and New York,[71] and the considerably larger populations of Russian émigrés in those cities, and the corresponding programs for young adults drawn from these communities.

Local lifestyles play a role in determining the nature of programs. Young people tend to be drawn to places like Denver, Seattle, and Phoenix, for example, because they offer magnificent settings for outdoor activities. Little wonder, then, that skiing and hiking trips are features of programs in Denver. Among the organizers of such trips is Rabbi Jamie Korngold, who bills herself as the "Adventure Rabbi." In her book, *God in the Wilderness:*

Rediscovering the Spirituality of the Great Outdoors with the Adventure Rabbi, she writes:

> Those of us who love wilderness excursions know that when we are open to spiritual experiences, hiking also exposes the layers of the soul. Perhaps this is why God chose to give us Torah in the wilderness to ensure that we were spiritually prepared to hear the teachings. . . . The point is not just Jewish people being outside. It's Jewish people doing Jewish stuff outside.

Before Rabbi Korngold's group of skiers starts down Copper Mountain on Shabbat, she reminds them: "It's the intention of Shabbat to have a day that's different from the rest of the week—and how do I make something holy?" Her answer: "By drawing closer to community and to God. To me, a powerful way to do that is to be outside in the natural world. It's a really powerful Shabbat experience."[72]

Hiking, climbing, biking, and skiing are also featured by Arizona Adventurers, which bills itself as "an all-volunteer Jewish outdoor club that just happens to draw many members from the local single population, not a singles group!"[73] The self-proclaimed goal of Arizona Adventures is "to build community, getting together for activities with other people in their twenties and thirties who identify themselves as Jewish."[74]

A very different set of preoccupations characterizes young adults migrating to New Orleans. Ever since Hurricane Katrina ravaged that city, it has been a magnet for service groups coming from around the country to help in the rebuilding. Hillels and volunteer programs such as the Jewish Funds for Justice service program and AVODAH: The Jewish Service Corps have directed young Jews to New Orleans during spring breaks and for more extended service trips. But the city is also attracting a small but perceptible influx of younger Jewish adults who are eager to stay for longer periods to work on policy and planning. As New Orleans Federation executive Michael Weil reports, the penchant for social service characterizing Jewish newcomers to New Orleans since the hurricane affects the tone of programs for Jewish younger adults overall in the Big Easy.

By contrast, the style of programs for younger Jews differs in other communities. A federation staff member in Dallas describes local young adult Jews as primarily business oriented. Federation programs therefore stress professional networking, helping connect Jewish peers to one another based on common business interests. In midwestern cities, young adults tend to marry at younger ages than in coastal cities. This has led to a greater emphasis on couples' programs and parenting advice in the offerings of Jewish organizations; it has also resulted in higher levels of interest in synagogues than one might find in the nation's average Jewish young adult population.

A very different dynamic is at work in Boston and the San Francisco Bay Area, where self-styled "progressive politics" are prominent features of local culture. Not surprisingly, federations there are more attuned to the GLBT community than in other places, and Jewish groups concerned with social action and also protesting against Israeli government policies have inevitably multiplied in those cities.[75]

Who sponsors programs and how they are delivered also depends on the local *Jewish* communal culture. In heavily centralized midwestern communities such as Chicago and Cleveland, the local Jewish federation dominates the landscape of activities. A Chicago young activist involved with the city's Jewish United Fund (JUF) nonetheless complains: "If you are not engaged with the JUF, they put a scarlet letter on you. JUF dominates like in no other city." It is also apparent that start-ups do not register with those cities' federation people, who speak about "our mainstream population" versus other types of younger Jews. And when a federation staff person pronounces that "so much more happens in Cleveland because of the federation," it seems doubtful that much thought is given to the possibility that innovators might be unleashed were federations to pull back and let them blossom. In short, the dominance of federations and the support they are prepared to offer innovators play a critical role in determining whether start-ups will have a chance to thrive.

As we consider the impact of local culture on the types of programs available to young adults, two further considerations warrant attention. One is the reality that some communities are gaining new populations, while others are watching their younger adults depart in large numbers. Among the latter cases are Long Island and other New York suburbs, where an exodus of young adults is depleting synagogues and other institutions (with the noteworthy exception of those neighborhoods attracting young Orthodox Jews). The other big losers of population are a number of midwestern cities. In an effort to stem the tide, the Cleveland Federation has created the staff position of "concierge" with sole responsibility to serve young Jewish adults. The idea is to work with younger Jews regardless of their level of interest in joining the Jewish community. As for the Young Leadership Division of the Cleveland Federation, it defines leadership in a particular way: leaders are those who can create networks and bring people to join. These efforts bespeak a deliberate plan to retain the younger generation and even to offer inducements to Jews from elsewhere to move to Cleveland. They also reflect worry about the future viability of the local Jewish community, as large numbers of younger adults depart and are not replaced.

In stark contrast, communities like Atlanta, the Bay Area, Denver, Seattle, Washington, D.C., and perhaps some Sunbelt communities have experienced a noticeable influx of younger adults. The mood of young leaders in such places seems far more upbeat. Not surprisingly, exciting programs have been created in those communities by innovators and establishment institutions alike, often in partnership, to draw newcomers into Jewish life. The point to be acknowledged is that some communities are winning, while others are losing. Yet as the case of Cleveland dramatizes, Jewish communities on the losing end of population movement are not at fault. The Cleveland Jewish Federation has invested heavily in efforts to retain young adults, including creating unusually large subvention programs for families sending children to Jewish day schools,[76] but the community is a victim of economic and social forces apparently beyond its control.

The second consideration concerns the difference between communities mainly offering establishment-sponsored activities for twenty- and thirty-year-olds and those with nonestablishment initiatives. With their concentration of independent minyanim, blogs, social actions groups, and even affinity organizations, some of the large coastal Jewish communities—those along the Boston–Washington, D.C., corridor in the East and San Francisco–Los Angeles on the other coast—offer far greater variety of programming for young adults than do many communities in the heartland. It is far more difficult for smaller communities with limited numbers of younger adults to mount a broad array of activities. E-3 cofounder Ezra Shanken puts this memorably: "I joke with my friends on the Upper West Side [of Manhattan] that it's hard to see Hadrian's Wall when you live in Rome. This [Denver] is where the battle is."

Still, as we conclude our mapping exercise of programs for this population, we need to acknowledge that—to use a military analogy—a large percentage of potential participants do not set foot on the battlefield. The communal survey conducted in Phoenix in 2002 estimated a population of 5,900 single and married households with no children in the younger than forty population, but the largest email list in the community only accounts for 1,800 of these households.[77] Ezra Shanken estimates that Denver has a population of 13,000 Jews in their twenties and thirties, but only four hundred are on the Facebook site of the Federation's Young Leadership Division and five hundred are on E-3's Facebook site. Even in the larger population centers, start-ups and federations tend to count attendance in the hundreds. Events in Manhattan such as the Matzo Ball and the Yom Ha'Atzmaut party sponsored by Dor Chadash are noteworthy for attracting several thousand individuals. But the potential market in Manhattan must be numbered in the many tens of thousands, if not more. Even with all the initiatives and programs that exist around the country, it is difficult to imagine that more than a fraction of the estimated one-and-a-quarter-million young Jewish adults participate in any meaningful fashion.

Given proportionally low attendance at Jewish events, those who do come out for events are most likely to participate in a social gathering, such as the Matzo Ball. Participation in more content-laden programs drops off as expectations increase. If the avenue for reaching young adults is to engage them in programs that are personally meaningful, small group activities and even one-on-one conversations are the most compelling. As a set of recommendations to Jewish communal organizations and funders puts it:

> Relationships are built one-by-one through face-to-face interactions, requiring time and resources and running counter to all of the social networking technologies like Facebook. But this low-tech approach is the only way to both make contact with individuals on the margins and to engage them in substantive conversations about their interests, concerns, and needs.[78]

This reality may help answer the question posed at the outset of this essay about the patterns of involvement exhibited by this generation as compared with earlier ones. The difference is not so much one of active participation but of joining. If the postwar generation flocked to take out memberships in organizations and the baby boomers have limited their involvement, this generation seems even more reluctant to join, but rather participates episodically and as the spirit moves them. Personal relevance, if not meaning, drives their willingness to engage.

Perhaps precisely for this reason, a plethora of alternatives has been created to draw potential participants into Jewish life. Where once formal organizations were the name of the game, today establishment institutions have been augmented and, in many cases, challenged by hundreds of start-ups and many new types of affinity organizations. A remarkable array beckons those who are interested.

Our mapping exercise also makes plain that the actual ecosystem of programs for young adults cannot easily be divided between establishment and nonestablishment. For one thing, participants go where they please with little regard for who is sponsoring an activity. They do not care whether a federation or a national organization is sponsoring an event, as opposed to the sponsor being a start-up. What matters is the quality of the experience, the presence of people with whom they wish to associate, and the meaning they can derive from an event. For another, the leaders and organizers of these programs themselves move fluidly from one to the next. Founders of start-ups join establishment organizations, and in some cases the reverse movement is evident: innovators are initially drawn into Jewish activity by exposure offered through a formal federation program or sponsored by an affinity group.

When interviewed, quite a few young leaders have marveled at how far they have come. "If you had told me when I was in college that I would have ended up this Jewish, I never would have believed you," is a refrain sounded by a segment of younger leaders. To be sure, others are more clearly groomed for such leadership roles, but a variety of circumstances and Jewish experiences have helped draw young Jews—both leaders and followers—to participate, the most frequently cited among them being Birthright Israel, Wexner Heritage Programs, Orthodox outreach efforts, and federation-sponsored missions. Indeed, quite a few current leaders of programs refer to such opportunities as "life-changing experiences." The mix of programs is noteworthy: some are for more Judaically knowledgeable and better educated individuals, and others are for all comers.

How, then, do today's young adults relate to organized activities? They opt to participate based on individualized interests and predispositions, moving fluidly from one set of experiences to the next with little regard for the sponsorship of programs. Establishment organizations, nonestablishment initiatives, and affinity groups are part of a growing set of Jewish options for a generation living in an age of ever-expanding choices. Though we cannot know for certain how many younger Jews avail themselves of these options, the numbers of attendees cited by organizers of social events, cultural programs, study and worship sessions, service days, lobbying and advocacy efforts, and other initiatives suggest that a proportion of Jews in their twenties and thirties continues to seek out places to associate with their Jewish peers, even if the nature of their connections to the Jewish community currently differs from that of previous generations.

NOTES

My thanks to the following individuals, all of whom serve as volunteer or professional leaders, for graciously agreeing to be interviewed about their work, organizations, and communities: *Atlanta*: Wendy Bearman, Seth Cohen, Cobi Edelson, Randy Gold, Ross Kogon, Rabbi Hirshy Minkowitz, Eileen Price, Rabbi Ari Solish, Dov Wilker, Alana Zavett. *Boston*: Irene Belozersky, Ed Case, Rachel Glazer, Orly Jacobowitz, David Perla, Nancy Viner. *Chicago*: Becky Adelsberg, Adam Davis, Jason Freedman, Caryn Peretz, Stefanie Pervos. *Cleveland*: Abby Hirsch, Matthew Klein. *Dallas*: Rabbi Zvi Drizin, Regan Wagh. *Denver*: Gregg Drinkwater, Eric Elkins, Shawna Friedman, Eli Hirsch, Ezra Shanken, Lisa Feiner Walko. *Los Angeles*: Esther Kustanowitz. *New Orleans*: Amy Berins Shapiro, Michael Weil, Rachel Zoller. *New York*: Matt Abrams, Matthew Ackerman, Roger Bennett, Rabbi Daniel Bronstein, Nina Bruder, Audrey David, Brigitte Dayan, Sarah Eisenman, Rachael Ellison, Matthew Gerber, Inna Goryachkovskaya, Elana Stein Hain, Deborah Lauter, Naomi Less, Meira Levinson, Erik Levis, Rebecca Neuwirth, Anna Rachmansky, Rabbi Pinny Rosenthal, Miryam Rosenzweig, Jodi Samuels, Biana Shilshut, Ari Teman, Jos Thalheimer, Julia Volpin, Bram Weber. *Philadelphia*: Ross Berkowitz, Jennifer Birch, Mira Colflesh, Jon Erlbaum, Rabbi Lauren Grabelle-Herman, Alison Margulies.

Phoenix: Rabbi Zvi Holland, Rabbi Elana Kanter, Virginie Polster. *San Francisco*: Elina Kaplan. *Seattle*: Rabbi Chaim Levine, Ilana Mantell, Rabbi Rachel Nussbaum, Noam Pianko, Masha Shtern. *St. Louis*: Heather Paperner, Marisa Reby. *Washington, D.C.*: Melanie Maron Pell. *Israel*: Ariel Beery, Rachel Fish, Dyonna Ginsburg, Aharon Horwitz, Haviv Retig.

1. Harold Weisberg, "Ideologies of American Jews," in *The American Jew: A Reappraisal*, ed. Oscar Janowsky (rev. ed.). Philadelphia: Jewish Publication Society, 1972, p. 344.

2. Marshall Sklare and Joseph Greenblum, *Jewish Identity on the Suburban Frontier: A Study of Group Survival in the Open Society*. New York: Basic Books, 1967, chapter 7, especially pp. 250–52.

3. Steven M. Cohen and Arnold Eisen, *The Jew Within: Self, Family, and Community in America* (Bloomington: University of Indiana Press, 2000), 152–54.

4. Robert D. Putnam, *Bowling Alone: The Collapse and Revival of American Community* (New York: Simon & Schuster, 2000).

5. We base ourselves on an estimate of the eighteen- to thirty-nine-year-old population made in 2006, which itself was calculated using data from the 2000–2001 National Jewish Population Survey. Assuming roughly the same numbers four years later and subtracting the eighteen- to twenty-one-year-old college cohort, we arrive at a rough figure of one and a quarter million. See Jacob B. Ukeles, Ron Miller, and Pearl Beck, *Young Jewish Adults in the United States Today* (New York: American Jewish Committee, September 2006).

6. Interviewees were not chosen randomly but rather with the goal of providing an equal mix of professionals and volunteers, and of encompassing a wide spectrum of activities. Interviews focused mainly on the programs and secondarily on the leadership activities of the interviewees. On average, each interview lasted an hour. The majority were conducted over the telephone. Because some interviewees wished to remain anonymous, their perceptions are not ascribed to any one particular person. This essay also relies upon written reports, which are duly footnoted. Some observations, though, appear without attribution when based on the comments of interviewees.

7. To illustrate how difficult it is to come by numbers for different subpopulations based on their marital and religious status, we note the range of percentages offered by Ukeles Associates in 2006: the estimated breakdown of Jewish adults between ages eighteen and thirty-nine who are married with children ranges from 13 to 24 percent of the total, unmarried Jewish adults without children range from 39 to 56 percent, the intermarried range from 10 to 20 percent, and the Orthodox range.from 11 to 27 percent. Ukeles et al., *Young Jewish Adults in the United States Today*, p. 62.

8. Sharna Goldseker, "Being the Next Generation," *Sh'ma*, October–November 2001, p. 1.

9. Steven M. Cohen and Ari Y. Kelman, *The Continuity of Discontinuity: How Young Jews Are Connecting, Creating, and Organizing Their Own Jewish Lives.* (New York: Andrea and Charles Bronfman Foundation and 21/64, n.d), 64.

10. This theme is discussed by Tamar Snyder, "Young Leaders Pushing for Seat at Table," *Jewish Week* (New York), June 30, 2010, p. 1.

11. Sacha Feiffer, "Philanthropic Shift: Young Jewish Donors Go Beyond Traditional Groups," *Boston Globe*, December 13, 2007, www.grandstreetnetwork.net.

12. In addition to marrying at a young age and having children in their twenties, tendencies that draw them into synagogue life, Orthodox Jews are motivated by a religious obligation to engage in public prayer—hence their congregations have done far better at attracting singles and young families than synagogues of other denominations. If anything, Orthodox synagogues generally are teeming with young families.

13. On the Riverway Project, see www.riverwayproject.org, as well as a report by Rabbi Morrison at the Synagogue 3000 website: "The Riverway Project: Engaging Adults in Their 20s and 30s in the Process of Transforming the Synagogue," www.synagogue 3000.org.

14. The success of Temple Israel in attracting between 150 and 200 people of the Riverway Project to join the congregation has drawn attention. We should note, though, that more than half of the participants are married or in long-term relationships, and quite a few are parents of young children. Singles seem less likely to join.

15. On Brooklyn Jews, see www.brooklynjews.org. Rabbi Daniel Bronstein, an associate rabbi at Congregation Beth Elohim, provided information on the types of programs offered at the synagogue for Jews in their twenties and thirties.

16. For a listing of these events, see www.atidla.com/history.php. See also J. Liora Gubkin, "Friday Night Live: It's Not Your Parents' Shabbat," in *Gen X Religion*, eds. Richard Flory and Donald Miller (New York: Routledge), 199–210.

17. Adas Israel of Washington, D.C., www.adasisrael.org.

18. Kol Tzedek, Philadelphia. www.kol-tzedek.org.

19. An organization called Let My People Go claims its New York City event attracted 4,200 people in 2008. See www.letmypeoplego.com/theball.html. For an overview of such events held in New York City, see Jacob Berkman and Ben Harris, "The Search for the Better Matzo Ball Leads to a Tour of Manhattan Debauch," *JTA*, December 27, 2007,

20. GesherCity, www.geshercity.org.

21. See the "About" section of ibid.

22. Friends of the Israeli Defense Forces, www. israelsoldiers.org/young_whoweare.php.

23. On the new JNFuture, see Tamar Snyder, "Lay Leader, Professional Create New Young Leadership Model," *Jewish Week* (New York), June 15, 2010, p. 27, and David Feith, "Giving Trees," *Wall Street Journal*, July 25, 2008, http://online.wsj.com.

24. In the past, establishment Jewish organizations relied heavily on the children of older leaders to restock their leadership cadres. Anecdotal information suggests this pattern still obtains to some extent but that established organizations can no longer rely heavily upon generational succession from stalwart families. The recruitment of leaders for the establishment sector—Who is courted? Where are they situated? What are their occupations in the main? From what socioeconomic and occupational backgrounds are they drawn?—warrants study.

25. See, for example, text from the website of the AJC Access program in Washington: "ACCESS DC members also interact with the general AJC Chapter by attending chapter programs and networking with seasoned AJC Board Members." Opportunities for learning from mentors are touted by professionals working with younger Jews. See www.ajc washington.org.

26. Contrary to the assumption that establishment organizations are oblivious to the new social media, an AJC Access program staff person states categorically: "If you are not on Facebook, you are invisible to this age group."

27. For a historical analysis of the minyan phenomenon, see Riv-Ellen Prell, "Independent Minyanim and Prayer Groups of the 1970s: Historical and Sociological Perspectives," *Zeek*, January 2008, www.zeek.net/

28. Elie Kaunfer, *Empowered Judaism: What Independent Minyanim Teach Us about Building Vibrant Jewish Communities* (Woodstock: Jewish Lights Publishing, 2010), especially pp. 61–71, and Steven M. Cohen, J. Shawn Landres, Elie Kaunfer, and Michelle Shain, *Emergent Jewish Communities and Their Participants: Preliminary Findings from the National Spiritual Communities Study of 2007* (New York: Mechon Hadar, November 2007), www.bjpa.org.

29. We can only speculate as to what might be "threatening" about establishment programs. The control exercised by conventional organizations over programming? The expectation of having to contribute funds to establishment organizations—i.e., pay to play? The dominance of baby boomer culture and the lack of opportunity for younger Jews to satisfy their own sensibilities?

30. The Denver Jewish community conducted a systematic study in 2007 of how Jews in their twenties and thirties engage with Jewish life. See Jacob B. Ukeles, *Connecting and Engaging Jewish 20s and 30s in Metro Denver/Boulder: Denver: Allied Jewish Federation of Colorado, May 2008*. The author graciously shared this report with me.

31. On the Dawn Festival, www.dawnfestival.org/about#dawn.

32. As this chapter discusses the types of programs available to younger Jews, rather than the infrastructure to nurture those programs, this essay does not explore the various support groups for younger Jewish leaders, ranging from leadership training programs to seed funders to networks of innovators. See Shaul Kelner's essay in this volume on leadership training efforts and especially the active role of Jewish foundations in encouraging younger innovators.

33. See "Theory of Change," www.moishehouse.org/data/MoisheHouseEvaluation Outline.pdf

34. See the kibbutz website, www.ravennakibbutz.org, and Carol Tice, "Ravenna Kibbutz: A Magnet for Jewish Newcomers," *Seattle Times*, June 20, 2009, http://seattletimes .nwsource.com.

35. On the cohousing movement in general, see the website of the Cohousing Association of the United States: www.cohousing.org.

36. The principles are found at www.cohousing.org/six_characteristics.

37. The role of the grandparent generation is probably attributable to a concern with "Jewish continuity"—i.e., a desire to see grandchildren raised in a Jewish ambience likely to nurture connection to Jewish life.

38. Rachel Nussbaum, "Demanding More of Community," *Sh'ma*, February 3, 2010, www.shma.com.

39. For an overview of its programs and a biography of its founder, Ari Teman, see "36 under 36: The Next Wave of Jewish Innovators," *Jewish Week* (New York), May 21, 2008, as posted at www.jcorps.org.

40. JCorps, www.jcorps.org.

41. For an example of a considerably smaller, and suburban, program for young Jewish singles, see the story on Jersey Tribe by Johanna Ginsburg, "'Tribe' Hunts an Elusive Cohort: Generation X," *New Jersey Jewish News*, January 6, 2010, http://njjewishnes .com/article/stateede/tribe-hunts-an-elusiveochort/.

42. On the Jewish Service Corps program, see www.jewishjustice.org.

43. On AVODAH, see www.avodah.net/history.

44. See the "About" page on the Progressive Jewish Alliance (PJA) website, www.pj alliance.org. PJA does not appeal only to twenty- and thirtysomethings, but we mention it because a substantial portion of its volunteers come from this age group. Hazon, by contrast, a national effort focused on Jewish environmental education, draws participants from all age groups. Founded in late 1999, Hazon is a noteworthy nonestablishment organization whose appeal transcends any particular age segment.

45. Significantly, a recent report on Jewish Service Learning features eight programs, half of which are start-ups and the other half organized by establishment organizations such as the Joint Distribution Committee, the American Jewish World Service, Hillel, and the Jewish National Fund. See Sarah Jane Rehnborg et al., *Young, Jewish, and Working for Change: Jewish Service Learning, An Analysis of Participant Jewish Identity and Program Characteristics*. Austin: The RGK Center for Philanthropy and Community Service, University of Texas, October 2008, p. 12.

46. On Encounter, see www.encounterprograms.org.

47. On the scope of work done by the David Project, see www.thedavidproject.org.

48. On the activities of Stand With Us, see www.standwithus.com.

49. Feiffer, "Philanthropic Shift."

50. On Grand Street, see www.grandstreetnetwork.net.

51. On givers' circles, see Tamar Snyder, "The Power of the Circles: The Next Phase in Jewish Philanthropy," *Jewish Week* (New York), August 25, 2009, www.thejewishweek .com/viewArticle/c36_a16598/News/New_York.htm.

52. On Reboot, see http://rebooters.net.

53. Adam Kredo, "Fellowship Places Community Organizing Skills in Jewish Context," *Jewish Week* (Washington, D.C.), May 19, 2010, www.jeremiahfellowship.org/in-the -news.html.

54. The Wexner Foundation, www.wexnerfoundation.org.

55. Shawn Landres and Joshua Avedon, *The Innovation Ecosystem: Emergence of a New Jewish Leadership Landscape*. Los Angeles: Jumpstart, the Natan Fund, and the Andrea and Charles Bronfman Foundation, 2009, p. 9, www.jewishjumpstart.org/documents/ InnovationEcosystem_WebVersion.pdf.

56. See www.sixpointsfellowship.org.

57. See *Resource Guide to Young Adult Jewish Boston*. Boston: Combined Jewish Philanthropies, n.d., downloaded in July 2009.

58. Jonathan Ament, *Jewish Immigrants in the United States*, report no. 7, United Jewish Communities Report Series on the National Jewish Population Survey, New York: United Jewish Communities, October 2004, p. 7.

59. See www.rjeneration.org. R Jeneration's tag line is "Born in the Soviet Union, made in the USA."

60. See Ezra USA, www.ezraus.org.

61. On RAJE, see www.rajeusa.com.

62. On Dor Chadash, see www.dorchadashusa.org.

63. See chapter 4 in this study, which refers to the second-generation Iranian Jewish community in Los Angeles, an important subpopulation among L.A.'s younger Jews.

64. Carolyn Slutsky, "Call of the Wildes: In the Battle for Unaffiliated Jewish Souls, the Manhattan Jewish Experience Is Expanding Its Reach Downtown," *Jewish Week* (New York), November 24, 2006.

65. A few institutions address a population moving in the opposite direction—abandoning Orthodox Judaism for a freer lifestyle. At a social meeting place in Manhattan known as Chulent, a reference to the traditional Sabbath stew, refugees from Haredi and Hasidic forms of Orthodoxy gather to compare notes with others struggling with the common experience of either having left Orthodox observance completely or living a dual life as a public Orthodox Jew and a private defector from at least some observance of Jewish rituals. See Jennifer Bleyer, "City of Refuge," *New York Times*, March 18, 2007, www.nytimes.com. A second organization named Footsteps offers lapsed Orthodox Jews training and guidance in how to adapt to larger American society. See http://chassidic .blogspot.com/2009/02/footsteps-interview-on-zev-brenner.html. Both efforts are directed mainly to Jews in their twenties and thirties.

66. On this effort, see Welcoming Synagogues Project, http://huc.edu.

67. Keshet defines itself first and foremost as working to achieve GLBT inclusion, but it also organizes social events. See www.keshetonline.org. As this project neared completion, some of these groups merged, principally Mosaic and Keshet. Significantly, the merger was aided by the Schusterman Foundation, yet another example of the crossing of institutional boundaries. Jacob Berkman, "Keshet and Jewish Mosaic to Merge," JTA, June 18, 2010, http://blogs.jta.org.

68. Other affinity groups provide forums for women sharing an interest in issues associated with their gender. Establishment organizations such as Hadassah, the National Council of Jewish Women, and the Jewish Orthodox Feminist Alliance (JOFA) all attract women in their twenties and thirties, though they do not necessarily create special programs for this age group. Conversely, some nonestablishment organizations have gender-segregated auxiliaries, often named ironically to refer to the older model of men's clubs and sisterhoods prevalent in synagogues of an earlier era. These include the men's club at IKAR, an independent minyan in Los Angeles, and the women's club at the Mission Minyan in San Francisco.

69. See the Half-Jewish Network website, www.half-jewish.net.

70. Julie Wiener, "'Half,' Whole or Neither?" *Jewish Week* (New York), July 1, 2009, www.thejewishweek.com.

71. For an overview of the activities of 30 Years After, an organization of second-generation Iranian Jews, see Sharon Udasin, "Young Iranian Jews Now Pushing Beyond Old Boundaries," *Jewish Week* (New York), January 29, 2010.

72. Korngold is quoted in Amy Klein, "Looking for Adventure with Outdoor Groups," JTA, February 5, 2009, www.jta.org. The article refers to a number of outdoor adventure trips—some for singles, some for entire families; some for younger adults, some for a range of ages.

73. Arizona Adventurers, www.arizonaadventurers.org.

74. Rachel Silverman, "Adventure Groups Take Spirituality Outdoors," *Jewish News of Greater Phoenix*, June 30, 2006, www.jewishaz.com.

75. Still another variable may be at work: in smaller Jewish communities or those in which Jews worry more about antisemitism, programs focusing on the security of American

and Israeli Jews may resonate far more than in communities where Jews feel well accepted and secure. Data on this question were not gathered, but the correlation between higher levels of insecurity and the popularity of particularistic Jewish programming is worthy of further investigation.

76. The Cleveland Federation offers a $5,000 per child tuition subsidy for day school, a larger subvention than that offered by most federations. Ellen Schur Brown, "Day Schools Holding Their Own Even in This Economy," *Cleveland Jewish News*, February 6, 2009, www.clevelandjewishnews.com.

77. Leisah Namm, "Groups Seek Jewish Young Adults," *Jewish News of Greater Phoenix*, August 22, 2003, www.jewishaz.com.

78. Ari Y. Kelman and Eliana Schoenberg, *Legwork, Framework, Artwork: Engaging the Next Generation of Jews: A Report on Rose Community Foundation's Next Generation Initiative* (Denver, Co: Rose Community Foundation, June 2008), 17.

STEVEN M. COHEN

2 From Jewish People to Jewish Purpose

Establishment Leaders and Their Nonestablishment Successors

Establishment Jewish Life—In Decline?

S INCE 1990 OR BEFORE, the landscape of organized life has been creaking and shifting. Since well before the economic downturn of 2008–2010, signs have been accumulating, generally pointing in the same direction and toward the same conclusion: The fabled "establishment Jewish communal system"—the vast continental network of long-established Jewish communal agencies and institutions—is in decline.

A decade after the turn of the twenty-first century, these organizations' members, donors, and resources (all of which can be measured) are diminishing; so too are their passion, energy, and moral purpose (more ephemeral and less quantifiable attributes, for sure). Almost all the older, veteran agencies seem reduced in scope, influence, and resources, especially when seen against the post–Six Day War period, which lasted through the 1980s.

To take some specifics: Jewish federations, the financial heart of this system, have seen their donors slowly shrink in numbers and gradually advance in age. While federations regularly proclaim new "record" levels of giving, the purchasing value of dollars contributed to the annual campaigns has drifted downward over the years. The federation system provides Israeli charities, once the moral heart of its fundraising, with only about one third the inflation-adjusted dollars that it did in the 1980s. Federation leaders point to their growing endowment funds as guarantors of their continued significance, especially after the wave of megadonors (such as Bernstein, Joseph, Wexner, Schusterman, Steinhardt, Grinspoon, Bronfman, and Bronfman) and their foundations (possibly a one-generation phenomenon) pass from the scene. But staking one's claims for continued vitality to the legacy of endowments suggests an implicit concession that younger donors are both less numerous and less generous than their grandparents.

In the denominational domain, with the exception of Orthodoxy, the available evidence points to weakened movements and shrinking membership in the congregations that constitute them. The Conservative membership base has been shrinking, marked by rapidly falling numbers of congregants (and their rising ages), closing or merging congregations, fewer participants in Conservative youth movements, and fewer students in Conservative schools, both day and supplementary. To take one example: In Philadelphia, those identifying as Conservative drops from 38 percent among those sixty-two and older to 18 percent among those under forty (Jewish Federation of Greater Philadelphia, 2009). Underscoring the significance of these findings for Conservative Judaism, Philadelphia has functioned as a virtual Conservative institutional capital for much of the twentieth century.

Until recently, the Reform movement seemed somewhat healthier, but the economic downturn exposed evidence of weak commitment on the part of its membership base. Thousands of congregants failed to renew their membership, resulting in drastic declines in the central Reform denominational body. The apparent numerical stability in congregants rests on what may be shifting sand. Reform household numbers certainly have been holding steady, albeit with increases in mixed married families. This trend translates into far fewer Reform Jewish individuals. By definition, an in-married couple consists of two adult Jews; a mixed married couple means only one Jewishly identifying adult. With more and more Reform households consisting of mixed married families (perhaps half of newly enrolled members in the last decade), fewer Jewish adults belong to Reform congregations today than in the 1980s and 1990s. Moreover, the mixed married families, as compared with their in-married counterparts, depart sooner—often just after their youngest child undergoes the requisite Bar or Bat Mitzvah ceremony. The increasing proportion of mixed married Jews in Reform congregations directly implies both shorter connection and lower average levels of commitment and involvement.

Jewish Community Centers (JCCs) have been a mainstay of Jewish life in North America for the greater portion of the twentieth century. Providing preschools, day camps, fitness facilities, cultural services, and more, JCCs today embrace more members than any denominational movement, constituting another vital component of the Jewish institutional establishment in North America. How fares the JCC movement? Notwithstanding scattered closings and reports of financial strain, they seem to be holding their own. But not unlike the Conservative movement (whose members constitute the plurality of JCC members), JCC constituencies are also aging gradually, as JCCs have made little headway in attracting young adults as members or users. JCCs remain attractive to parents of young children, at a time when Jews are marrying later (if at all) and bearing children well into what was once regarded as middle age. Certainly, even insider-advocates agree that the JCC heyday of the mid-twentieth century, with its residentially concentrated Jewish neighborhoods and inner-ring suburbs that contained these Centers of the Jewish Community, is long past and never to return. These venerable institutions, faced with financial challenges, have also experienced significant cutbacks in recent years in federation funding—further testimony to the withering of the interdependent "system" of established Jewish institutions.

Jewish membership organizations have long been a testimony to Jewish exceptionalism in America, and American exceptionalism in the Jewish world. Voluntary organizations—fraternal, Zionist, charitable, and otherwise—find no counterpart for their number, scope, and complexity among other American religious or ethnic groups. Notwithstanding its fabled history throughout the twentieth century, this "alphabet soup" of major Jewish organizations has been experiencing the same trends as other collective endeavors: shrinking numbers and aging constituencies.

Elsewhere, the outlook for Jewish organizational life is hardly much brighter. With the possible exception of AIPAC, the long-enduring communal "defense" agencies can no longer count on a fully mobilized American Jewry, whether in support of liberal causes (as in midcentury) or for defending Israel (as in the 1970s and 1980s). The mixed condition of pro-Israel and communal defense agencies suggests everything from a diminished enthusiasm for Israel to a diminished sense of marginality and vulnerability (perhaps well founded in social reality). Collective Jewish causes, large and small, no longer seem to animate American Jews as much as they once did (Cohen and Wertheimer 2006). Jewish human service agencies continue their valued role in helping Jews and (more often) non-Jews alike. But their funding derives heavily from government and non-Jewish sources, rather than from generous Jewish donors.

In short, none of the components of the so-called establishment community is in particularly good shape; all seem stable at best or challenged at worst.

"Nonestablishment" Phenomena—On the Rise?

At the same time as the organized Jewish community (OJC) of old has stumbled, the last decade has witnessed the substantial rise of a wide variety of phenomena that may be called "nonestablishment" (other possibilities:

"start-up," "emergent," "countercultural," or "innovative"). These embrace a diversity of events, projects, organizations, and communities. More concretely, they include independent minyanim, social justice projects, cultural events (music, art, filmmaking), learning initiatives (by individuals, in small groups, or at massive learning festivals), and Jewish life online (where the once-virtual is now very real indeed). Taken together, all speak to a newfound and newly expressed energy, largely by Jewish social, cultural, spiritual, and educational entrepreneurs mobilizing like-minded leaders, activists, and constituencies. To call them "followers" might be a misnomer, as the very nomenclature of "membership" and "leaders," or the hierarchy models of yesteryear, hold little appeal for this nonestablishment sector.

By any measure, these variegated nonestablishment phenomena have grown substantially in number and scope. One study of new self-styled spiritual communities, largely outside Orthodoxy, identified about eighty founded between 1998 and 2007 and still functioning (Cohen et al. 2007). The greatly reduced costs of cultural production and distribution have helped prompt the flourishing of Jewish-oriented music, theater, and video (Cohen and Kelman 2006). The web now hosts billions of pages with Jewish content, obviously all created since the early 1990s. While social service and social justice activities have long been a staple of Jewish life (Fein 1994; Vorspan and Saperstein 1992), the latter third of the twentieth century saw a reduction in such passions and activities, with the waning of the civil rights and antiwar movements (Diner 2004). But, as one comprehensive study has demonstrated (Bronznick and Goldenhar 2008), the extensive cottage industry in local and some national social service and social justice activities has expanded in diversity, number, budget, staff, and, presumably, constituency. Adult Jewish learning constitutes a major domain of the nonestablishment collective endeavor in recent years, and is perhaps best illustrated by the international rise of Limmud, a string of local initiatives that staged approximately thirty Jewish learning festivals around the world last year, each reaching hundreds of participants for two- to five-day encampments. Landres and Avedon (2009) speak of a Jewish Nonestablishment Ecosystem encompassing more than three hundred groups, with $100 million of expenditure, and upwards of 400,000 followers—maximal estimates to be sure.

To these clearly nonestablishment phenomena must be added several initiatives by establishment organizations to engage Jews under the age of forty. Congregations, federations, JCCs, fraternal organizations, and others have—with varying success—undertaken efforts to involve younger adult Jews directly in their operations, or to hold age-targeted events and programs comparable to the "church within a church" model long extant among Christian congregations in North America.

Two Camps: Each Diverse

Establishment and nonestablishment encompass two broad and diverse aggregates of Jewish collective enterprise. Not all establishment Jewish organizations are the same: A local Jewish federation, an Anti-Defamation League (ADL) regional chapter, and a Conservative congregation are far from identical. The same can be said for such representatives of the nonestablishment camp as an edgy Jewish film production, a Jewish social justice group, and an independent minyan. The pattern of leadership sharing, overlap, and rotation is suggestive. One would not be surprised to hear of someone occupying leadership in several establishment entities, or of a younger activist participating in many of the nonestablishment venues. People, issues, motivations, and culture vary within these two camps as well as between them. At the same time, some broad and identifiable distinctions in ethos and organizational culture divide, albeit loosely, the establishment from the nonestablishment camps. In very broad terms, establishment leaders, as a group, differ from their nonestablishment (and often younger) counterparts.

Insofar as we can speak meaningfully of the establishment and nonestablishment camps, we ask: What are the most significant differences between these two camps? How do establishment and nonestablishment leaders' hopes, fears, and objectives resemble and contrast with one another? In what ways do the two groups broadly differ in terms of their Jewish involvement, socio-demographic character, Jewish upbringing, and, most critically, their approach to Jewish life? What issues and developments in Jewish life concern, disturb, and even worry them? Where do they stand on Jewish continuity, survivalism, collective identity, Israel, in-marriage, outreach, and making Jewish life meaningful to the unengaged and uninvolved?

Scattered research over the last few years suggests some ways in which nonestablishment Jews differ from their older establishment counterparts. Younger adult Jews are more often single and without children (Cohen 2005; Cohen and Kelman 2008; Ukeles et al. 2006). In parallel with their Christian counterparts for whom singlehood is proving an obstacle to church affiliation (Wuthnow 2008), they refrain from joining congregations and other Jewish institutions. If and when younger Jews marry, more often than in the past, they marry non-Jews, and they find more of their friends among non-Jews. As a result or a corollary, they maintain fewer (or lower) social, cultural, and psychological boundaries differentiating Jews from non-Jews.

Younger Jews express less attachment to Jewish collectivity and peoplehood generally (Cohen 1998), and less attachment to Israel specifically (Cohen and Kelman 2007b; for an alternative view, see Sasson et al. 2008). They express greater readiness to fashion and refashion their social identities, including their approaches to being Jewish (Cohen and Kelman 2007a). They more often resent the explicit articulation of Jewish social and cultural expectations as judgmental (e.g., marry Jewish; donate to Jewish causes; join Jewish institutions; support the State of Israel), if not unduly coercive and exclusionary (Cohen and Kelman 2006).

Do these and related distinctions among the population at large extend to those organizing and leading entities of highly engaged Jews? And do the variations that characterize the comparisons of young(er) with old(er) Jews also extend to distinctions between nonestablishment and establishment camps?

Insofar as we uncover distinctions in attitudes, do they owe primarily to age (young vs. old) or to camp (nonestablishment vs. establishment) or to both—and for which attitudes? In other words, do nonestablishment leaders differ from establishment leaders because they are generally younger; or do younger leaders differ from older leaders primarily because the former are more often found in the nonestablishment camp? Or do both age/generation and camp (nonestablishment vs. establishment) work largely hand-in-hand to reinforce one another?

Analytic Strategy: Older Establishment vs.
Younger Nonestablishment

The analysis addresses these substantive questions by comparing older with younger leaders, as well as establishment with nonestablishment poles, along with a middle category of "mixed" for those with leadership positions in both camps or for the few leaders whose domains are not represented in either. The analysis focuses upon and repeatedly contrasts two polar opposite groups: establishment leaders who are forty-plus and nonestablishment leaders who are younger than forty.

As we will learn, both age and sector or camp (establishment vs. nonestablishment) operate in similar fashion and differentiate leaders in similar ways. Thus, of all four possible combinations (older vs. younger crossed with establishment vs. nonestablishment), the contrasts between older establishment and younger nonestablishment leaders are the most pronounced and the most illuminating.

In fact, these particular contrasts may be most indicative of the directions in which American Jewish leadership has been headed. There is no doubt that, in time, younger people are destined to supplant their elders. In like fashion, one could readily argue that nonestablishment leaders embody the future. The nonestablishment organizations are not only newer, but, as we demonstrate presently, they are more likely to have younger leaders.

The logic here, while imperfect, can be illustrated by the contrasts between the older people who now run federations (for example) and the younger people who lead independent minyanim (to take another example). These contrasts should yield provocative and indicative clues to changes in American Jewish leadership. With some caution and audaciousness, we may also deduce from them potential changes in the thinking, structure, culture, and ethos of American Jewry more generally.

The Survey, Sampling, and Data Collection

To address these and related issues, we conducted an opt-in, web-based survey of Jewish leaders, young and old, from organizations that we would eventually classify as establishment, nonestablishment, or otherwise. We distributed our survey invitations virally, sending the email to hundreds of potential respondents using lists providing by a variety of sources.

List gatekeepers are understandably reluctant to share (or, for privacy reasons, are barred from sharing) their lists with outsiders. As a result, we importuned list gatekeepers to send our email invitations to their lists. We secured cooperation from both establishment gatekeepers (e.g., the JCC Association, AJC Access, Synagogue 3000, and selected local Jewish federations) and nonestablishment gatekeepers (e.g., Encounter, independent minyanim, JDub Records, Hazon, and Jewish Jumpstart). We also received referral recommendations from our respondents and sent follow-on invitations to a small number of individuals (fewer than one hundred).

The Questionnaire

In addition to asking the usual Jewish identity profile questions, our survey explored:

Types of organizations where respondents serve as lay or professional leaders
Demographic characteristics (age, sex, education, income, region, etc.)
Patterns of Jewish upbringing (denomination, parental involvement, Jewish education)
Leadership program participation in the past
Issues and challenges in Jewish life that cause worry or concern
Commitment to a variety of objectives and missions in Jewish life
Positions on major Jewish communal policy questions

In more colloquial terms, we asked: Where do you now serve as a leader? Who are you and how were you raised? How did you become the leader you are today? What Jewish causes do you care most about? What worries or bothers you with respect to Jews, Judaism, and Jewish life? What do you think about Israel, Jewish education, Jewish philanthropy, intermarriage, and other "hot button" issues?

The Respondents

In all, 6,773 respondents completed the questionnaire. Of these, 4,466 qualified as "leaders" by their own testimony. The survey provided them a list of fifteen areas of leadership involvement: a conventional congregation, an independent minyan or similar community, a Jewish federation, a JCC, a Jewish human services agency, a Jewish day school or religious school, a Jewish social justice organization or initiative, an adult Jewish learning initiative, a Jewish cultural organization or initiative, an Israel advocacy organization, another Israel-oriented project, a group for people primarily under forty sponsored by an "established" Jewish organization, a philanthropic foundation, a national Jewish organization, and a local Jewish organization. We classified a respondent as a "leader" if in at least one such instance he or she claimed to serve as the organization's principal professional leader (e.g., chief executive officer), principal lay leader (e.g., chair), or lay leader (e.g., officer or board member).

The three other possible choices were: not involved, involved but not a leader, and a professional leader serving below the top position (i.e., CEO). After some investigation, we decided *not* to regard those citing "professional leader" as their only qualification for leadership as leaders for this chapter. Preliminary analysis we conducted demonstrated that many communal professionals lacking genuine leadership credentials might have checked the category. The preliminary analyses demonstrated further that "lay leader" served as a better and more consistent predictor of the characteristic attitudes linked with a particular area of involvement than did the "professional leader" response. Thus, if respondents were professionals below the CEO level and claimed no role as a lay leader anywhere in Jewish life, then they did not qualify as a leader for the purposes of this chapter. This restrictive definition may have excluded some respondents deserving to be included, but a more expansive definition would have included many respondents who should have been excluded.

Were the universe of Jewish communal leaders known and bounded, and if it were possible to obtain a reasonably diverse and random sampling of their email addresses, we could have relied upon more customary, and more rigorous, sampling methods. But in this case, the ambiguous and diverse world of establishment Jewish organizations—a characterization that applies even more powerfully to the nonestablishment enterprises—made the viral sampling technique the only economical and expedient choice. In fact, one purpose of the study was to determine the content and boundaries of the establishment and nonestablishment domains.

The impossibility of following more standard sampling techniques both underscores and heightens all the usual qualifications regarding the reliability of survey data and the need to carefully and cautiously interpret their implications. In all social scientific studies, especially this one, we would like to see inferences from the survey data buttressed by sound theory, side literature, and in-depth qualitative interviews with representatives of the respondent pool. Ideally, the survey findings will extend and deepen insights and inferences drawn from other sources, rather than contradict them. In the current instance, the survey data, as cautious as we need to be about them, largely find corroboration—and validation—from other sources and other contexts, including most notably the other papers in this project.

The Findings

ESTABLISHMENT VS. NONESTABLISHMENT CAMPS: DEFINING FEATURES

As noted before, we asked respondents their extent of involvement and leadership engagement in fifteen areas of Jewish collective endeavor. The distribution of responses is shown in table 2.1.

We built these two camps guided in part by the age distributions of their component organizations' leaders, in part by their patterns of overlap in leadership positions, and in part by field research pointing to the contours of the two camps. In fact, all these considerations suggested the same sorts of groupings and boundaries between the camps.

We excluded several types of organizations from the establishment/nonestablishment classification entirely. These consisted of philanthropic foundations, religious schools, adult learning initiatives, unspecified national organizations, and unspecified local organizations. These areas of engagement were not particularly distinguished either by older or younger age profiles, or by much systematic overlap with one camp or the other, or by distinctive social attitudes.

Some leaders hold leadership positions in one of the two main camps. Most of the others hold positions in both camps, and a small fraction hold leadership positions exclusively in institutions that did not fall neatly into either camp. By counting the institutional leadership positions in one camp

TABLE 2.1

Distribution of Lay, Professional, and Other Involvement with 15 Areas of Engagement

Area	Not Involved (%)	Involved, Not Leader (%)	Professional Leader (%)	Lay Leader (%)	Top Professional Leader (%)	Top Lay Leader (%)
Establishment organizations						
Congregation	23	29	6	27	10	6
Jewish Federation	55	26	5	11	2	2
A philanthropic foundation	65	18	4	8	3	3
JCC	68	21	3	5	2	1
Jewish human services agency	72	16	4	5	2	1
Israel advocacy organization	55	28	3	3	10	2
Nonestablishment organizations						
Independent minyan	64	16	1	13	2	5
Jewish social justice organization	47	30	5	12	3	
Jewish cultural organization or initiative	50	26	5	10	5	4
Other						
Jewish day school or religious school	56	18	9	10	4	2
Adult Jewish learning initiative	41	28	8	12	7	4
Another Israel-oriented project	56	25	5	8	3	3
Group for people primarily under 40	72	11	3	7	4	3
National Jewish organization	57	20	6	11	4	3
Local Jewish organization	62	18	4	10	3	3

Note: Total = 100%

TABLE 2.2
Distribution of Establishment and Nonestablishment Leaders

Leadership Classification	Number of Cases	Percentage
Establishment	1,690	38
Mixed	1,702	38
Nonestablishment	1,074	24
Total	4,466	100

or another, and by weighting more heavily the occupancy of the top lay or professional leadership positions, we assigned the vast majority of the leaders into either of these two camps (38 percent establishment and 24 percent nonestablishment, with 38 percent equally situated in both camps or neither camp but holding leadership elsewhere).

By virtue of these classificatory manipulations, the establishment classification consists of people who heavily hold leadership positions in conventional congregations (about two-thirds). About a quarter of the establishment leaders exercise leadership in federations, and smaller numbers are found leading JCCs, human service agencies, and Israel advocacy groups. Beyond these types of agencies that constitute our operational definition of "establishment," such leaders infrequently hold leadership positions in agencies that are not clearly establishment or nonestablishment, such as schools, adult learning initiatives, and miscellaneous organizations.

For its part, the nonestablishment category (Cohen and Kelman 2007a) consists of leaders in independent minyanim (see Cohen et al. 2007; Kaunfer 2010), as well as of cultural initiatives (Cohen and Kelman 2006) and social justice groups (Bronznick and Goldenhar 2008). A very small number of nonestablishment leaders are found leading "pro-Israel, pro-peace" groups.

Older Establishment and Younger Nonestablishment Leaders

The shift both over time and generationally from establishment to nonestablishment organizations emerges quite clearly in the age contours associated with each camp. Older leaders are heavily establishment, while younger leaders are heavily nonestablishment. Similarly, establishment leaders are older, and nonestablishment leaders are much younger. Those in the mixed category are neither much older nor much younger than the average respondents in this leadership sample. As shown in table 2.6, among those in their sixties, 50 percent are establishment, and 14 percent are nonestablishment.

TABLE 2.3
Areas of Involvement among Leaders

Establishment Organizations	Non-establishment		Mixed		Establishment	
	Young (%)	Old (%)	Young (%)	Old (%)	Young (%)	Old (%)
Conventional congregation	0	0	32	50	66	74
Federation	0	0	15	19	22	21
JCC	0	0	10	11	8	12
Human service agency	0	0	11	13	7	10
Israel advocacy	0	0	11	16	12	11

TABLE 2.4
Areas of Involvement among Leaders

Nonestablishment Organizations	Non-establishment		Mixed		Establishment	
	Young (%)	Old (%)	Young (%)	Old (%)	Young (%)	Old (%)
Independent minyan	48	46	21	22	0	0
Social justice	39	24	29	29	0	0
Jewish cultural initiative	30	37	31	29	0	0
Pro-peace	8	7	4	7	0	0

Among those in their twenties, the proportions are almost reversed: just 13 percent establishment and 48 percent nonestablishment.

Correlatively, among establishment leaders, 62 percent are fifty and older and just 19 percent are under forty. For the nonestablishments, we find respective figures of 29 percent and 56 percent—essentially the reverse. The mixed group's age profile is situated midway between the older establishment leaders and the younger nonestablishment leaders. Accordingly, we find significant numbers of leaders, both older (forty-plus) and younger (under forty), among all three sectors: nonestablishment (417 older, 537 younger), mixed (944, 522), and establishment (1191, 282).

TABLE 2.5
Areas of Involvement among Leaders

Mixed Organizations	Non-establishment		Mixed		Establishment	
	Young (%)	Old (%)	Young (%)	Old (%)	Young (%)	Old (%)
Philanthropic foundation	8	9	16	19	7	12
Other Israel-oriented	5	2	17	16	13	10
Jewish day school/religious school	8	14	15	25	20	16
Group for those under 40	21	10	38	8	28	3
National organization	12	14	18	26	12	16
Local organization	15	15	22	22	13	12
Adult Jewish learning	23	24	27	34	13	17

TABLE 2.6
Leadership Sector by Age

Age	Leadership Sector		
	Establishment (%)	Mixed (%)	Nonestablishment (%)
60+	50	36	14
50–59	48	38	15
40–49	41	38	22
30–39	27	39	34
29 and under	13	39	48

Note: Total = 100%

Establishment More Male and Nonestablishment More Female

Beyond age variations, the two camps exhibit quite different demographic profiles in other ways. Both age (being young) and camp (being nonestablishment) are associated with the greater presence of women. Younger nonestablishment leaders are mostly women (very much so: 65 percent), while older establishment leaders are mostly men (56 percent). Gender distributions for all other groups tilt toward women as well. In short, the transitions

TABLE 2.7
Age by Leadership Sector

	Leadership Sector		
Age	Nonestablishment (%)	Mixed (%)	Establishment (%)
60+	29	21	13
50–59	33	26	16
40–49	19	17	15
30–39	14	20	28
29 and under	5	15	29

Note: Total = 100%

from establishment to nonestablishment and from older to younger leaders are associated with a growing presence of women and diminished presence of men. Whether the mobilization of women, or the relative departure of men from Jewish life, underlies these shifts remains to be explored and clarified.

That said, several explanations for the over-time and over-camp shift toward women leaders come to mind. Among them are the Jewish feminist movement that advanced women's participation in Jewish communal and religious life; the ordination of women rabbis that endowed women with the skills, connections, and credentials to lead; and the acculturation of Judaism to American religious patterns according to which women consistently participate in religious life more than men. A related factor is that relatively few of the younger nonestablishment leaders are married (50 percent), as contrasted with the vast majority (90 percent) of older establishment leaders. Among the nonmarried, women participate in a variety of Jewish contexts more than men, with marriage seeming to boost male participation in Jewish life more than it does for women.

Clearly, the gender shift noted here lends itself to several explanations— all of which touch upon larger issues in contemporary Jewish life.

As might be expected, older leaders report higher incomes than younger leaders, while establishment leaders report higher incomes than nonestablishment leaders in the same age group, with mixed leaders falling between the two main camps in income. Accordingly, large income gaps separate older establishment leaders from younger nonestablishment leaders.

Finally, several cities show notable concentrations of leaders who are younger and more nonestablishment. Most prominent among these are New York, Boston, San Francisco, and Los Angeles. Likewise, these areas report

TABLE 2.8
*Selected Demographic Characteristics for Nonestablishment and
Establishment Leaders*

	Non-establishment		Mixed		Establishment	
	Young	Old	Young	Old	Young	Old
Gender						
Male	35	44	37	50	46	56
Female	65	56	63	50	55	44
Marital status						
Married (%)	50	82	56	87	75	90
Annual income (%)						
>$100K	12	36	14	49	27	56
$60–$99K	21	33	27	23	33	24
<$60K	67	31	60	28	40	20
Residence (%)						
New York	32	20	28	19	21	16
Boston	12	10	8	5	4	3
San Francisco	6	4	5	3	6	3
Los Angeles	6	6	6	6	4	4
Outside major Jewish population areas	37	49	46	57	56	61

relatively fewer leaders who are older and establishment oriented. Outside the major U.S. areas of Jewish population, leaders are more often older, and more often establishment rather than nonestablishment.

Shifting Identities: A New Generation Moves toward the Nonestablishment Camp

Shifts in denominational identity from childhood to the present—and how they vary among establishment and nonestablishment leaders—tell us not only about the origins of leaders in both camps; they also tell us about their varying sensibilities and identity preferences. We find that, for all camps of leaders, Conservative is the most frequent childhood denomination, followed by Reform and Orthodoxy.

Although nonestablishment and establishment leaders, both old and young, share fairly similar distributions of denominational identities in their childhood years, they adopt very different denominational choices in their adult years. In comparing childhood with current patterns of identity, establishment Jews maintain or move toward Conservatism and the younger nonestablishment leaders toward Orthodoxy, albeit with a slight growth as well in "postdenominational" identity. At the same time, they move away from Reform.

Relative to their patterns in childhood, nonestablishment leaders identify far less often as Conservative or Reform and much more often as postdenominational or with other nondenominational identities. While the independent minyan movement has been seen as competitive with Conservative identity, the results here show that leadership in a nonestablishment organization is highly incompatible with a Reform identity: among younger nonestablishment leaders, two thirds of those raised Reform shift to another identity as adults.

While 91 percent of the older establishment leaders identify with a denomination, about half that number (45 percent) of the younger nonestablishment leaders so identify. For the older establishment leaders, denominational identity is a prevalent, if not necessary, social location. For the younger nonestablishments, it is an option but clearly not compelling.

As Christian religious and denominational identities are more fluid and transitory than in the past (Pew Religious Landscape Survey 2008; 2009), it

TABLE 2.9

Denominations in Which Respondents Were Raised

	Non-establishment		Mixed		Establishment	
	Young (%)	Old (%)	Young (%)	Old (%)	Young (%)	Old (%)
Orthodox	11	13	9	13	12	14
Conservative	46	42	41	49	44	49
Reform	27	25	27	21	28	22
Reconstructionist	2	1	3	1	0	1
Post-denominational	2	1	3	0	2	0
Other Jewish	10	15	13	12	10	11
Not Jewish	2	4	4	4	5	4

Note: Total = 100%

TABLE 2.10
Denominational Identities Now

	Non-establishment		Mixed		Establishment	
	Young (%)	Old (%)	Young (%)	Old (%)	Young (%)	Old (%)
Orthodox	9	11	15	10	20	10
Conservative	21	30	29	44	40	53
Reform	9	10	17	20	19	23
Reconstructionist	6	10	4	6	5	5
Post-denominational	35	23	18	13	6	5
Other Jewish	20	16	17	7	10	3.8

Note: Total = 100%

is no surprise to see evidence of a similar transition in the contrasts between the older establishment leaders, on the one hand, and their younger non-establishment counterparts, on the other.

Younger Leaders: More Jewishly Socialized and Educated

In moving from older to younger leaders, we note perceptible increases in Jewish socialization and education in the childhood and adolescent years. As children, younger leaders attended religious service more often—as did their parents—and experienced other forms of parental religious involvement. In addition, we largely find growth among the younger leaders (of all camps) with respect to such Jewish educational experiences as day school, camp, youth groups, and Hillel.

At the same time, in contrast with the age-related patterns for socialization and education, we find that social segregation from non-Jews (a standard barometer in the assessment of group cohesiveness and distinctiveness) operates in the other direction. However we measure close ties with Jews and non-Jews, the young nonestablishment leaders are more integrated/less segregated than older establishment leaders. The differences can be small, but they all fall in the same direction. As we move from older to younger, from establishment to nonestablishment, we find reports of more non-Jewish parents, high school friends, and romantic partners.

In the Jewish population at large, those who are more socially segregated also report higher levels of childhood socialization with other Jews and Jewish educational experiences. Here, perhaps paradoxically, younger leaders, in comparison with their elders, report higher socialization and education but lower levels of social segregation. As we shall see, the greater integration (i.e., number of non-Jewish intimates) of younger leaders and of nonestablishment leaders comports with age-related and camp-related variations in attitudes toward various aspects of Jewish collectivity.

A long line of research on the larger population of American Jews finds that parents, socialization, and the various instruments of Jewish education all operate to produce higher levels of Jewish identity outcomes in adulthood. More engaged parents are indeed more likely to provide their children with more intensive and extensive forms of Jewish education. But the independent statistical impact of education, net of their parental background characteristics, is quite apparent and significant. By definition, all these respondents are "leaders," so we are unable to analyze the impact of childhood experiences upon the likelihood of becoming a leader. But the high levels of parental engagement and Jewish educational experiences observed here are consistent with the general finding observed elsewhere: parents and Jewish educational experiences operate jointly to elevate Jewish engagement in adulthood.

We combined several Jewish educational experiences into an overall index ranging from "very high" to "low." The contrasts between younger nonestablishment leaders and older establishment leaders are most striking. Among the former, the balance between very high and low levels stands at 31 percent versus 17 percent. For the older establishment leaders, meanwhile, the numbers are basically reversed: 10 percent very high versus 38 percent low. By any measure, the extent of Jewish educational experience grows from older to younger (younger establishment leaders also report high levels of Jewish education).

Several observations may be drawn from these patterns:

1. Educational enrollment has significantly expanded among American Jews over the years.
2. Jewish education, in all its varieties, became both more of a conduit to and a functional prerequisite for attaining and assuming Jewish leadership.
3. Younger Jewish leaders are indeed more Jewishly educated than their elders, setting higher standards for leadership and producing a Jewish leadership culture and ethos that may further set it apart from the more poorly educated Jewish rank-and-file.

TABLE 2.11

Jewish Socialization, Education, and Integration for Establishment and Nonestablishment Leaders

Jewish Socialization	Non-establishment		Mixed		Establishment	
	Young	Old	Young	Old	Young	Old
Attended services > twice a month						
Mother	36	25	31	27	38	23
Father	35	30	34	32	38	29
Self	42	39	37	42	44	36
Judaism at home						
Parents were communal professionals	24	10	20	11	20	6
Parent active in Jewish life	63	56	61	60	64	55
Lit Shabbat candles	67	63	64	67	66	61
Jewish Education						
Day school	40	21	34	21	38	17
Jewish youth group	69	71	67	71	72	68
Jewish camp	71	68	70	65	71	57
Hillel	80	51	72	52	74	46
Worked as Jewish educator	70	67	69	61	65	46
Social integration						
Both parents Jewish	89	95	89	94	89	95
High school friends mostly Jewish	52	68	52	69	52	70
Romance with a non-Jew	70	67	68	59	57	58

Leadership Programs Produce Leaders, Especially among the Young

The last two decades have seen growing numbers of leadership development programs, significantly augmenting the handful extant in prior years. Some are explicitly labeled or characterized as leadership programs. The

TABLE 2.12
Level of Jewish Educational Experiences

Level	Non-establishment Young (%)	Old (%)	Mixed Young (%)	Old (%)	Establishment Young (%)	Old (%)
Very high	31	13	25	15	28	10
High	32	30	32	28	33	28
Moderate	20	28	20	26	20	24
Low	17	29	23	31	19	38

Note: Including day school, camp, youth group, Hillel, Jewish studies, Israel, etc.
Total = 100%

Wexner programs come to mind, as do Joshua Ventures, Dorot, Bronfman, and Mandel fellowships—to name just a few (apologies to all the others!). Programs with an implicit leadership-development impact consist of intensive Jewish learning (Pardes, Limmud). Yet others are more experiential (Birthright for the "masses," and American Jewish World Service [AJWS] fellowships or Encounter for far more selective constituencies). Taken together, the programs represent a significant investment on the part of philanthropists and Jewish communal agencies. One wonders, is the investment paying off?

The findings certainly point in that direction. Younger leaders report these experiences far more than their elders. For example, the number of leadership development experiences doubles as we move from establishment leaders over forty (an average of 1) to nonestablishment leaders in their twenties and thirties (an average of 2.2). Participation in these programs is far more a matter of age than of sector, but nonestablishment leaders participated in such programs more than nonleader counterparts their age, with the mixed sector reporting intermediate levels of participation.

Apparently, the growing number of leadership development programs is having an impact on the pool of Jewish leaders. These programs not only impart skills, knowledge, and motivation. They also inaugurate their participants into networks of social ties among the "leadership class, networks that are reinforced for the most involved by repeated leadership experiences where they engage with circles that overlap with those they have encoun-

TABLE 2.13
Average Number of Leadership Programs Experienced

Younger nonestablished	2.2
Older nonestablished	1.1
Younger mixed	1.9
Older mixed	1.3
Younger established	1.6
Older established	1.0

tered before" (see the chapter in this volume by Shaul Kelner). (Not coincidentally, the three thirtysomething scholars in this project have all engaged in multiple Jewish leadership development experiences, including Reboot and the Wexner Graduate Fellowship Program.)

We find similar age-linked patterns with respect to long-term study (or work) in Israel. Almost *all* Jewish leaders, young or old, nonestablishment or establishment, have spent time in Israel (92 to 96 percent), about two-and-a-half times the average for all American Jews. Birthright Israel contributed to Israel visits, although its presence is limited to those under forty in all three sectors (15 percent of the establishment younger leaders, 22 percent of the mixed, and 21 percent of the nonestablishment leaders under forty). This makes sense given that Birthright was founded in the 1990s.

More remarkable still is the large number of leaders who have spent time in an Israel-based program lasting four months or more. Studying at a university or in a yeshiva is an option, but numerous other programs exist as well. About 56 percent of younger Jewish leaders, from all camps, have participated in such long-term programs. By comparison, about half as many older establishment leaders (30 percent) have spent as much time in Israel on a single visit.

When coupled with the findings on socialization and education, those on leadership program participation and Israel-based study all point to a more culturally proficient leadership among younger adults, be they establishment, nonestablishment, or mixed. In the 1970s, young activists in Jewish life (who constitute many of today's baby boomer Jewish leaders) bemoaned what they saw as relatively low levels of Jewish knowledge and erudition among the establishment leaders of their time. If the results here are any indication, opportunities for Jewish education, both formal and informal, have widened steadily in the intervening decades, along with far broader and higher levels of participation in leadership development experiences by a more Judaically proficient and better-connected leadership.

TABLE 2.14
Study- or Work-Related Trips to Israel

	At Least 1 Trip of >4 Months (%)	At Least 1 Trip of <4 Months (%)	Never Visited (%)
Younger nonestablished	56	40	4
Older nonestablished	46	46	8
Younger mixed	56	38	6
Older mixed	42	53	6
Younger established	55	37	8
Older established	30	62	8

Note: Total = 100%

Strong Sense of Belonging by All

While younger American Jews in general may be less connected to people-hood and community (Cohen and Wertheimer 2006), younger leaders are by definition unlike the Jewish public or rank-and-file from which they have emerged. By their very nature, they are a selective group, such that patterns observed in the general population may not extend to those highly involved in Jewish life. Indeed, when we asked about respondents' ties to the Jewish people and the Jewish community, all four groups—young or old, nonestablishment, mixed, and establishment—provided fairly similar answers. All frequently claimed to feel a strong sense of belonging to the Jewish people and to feel part of the Jewish community. That said, the older establishment leaders did outpace the younger nonestablishment leaders on the questions on belonging to the Jewish people and feeling part of the Jewish community.

However, feelings of attachment do not always translate into normative commitment. Although expressed feelings of attachment may characterize all leadership groups, younger nonestablishment leaders are far less likely than the others to strongly agree that they "have a responsibility to take care of Jews in need around the world." In general, younger people within each sector feel less of a responsibility to Jews globally, consistent with similar characterizations of American Jewish young people on the whole (Cohen and Wertheimer 2006). As we shall see, several other differences separate the young nonestablishment leaders at one extreme from the older establishment leaders at the other.

TABLE 2.15

Percentage Who "Strongly Agree" with Selected Issues Related to Jewish Collective Identity

	Non-establishment		Mixed		Establishment	
	Young	Old	Young	Old	Young	Old
I have a strong sense of belonging to the Jewish People	73	80	77	86	75	83
Feel part of the Jewish community	64	70	71	79	73	78
Have responsibility to take care of Jews in need around the world	33	48	47	57	49	51

Continuity: Less Concern among the Younger Nonestablishment Leaders

The 1990 National Jewish Population Survey (Kosmin et al. 1991), with its finding of a high intermarriage rate (first reported at 52 percent and later revised to 43 percent), produced a surge of anxiety and a flurry of communal activity marked by the emergence of a new phrase in the communal lexicon: Jewish continuity. Scores of "Jewish continuity" commissions sprang up in the federation world and elsewhere in response to the perceived demographic threat to the very future of a large American Jewish population and, by extension, to the cultural vitality of the community. Leaders at the time largely agreed that intermarriage signified the weakening of communal bonds and Jewish community. Some saw its rise as portending further erosion of Jewish connection and Jewish commitment.

Our survey asked, "To what extent are you personally worried or bothered by each of the following issues, challenges, or problems in Jewish life?" The option "very worried/bothered" was the bleakest response. One cluster of questions revolved around the classic issues in the continuity discourse: ignorance and apathy among the young, high intermarriage, low birthrates, and distancing from Israel. On *all* these items, fewer young nonestablishment leaders expressed worries than older establishment leaders. More than twice as many of the older establishment leaders were very worried by intermarriage; twice as many were worried by distancing from Israel; and twice

TABLE 2.16

Percentage "Very Worried/Bothered" by Selected Continuity-Related Issues

	Non-establishment		Mixed		Establishment	
	Young	Old	Young	Old	Young	Old
Jewish ignorance/lack of Jewish education	40	52	48	60	49	59
Young Jews not interested in Jewish life	33	45	49	61	56	65
High intermarriage	17	25	29	38	35	43
Low Jewish birthrates (very + somewhat)	5	12	10	15	13	15
Distancing from Israel	15	30	25	43	34	39

as many were at least somewhat worried by low Jewish birthrates. Conversely, more than twice as many younger nonestablishment leaders as older establishment leaders expressed no concern about low Jewish birthrates.

Clearly, the various components of the Jewish continuity concern are the province of older leaders, particularly establishment leaders. The notion that leaders should worry about whether Jews will continue as such in large number seems uninteresting if not alienating to many younger nonestablishment leaders.

Do Paranoids Have Enemies? Contrasting Reactions to
External Threat

Older establishment leaders express keen sensitivity to antisemitism (in the United States and more so in Europe) and even greater concern regarding threats to Israel's security and, in particular, critics of Israel's right to exist as a Jewish state. On all these interrelated questions, the nonestablishment leaders are less disturbed than the establishment leaders, and the young are less worried than the old. To take the question on "threats to Israel's security" as a useful bellwether in this domain: as many as 59 percent of the older establishment leaders are very worried, as are 43 percent of their younger counterparts, 39 percent of the older nonestablishments, and just 23 percent of the younger nonestablishment leaders. Reactions to other embodiments of external threats to Jews and Israel follow a similar contour. In short, the percentage of those who are very worried about threats to Israel's security is

TABLE 2.17
Establishment Leaders Worried about Security Threats

	Non-establishment		Mixed		Establishment	
	Young (%)	Old (%)	Young (%)	Old (%)	Young (%)	Old (%)
Threats to Israel's security	23	39	39	56	43	59
Critics of Israel's right to exist as a Jewish state	24	41	38	53	45	57
U.S. antisemitism	9	14	13	19	19	19
Antisemitism in Europe	13	28	21	34	24	33
Remembering the Holocaust	23	36	35	45	39	45
Fighting antisemitism	23	32	38	45	49	49

almost three times as great among older establishment leaders as among younger nonestablishment leaders. This gap between the two groups compares to that regarding worries over critics of Israel's right to exist as a Jewish state, and is almost as large with respect to concerns about antisemitism, be it in the United States or Europe.

For the older establishment, then, the world is still a very dangerous place, with real enemies who would do harm to Jews and to Israel. While some young nonestablishment leaders might agree, far fewer are as easily provoked or mobilized by threat—perhaps because they see less threat, or perhaps because they feel less attached to Israel.

Quite possibly, chronological distance from the Holocaust constitutes part of the explanation for a diminished sense of threat and vulnerability, as does a greater sense of full acceptance in American society; but other factors are no doubt at work as well, such as possibly less widespread personal experience with antisemitism.

The "System"—and Its Older Establishment Custodians

We asked respondents to examine a list of activities and to report on which represent their main work in Jewish life. For those items that were not their main work, we asked leaders to evaluate the importance of the objectives they embodied. Two answers, then, reflect a high valuation of a particular mission: one in which the leader him or herself claimed personal engagement and, absent that, one in which the respondent saw the work as very important.

Several of these questions reflect a high valuation of the "system"—the organized Jewish community in which establishment leaders invest their volunteer and professional energies. These particular survey questions are as follows:

· Supporting the organized Jewish community;
· Providing or raising philanthropic support for Jewish life;
· Making Israel engaging for American Jews, defending Israel against unfriendly critics;
· Encouraging Jews to in-marry;
· Providing Jewish education for children and teens; and
· Providing social services for Jews in need.

These half-dozen objectives correspond to the overall missions of the various types of organizations headed by establishment leaders (e.g., federations, congregations, JCCs, Israel advocacy organizations, and human services agencies).

Not surprisingly, older establishment leaders react very positively to these objectives; in contrast, younger nonestablishment leaders are far more unmoved. To take one telling example—supporting the organized Jewish community—we find predictable contrasts. As many as 65 percent of the older establishment leaders value this area highly as compared with just 20 percent of the younger nonestablishment leaders.

To older establishment leaders, the system of agencies constructed by their parents' generation (and those before), and sustained and expanded by them, is self-justifying. These institutions' histories of good deeds and good community endow them with evident legitimacy and value. For the younger nonestablishments, the value of these agencies is far from self-evident; their objectives are not immediately compelling or mobilizing.

Universalist Charitable Giving among Younger and Nonestablishment Leaders

Patterns of charitable giving offer a window onto larger issues. We asked respondents about the extent to which they devote their charitable giving to Jewish causes, and the extent to which their giving to Jewish agencies eventually goes to benefit non-Jews (the American Jewish World Service may be the most prominent example of a so-called universalist cause with Jewish sponsorship).

TABLE 2.18

Percentage Who Find Community-Related Objectives Very Important

	Non-establishment		Mixed		Establishment	
	Young	Old	Young	Old	Young	Old
Support the organized Jewish community	20	40	45	60	57	65
Philanthropic support for Jewish causes	26	39	41	60	47	53
Engaging the unaffiliated	40	49	53	56	55	57
Making Israel engaging for American Jews	31	42	47	61	51	56
Jewish education for children and teens	48	59	57	71	69	76
Social services for Jews in need	25	40	35	50	45	52

By assigning numerical values to the answer categories, we were able to directly estimate the proportion of respondents' charitable giving that is devoted to Jewish causes and to universalist causes, albeit Jewishly sponsored. The difference (see third column in table 2.19, following) represents the proportion of total charitable giving to Jewish causes whose beneficiaries are primarily Jewish.

The results point to remarkably consistent patterns in which age (older vs. younger) and leadership camp (established vs. mixed vs. nonestablished) operate in parallel directions. The comparisons between older established and younger nonestablished leaders are most instructive. The former give more of their charity to Jewish causes, and the latter, when they give to Jewish causes, give more to those benefiting primarily non-Jews. Among older establishment leaders, giving to Jewish causes to benefit Jews equals 60 percent of total giving; for the younger nonestablishment leaders, it comes to half that amount—just 30 percent. A closer inspection of the figures for older and younger, and for established, mixed, and nonestablished camps, shows that both age and camp influence the universalist/particularist mix of giving.

These patterns speak not only to charitable giving but also to larger visions of Jewish life. For younger people, and for those associated with the nonestablishment camp—be they leaders or the rank and file—the more

TABLE 2.19

Giving to Jewish Charities, for Universalist Purposes and to Benefit Jews in Need

	Jewish Causes (%)	Universalist Causes with Jewish Sponsorship (%)	Percent of Charity to Jewish Causes for Jews
Younger nonestablished	56	29	30
Older nonestablished	66	23	44
Younger mixed	64	22	44
Older mixed	77	21	57
Younger established	71	18	54
Older established	77	17	60

compelling features of Jewish life are those that cross the boundaries between Jews and non-Jews, between the Jewish community and the larger world.

Alienation of the Nonestablishment

At the heart of many innovations and change efforts is a sense of dissatisfaction with the current reality or available options. It comes as no surprise, therefore, that younger nonestablishment leaders express more dissatisfaction with synagogues, federations, and the organized system than do older establishment leaders. They are more than twice as likely as older establishment leaders to agree that "most synagogues fail to provide a sense of real meaning and purpose" (58 percent vs. 39 percent) and to have similar views of federations (46 percent vs. 35 percent).

Of interest is that these more critical attitudes are more a function of sector (nonestablishment vs. establishment) than of age. In other words, insofar as young people are more critical of the current establishment, either their views reflect their involvement in nonestablishment activities or (more likely) they have gravitated to the nonestablishment sector owing in part to dissatisfaction with prevailing options in establishment life.

Younger Nonestablishment Leaders Are "Out" on In-Marriage

Consistent with their relative lack of concern for Jewish continuity per se, younger nonestablishment leaders differ from other Jewish leaders in their far greater acceptance of mixed marriage. In fact, they part company not only from older establishment leaders but also from older nonestablishment leaders (i.e., those who share their leadership camp) and from younger es-

TABLE 2.20

Alienation from Organized Jewish Life

	Non-establishment		Mixed		Establishment	
	Young (%)	Old (%)	Young (%)	Old (%)	Young (%)	Old (%)
Synagogue fails to provide meaning	58	50	49	45	35	39
Federation lacks real meaning	46	41	40	39	35	35

tablishment leaders (who share their age cohort). In short, younger non-establishment leaders are especially accepting of mixed marriage—their youthfulness and their association with the nonestablishment ethos combine to exert similar effects on these attitudes.

The responses to several questions related to in-marriage and mixed marriage point in the same direction. One is especially noteworthy. We asked respondents if they agreed that "Jews should marry whoever they fall in love with even if they're not Jewish." By disagreeing, a respondent indicates support for the conventional position against intermarriage. Just under a quarter (24 percent) of the younger nonestablishment leaders disagreed with the proposition, in contrast with almost twice as many (46 percent) among older establishment leaders. In like fashion, the younger nonestablishment leaders were least likely to consider encouraging Jews to marry Jews important (18 percent). In sharp contrast are the older establishment leaders, where far more (48 percent) see encouraging in-marriage as an important communal or personal objective.

The variations in attitudes toward intermarriage are not at all attributable to variations in intermarriage among the leaders. Overall, of those married, 94 percent are in-married. In-marriage rates are ever so slightly higher among the establishment leaders, but young-old variations by sector hardly mirror the national pattern for the rank and file. Even younger Jewish leaders are drawn almost exclusively from the in-married. For example, 93 percent of younger nonestablishment leaders are in-married as compared with 96 percent of their establishment-age peers.

The older establishment leaders tend to view intermarriage as a threat to Jewish life and as a violation of long-standing communal norms. The younger nonestablishment leaders see intermarriage as an obstacle to Jewish

TABLE 2.21
Attitudes Related to Intermarriage

	Non-establishment		Mixed		Establishment	
	Young (%)	Old (%)	Young (%)	Old (%)	Young (%)	Old (%)
Jews should marry whomever they fall in love with, even if not Jewish (DS + D)	24	33	39	45	47	46
Upset if my child were to marry a non-Jew who didn't convert (AS + A)	50	61	62	69	68	71
Important to encourage Jews to marry Jews	18	27	36	44	41	48

Note: AS = Agree strongly; A = Agree; D = Disagree; DS = Disagree strongly; entries are reported so as to indicate pro-in-marriage attitudes

involvement, but one that can be overcome with genuine commitment and involvement. Moreover, they are less inclined to believe that Judaism or the Jewish community is legitimately entitled to sanction personal choices such as marriage.

Previous research has pointed to the declining commitment to in-marriage among the American Jewish public, but it has generally suggested that the leadership remained committed to endogamy. These results suggest sharp erosion in sentiment supportive of in-marriage, as the young inevitably replace the old and the establishment ethos appears to give way to that embodied in the newly emergent groups in the nonestablishment sector.

Distancing from Israel among the Young, Especially Nonestablishment Leaders

Younger leaders are less attached to Israel than their older counterparts, a finding that largely recapitulates data from the study of the population at large (Cohen and Kelman 2007b). This straightforward inference rests on the responses to two pertinent questions. One asked for reactions to the

TABLE 2.22

Israel Attachment among Nonestablishment and Establishment Leaders

	Non-establishment		Mixed		Establishment	
	Young (%)	Old (%)	Young (%)	Old (%)	Young (%)	Old (%)
Caring about Israel a very important part of my being a Jew (AS)	32	52	48	64	51	56
Very emotionally attached to Israel	56	64	64	78	64	70

Note: AS = Agree strongly

statement "Caring about Israel is a very important part of my being a Jew." The other asked, "How emotionally attached are you to Israel?" The patterns for the four leadership groups are roughly the same for both questions.

Left-Right Gaps on Israeli Policies and Advocacy

Set against the modest gaps between nonestablishment and establishment leaders in their attachment to Israel, with age held constant, are variations far more pronounced with respect to policy-related issues and advocacy on behalf of Israel. Younger nonestablishment leaders and older establishment leaders offer dramatic contrasts with respect to the importance of defending Israel, freezing settlement expansion, and Israel advocacy groups versus pro-Israel, pro-peace organizations.

Thus, while 53 percent of older establishment leaders think it important to defend Israel against unfriendly critics, just 18 percent of the younger nonestablishment leaders think likewise. A very large majority of nonestablishment leaders support a settlement freeze (77 percent among the young), in contrast with about an even division among the establishment leaders, be they old or young. Just about 20 percent of establishment figures are "bothered" by Israel's treatment of the Palestinians, in contrast with more than twice as many among the nonestablishment leaders, both old and young. The nonestablishments feel more warmly toward so-called pro-Israel, pro-peace groups than do establishment or mixed leaders. As might be expected, views

TABLE 2.23

Israel-Related Policy Positions

	Non-establishment		Mixed		Establishment	
	Young (%)	Old (%)	Young (%)	Old (%)	Young (%)	Old (%)
Important to defend Israel against un-friendly critics (A)	18	29	35	51	39	53
Bothered by Israel's treatment of Pales-tinians (A)	48	47	28	29	21	20
Israel should freeze settlements (A)	77	74	58	61	45	55
Pro-Israel/pro-peace groups injure image of Israel (D)	7	10	12	16	20	16
Israel advocacy groups injure chances of engaging young Jews with Israel (D)	34	21	21	15	13	11

Note: A = Agree; D = Disagree

are reversed with respect to whether Israel advocacy groups are injuring "the chances of engaging younger Jews with Israel." Just 11 percent of older establishment leaders agree with this view, in contrast with three times as many among the younger nonestablishment leaders.

The differences on these policy issues are not so much attributable to age (which exerts a small effect) as to camp, according to which the non-establishment leaders are more "dovish" and the establishment leaders more "hawkish" on Israeli policy and on the preferred nature of Israel advocacy in America. The presence of leaders of pro-Israel, pro-peace groups in the nonestablishment camp is hardly a factor, given that these leaders constitute such a tiny proportion of the nonestablishment camp. Rather, as we demonstrate, the two camps are divided politically, with the nonestablishment leaders leaning left and the establishment leaders closer to the political center (or left-of-center).

Left-Center Gap on Worldviews

American Jews have long been situated on the center-left of the political spectrum, with a possibly exaggerated reputation for liberalism owing in large part to their firm support for the Democratic Party (Cohen and Liebman 1997). Jews, especially non-Orthodox Jews, have voted in lopsided proportions for Democratic presidential candidates. And even as Jews have figured prominently in the funding of both major parties, they have supported Democrats far more often than Republicans. With all this said, detailed analysis of public opinion surveys demonstrates that Jews are not all that liberal on many issues, especially taking into account their education levels and regional distribution, but they do, indeed, identify politically as very liberal (Cohen and Liebman 1997; Cohen and Abrams 2008). That is, they identify with the Democrats and other groups in the liberal camp to an extent surpassing their liberalism on the issues.

Three factors, though, diminish Jews' liberal political identity: Orthodoxy, significant wealth, and intermarriage. In comparing nonestablishment leaders with establishment leaders, neither Orthodoxy nor intermarriage has much effect on political leanings. Few are Orthodox in either camp and even fewer are mixed married. Obviously, though, establishment leaders are far wealthier.

For all these reasons, it comes as no surprise to find hardly any Republicans among nonestablishment leaders, and a small number (about 10 percent) among establishment leaders. Conversely, with more than 80 percent of the nonestablishment leaders identifying as Democrats, somewhat fewer are found in establishment circles. Sharper differences, though, emerge with respect to political ideology. While hardly any nonestablishment leaders (less than 5 percent) call themselves conservative (politically), nearly twice as

TABLE 2.24
Political Orientation

	Non-establishment		Mixed		Establishment	
	Young (%)	Old (%)	Young (%)	Old (%)	Young (%)	Old (%)
Democrats	84	82	75	77	72	72
Liberals	83	75	68	61	56	54

many of the establishment leaders so identify. And while over three quarters of the nonestablishment see themselves as liberal, just over half the establishment leaders describe themselves as having liberal views. Liberal political identity is slightly a function of youthfulness, but very much a function of organizational camp, with the nonestablishment the most liberal, the establishment the least liberal, and the mixed camp situated between the two poles.

Jewish Progressives in the Nonestablishment

Accordingly, the three camps are arrayed as might be anticipated with respect to Jewishly connected social causes. Nonestablishment leaders score higher on socially progressive attitudes than do establishment leaders, with only minor or nonuniform variations between older and younger. This generalization extends to such items as the importance of Jews working for social justice causes to Jewish environmentalism to gender equality. For example, just 39 percent of older establishment leaders think it important for Jews to work for social justice causes, while the figure for younger nonestablishment leaders reaches 64 percent. The more pronounced left-liberal tendencies among nonestablishment leaders, both young and old, then, find expression in their sympathies for progressive causes.

Similarities in Many Other Areas

The foregoing text has highlighted the major points of variation between nonestablishment and establishment leaders, and especially between younger

TABLE 2.25
Social and Cultural Issues

	Non-establishment		Mixed		Establishment	
	Young (%)	Old (%)	Young (%)	Old (%)	Young (%)	Old (%)
Jewish environmentalism	30	33	29	28	21	20
Gender equality and women's leadership in Jewish life	47	47	41	44	34	37

TABLE 2.26
Importance of Selected Objectives in Jewish Life

	Non-establishment		Mixed		Establishment	
	Young (%)	Old (%)	Young (%)	Old (%)	Young (%)	Old (%)
More welcoming, inclusive	83	73	79	78	75	78
Text learning and Torah study for adults	41	53	46	56	52	52
Engaging prayer	50	52	46	57	53	60
Jewish spirituality	45	57	47	58	50	55
High-quality culture	52	57	57	55	46	49

Note: Percentage who say "best describes" their main work + those who say the objective is very important

nonestablishment leaders and older establishment leaders. But these differences ought not to obscure many areas where their differences range from small to nonexistent. Among those areas they value nearly equally are:

Helping Jews find real meaning in being Jewish
Promoting a more welcoming, inclusive, and diverse community
Text-learning and Torah study
Engaging prayer and worship services
Jewish spirituality
High-quality cultural experiences

All of these items are near-consensus matters earning majority to almost-unanimous endorsement by Jewish leaders.

Conclusion

The analysis in this chapter demonstrates that younger leaders do, in fact, differ from their older counterparts, and that the nonestablishment initiatives in which many of them are involved differ likewise from those of the establishment organizations, which are more characteristic of middle-age and older Jews. All these trends are interrelated and mutually supportive. Older leaders more often head establishment organizations, and younger leaders tend toward the nonestablishment camp. The differences between older and younger Jews (be they establishment or nonestablishment in involvement) resemble the differences between establishment and nonestablishment leaders (be they older or younger). In fact, on the many attitudinal dimensions on which we found differences by age and by organizational camp (i.e., established, mixed, and nonestablished), the polar positions were occupied by older establishment leaders on the one hand and younger nonestablishment leaders on the other.

To recall, the numerous attitudes on which these sorts of differences emerged included the following:

Commitment to Jewish peoplehood
Concern for Jewish demographic continuity
Fears for the security of Israel and regarding antisemitism more generally
Devotion to the sustenance of the Jewish establishment itself
Charitable commitment to Jews in need as opposed to others in need
Privileging of in-marriage as an explicit objective
Support for policies of the Israeli government

The findings in this chapter need to be understood in the larger context of social change now under way in American Judaism. As noted at the outset, the vast institutional infrastructure of American Jewry is in decline. With the exception of institutions associated with Orthodoxy, the diverse array of denominational congregations, philanthropic federations, human service agencies, so-called fraternal organizations (populated mostly by women), and defense agencies generally seem to be losing members, money, and mission. Some, indeed, are holding their own or possibly even growing a bit stronger. But, in recent years, several notable institutions have shed staff and organizational objectives amid significant budget cutbacks. Decline of the organized Jewish infrastructure does not translate into bankruptcy or disappearance, at least not in the foreseeable future or for the great majority of venerable and once-powerful institutions. But decline does signify an overall weakening in appeal to American Jews—as members, activists, and donors—and a diminished capacity to achieve organizational and communal objectives.

At the same time as the historic Jewish establishment has retreated and witnessed an aging of members and supporters, "new Jewish organizing" has flowered in the past decade. Whether the full weight and significance of these new forms of Jewish collective expression will entirely compensate for the likely losses in the establishment is an open question.

Led primarily by Jews in their twenties and thirties, the phenomenon encompasses five domains: spiritual communities (independent minyanim, rabbi-led emergent communities); culture (e.g., filmmaking, magazines, music, drama); learning (e.g., Limmud); social justice (many areas); and new media (e.g., Jewish-oriented pages on the Web, social networking).

The new forms of organizing consist almost entirely of small-scale projects and communities—at least for now. They tend to center on energetic social and cultural entrepreneurs who recruit small circles of staff and volunteers who in turn reach out to specialized constituencies. All are still low-budget operations with small paid staffs. They are funded in large measure by third parties, often well-known philanthropists in Jewish life, and their leaders have benefited from numerous leadership development programs launched and supported by the philanthropic class (see Shaul Kelner's chapter in this volume).

With all its variety, this "innovation ecosystem" sets a priority on purposeful activity: "high-quality davening"; self-empowered Jewish learning; creative Jewish music; access to meaningful Judaism; serving the developing world in authentic ways; Jewish environmentalism; and so on. Consistent with the findings in this survey, few such endeavors deal directly with the principal, animating issues on the twentieth-century Jewish communal agenda—those focused on bolstering the chances for survival, continuity, security, and collective identity.

Instead, consistent with our survey findings, younger adult activists focus on delivering Jewish meaning and purpose to niche constituencies that share common concerns and cultural styles. The newer forms of Jewish community blur the boundaries between education and entertainment, prayer and social justice, learning and spirituality. For the nonestablishment leaders and activists, social justice advocacy, text study, passionate prayer, and good music can and should be interwoven in a single experience.

To many nonestablishment figures, the establishment Jewish world is overly preoccupied with sustaining historic and needless social and ideological divisions, such as those between Jews and non-Jews, or amongst Jews themselves (by denomination, gender, age, class, etc.). As in our survey, many engaged Jews younger than forty see these distinctions as exclusive, judgmental, and coercive. Accordingly, the nonestablishment personalities maintain stances that strike the establishment leaders as too lax on intermarriage, denominational identities, and institutional loyalties.

One wonders: why now? Why are we in the midst of this period of innovative organizing, dating back only to the late 1990s? Several answers come to mind.

On the broadest scale, NGOs have exploded in number. In 2000, Robert Putnam's *Bowling Alone* charted declining national organizations with local chapters. At about the same time, the Internet helped propel a massive increase in small-scale organizing around the globe. Jewish start-ups are part of that development, one in which major entities are being challenged by smaller, more nimble, and niche-specific start-ups (see Chris Anderson's "long-tail" phenomenon: Anderson 2006).

In addition, as the survey results demonstrate, educational and demographic factors have come into play. The last thirty years have seen expanded participation in day schools, Jewish camp, Hillels, Jewish studies, and Israel travel. At the same time, philanthropists have launched numerous initiatives for young adults. This expanded educational infrastructure substantially enriched the Jewish cultural and social capital of those in their twenties and thirties. Meanwhile, this generation postponed marriage. Today, most non-Orthodox Jews ages twenty-five to thirty-nine are nonmarried, differentiating them from those who typically join conventional Jewish institutions. The combination of strong Jewish sociocultural capital and a demographic disconnect from existing establishment institutions ultimately has created a vast potential market for innovations and alternatives to prevailing communal offerings.

Looking forward, caution and experience demand resisting the temptation to engage in "straight-line" forecasting. We cannot tell what the future will bring, whether we are on the cusp of further significant expansion of the nonestablishment or approaching a leveling off of the innovative period in leadership, organization, and ethos. We only know for sure that the first decade of the twenty-first century has brought a new wave of Jewish organizing, one that simultaneously challenges, augments, enriches, and relies upon the long-standing Jewish communal establishment. This wave has already left a profound imprint on the origins, nature, interests, and capacities of a younger generation of Jewish leaders and the endeavors they have founded.

REFERENCES

Anderson, Chris. *The Long Tail*. New York: Hyperion, 2006.

Bronznick, Shifra, and Didi Goldenhar. *Visioning Justice and the American Jewish Community*. New York: Nathan Cummings Foundation, 2008.

Cohen, Steven M. "Engaging the Next Generation of American Jews: Distinguishing the In-Married, Inter-Married, and Non-Married," *Journal of Jewish Communal Service* (Fall/Winter 2005): 43–52.

Cohen, Steven M., and Ari Y. Kelman. "Cultural Events and Jewish Identities: Young Adult Jews in New York." Pamphlet. New York: National Foundation for Jewish Culture and The UJA–Federation of New York, 2005.

Cohen, Steven M., and Ari Y. Kelman. "The Continuity of Discontinuity." Pamphlet. Andrea and Charles Bronfman Philanthropies, 2007a.

Cohen, Steven M., and Ari Y. Kelman. "Beyond Distancing: Young Adult American Jews and Their Alienation from Israel." Pamphlet. New York: Jewish Identity Project of Reboot, 2007b.

Cohen, Steven M., and Ari Y. Kelman. "Uncoupled: How Our Singles Are Reshaping Jewish Engagement." New York: Jewish Identity Project of Reboot, 2008.

Cohen, Steven M., J. Shawn Landres, Elie Kaunfer, and Michelle Shain. "Emergent Jewish Communities and Their Participants." Pamphlet S3k. Synagogue Studies Institute and Mechon Hadar, 2007.

Cohen, Steven M., and Jack Wertheimer. "Whatever Happened to the Jewish People?" *Commentary* (June 2006): 33–37.

Diner, Hasia. *In the Almost Promised Land: American Jews and Blacks, 1915–1935.* Baltimore: Johns Hopkins University Press, 1995.

Fein, Leonard. *Smashing Idols and Other Prescriptions for Jewish Continuity.* New York: The Nathan Cummings Foundation, 1994.

Jewish Federation of Greater Philadelphia. *Jewish Population Study of Greater Philadelphia: 2009 Summary Report.* Philadelphia: Jewish Federation of Greater Philadelphia, 2009.

Kaunfer, Elie. *Empowered Judaism: What Independent Minyanim Can Teach Us about Building Vibrant Jewish Communities.* Woodstock, VT: Jewish Lights, 2010.

Landres, Shawn, and Joshua Avedon. *The 2008 Survey of New Jewish Organizations.* Los Angeles: Jumpstart 2009.

Sasson, Theodore, Charles Kadushin, and Leonard Saxe, "American Jewish Attachment to Israel: An Assessment of the 'Distancing Hypothesis.'" Report. Steinhardt Social Research Institute, Brandeis University, 2008.

Ukeles, Jacob B., Pearl Beck, and Ron Miller. *Young Jewish Adults in the United States Today.* New York: American Jewish Committee, September 2006.

Vorspan, Albert, and David Saperstein. *Tough Choices: Jewish Perspectives on Social Justice.* New York: URJ Press, 1992.

Wuthnow, Robert. *After the Baby Boomers: How Twenty- and Thirty-Somethings Are Shaping the Future of American Religion.* Princeton, NJ: Princeton University Press, 2007.

STEVEN M. COHEN

3   Expressive, Progressive, and Protective

Three Impulses for Nonestablishment Organizing among Young Jews Today

A S ILLUSTRATED in the previous chapter (and others in this volume), the people linked to Jewish groups we have labeled "establishment" and "nonestablishment" differ in significant and sizable ways. Without denying all the possibilities for overlap, and all the fuzziness in the imputed boundaries between the two categories, we can discern rather striking tendencies dividing establishment and nonestablishment group members.

For the most part, those who lead the establishment camp—as embodied in federations, congregations, human service agencies, Jewish Community Centers (JCCs), and defense organizations—*tend* to share several passions and perspectives. They are Jewish survivalists—they see the continuity of Jewish life threatened by high rates of intermarriage and low rates of communal affiliation. They are Jewish communalists—they are committed to supporting and strengthening the institutional features of American Jewish life. They are Jewish protectivists—they see great need to defend Jewish interests at home, in Israel, and around the world against threats from various antisemitic and anti-Israel forces. More than their nonestablishment counterparts, establishment Jews' political inclinations are decidedly more centrist and may, for some, lean toward being conservative.

In contrast stand the leaders of nonestablishment organizations: independent minyanim, social justice projects, cultural endeavors, learning initiatives, and the "pro-Israel, pro-peace" brand of Israel advocacy. These leaders see the establishment camp as overly concerned with threats to continuity, survival, and Jewish interests; unduly insistent upon preserving boundaries between Jews and non-Jews; disturbingly preoccupied with institutional survival rather than the achievement of higher Jewish purpose (whatever that purpose may be); and excessively defensive in its political stance.

Instead, leaders of the nonestablishment sector consider it their mission to express and deliver genuine Jewish meaning—to themselves or others—

through enriching experience, be it in prayer, learning, culture, or social justice. They reject seeming tribalism for more fluid intergroup boundaries and greater involvement in the larger world. Their more universalist social justice interests, bound with their sense of Judaism's particular mission in the world, lead them to value Jewish engagement in addressing society's greater ills. For these and other reasons, they tend to be situated on the liberal-left of the political spectrum; many see themselves as socially, culturally, and politically progressive.

Broadly speaking, leaders from both camps come from similar Jewish formative experiences. They report having parents who, as a group, were more engaged in Jewish life than other American Jews their age; their childhood denominational spectrum finds its center of gravity in the Conservative movement; and they benefited from more numerous and more intensive Jewish educational experiences than most Jews of their generation. That said, the two camps part company in their current identification, with many more establishment leaders retaining conventional denominational labels (even moving a bit toward Orthodoxy) while nonestablishment leaders tend to abandon the denominational affiliations of their childhood years, preferring "post-denominational" or other nondenominational labels. Moving beyond this distinction, we may extrapolate that establishment leaders prefer (and perhaps preserve) inherited categories of identity, whereas nonestablishment leaders prefer (and perhaps privilege) newly constructed and individually selected modes of identity and affiliation.

Yet we should be mindful not to infer too much homogeneity within each camp. Any moderately experienced Jewish communal insider can readily speak to variations within the establishment camp. Leaders of JCCs, congregations, local federations, defense agencies, and human service providers maintain different perspectives and commitments. Likewise, diversity exists among so-called nonestablishment endeavors, whose different ultimate objectives are reflected in leaders and constituencies who exhibit different values, interests, and backgrounds.

The distinction between the establishment and nonestablishment camps may thus be less sharp than we imagine. Establishment leaders, for their part, bristle at the implicit suggestion that all innovation takes place in the nonestablishment camp, in effect challenging the very nomenclature of "establishment" and "nonestablishment." As some establishment leaders certainly qualify as nonestablishment (either through nonestablishment behavior or sharing the worldviews of many in the nonestablishment camp), so too would we expect to find establishment-like individuals in the nonestablishment camp.

The very distinction between establishment and nonestablishment is muddied further not only by the diversity within these camps or the overlap between them but by the lack of a clear formal definition of each camp. Not everything old in Jewish life is establishment, and not everything new is non-establishment.

Such considerations suggest variations within the nonestablishment camp and point to a lack of clarity in the boundary separating the nonestablishment from the establishment camp. To what extent and in what fashion do nonestablishment camp members or participants differ in their views, perspectives, and objectives?

While the previous chapter drew and emphasized the distinctions between the two large camps (establishment and nonestablishment), this chapter seeks to explore the diversity under the surface—and to caution against both assuming uniformity within the camps and assuming an automatic identity for new groups with the nonestablishment ethos and, by extension, groups with establishment thinking and concerns. We will find that genuinely new and nonestablishment groups differ amongst themselves and that some young Jewish adults have initiated endeavors that are very establishment in their orientation and appeal.

The exploration that follows, then, will help us draw a more accurate, precise, and nuanced portrait of the establishment and nonestablishment camps, and will serve to correct an excessively uniform portrait of the nonestablishment camp.

Analytic Strategy: Exploring the Rank and File

To explore these issues, we examine rank-and-file members associated with seven nonestablishment groups (or classes of groups), selected to represent diversity in purpose and geographic location. The seven groups are as follows:

Independent minyanim—"Members" of independent minyanim across the country, as self-defined in responses to the survey, excluding those who claimed any lay or professional leadership role in minyanim. This category, of course, embraces minyanim of quite varied character in terms of size, geography, and denominational provenance or style.

Encounter—Participants on Encounter-sponsored trips to meet with Palestinian spokespeople in Bethlehem, including overnight home hospitality stays in Palestinian homes. For sure, Encounter is more of a program or an experience than a traditional organization.

Hazon—Participants in any of Hazon-sponsored programs (bike rides, food conferences, etc.).

Limmud—Attendees at any Jewish learning conferences sponsored by local Limmud operations around North America, including in New York, Los Angeles, and Atlanta.

AJC Access—Participants in the American Jewish Committee (AJC) Access
program, an initiative to engage Jewish young adults. Respondents were
drawn primarily from the Access efforts in New York, Los Angeles, and
Atlanta. AJC Access is "nonestablishment" in that it appeals entirely to
Jews younger than forty; at the same time, AJC is surely in the heart of
the Jewish communal establishment.

E-3 Events—Mailing list members from a project aimed at Jewish young
adults in the Denver area.

JDub Records—Mailing list members who are associated with this
nonestablishment promoter of Jewish musical artists, concerts, and
related events.

In part because none of these groups is entirely antithetical to the others,
a good number of respondents are associated with more than one. The analysis treats each of the seven groups separately, essentially going through the
full data set seven separate times.

To remove the complications and confounding effects of age, the analysis
is limited to those younger than forty, be they members of the seven nonestablishment groups or leaders from the establishment or nonestablishment
sectors.

We sent survey invitations directly to members of six of the groups: AJC
Access (New York, Los Angeles, and Atlanta chapters), E-3, Hazon, Encounter, JDub Records, and Limmud New York (with members from the last
constituting the large majority of participants under the Limmud rubric).
Between respondents drawn from these lists, and those attracted through
other lists or virally transmitted invitations, the number associated with each
constituency appears as follows:

TABLE 3.1
Number of Cases, Ages 21–39 and 40-plus, for the Seven Selected
Nonestablishment Groups

Group	Number of Cases, 21–39	Number of cases, 40-plus
Independent minyanim	539	471
Encounter	153	42
Limmud	350	388
Hazon	230	673
AJC Access	225	47
E-3 Events	56	16
JDub	209	185

Those associated with independent minyanim, JDub, and Limmud are split about evenly between those over and under forty, while Hazon participants are predominantly over forty.

The analysis proceeds by examining survey responses for constituencies associated with each of the seven groups and comparing them with those of leaders surveyed in the establishment and nonestablishment sectors. For each group, the analysis asks: do members of the group more closely resemble their age peers who are nonestablishment leaders or those who are establishment leaders. It also seeks to discern the distinctive features of each group.

To anticipate the findings, we will learn that:

> The seven groups each offer a distinctive configuration of attitudes, albeit with points of similarity among some of them.
>
> Not all the seven so-called nonestablishment groups share the attitudes and perceptions associated with nonestablishment leaders. For some of these groups, the thinking and attitudes of members actually place them in the establishment rather than the nonestablishment camp. To be sure, the entire classification is murky, and one that this chapter may help clarify. In particular, AJC Access stands out as the one group initiated by a veteran, establishment agency.
>
> Most of the groups bear evidence of what may be called a "signature issue," testifying to the power of different groups to attract like-minded members, supporters, and affiliated individuals.
>
> Finally, distinct objectives motivate various constituencies to affiliate with certain groups. Some initiatives focus primarily upon expressing leaders' and constituents' spiritual, intellectual, or cultural interests; others engage in progressive social justice activities; and still others are motivated heavily by a protective urge to defend Jews, and especially Israel, in a threatening environment. In short, as we shall see, respondents' answers and the groups with which they are associated suggest a division into what can be called "expressive," "progressive," and "protective" groups, leaders, individuals, and motivations.

The Seven Groups

Independent Minyanim

Members of independent minyanim who are younger than forty share the early life-stage characteristics of nonestablishment sector leaders: they are disproportionately younger (i.e., under thirty), single, and relatively low-income.

Along with nonestablishment and establishment leaders, minyan members exhibit relatively high rates of religious and ritual involvement. On several indicators of Jewish involvement, minyan members resemble leaders from both the nonestablishment and establishment sectors. To take one example: among minyan members, 76 percent celebrate Shavuot, more than among establishment leaders (61 percent) and even nonestablishment leaders (73 percent). On a variety of Jewish education measures, minyan members are not particularly distinguishable from nonestablishment and establishment leaders, although, to be sure, all report more frequent and more intensive educational experiences than American Jews overall in their twenties and thirties.

In several measures of attitude, the minyan members are situated somewhere between the nonestablishment and establishment poles, including with regard to feelings of attachment to the Jewish people, concerns about intermarriage, and attachment to Israel (though in no areas do they fall *closer* to the establishment pole than to the nonestablishment). Yet in several other areas, minyan members closely resemble the nonestablishment leaders, such as the following:

> Minyan members evince a relative lack of concern with antisemitism, be it in the United States or Europe. Like nonestablishment leaders, they are decidedly less protective of Jewish interests than are establishment leaders.
>
> Minyan member express only a limited interest in sustaining the organized Jewish community or in "engaging the unaffiliated," principal concerns of establishment Jewish leaders. Just 30 percent of minyan members consider it very important to support the organized Jewish community (as do 22 percent of nonestablishment leaders) compared to twice as many (57 percent) of younger establishment leaders—a stark contrast.
>
> They reflect a decided left-of-center tilt in their thinking about Israel, as manifest in their answers to several questions. An illustration: of minyan members, 66 percent support a freeze in settlement construction, compared with 48 percent of establishment leaders. Asked whether they were very bothered by Israel's treatment of the Palestinians, minyan members assented more than twice as often as did the establishment leaders.
>
> Minyan members' progressive political views on Israel comport with their political identities. Contrasting minyan members with establishment leaders, more of the former identify as liberal (73 percent vs. 57 percent), see social justice work as very important (58 percent vs. 44 percent), and regard advancing gender equity in Jewish life as very important (46 percent vs. 33 percent).
>
> Their charitable choices also speak to a greater universalism among minyan members as contrasted with establishment leaders. Far fewer minyan members give almost all their charity to Jewish causes (24 percent vs.

TABLE 3.2

Minyan Members in Comparison with Nonestablishment and Establishment Leaders

	Minyan Member (%)	Nonestablishment Leader (%)	Establishment Leader (%)
Female	64	64	55
Age <30	53	50	24
Married	50	56	76
Income $80,000+	21	19	43
Almost all friends Jewish	32	32	39
Attend weekly services	36	42	42
Do you participate in a Shabbat dinner at least monthly?	88	88	84
When eating at home, do you refrain from combining meat and dairy?	78	76	67
Did you celebrate Shavuot this year?	78	74	62
Do you regularly read a major Jewish news source?	59	53	60
Do you regularly read any Jewish blogs on Jewish themes?	56	53	45
Do you read Jewish literature?	40	39	44
Jewish people belonging	73	76	73
Feel part of the Jewish community	65	68	74
Responsible for Jews in need	41	33	49
Worried about			
Young Jews not interested	44	36	54
High intermarriage	24	19	34
Jews distant from Israel	23	16	28
Threats to Israel	31	23	44
Critics of Israel right to exist	33	24	41
Antisemitism in U.S.	9	7	17
Antisemitism in Europe	16	13	24
Remembering the Holocaust	29	21	39
Supporting the organized community	30	24	58
Philanthropy for Jewish causes	28	28	50
Social services for Jews in need	36	26	42
Engaging the unaffiliated	44	42	59
Making Israel engaging	43	31	48

TABLE 3.2 (CON'T.)

	Minyan Member (%)	Nonestablishment Leader (%)	Establishment Leader (%)
Marry whomever (disagree)	36	28	46
Upset if child mixed married	59	51	68
Upset if fewer U.S. Jews	73	65	83
Encouraging Jews to marry Jews	29	18	41
Israel important to my sense of being Jewish	42	36	48
Very attached to Israel	61	55	66
Defending Israel against critics	27	16	37
Israel should freeze settlements	68	75	48
Israel treatment of Palestinians— bothered	43	48	18
Pro-peace groups injure Israel among youth	10	8	16
Advocacy groups injure chances of engaging young with Israel	27	32	13
Democratic	81	83	73
Liberal	73	80	58
Helping Jews work for social justice	57	61	45
Supporting Jewish environmentalism	33	27	26
Advancing gender equity	46	51	32
Jewish causes—almost all charity	24	25	47
Jewish causes for non-Jews—half or more	29	33	21

45 percent), while more give half or more of their charity to Jewish-sponsored causes that benefit mostly non-Jews (29 percent vs. 21 percent).

Encounter

"Encounter is an educational organization dedicated to providing Jewish Diaspora leaders from across the religious and political spectrum with exposure to Palestinian life. . . . Encounter has brought over 750 Jewish leaders from diverse religious and political backgrounds on one and two-day journeys to Bethlehem, Hebron, and East Jerusalem" (http://encounterprograms.org, January 13, 2010).

Encounter recruits participants from those already visiting or studying in Israel, largely American Jewish communal professionals and lay leaders who have been to Israel several times. Given their background, Encounter participants may be considered "followers" in the Encounter program, but most would qualify as leaders of other endeavors, both establishment and non-establishment. In fact, more than 90 percent of young Encounter participants in this sample have spent four months or more in Israel, a far higher proportion than among nonestablishment or establishment leaders (55 percent). In fact, their extensive Israel involvement, no doubt reinforced by the Encounter program itself, underlies a distinctive pattern of views related to Israel—a "signature" issue for Encounter participants.

With the program's focus upon young adults studying in Israel, Encounter's participants are also exceptional for exhibiting several signs of their early life stage: youthfulness, singlehood, and limited affluence.

Encounter participants report very high rates of religious engagement. As many as 67 percent attend services weekly, as compared with just 34 percent for the nonestablishment leaders and 42 percent for the establishment leaders. Nearly all Encounter participants (92 percent) celebrated Shavuot as compared with about two-thirds of the leaders in both camps. They also report rather high rates of other Jewish engagement, surpassing both nonestablishment and establishment leaders, for example, in having almost entirely Jewish friends (41 percent) and regularly reading a major Jewish news source (60 percent).

Notwithstanding these high rates of Jewish involvement, Encounter participants score lower than establishment leaders on indicators of Jewish peoplehood commitment. For example, just 35 percent "strongly agree" that they are responsible for Jews in need around the world as contrasted with 51 percent of establishment leaders.

Encounter participants, like nonestablishment leaders, are considerably less "survivalist" in their orientations than are establishment leaders. They express fewer worries about young people's lack of engagement in Jewish life, distance from Israel, low birthrates, or high intermarriage. On the last issue, twice as many establishment leaders are very worried as are Encounter participants (34 percent vs. 15 percent).

On several matters pertaining to external threats to Jews and Israel, Encounter participants register far lower levels of concern than establishment leaders, and even trail the nonestablishment leaders. For example, on worries about critics of Israel's right to exist, levels drop from 42 percent for the establishment leaders to 27 percent for nonestablishment leaders to a tiny

12 percent for Encounter participants. In short, Encounter participants rank very low on Jewish protectivism.

Several indicators reflect Jewish communalism—the complex of attitudes associated with engagement with the organized Jewish community and its predominant rhetoric and concerns. On all these indicators, these young, Jewishly active, and Israel-experienced Encounter participants score far lower than establishment leaders. On the key question about whether they regard supporting the organized Jewish community as very important, just 22 percent of the Encounter participants answer affirmatively as contrasted with more than twice as many (56 percent) establishment leaders.

Consistent with their lack of survivalism and low levels of protectivism, Encounter participants are singularly unimpressed with pro-endogamy (in-marriage) stances. Just 15 percent think it important to encourage Jews to marry Jews, in contrast with nearly three times as many establishment leaders (41 percent).

It is with respect to Israel that Encounter participants display truly distinctive attitudes. They are very much unmoved by the importance of defending Israel against unfriendly critics. They almost uniformly support the freezing of Israeli settlements—at a level twice that among establishment leaders (91 percent vs. 47 percent). Far more of them are bothered by Israel's treatment of Palestinians (69 percent vs. 18 percent), and they are far more concerned that traditional Israel advocacy groups harm young American Jews' chances of engaging with Israel (strongly agree: 48 percent vs. 14 percent). In short, Encounter participants manifest a strongly progressive approach to Israeli political issues.

This stance finds parallels elsewhere. Encounter participants report high levels of identification as Democrats and liberals, and high levels of support for a variety of progressive social causes. On the importance of helping Jews work for social justice causes, they outscore establishment leaders 67 percent to 45 percent. Compared to establishment Jewish leaders, Encounter participants are far less likely to give almost all their charity to Jewish causes, and far more likely to fund charities that benefit non-Jews.

Unquestionably, Encounter participants display a remarkable configuration of characteristics. They are highly engaged in Judaism, Jewish life, and Israel, and committed to prayer and learning. They display little conventional concern for threats to Jews or Israel, and little attachment to organized Jewry. They take politically progressive positions on a variety of issues, especially with respect to Israel. This configuration distinguishes Encounter participants from both nonestablishment and, especially, establishment leaders, such that Encounter participants display a nonestablishment ethos even more distinctly and acutely than nonestablishment leaders generally.

TABLE 3.3
Encounter Participants in Comparison with Nonestablishment and Establishment Leaders

	Encounter Participant (%)	Nonestablishment Leader (%)	Establishment Leader (%)
Female	57	67	55
Age <30	62	50	27
Married	49	53	73
Income $80,000+	12	19	43
Almost all friends Jewish	42	29	39
Attend weekly services	68	35	44
Do you participate in a Shabbat dinner at least monthly?	97	87	84
When eating at home, do you refrain from combining meat and dairy?	81	74	70
Did you celebrate Shavuot this year?	92	72	66
Do you regularly read a major Jewish news source?	64	53	61
Do you regularly read any Jewish blogs on Jewish themes?	60	53	47
Do you read Jewish literature?	44	38	45
Participate in Jewish groups	44	49	45
Jewish people belonging	68	77	75
Feel part of the Jewish community	67	68	75
Responsible for Jews in need	35	34	52
Worried about			
Young Jews not interested	37	35	57
High intermarriage	15	19	35
Birthrates	3	6	12
Jews distant from Israel	18	17	28
Threats to Israel	20	25	44
Critics of Israel right to exist	13	27	42
Antisemitism in U.S.	2	8	16
Antisemitism in Europe	6	14	23
Remembering the Holocaust	20	23	38
Supporting the organized community	22	22	56
Philanthropy for Jewish causes	20	28	49

TABLE 3.3 (CON'T.)

	Encounter Participant (%)	Nonestablishment Leader (%)	Establishment Leader (%)
Social services for Jews in need	31	26	42
Engaging the unaffiliated	39	43	59
Making Israel engaging	36	33	49
Marry whomever (disagree)	24	28	47
Upset if child mixed married	52	51	69
Upset if fewer U.S. Jews	60	68	84
Encouraging Jews to marry Jews	15	19	42
Israel important to my sense of being Jewish	39	38	48
Very attached to Israel	65	57	66
Defending Israel against critics	10	19	36
Israel should freeze settlements	91	74	46
Israel treatment of Palestinians— bothered	69	47	16
Pro-peace groups injure Israel among youth	6	8	17
Advocacy groups injure chances of engaging young with Israel	47	31	14
Democratic	89	82	73
Liberal	86	80	57
Helping Jews work for social justice	66	63	45
Supporting Jewish environmentalism	36	29	25
Advancing gender equity	58	48	34
Jewish causes—almost all charity	19	25	45
Jewish causes for non-Jews—half or more	36	31	21

Hazon

"Hazon works to create a healthier and more sustainable Jewish community and a healthier and more sustainable world for all. . . . The following values underpin our programs:

A strong commitment to inclusive community; . . .
Being Jewishly serious *and* deeply engaged with the world around us;

We believe in reaching people where they are and not where we might like
   them to be" (http://www.hazon.org, January 13, 2010).

Hazon's program comprises, in large part, outdoor environmental education and various activities around food and Judaism.

Hazon participants younger than forty display demographic characteristics that place them somewhere between nonestablishment and establishment
leaders. On most measures of Jewish engagement, they resemble both nonestablishment and establishment leaders' relatively high rates of engagement.

On those attitudes on which nonestablishment and establishment leaders
differ, Hazon participants are generally situated far closer to the nonestablishment pole. For example, voicing particular worry about threats to Israel are
31 percent of Hazon participants, 23 percent of nonestablishment leaders,
and 44 percent of establishment leaders. On whether supporting the organized Jewish community is important, the numbers are 32 percent (Hazon),
20 percent (nonestablishment), and 55 percent (establishment). This pattern generally holds on questions bearing upon Jewish survivalism, communalism, and protectivism, as well as in-marriage attitudes and Israel-related
attitudes. Hazon participants' politics reflect a progressive tilt, very much
resembling nonestablishment leaders: Just over 80 percent of both groups
are self-identified liberals, as compared with 57 percent of the establishment
leaders.

On one issue, not surprisingly, Hazon participants are "off the charts":
Jewish environmentalism. Just 24 percent of establishment leaders think it
very important to support Jewish environmentalism, as does just a slightly
higher proportion (27 percent) of the nonestablishment leaders. But fully 50
percent of Hazon participants endorse the importance of Jewish environmentalism. Clearly, Hazon has attracted or educated a constituency based on
one of its signature issues.

In short, whereas Hazon participants' profile generally resembles that of
nonestablishment leaders, their commitment to Jewish environmentalism
represents an exception. This core issue differentiates Hazon participants
from Jewish leaders their age, both in the nonestablishment and establishment sectors.

Limmud

"We are a conference, a festival, a gathering of hundreds of Jews from all
walks of life, all Jewish backgrounds, all lifestyles, and all ages. Limmud is
four days of lectures, workshops, text-study sessions, discussions, exhibits,
performances and much more—all planned by a community of volunteers.

TABLE 3.4
Hazon Participants in Comparison with Nonestablishment and Establishment Leaders

	Hazon Member (%)	Nonestablishment Leader (%)	Establishment Leader (%)
Female	67	65	54
Age <30	38	51	30
Married	57	54	73
Income $80,000+	24	18	42
Almost all friends Jewish	29	31	40
Attend weekly services	37	38	44
Do you participate in a Shabbat dinner at least monthly?	87	88	85
When eating at home, do you refrain from combining meat and dairy?	77	74	71
Did you celebrate Shavuot this year?	73	74	67
Do you regularly read a major Jewish news source?	46	55	62
Do you regularly read any Jewish blogs on Jewish themes?	52	53	48
Do you read Jewish literature?	35	39	45
Jewish people belonging	72	76	74
Feel part of the Jewish community	62	68	76
Responsible for Jews in need	37	33	50
Worried about			
Young Jews not interested	40	35	57
High intermarriage	23	18	34
Birthrates	6	5	12
Jews distant from Israel	20	16	28
Threats to Israel	30	24	44
Critics of Israel right to exist	31	24	42
Antisemitism in U.S.	11	7	16
Antisemitism in Europe	18	12	24
Remembering the Holocaust	26	22	39
Supporting the organized community	31	21	55
Philanthropy for Jewish causes	31	28	48
Social services for Jews in need	37	27	41
Engaging the unaffiliated	33	43	61
Making Israel engaging	37	32	51

(*continued*)

TABLE 3.4 (CON'T.)

	Hazon Member (%)	Nonestablishment Leader (%)	Establishment Leader (%)
Marry whomever (disagree)	33	25	47
Upset if child mixed married	61	49	69
Upset if fewer U.S. Jews	67	65	82
Encouraging Jews to marry Jews	28	17	41
Israel important to my sense of being Jewish	37	37	50
Very attached to Israel	62	58	66
Israel-engaged	54	56	62
Pro-Israel	50	42	63
Defending Israel against critics	23	17	37
Israel should freeze settlements	68	76	47
Israel treatment of Palestinians— bothered	44	51	17
Pro-peace groups injure Israel among youth	6	8	17
Advocacy groups injure chances of engaging young with Israel	19	35	15
Democratic	85	81	73
Liberal	82	80	57
Helping Jews work for social justice	67	62	44
Supporting Jewish environmentalism	51	27	23
Advancing gender equity	43	50	34
Jewish causes—almost all charity	25	25	46
Jewish causes for non-Jews—half or more	25	33	21

In Hebrew, Limmud means "learning"—and that's what it's about. An opportunity to craft your own Jewish world. Explore your connection to Jewish ideas and tradition. Meet people who share your curiosity and enthusiasm. Relax, reflect, and celebrate" (http://www.limmudny.org/content/view/13/33/ January 14, 2010).

This description of Limmud New York applies, as well, to numerous other Limmud gatherings around the United States and around the world. The New York event attracts about 700 participants annually, a number that is nearly matched in Los Angeles, Denver, Atlanta, Philadelphia, Chicago, and, most recently, New Orleans.

Demographically, those Limmud attendees under age forty have features that situate them between nonestablishment and establishment leaders, though closer to the nonestablishment.

Limmud attendees match or surpass both leader groups with respect to religious engagement. For example, they attend Shabbat dinners slightly more often than both leadership groups, keep a level of kashrut more widely than either nonestablishment or establishment leaders (79 percent vs. 72 percent and 70 percent), and more Limmudniks than others observe Shavuot. Significantly, they also lead, albeit with small gaps, on every measure of Jewish knowledge consumption: reading news sources, Jewish blogs, and Jewish literature, as well as participating in Jewish online groups.

Limmud participants situate themselves somewhere between nonestablishment and establishment leaders on a variety of survivalist concerns, including in-marriage. They share the former's diminished sense of threat, and limited interest in the organized Jewish community.

The one critical feature that Limmud attendees share with establishment leaders is an attachment to and engagement with Israel. Yet, resembling the pattern found among Encounter participants (albeit far less pronounced), Limmudniks adopt a variety of progressive positions on Israel-related political issues. In other matters of political identity as well, Limmud participants tilt largely toward the more progressive positions more widely favored by nonestablishment leaders than by establishment leaders.

The overall impression one gains from these findings is that Limmud participants are Jewishly committed and culturally engaged, with a sociocultural cast that is moderated from the progressive stance associated with nonestablishment leaders.

AJC Access

"ACCESS, AJC's new generation program, inspires and empowers young professionals to engage in today's critical domestic and international issues. Working at the nexus between the Jewish community and the world, we reach out to diplomats, policy makers and young leaders of diverse religious and ethnic communities and strive to re-envision the role of young Jewish leaders in global affairs" (http://www.ajc.org/site/c.ijITI2PHKoG/b.4203673/k.E5F1/ACCESS_NY.htm January 14, 2010).

In almost all ways, AJC Access members look like establishment leaders. In fact, in some distinctive ways, their views go beyond those held by establishment camps in contrast with nonestablishment.

TABLE 3.5

Limmud Participants in Comparison with Nonestablishment and Establishment Leaders

	Limmud (%)	Nonestablishment Leader (%)	Establishment Leader (%)
Female	65	66	56
Age <30	44	52	28
Married	53	54	74
Income $80,000+	25	18	42
Almost all friends Jewish	39	29	39
Attend weekly services	41	38	44
Do you participate in a Shabbat dinner at least monthly?	91	87	84
When eating at home, do you refrain from combining meat and dairy?	81	72	70
Did you celebrate Shavuot this year?	80	70	66
Do you regularly read a major Jewish news source?	62	52	60
Do you regularly read any Jewish blogs on Jewish themes?	60	50	47
Do you read Jewish literature?	46	35	43
Jewish people belonging	78	76	74
Feel part of the Jewish community	73	67	74
Responsible for Jews in need	43	32	51
Worried about			
Young Jews not interested	44	34	58
High intermarriage	23	17	36
Jews distant from Israel	23	15	29
Threats to Israel	34	23	44
Critics of Israel right to exist	32	25	42
Antisemitism in U.S.	8	8	17
Antisemitism in Europe	16	12	23
Remembering the Holocaust	25	22	38
Supporting the organized community	30	24	55
Philanthropy for Jewish causes	32	28	48
Social services for Jews in need	32	27	42
Engaging the unaffiliated	48	41	59
Making Israel engaging	38	33	50

TABLE 3.5 (CON'T.)

	Limmud (%)	Nonestablishment Leader (%)	Establishment Leader (%)
Marry whomever (disagree)	35	26	47
Upset if child mixed married	62	49	69
Upset if fewer U.S. Jews	72	67	82
Encouraging Jews to marry Jews	26	18	42
Israel important to my sense of being Jewish	46	36	47
Very attached to Israel	67	57	65
Defending Israel against critics	23	18	37
Israel should freeze settlements	67	77	46
Israel treatment of Palestinians— bothered	40	51	16
Pro-peace groups injure Israel among youth	8	8	18
Advocacy groups injure chances of engaging young with Israel	29	35	14
Democratic	81	83	74
Liberal	74	82	57
Helping Jews work for social justice	56	64	44
Supporting Jewish environmentalism	34	30	23
Advancing gender equity	47	48	33
Jewish causes—almost all charity	30	23	46
Jewish causes for non-Jews—half or more	29	32	21

Although they are more religiously engaged than the young Jewish public at large, Access members are less religiously active than either nonestablishment or establishment leaders. Just 15 percent attend services weekly (vs. 40 percent for nonestablishment and 47 percent for establishment); and under half (45 percent) celebrated Shavuot (vs. 74 percent and 70 percent).

Like establishment leaders, AJC Access members are highly sensitive to threats to Jewish interests, very survivalist-oriented, heavily pro-Israel, very protectivist, and very distant from the progressive politics (be it on Israel or other matters) that characterize younger nonestablishment leaders.

As noted, on several bellwether issues, AJC Access members actually surpass establishment leaders. These include worries about high intermarriage, distancing of Jews from Israel, threats to Israel, critics of Israel's right to exist, and antisemitism (in both the United States and Europe). In short, AJC Access members worry more than even other establishment leaders about external threats to Jewish security. AJC Access members reflect "protective" impulses, scoring high on concern for every threat to Jewish existence and endorsing strong responses to those threats. The resemblance to establishment leaders extends to several positions, among them the importance of raising philanthropic dollars for Jewish causes, making Israel engaging for American Jews, encouraging Jews to marry Jews, and defending Israel against unfriendly critics.

Few Access members take progressive stands on political issues. In like fashion, they less often identify as Democrats or liberals than do establishment leaders, who, in turn, are situated to the right of nonestablishment leaders (although still more than half liberal).

In short, AJC Access members resemble the organizational culture and positions associated with the American Jewish Committee itself. Access members hardly share in the worldviews associated with nonestablishment leaders. This recently founded endeavor for young adults (albeit by a very establishment agency) manages to attract a sizable number of young adults who share a establishment worldview—or else it influences them to adopt that worldview.

More broadly, AJC Access members provide an example of an impulse for organizing among Jewish young adults not seen in the previous examples, or in much of this larger project's work on young adults (except in Sarah Benor's essay in this volume).

E-3 Events

"E-3 Events bridges the gap between popular culture and traditional Jewish values while providing connections and exploring Jewish identity. . . . With cocktails" (http://www.e-3events.com, January 14, 2010).

This Denver-based effort uses social and cultural events (parties and music, concerts and cocktails) to engage Jewishly uninvolved people in their twenties and thirties.

About half of E-3 Events members are married, and they are not particularly affluent. On all measures of Jewish involvement, they report scores far lower than those reported by either nonestablishment or establishment Jewish leaders. Very few E-3 participants have entirely Jewish friendship circles, and hardly any attend services weekly. They report low levels of belonging

TABLE 3.6

AJC Access Members in Comparison with Nonestablishment and Establishment Leaders

	Access Member (%)	Nonestablishment Leader (%)	Establishment Leader (%)
Female	56	66	55
Age <30	43	52	27
Married	44	53	77
Income $80,000+	32	18	41
Almost all friends Jewish	27	31	41
Attend weekly services	15	41	49
Do you participate in a Shabbat dinner at least monthly?	66	89	90
When eating at home, do you refrain from combining meat and dairy?	49	76	75
Did you celebrate Shavuot this year?	46	76	70
Do you regularly read a major Jewish news source?	57	54	62
Do you regularly read any Jewish blogs on Jewish themes?	43	55	48
Do you read Jewish literature?	34	40	47
Jewish people belonging	72	76	76
Feel part of the Jewish community	61	68	75
Responsible for Jews in need	47	32	52
Worried about			
Young Jews not interested	46	34	57
High intermarriage	40	16	33
Jews distant from Israel	37	15	26
Threats to Israel	54	21	40
Critics of Israel right to exist	57	22	38
Antisemitism in U.S.	26	6	14
Antisemitism in Europe	38	11	19
Remembering the Holocaust	46	21	33
Supporting the organized community	46	21	52
Philanthropy for Jewish causes	50	25	46
Social services for Jews in need	38	27	41
Engaging the unaffiliated	44	41	59
Making Israel engaging	56	31	48

(*continued*)

TABLE 3.6 (CON'T.)

	Access Member (%)	Nonestablishment Leader (%)	Establishment Leader (%)
Marry whomever (disagree)	40	25	46
Upset if kid mixed married	60	49	71
Upset if fewer U.S. Jews	86	64	83
Encouraging Jews to marry Jews	46	17	38
Israel important to my sense of being Jewish	54	35	47
Very attached to Israel	61	56	68
Defending Israel against critics	56	15	32
Israel should freeze settlements	50	78	51
Israel treatment of Palestinians— bothered	19	52	19
Pro-peace groups injure Israel among youth	17	8	16
Advocacy groups injure chances of engaging young with Israel	14	35	16
Democratic	65	83	78
Liberal	51	83	62
Helping Jews work for social justice	46	65	47
Supporting Jewish environmentalism	23	32	25
Advancing gender equity	27	52	37
Jewish causes—almost all charity	35	22	43
Jewish causes for non-Jews—half or more	18	35	21

to the Jewish people or Jewish community. They score low on concerns for Jewish continuity, on commitment to in-marriage, and on attachment to Israel (i.e., relative to the Jewish leaders in this chapter, both nonestablishment and establishment). Their political views fall far closer to those of the more centrist establishment leaders than to those of the fairly progressive nonestablishment leaders.

With all this said, E-3 Events participants stand out in a few notable ways. They are very worried by external threats of all kinds—threats to Israel, delegitimization of Israel, and antisemitism in the United States and Europe.

With respect to antisemitism, they are more worried than even the establishment leaders. They are more likely to find remembering the Holocaust important than establishment leaders and, certainly, than nonestablishment leaders. E-3 Events participants are also notable for the extent to which they see themselves as "cultural Jews," no doubt reflecting the influence of aligning with a group that is explicitly cultural in purpose and character.

The high levels of sensitivity to antisemitism and related threats among E-3 Events participants warrant an attempted explanation, even if speculative. One factor may be location. All reside in the Denver area, where Jewish population concentration is far lower than in the areas where most other survey respondents reside. Possibly, E-3 Events participants feel more vulnerable and exposed as a minority group. Another possibility is that E-3 Events participants experience an elevated sensitivity to antisemitism for lack of other ways to express their Jewish identity. They are not especially well-educated in Jewish terms, nor particularly religious, nor highly committed to Jewish social justice causes. Perhaps their sensitivity to antisemitism is an expression of their group identity that does not find outlet in other ways.

JDub Records

"JDub [to which its name has been shortened] is a not-for-profit record and event production company for nonestablishment Jewish music, community, and cross-cultural dialogue. Founded in December 2002 by two NYU students . . . JDub has grown into an internationally recognized brand and has introduced proud Jewish voices squarely into establishment culture, offering young adults opportunities to connect with their Judaism in the secular world in which they live. In its start-up phase, JDub focused on developing a small cadre of artists . . . and introducing its unique programming to its target audience, primarily through events in New York City, festivals . . . , national CD releases, and via national media outlets. . . . Since that time, JDub's artist roster has grown to 12, spanning Israeli hip hop, Biblical indie rock, Yiddish Punk, Cantorial afro-punk, Sephardic rock, and Jewish Kids music, and the organization has executed marketing campaigns and produced events for Random House, New Israel Fund, Nextbook, and others" (http://jdubrecords.org, June 27, 2010).

JDub participants in this survey are those on the company's mailing list, one that includes some non-Jews, who for the most part refrained from answering our opt-in survey invitation.

Demographically, JDub participants resemble leaders from the nonestablishment camp rather than the establishment leaders. They are disproportionately young, single, and earn relatively low incomes.

TABLE 3.7

E-3 Events Participants in Comparison with Nonestablishment and Establishment Leaders

	E-3 Member (%)	Nonestablishment Leader (%)	Establishment Leader (%)
Female	70	65	54
Age <30	25	52	29
Married	47	53	72
Income $80,000+	18	18	42
Almost all friends Jewish	11	31	41
Attend weekly services	5	39	46
Do you participate in a Shabbat dinner at least monthly?	62	89	86
When eating at home, do you refrain from combining meat and dairy?	32	75	72
Did you celebrate Shavuot this year?	27	75	69
Do you regularly read a major Jewish news source?	36	55	62
Do you regularly read any Jewish blogs on Jewish themes?	29	54	48
Do you read Jewish literature?	38	38	46
Jewish people belonging	43	77	76
Feel part of the Jewish community	41	68	76
Responsible for Jews in need	21	34	52
Worried about			
Young Jews not interested	27	35	57
High intermarriage	18	17	35
Jews distant from Israel	13	16	29
Threats to Israel	34	24	43
Critics of Israel right to exist	43	25	41
Antisemitism in U.S.	30	7	15
Antisemitism in Europe	32	13	22
Remembering the Holocaust	59	21	37
Supporting the organized community	39	22	55
Philanthropy for Jewish causes	41	27	48
Social services for Jews in need	52	27	40
Engaging the unaffiliated	36	41	60
Making Israel engaging	38	33	49

TABLE 3.7 (CON'T.)

	E-3 Member (%)	Nonestablishment Leader (%)	Establishment Leader (%)
Marry whomever (disagree)	21	26	47
Upset if child mixed married	39	50	69
Upset if fewer U.S. Jews	73	66	83
Encouraging Jews to marry Jews	32	17	42
Israel important to my sense of being Jewish	25	38	49
Very attached to Israel	34	58	67
Defending Israel against critics	32	18	35
Israel should freeze settlements	46	77	49
Israel treatment of Palestinians—bothered	27	50	19
Pro-peace groups injure Israel among young	11	8	17
Advocacy groups injure chances of engaging young with Israel	20	34	15
Democratic	70	83	74
Liberal	63	81	60
Helping Jews work for social justice	45	64	46
Supporting Jewish environmentalism	25	31	25
Advancing gender equity	25	51	36
Jewish causes—almost all charity	11	24	45
Jewish causes for non-Jews—half or more	18	33	21

Relative to both nonestablishment and establishment leaders, JDub members score low on indicators of Jewish religious activity and lower on many measures of Jewish educational experience. Nevertheless, as they are by definition Jewish cultural consumers, JDub participants report levels of "Jewish reading" comparable to the leaders.

In many areas where nonestablishment and establishment leaders differ, JDub participants' attitudes come closer to those of the nonestablishment leaders. Thus, they report feeling relatively low levels of responsibility for Jews in need and of worries about intermarriage, young people's distance from Israel, or their lack of interest in Jewish life. Like the nonestablishment

TABLE 3.8

JDub Participants in Comparison with Nonestablishment and Establishment Leaders

	JDub Participants	Nonestablishment Leader	Establishment Leader
Female	54	66	55
Age <30	48	51	29
Married	54	53	73
Income $80,000+	23	18	41
Almost all friends Jewish	18	31	40
Attend weekly services	21	39	45
Do you participate in a Shabbat dinner at least monthly?	62	88	86
When eating at home, do you refrain from combining meat and dairy?	53	75	71
Did you celebrate Shavuot this year?	43	75	67
Do you regularly read a major Jewish news source?	51	55	61
Do you regularly read any Jewish blogs on Jewish themes?	53	54	48
Do you read Jewish literature or participate?	44	39	46
Jewish people belonging	65	77	75
Feel part of the Jewish community	44	68	75
Responsible for Jews in need	35	34	51
Worried about			
Young Jews not interested	34	35	57
High intermarriage	22	18	34
Jews distant from Israel	19	16	28
Threats to Israel	35	24	43
Critics of Israel right to exist	39	25	41
Antisemitism in U.S.	24	7	16
Antisemitism in Europe	31	12	23
Remembering the Holocaust	40	22	37
Supporting the organized community	31	22	55
Philanthropy for Jewish causes	32	27	48

TABLE 3.8 (CON'T.)

	JDub Participants	Nonestablishment Leader	Establishment Leader
Social services for Jews in need	41	27	41
Engaging the unaffiliated	35	42	59
Making Israel engaging	36	33	49
Marry whomever (disagree)	23	27	46
Upset if child mixed married	42	51	68
Upset if fewer U.S. Jews	71	66	82
Encouraging Jews to marry Jews	26	18	41
Israel important to my sense of being Jewish	33	37	48
Very attached to Israel	49	58	66
Defending Israel against critics	36	18	35
Israel should freeze settlements	57	76	48
Israel's treatment of Palestinians—bothered	40	49	19
Pro-peace groups injure Israel among youth	14	8	17
Advocacy groups injure chances of engaging young with Israel	21	33	15
Democratic	65	83	74
Liberal	67	81	59
Helping Jews work for social justice	55	64	45
Supporting Jewish environmentalism	28	30	25
Advancing gender equity	41	50	35
Jewish causes—almost all charity	17	24	43
Jewish causes for non-Jews—half or more	28	33	21

leaders, they are not particularly disturbed by intermarriage or matters attached to Israel.

JDub members' participation in the nonestablishment culture does not extend to political identities or social causes, where their views fall somewhere between the centrist-liberalism of the establishment leaders and the social progressivism typical of nonestablishment leaders.

In one area, sensitivity to antisemitism, JDub participants resemble the establishment leaders and depart from the nonestablishment camp. JDub participants express rather high levels of concern about antisemitism in Europe and the United States as well as keen interest in remembering the Holocaust. In these respects they resemble E-3 Events participants, who are also loosely affiliated with a Jewish cultural group and score relatively low on religious observance and Jewish educational experiences.

Conclusion

Far from displaying uniformity, or even near-similarity, the seven groups of constituents under close scrutiny exhibit considerable diversity in values and attitudes. They range in the extent to which they are religiously engaged, with Encounter participants at the highest end, joined by minyan members, Limmud participants, and Hazon members; AJC Access members at a somewhat less engaged level; and JDub and E-3 Events participants showing the rarest signs of conventional Jewish involvement.

The groups range, as well, with respect to matters of Jewish survivalism, communalism, and protectivism. On most of these issues, Encounter occupies one end of the spectrum and AJC Access stands at the other end. The JDub and E-3 participants share some of the Access constituency's sensitivity to external threat. Joining Encounter participants on these issues are Hazon, the minyan members, and, to a lesser extent, the learners of Limmud.

Politically, Encounter and Hazon are strongly progressive; minyanim and Limmud participants are less so; and the AJC Access people are, compared to the left-of-center Jewish population from which they are drawn, not at all progressive politically, with the same characterization holding for E-3 Events participants. JDub members take a moderate political posture.

In short, not all nonestablishment groups share the ethos of nonestablishment leaders; some (two in this particular study) exhibit attitudes akin to those shared by establishment leaders.

The results outlined here also prompt the question of what constitutes the "nonestablishment" or "establishment" camps. According to one definition of "nonestablishment," such groups are strongly purpose-driven rather than affiliatory in motivation; recently created; appealing to Jews in their twenties and thirties; and initiated and led by young adults. Using these criteria, Encounter, independent minyanim, and Limmud seem to qualify fully. While AJC Access satisfies two or three of these criteria, other enterprises with a like-minded sociopolitical agenda meet all of them: Friends of the IDF may be such an example, as may be Fuel for Truth, a pro-Israel advocacy organization. One upshot of these findings, then, is that our working definition of "nonestablishment" and "establishment" is not all that precise; correlatively, the world is not all that neatly ordered, with an array of collective Jewish endeavors resisting easy classification.

Perhaps the signal contribution of this chapter is to point out that prevailing concepts of the nonestablishment fail to embrace those innovating out of what I have called the "protective" motivation. The major institutions in the "nonestablishment ecosystem" and their funders have clearly recognized innovators in spirituality, learning, and culture—areas that may be grouped in the "expressive" dimension of innovation in that they allow for leaders and participants to explore their personal Jewish interests and motivations. And the prevailing rhetoric certainly has recognized the wide swath of social justice initiatives, or what may be seen as embodiments of the "progressive" dimension.

But, for understandable reasons, much of the current thinking, writing, and speaking has failed to encompass groups that advance particularist visions of Jews in the world and a sense of an embattled and threatened Jewry—those embodying the protectivist dimension. A truly inclusive definition of contemporary innovation among younger adult Jews ought to extend to this dimension as well, even though (or especially because) it stands in political and cultural tension with the explicitly or implicitly progressive forces found elsewhere in Jewish nonestablishment camps today. In short, the "innovation ecosystem" embraces—or ought to be seen as embracing—not only expressive and progressive endeavors but protective initiatives as well.

4 Young Jewish Leaders in Los Angeles

*Strengthening the Jewish People in Conventional
and Unconventional Ways*

O N A BEAUTIFUL Sunday afternoon in 2009, I took the 405 Freeway to
the Skirball museum and followed the signs for "PJA 10 Live: Advocacy for a New Era," the Progressive Jewish Alliance annual dinner.
As I parked my Prius in the lot, I noticed several other Priuses, some with
Obama or Jewish social justice bumper stickers. I went up the stairs to the
cocktail area and found a crowd that was diverse in age but that included many
people under forty. Most attendees were white, but a number of other ethnic
backgrounds were represented as well. A lesbian couple walked in hand-in-
hand. I noticed a few knit yarmulkes, mostly on non-Orthodox rabbis I know,
including one woman. Most men wore suits; women wore suits or dresses.

I chatted with some of my faculty colleagues from Hebrew Union College, as well as several friends from the Shtibl Minyan and IKAR (nondenominational, traditional, egalitarian spiritual communities geared toward
social action) who are Jewish professionals and other nonprofit workers,
artists, filmmakers, and lawyers. I talked to a young man who had completed PJA's Jeremiah Fellowship and works for a Jewish cultural organization. And I met a young woman who was not involved in Jewish life until she
did the Jeremiah Fellowship.

I walked past the DJ, who was spinning some funky beats, and snacked
on chips and dips at the hors d'oeuvres table. I talked to the volunteers man-
ning the table with information on PJA's action campaigns, and I signed
petitions to legalize same-sex marriage and mandate affordable housing.
I browsed through decorated sneakers and basketballs at an exhibition of
fair-trade sports goods.

We were ushered into the dining area and found the dozens of tables
(almost five hundred guests attended) decorated with centerpieces highlight-
ing social justice heroes, including Betty Friedan and Harriet Tubman. Signs
on the wall invoked Martin Luther King, Jr. ("What would MLK do? Stand

up for health care."), and Gandhi, as well as the Babylonian Talmud and the prophet Jeremiah. As the guests found their tables, the hip-hop music started, and a troupe of young African American performers danced in a style they told us was called "krump," including a dance to a recording of MLK's "I Have a Dream" speech.

The dinner chairs, two young PJA lay leaders, came to the stage and pumped up the crowd: "Let's get some *ruach* in this room!" Thus began a series of speeches clearly geared toward a mostly young, Jewishly knowledgeable, left-wing audience. A young female rabbi and an older male pastor gave a joint invocation. The rabbi said, "Hold up your hands: these are hands that do the work of justice. Now touch someone: these are your partners in this work." She said *hamotzi* in Hebrew and English.

A black politician spoke next. She asked how many people were at Obama's inauguration, and several hands went up. She revved up the crowd with passionate talk of justice and support for local progressive politicians and propositions; for a few minutes I felt like I was at a Democratic pep rally.

A PJA professional leader recognized the staff and talked about PJA's accomplishments, focusing on the "next generation of Jewish leaders." She asked us to raise our glasses and say "a *l'chaim* to ten years [of PJA] and over a hundred and twenty more." In a video presentation, a Jewish history professor talked about the Jewish historical mandate for justice. He talked about immigration and sweatshops and quoted the Prophets: "Justice, justice shall you pursue."

Another PJA professional mentioned PJA's allies, including Jewish Funds for Justice, the American Jewish World Service, AVODAH, and the Muslim Public Affairs Council. She talked about various groups who are suffering injustice and said after each one, "We are you and you are us." She declared, "There is no us versus them, there is we—*si, se puede*, together we can." She talked about Tookie Williams, a death row inmate who "sought to practice *tshuva* [repentance]." She teared up when she mentioned the recently passed Proposition 8, which made same-sex marriage illegal in California. To mark the special moment of this annual dinner, she sang "*Shehechiyanu*," and many of the attendees sang along.

Dinner was served. It was standard gala fare—rolls, salad, chicken, and roasted vegetables—with a trendy, international flair, including seaweed and sesame oil in the salad and cucumber-infused water with lemon. During dinner, the screen onstage featured profiles of people involved with PJA, mostly under forty, including the founder-rabbi of IKAR, the founder-CEO of JDub Records, and a Muslim man involved in the NewGround Muslim-Jewish dialogue group. A brief slide show, set to classical music, honored an older couple who funded some PJA programs.

I flipped through the tribute journal, a narrow, ninety-one-page booklet with an edgy, graffiti-esque cover and filled with ads from individuals, organizations, and politicians congratulating PJA and the evening's honorees. There were many *mazel tov*s and *yasher koach*s, Hebrew-origin phrases of congratulations. A staff member wrote about "Abraham Joshua Heschel's exhortation to 'pray with our feet.'" And one of the honorees expressed an aspiration: "In ten years, Jews will be to justice and service what Quakers are to peace."

The main event of the evening began: a discussion forum, moderated by the editor of the local Jewish newspaper, with the two honorees: the forty-year-old past executive director of PJA and a middle-age lawyer and law school dean who has worked to advance civil liberties. One was introduced as "working to return social justice to its rightful place at the forefront of the Jewish agenda" and the other as "author, agitator, mensch." The honorees talked about their past, present, and future work for social justice and its relation to Jews, and they answered the moderator's questions about justice, fundraising, and Obama.

After the forum, a PJA professional publicly thanked the kitchen staff in English and Spanish, and she asked attendees to consider joining one of PJA's several working groups, "the way we get our *tachlis* [practical work] done." She then invited guests into the lobby for dessert and coffee, and a Korean percussion ensemble began its performance of loud, rhythmic drumming.

A few weeks later, on a beautiful Monday afternoon, I got into my Prius and drove down the Avenue of the Stars to the Century Plaza Hotel. I passed a line of Lexuses, BMWs, and Audis inching up to the valet at the main entrance, and I drove behind the hotel and parked in the lot next to a Mercedes. I followed signs for "Gala of the Legends," the Jewish Federation Real Estate and Construction Division Annual Dinner. On the way up to the hotel, I chatted with a middle-age non-Jewish woman who said she attends this event every year and sits with some of her clients at a table purchased by her financial firm. I entered the cocktail area and said hi to several Federation staff members and lay leaders whom I knew either because they were my former students at Hebrew Union College or because I had interviewed them for this research project.

The lobby was filled with hundreds of people of all ages, mostly white but also some of Middle Eastern, African American, Latino, and Asian origin. Men wore suits; women wore suits or cocktail dresses. I saw a number of men in yarmulkes, including a few black velvet ones. Cocktails in hand, attendees chatted and exchanged business cards. I met a young woman who designs the interiors of office buildings. She said she is not involved with the

Federation but attends this and several "other industry events" every year. I talked to a young man who I knew was a Real Estate and Construction (REC) Division leader because of the ribbons on his name tag. He said he goes to many fundraising dinners like this: "It's an L.A. thing, you know, the red carpet, being seen." He loves the Federation because it is a "very efficient philanthropy" with "little overhead," and he has really enjoyed serving on a committee and making friends. He hopes to build relationships for his career in investment banking and meet a woman who is "young and successful."

A large wide-screen TV featured a slide show of Federation beneficiary agencies ("Thanks to you, 35,000 medical visits were subsidized . . ."), interspersed with thank-yous to the event sponsors. Tuxedoed servers circulated plates of beef skewers with peanut sauce and other hors d'oeuvres, and a huge banner congratulating the evening's honorees hung overhead.

We were ushered into the elegant ballroom through security scanners. There were several dozen tables (over a thousand guests attended). Up front were the major donors and other VIPs, then the tables purchased by individuals and companies, then the members of the Young Leadership Development Institute (a minimum-gift fellowship program started in L.A. and replicated by federations around the country), and then the rest of the attendees, including a few more tables of young people at the back. The tables looked elegant; centerpieces were decorated baskets of kosher food to be donated to SOVA, a Federation-beneficiary food bank.

I was seated in the back at a table with other young people, mostly real estate professionals. Three young men were leafing through the stacks of business cards they had just collected. One pointed out a young woman at the next table with a large diamond ring. "Her husband must be making seven figures," he whispered. He suspected based on her mannerisms that she did not grow up wealthy.

The official events opened with a lay leader introducing the cantorial soloist from Beit T'shuva (a Federation-supported addiction recovery organization), who stood between the Israeli and American flags and sang the two national anthems. The middle-age lay leader dinner chair welcomed "distinguished guests," including several Jewish and non-Jewish politicians. He congratulated dinner attendees on raising more than $640,000, an impressive amount in any year and especially during the economic downturn. He thanked REC donors for their gifts over the past year, which totaled $9.1 million: "You generous people raised 18 percent, or *chai*, of all the money raised by the Federation." He recalled how he had reluctantly agreed to chair the dinner: "You just want a poor *shmuck*, I'm not *meshugenneh*." He promised he would "keep the speeches short and the networking long" and

invited another lay leader to say *hamotzi* over a challah so large that someone suggested it could make it into the *Guinness Book*.

Dinner was typical for a gala: a salad of mixed greens with candied pe-
cans, an entrée of chicken with potatoes and vegetables. During dinner, I
chatted with the young men at my table. One asked me about my research,
and I told him I am interviewing leaders of several Jewish organizations. He
had not heard of PJA, so I explained that it works for social justice. He said
with a smile, "That's better than us—we're just in it for the networking." He
explained: "Young people do it for the networking; older people don't need
the networking—they do it to be good. When young people do it to be good,
that's when the deals come."

During a lull in the conversation, I skimmed the heavy, glossy tribute
book. It featured pictures from REC's social service events, such as the "Senior Prom" at a Jewish Community Center (JCC), the "Festival of Lights
Toy Drive," and the mission to Cuba (including a sampling of local cigars).
And it offered information about the Federation: "Just because we're almost
100 doesn't mean we don't think about the future. In fact, we think about
it all the time, which is why The Jewish Federation has so many ways for
young people to get involved throughout Los Angeles and the Valley." The
majority of the 224-page book was filled with tribute ads, divided according
to amount of donation. Ads mentioned the four honorees' success as real
estate developers, their generosity to the Jewish community, or both. There
were many *mazel tov*s and *yasher koach*s. Another section listed REC Division donors divided by ranges of contribution to the Federation's annual
campaign.

The MC returned to the stage and introduced a young woman wearing a
striking red dress—the first woman, he said, to give the appeal at the annual
REC dinner. She started by talking about her negative childhood experiences
with Judaism. After going on a Birthright Israel trip, however, she came back
"connected to the State of Israel" and got involved with the Federation. She
talked about the work of the Federation: feeding the poor, offering a safety
net, fulfilling the "mandate of *tikkun olam*, repairing the world." She said
that by giving to the Federation we can honor our ancestors who died in the
Holocaust, and we can ensure continuity. After a rousing round of applause,
attendees were asked to fill out the pledge cards at their table, and Federation staff members circulated to collect them.

The main event of the evening was the ceremony inducting the honorees,
four octogenarian real estate giants who have been major Federation donors,
into the REC Hall of Fame. They were acknowledged with video presenta-
tions featuring relatives and friends praising them for their professional and
philanthropic accomplishments, interspersed with pictures of the Federation

office and other Jewish communal buildings imprinted with their names. One man in a video tribute used the Yiddish phrase for "may you live until 120"—*Biz hundert tsvantsik*—and then added, "May you feel like twenty." Each inductee came to the stage to accept a plaque and pose for photographers.

The official portion of the event ended when the dinner chair said, "We're going to have dessert, drinks, and transactional activity in the lounge." He exhorted guests: "If you guys get a deal tonight . . . [make a] supplemental donation to the Federation." I checked the program's order of events, and, indeed, it ended with "Dessert, drinks, & deals in the California Lounge."

Two annual dinners of Jewish nonprofit organizations. Both were intended to motivate members and supporters, honor leaders, and raise much-needed funds. Both attracted hundreds of Jews, including many in their twenties and thirties. And both included a good deal of Jewish content, as well as English peppered with Hebrew and Yiddish. But it is clear from the thematic emphases and aesthetic orientations of these events that the Federation and the Progressive Jewish Alliance attract and cater to very different crowds. The Federation is geared toward conventional Jews who are wealthy or striving to be wealthy, especially those with a desire to contribute to Jewish causes, and PJA is geared toward young, progressive Jews with a desire to work toward justice for all. The Federation attracts Jews who are also involved with other organizations that support Israel and local Jewish causes, especially through philanthropic engagement, and PJA attracts Jews who are also involved with IKAR and independent minyanim, as well as Jewish cultural organizations.

As I found in my research, the differences between these Federation and PJA events are not limited to these two organizations but typify what leaders call "mainstream" or "establishment "Jewish organizations on the one hand and "innovative" or "nonestablishment" Jewish "start-ups" on the other hand. This chapter examines these organizational spheres by analyzing discourse about them and the views of their young leaders. I found that, for some leaders, especially those of social justice and cultural groups, the dichotomy between "establishment" and "innovative" organizations is salient and serves as a driving force behind their work. And I found that the spheres differ in several ways but that there is also a good deal of overlap in participation, leadership, and collaboration.

We know from previous work that there is great diversity among Jews in their twenties and thirties. Although this age cohort is less engaged in organizational life than their parents and grandparents, and many young Jews prefer episodic engagement over formal membership and leadership roles

(Cohen and Kelman 2005), some Jews in their twenties and thirties are strongly committed to Jewish organizations. Ukeles, Miller, and Beck (2006) found a hierarchy of engagement: Orthodox Jews are most strongly connected, followed by non-Orthodox in-married Jews with children, non-Orthodox singles and in-married couples without children, and finally intermarried couples. Even so, as I found in my research, members of all these groups are participating in the leadership of Jewish organizations.

From January to September 2009, I conducted ethnographic research in Los Angeles to study these diverse leaders. I began my research with three questions: How do young Jewish leaders get involved with Jewish organizations? How do leaders of establishment and nonestablishment organizations differ? And how is that distinction constructed rhetorically? To answer these questions, I carried out a three-tiered approach, looking at seventeen organizations in the cultural, political, social, and philanthropic spheres that are attracting many young Jews to leadership roles (see Appendix):

1. Interviews with forty Jews, mostly in their twenties and thirties, who are professional or volunteer leaders of at least one organization, including presidents, board members, and founders of young adult divisions.[1]
2. Observation of more than a dozen meetings and events.
3. Analysis of websites and other promotional materials.

The young leaders I interviewed are extremely diverse. They range from secular to observant and from liberal to conservative. In this nonrandom sample, about half are single, and half are married or partnered. While most are Ashkenazim, several are Sephardi/Mizrahi (including a few Persian and Israeli Jews) or of mixed heritage. The sample includes immigrants and children of immigrants, gay and lesbian Jews, Jews of color, and Jews originally from other parts of the country. Interviews lasted an average of sixty-six minutes (range: thirty-three minutes to one hour, fifty-four minutes) and were recorded, transcribed, and analyzed.

Los Angeles as a Case Study

In this type of study, it is fruitful to focus on one locale: to observe and analyze the local dynamics among organizations, leaders, participants, funders, and the local industrial, cultural, and political landscape. Los Angeles was an obvious choice because I live here. But it is also appropriate for other reasons. People talk about L.A. as prefiguring Jewish and general trends (e.g., Phillips 2007; see also Dear and Flusty 2002). A great deal of innovation happens in L.A.—both in long-standing and new organizations—that is later replicated in other cities. Examples include the social justice–based spiritual community IKAR, the action-based social justice group PJA, the grass-roots unity-oriented social/educational/cultural/religious group JConnect, and the Federation's Real Estate and Construction Division's Young Leadership Development Institute. L.A. is also a hub for umbrella organizations and institutes that study and encourage innovation, including Hebrew Union College's School of Jewish Nonprofit Management, the Professional Leaders Project, and Jumpstart—a "thinkubator for sustainable Jewish innovation."[2] As I heard the new CEO of the L.A. Federation say at his first public speaking engagement in 2009, "What Jews do in Los Angeles will have an impact around the world."

L.A. is clearly an important player in the American Jewish community. At the same time, it is unique in a number of ways. First, L.A. is second only to New York in community size; current estimates range from 519,151 to 668,000 Jews (Herman 1998, DellaPergola 2007: 599).[3] Like New York, parts of L.A. are densely Jewish. On the Westside, Jews constitute 22–26 percent of the population, and in parts of the San Fernando Valley, that percentage is as high as 48 percent (Phillips 2007).

Second, as part of an international city, the L.A. Jewish community includes several streams of recent immigrants, including Jews from Iran, Israel, the former Soviet Union, Latin America, South Africa, and, more recently, France. Jews from these groups are represented to varying extents in organizational life,[4] but the most prominent group is Iranian/Persian Jews. Immigrants from Iran and their children tend to be wealthy, pro-Israel, and politically conservative. Many are involved in mainstream organizations like the Federation, Friends of the Israel Defense Forces (FIDF), Hadassah, and the American Israel Public Affairs Committee (AIPAC), and young Iranian Jews have created their own groups, including young adult divisions of Iranian American organizations and three new groups: 30 Years After (referring to the date of the Iranian revolution, which sparked Jews' emigration), the Lev Foundation (founded in memory of a young man named Daniel Levian), and Ledorvador ("from generation to generation").

Entertainment Industry, Red Carpet Phenomenon

Like in other cities, Jews in Los Angeles are overrepresented in legal, medical, and business professions.[5] In addition, many local Jews are involved in the entertainment industry. I have met Jews who are writers, producers, directors, actors, agents, casting professionals, post-production editors, cameramen, financiers, and film critics. Some Jewish organizations reach out to Jews in the entertainment profession, and those that do not inevitably find that some of their participants are "in the industry."

Partly due to influence from the entertainment industry, the "red carpet" phenomenon is ubiquitous in Los Angeles Jewish life. Perhaps even more than in other wealthy communities, "being seen" is central to social life. At a few of the Jewish events I attended, there was an actual red carpet, as well as a photography area near the entrance.

In the driving culture of L.A., much attention is given to cars. In wealthy circles, Mercedes, BMW, Lexus, and Audi are popular, and every once in a while one sees a Bentley or an Italian sports car. In Orthodox circles, because large families are the norm, so are minivans; and in left-wing activist circles, Priuses, Smart Cars, and other environmentally friendly vehicles are common. In other cities, cars are certainly important indicators of identity, but in L.A. they are especially salient.

City of Transplants

In contrast to some cities, like Detroit and Chicago, Los Angeles is home to many Jews who grew up elsewhere, a trend that goes back to the postwar influx from the Northeast and Midwest (Moore 1994). While the forty leaders I interviewed by no means represent a random sample, it is interesting that the vast majority of professionals did not grow up in Los Angeles but the vast majority of lay leaders did. Perhaps young Jews are more attuned to local lay leadership opportunities if their parents and longtime friends are involved.

Certainly, the lack of familial continuity in Los Angeles has ramifications for Jewish engagement. One Federation professional says that many young Jews here "don't have family, they don't have friends, they don't have people to go to temple with . . . so they kind of just lose their Jewish life." Some young transplants seek out organizations or types of organizations with which they are familiar from other cities, including the Federation, AIPAC, denominational synagogues, or independent minyanim. GesherCity, the "bridge to the local Jewish scene," caters partly to transplants: "Whether you're a native Angelino [sic] or new in town, GesherCity L.A. is going to help get you connected."[6]

Fragmented City

The Los Angeles Jewish community is very spread out. Jews live and run institutions in the Valley, the Westside, Mid-City, the Eastside, the South Bay, Orange County, and several other regions (see Phillips 2007 for a regional mapping). Because of traffic and perceived cultural differences and geographic barriers, Jews in some areas rarely visit others. While downtown serves as a hub for some cultural events (theater, orchestra, etc.), no central area serves as a hub for Jewish life. One lay leader who has also lived in Washington, D.C., and Chicago says that the L.A. Jewish community is comparatively dispersed. She feels that people in L.A. are more oriented toward their own lives than communal engagement: "In D.C. and Chicago, . . . more people are on the pulse of what's going on, versus L.A., [where] it's like, 'I'm at the beach.'" Similarly, an Orthodox professional originally from New York sees gaps between Orthodox, Conservative, and Reform Jews in Los Angeles. He says, "I think people here aren't even exposed [to other groups]. It's so cut off, you never really see people. In Manhattan, you're in daily contact with people." The fragmented nature of Los Angeles Jewish life likely stems from several factors, including the large size of the Jewish community, the reliance on cars for transportation, and the culture of individualism.[7]

Federation Not As Central

In some locales, including Chicago and smaller cities, one Jewish philan-thropic body (the Federation, United Jewish Appeal, Combined Jewish Phi-lanthropies) is the "central Jewish address" and the main or only show in town for Jews in their twenties and thirties. In Los Angeles, the Federation has struggled to maintain a position of centrality. Perhaps because of the factors discussed before, the independent mind-set characteristic of Califor-nia, and the dizzying array of organizations and engagement opportunities, the Federation is not necessarily the first place Jews turn when looking to get involved. Even so, as I explain in the passages to follow, it is still an impor-tant source of activity for some Jews in their twenties and thirties, and lead-ers of many groups talk about the Federation as emblematic of the Jewish establishment.

Discourse Surrounding Establishment vs. Nonestablishment Organizations

National Jewish Discourse

The discourse surrounding establishment and nonestablishment Jewish or-ganizations permeates the Jewish communal landscape. In national and local periodicals and research reports, new and niche organizations are often dis-cussed in contrast to "mainstream" Jewish groups. Independent minyanim and new spiritual communities are contrasted with "mainstream" congrega-tions;[8] the Jewish blogosphere and new Jewish media like *Heeb* magazine and *Guilt and Pleasure* are contrasted with the "mainstream Jewish media";[9] left-wing Israel groups like Americans for Peace Now and J Street and social justice groups like the American Jewish World Service (AJWS) and Jewish Funds for Justice (JFSJ) are contrasted with "mainstream Jewish organizations," especially AIPAC, the Anti-Defamation League (ADL), and the AJC;[10] congregations serving mostly gay, lesbian, bisexual, and transgender (GLBT) Jews are contrasted with mainstream synagogues;[11] and Black, Latino, and Asian Jews are contrasted with the "mainstream" (i.e., white) Jewish community.[12] We see this rhetoric in news stories as well as in opinion pieces from leaders of both "establishment" and "nonestablishment" groups. Jumpstart chief operating officer Joshua Avedon writes in a *Forward* op-ed, "If the mainstream Jewish community doesn't get hip to what is driving the new start-ups soon, a whole parallel universe of Jewish communal life might just rise up and make the old structures irrelevant." Using a tongue-in-cheek Darwinian metaphor, he goes on to contrast two species, "*Synagogus Mainstreamus*" and "*Synagogus Emergentus*," and argues that "they can (and should) interbreed."[13]

The term "organized Jewish community" is also common on both sides of the aisle. In the introduction to Cohen and Kelman's (2007) study of new Jewish organizations, Jeffrey Solomon and Roger Bennett of the Andrea and Charles Bronfman Philanthropies write (I italicize group/sphere descriptors in the many passages to follow):

> At first, most of us in the *organized Jewish community* wrote this *"New Jewish Identity"* off as a fad, lacking in depth that, like any trend, would prove to be a temporary phenomenon. This organizing, even if it was "an explosion," was taking place outside of the walls of the organizations and institutions we had dedicated our lives to building. (p. 4)

They go on to explain that they have embraced these "*new forms of Jewish organizing*."

From the other side, a report about Jewish social justice groups shows how such leaders see themselves in various relationships with the "organized Jewish community":

> Some Jewish social justice leaders take the position that, to build the field, it is crucial to develop relationships with the *organized Jewish community*. They view the organized Jewish community (OJC) as the source of money, power, and people that can be engaged in this work. Others see the OJC as increasingly irrelevant, and argue that these relationships should occupy low priority on the Jewish social justice agenda. (Bronznick and Goldenhar 2008: 50)

Bronznick and Goldenhar conclude that "The *Jewish social justice community* and the *organized Jewish community* have an unprecedented opportunity, to move from *shared interests* to a more profound appreciation of *shared values*" (p. 15). Similarly, AJWS head Ruth Messinger argues that service organizations should "be recognized as essential players in the *organized Jewish community.*"[14] While there are multiple views as to how much new organizations are or should be part of the establishment, it is clear that many leaders and observers recognize two contrasting spheres of Jewish communal life.

Other descriptors are also common. In a July 2009 op-ed in the *Forward*, J Street's Isaac Luria contrasts "*traditional,*" "*establishment,*" and "*old-style top-down institutions*" with "*an emerging new Judaism of independent minyanim, social justice and alternative Jewish culture.*"[15] A recent report on the Jewish "*innovation ecosystem*" discusses "*startups* and *established institutions*" (Jumpstart et al. 2009: 2). In its authors' characterization, "In and beyond the Jewish community, a new generation of *organic, decentralized,* and *flexible* structures is replacing the twentieth century's *mechanical, centralized,* and *top-down* organizations" (p. 1).

From this brief survey of discourse around the country, it is clear that journalists, researchers, and diverse Jewish leaders classify some Jewish organizations as "mainstream" or "establishment" and others as "innovative" or "start-ups." The establishment sphere includes long-standing groups like federations and other philanthropies that benefit mostly Jews, as well as Jewish communal defense and centrist or right-wing Israel advocacy groups. New spiritual communities, cultural initiatives, and social justice and left-wing Israel groups (both long-standing and new) are seen as constituting a separate sphere, an "innovation ecosystem," even as they are seen as making inroads into the "organized Jewish community."

Discourse among Young Jewish Leaders in Los Angeles

The distinction between establishment and nonestablishment organizations certainly came up in many of the interviews I conducted in Los Angeles. Leaders of both types of organizations contrasted them using a number of terms, referring primarily to three dimensions: how old they are ("long-standing," "established," "existing" organizations vs. "new," "young" "start-ups"), how conventional they are ("mainstream," "conventional," "traditional" groups vs. "innovative," "unconventional," "independent," "edgy" ones), and their size and structure ("large," "corporate," "bureaucratic," "hierarchical," and "institutionalized" vs. "small," "grassroots," and "organic"). Interviewees applied these labels to the organizations, their events and programs, and the people who participate in and lead them.

I heard this discourse of contrast many times in the interviews, but only from leaders of certain organizations. Leaders of PJA, JDub, Yiddishkayt

L.A., Reboot, JQ International, and JConnect contrasted their groups with mainstream ones. Leaders of the Federation, especially professionals, discussed these new groups in contrast to the Federation and other establishment groups. But leaders of new philanthropic and centrist/right-wing Israel groups (e.g., FIDF and Stand With Us) did not participate in this discourse of contrast. This is not surprising, considering that some are also involved in the Federation, AIPAC, and similar groups and have little knowledge of the new organizations.

I found many examples of the discourse of contrast. For example, a leader of Yiddishkayt L.A. says that the Jews involved with his organization "are not always people being reached by the *mainstream* Jewish community." This sentiment echoes the organization's promotional materials for a fellowship for young adults:

> For Jews with Yiddish heritage, understanding the riches and history of Yiddish culture leads to a deep and strong Jewish identity based in the achievements of a thousand years of Jewish civilization. Once ubiquitous, this pathway to Jewish identity is now *revolutionary*, an *alternative* to the narrative provided by the present-day *mainstream Jewish community*.

A professional who sees herself as a bridge between different types of organizations says, "Look at what all these Jewish *innovative* organizations are doing that's different from the *institutions* and the *bigger* organizations." One Federation professional says, "Certainly, federations are the more *corporate* of the Jewish engagement opportunities." Along the same lines, another Federation professional explains:

> There are certain people that just don't want to be part of the *mainstream*, and the Federation is *mainstream* to a large extent. So, I think there are some people that just would rather be with something *smaller* and maybe more *niche-focused* . . . that kind of personality that just *doesn't want to do what everyone else is doing*. They want to do something different.

A leader of JConnect, in explaining how his group—run by Orthodox Jews and geared toward Jewish unity—makes it "cool to be Jewish," says his programs have "a little bit of an *edge*." He uses a number of terms of contrast:

> We don't do stuff in . . . an *institutional* setting. For all the reasons that the *indie minyan*s are working and all the reasons the *grassroots* groups are working are all the things we carry with us. Even though at times we do partner with the *establishment*, we still carry with us sort of like this *anti-establishment*, *independent*, be who—you know, it's like, we're in the YouTube generation,

we're in the MySpace generation. We're in the generation of people who . . . want to *express themselves as an individual*. . . . They may not all want something prepackaged.

There is sometimes debate over whether or not a particular group is part of the organized Jewish community. A leader of the Progressive Jewish Alliance contrasts "the *organized Jewish community* and the *progressive-left community*." She says that PJA "represents a very particular perspective and . . . builds alliances that move the *mainstream Jewish community*" to incorporate progressive values. But in the same interview, she says:

> We're part of the *mainstream Jewish community*; we're an organization that people see as just one of the . . . Jewish communal representatives, and part of what we do is we work with our other *organized Jewish community institutions* to move them in that [progressive] direction.

She sums up PJA's situation by saying the organization has "one foot in the *organized Jewish community* and one foot out."

When I asked another PJA leader if she considers PJA to be part of the organized Jewish community, she responded, "That's a big question. I don't know. I mean, I think to some extent it is, and *we* sit at the table with *them*, and to another extent, we're so much *smaller*." Even as she posits that PJA is part of the organized Jewish community, she uses "us versus them" language, indicating PJA's ambiguous status with respect to other organizations. Similarly, a third PJA leader says, "We'd love to have a more symbiotic relationship with the *mainstream Jewish community*. We are mainstream. Being progressive is at the center of Jewish life." Within one utterance, this leader portrays her organization as being both outside and inside the mainstream. This seeming contradiction points to mixed feelings and multiple stances within PJA concerning how the organization should position itself with respect to the mainstream, as well as various views within the Federation and other establishment organizations concerning how to relate to PJA.

We find a similar tension in cultural organizations. Leaders of one new cultural organization talk about it in contrast to the mainstream Jewish community and its "reactive" Judaism based on discourses of antisemitism. But one person I talked to who has been involved both with this organization and with long-standing organizations says the dichotomy is overstated: "The truth is, when you have an organization whose funders are all Jewish, who are investing in you to reach the community, you therefore become part of the community."

A different rhetoric emerges among leaders of Jewish organizations that are new but have missions regarding Israel advocacy or social engagement rather than social justice or culture. One professional who was instrumental in bringing GesherCity, an initiative of the Jewish Community Center Association, to Los Angeles says he thinks GesherCity "wants to be" part of the organized Jewish community. "I don't know whether the organized Jewish community wants GesherCity to be a part of it," he continues. He goes on to say that he attends every meeting about young Jewish adults in Los Angeles and embraces any opportunity to collaborate, because he thinks GesherCity "really is a great tool that the Jewish community could use. And needs." Although this leader does not (yet) see his organization as part of the mainstream, he does not use the same language of contrast as the social justice and culture leaders discussed earlier.

A young lay leader who founded a young adult chapter of the pro-Israel group Stand With Us conveys a similar sentiment. She expresses concern that many people involved in other Jewish organizations do not know about Stand With Us but makes clear that she does not see her organization in contrast to a mainstream. Similarly, while I heard critiques of the Federation from leaders of the young divisions of FIDF and Guardians of the Jewish Home for the Aging (Guardians), I did not hear the discourse of contrast between different types of organizations. It seems that the "us versus them" language is limited to new organizations whose missions and constituencies are different from those of long-standing institutions, especially those that deal with Jewish culture, social justice, and GLBT Jews.

This rhetorical difference can be seen in the way leaders of justice and culture groups talk about innovation and transformation. Several talk about establishment organizations "*do[ing] what they've been doing for years*," while start-ups focus on "*R&D* [research and development]," "*challenge the norm*," and offer a "*groundbreaking*" approach to Jewish life. One non-establishment leader says she feels that "*edgy*" organizations are "*constantly asking questions*" like "What should the Jewish community do? What should be the focus?" She feels mainstream organizations are not asking these questions. Of course, every well-run organization engages in periodic strategic planning and implements changes intended to strengthen the organization and achieve its goals. But many of the leaders of organizations in the non-establishment sphere see establishment groups as continuing business as usual, while they see themselves—and often young Jews in general—as creating something new.[16]

Some establishment leaders reject the rhetoric of innovation. One Federation professional is uncomfortable with the notion of "innovation" as the distinguishing factor between long-standing and new organizations, as articulated in the Jumpstart report on the "innovation ecosystem" and elsewhere. "It makes it seem as though innovation only happens in new/smaller organizations," he wrote in an email to me. In fact, several Federation leaders emphasize the innovative work they are doing in the areas of programming, fundraising, marketing, and leadership training. One Federation professional believes that some young people prefer "*newer* organizations" because they think mainstream organizations are run by "leaders in their sixties and seventies who are too *established in their ways*" to allow for innovative ideas. She agrees that this may have been the case in the past but argues that the situation has changed in recent years. I did, in fact, find that some nonestablishment leaders I interviewed viewed the establishment as lacking a desire to change. One young man who is involved with a number of nonestablishment organizations said that he is only interested in new and constantly changing organizations and that he sees the Federation as too set in its ways to recreate itself for the changing times: "I enjoy building things; I don't enjoy sustaining things. I don't believe in perpetuating organizations for the sake of perpetuating organizations."

Finally, there is a sense that some mainstream organizations are large and bureaucratic. Leaders of a few nonestablishment organizations told me about their difficulties navigating the bureaucracy of the Jewish Federation in particular. One nonestablishment organization leader says, "It's been pretty challenging to get the Federation to send out anything through their list for us, even the stuff that they cosponsor." Leaders of two different nonestablishment organizations say they have had several great conversations with Federation professionals about collaboration, funding, and leadership development but that nothing ever comes to fruition because of what one calls the "unbelievable *bureaucracy*." One of these leaders points out that while his small organization can make decisions quickly over email, the Federation is a "much *heavier* organization" for which any action takes longer. Even one Federation lay leader mentions that some people avoid the Federation because they see it as "a big *bureaucracy*." Certain young Jews, especially, perhaps, those who work in the corporate world, do not mind the large and complex structure of the Federation. But others, including many who take a more independent and countercultural approach to life, consider it a turn-off and find opportunities for Jewish communal involvement elsewhere.

Among young Jewish leaders, the discourse is not limited to contrasting old and new organizations. It also extends to which Jews these groups attract. In discussing this issue, several leaders lumped certain organizations together in contrast to others. They described participants in the Federation, AJC, ADL, denominational synagogues, and Israel advocacy groups as conventional and centrist, while they characterized participants in PJA, IKAR, and cultural organizations as unconventional and liberal.

One leader who is involved with several Jewish organizations says:

> If you're a PJA person, your realm is sort of IKAR—and, I mean, I don't want to characterize—but it's like IKAR and then certain Jewish cultural things, certain Jewish political things. Whereas let's say you're an Orthodox person at Beth Jacob [a Modern Orthodox synagogue serving the Pico-Robertson neighborhood], you're going to be involved with, let's say, AIPAC, and you'll be involved with this religious entity and this Jewish school. . . .

The same leader feels that there is not enough interaction among these different types of Jews, and he sees himself as a bridge between Jewish communal spheres.

A woman who works at the Federation characterizes people involved with IKAR and PJA as "hippyish." She says her understanding of a hippy is epitomized by people she met from the Rainbow Coalition, a progressive organization. But she also uses the term "hippy" to describe rabbinical students she meets in L.A., as well as college students involved in her university's Hillel. This characterization stems from individuals' practice of waving their arms and dancing during services at Hillel or IKAR. Also, she says she uses the term "hippy" when people "try and do things alternatively, I guess. They try and create new things that aren't already done. . . . I think people strongly believe that the traditional is not cutting it anymore." She does see a bit of "hippy" in herself, but she contrasts herself with the people involved with those organizations. In this mainstream leader's discourse, the Rainbow Coalition, Hillel, rabbinical schools, IKAR, and PJA all attract people who have an unconventional orientation. In the same interview, she said that young Jews who attend Federation events also attend events of the Guardians, Hadassah, FIDF, (Conservative) Sinai Temple's young adult group Atid (Hebrew for "future"), and other organizations that have been characterized as mainstream.

Similarly, a man who works at the Federation talks about "mainstream institutional folks" who attend events at the Federation's Young Leadership Divisions, the ADL, the AJC, W Group (Reform temple Stephen S. Wise's young adult group), and Sinai Atid. A similar discourse was reported in a previous study of young Jewish adults in Los Angeles. Tobin Belzer's research found that "JDub staff characterize their audience as 'artsy, creative types' in contrast to the more 'conventional' types who are drawn to [Sinai Temple's] Friday Night Live" (Chertok et al. 2009).

Through the discourse of Jewish leaders, there emerge distinct spheres of Jewish organizational life. Organizations committed to raising and distributing funds for Jewish education and social services, combating antisemitism, or helping Israel from a centrist or right-wing perspective are seen as the establishment, while groups committed to social justice, Jewish culture, GLBT Jews, and left-wing Israel work[17] are seen as outside the establishment. Although I did not analyze the religious domain, interviewees made clear that denominational synagogues are seen as mainstream, while independent minyanim and the IKAR community are seen as innovative. Of course, not all groups are considered part of one sphere or the other, as the appendix that follows indicates.

It is interesting to note that, of the groups I studied in Los Angeles, the majority of the nonestablishment groups—and none of the establishment groups—are featured in *Slingshot*, the "guide to some of today's most inspiring and innovative organizations, projects, leaders and visionaries in the North American Jewish community," published by 21/64, a division of the Andrea and Charles Bronfman Philanthropies. An independent foundation is contributing to the formation of an "innovative" sphere of Jewish communal life (see Kelner, this volume), both rhetorically and financially.

How Separate Are the Spheres?

How distinct are the establishment and nonestablishment spheres that emerge from the discourse of young Jewish leaders? In Kelman's mapping of online networks (this volume), he found that nonestablishment organizations (both nationally and in San Francisco and Los Angeles) tend to cluster with each other but also connect with mainstream groups. Similarly, when we examine cosponsorship, participation, and leadership of Jewish organizations in Los Angeles, we find both differences and overlap.

Groups considered part of the nonestablishment sphere often cosponsor events together, and groups considered mainstream often do the same. Even so, the most common cosponsorship I noticed was between spheres, because some establishment groups offer much-needed funding and some new groups offer innovative ideas and a broader pool of potential participants.

Events of cultural and social justice organizations are often cosponsored by the Federation or Jewish Community Foundation[18] and sometimes Birthright Israel Next or GesherCity. For example, an evening with AJWS's Ruth Messinger was cosponsored by PJA, Temple Emanuel of Beverly Hills, the New Leaders Project (of the Federation), and the Federation itself. A pre-Passover arts seder was cosponsored by Yiddishkayt, PJA, the Jewish Artists Initiative, GesherCity, the Westside JCC, the Jewish Community Foundation, and some non-Jewish arts organizations. And a JDub event was cosponsored by Nextbook/Tablet and the Jewish Community Foundation. PJA has cosponsored events or collaborated in some way with most Jewish social justice organizations, including AJWS, JFSJ, and Jews United for Justice, as well as most other nonestablishment Jewish organizations, including IKAR, JDub, Yiddishkayt, and Reboot. But PJA has also collaborated with the Federation, Hebrew Immigrant Aid Society, ADL, and other establishment organizations. One PJA professional emphasizes that PJA often offers free cosponsorship to organizations in both spheres "to create greater collaboration with other groups." In fact, according to my research, every nonestablishment organization has "partnered" with establishment organizations in some way or another, a strong indication of the overlap between the two spheres.

In the domain of participation, the norm is also for people to attend events mostly in the establishment or nonestablishment sphere. Even so, overlap occurs. I saw a few of the same people at events run by both establishment and nonestablishment groups—for example, Yiddishkayt's arts seder and a Federation mixer or JConnect's Purimpalooza and IKAR's Purim justice carnival. At the PJA dinner described in the introduction to this chapter, I met people who had attended classes at Aish HaTorah (an Orthodox outreach group) and events at Sinai Atid. At a JDub concert cosponsored by Limmud and the Jewish Community Foundation, I met several people who are involved with PJA, IKAR, and alternative minyanim. And at a JDub bar night cosponsored by Nextbook/Tablet and the Jewish Community Foundation, attendees ranged from casually dressed "hipsters," including one with a mohawk, to financial consultants in suits. I met people there who had attended events with Birthright Next, Aish HaTorah, AIPAC, JConnect, Chai Center (an Orthodox outreach group), and the Federation. JDub, like a number of other organizations, seems to be succeeding in engaging diverse crowds. As one JDub leader says, the perception is that "JDub appeals to a certain type of person, the 'hipster' Jew. I think that JDub does appeal to the hipster Jew, but I think that JDub also appeals to the pretty mainstream, engaged Jew."

One PJA leader talks about a few of her friends who would be unlikely to go to Federation events: "Some of them have tattoo sleeves and mohawks. It just doesn't seem like that would fly at the Federation." On the other hand, she points out that one does not see many tattoos and mohawks at PJA either. And she says she could see some of her unconventional friends getting involved with certain Federation programs or agencies, like the New Leaders Project or Jewish Family Service. In short, different organizations are seen as attracting different types of Jews, and there is some perceived overlap.

When it comes to leaders, we see a similar pattern. A number of young leaders are involved with more than one of the nonestablishment organizations (e.g., PJA and Shtibl Minyan; PJA, Yiddishkayt, Reboot, and IKAR). And a number of people are involved in more than one of the establishment organizations (e.g., Federation and a Conservative synagogue; FIDF and Guardians; FIDF and AIPAC; Stand With Us and an Orthodox synagogue). Several leaders in mainstream organizations were not familiar with some of the social justice and culture groups, and some of the social justice and culture group leaders were not familiar with smaller philanthropic groups like Guardians and FIDF.

Yet we can also observe overlap, for example, in the leaders who have participated both in PJA's Jeremiah Fellowship and in the Federation's New Leaders Project (NLP), which is not surprising given the civic orientation of both programs. One lay leader is active in PJA, AIPAC, and the Federation, beyond the fellowship programs he participated in. He considers himself "progressive on domestic issues" but says he has an "AIPAC point of view on foreign policy." Another leader has worked for several Jewish organizations, including a politically progressive group and a mainstream Israel group. In addition, a number of young lay leaders at AJC, which is often seen as part of the Jewish establishment, are also involved with mainstream or new organizations or both, including the Federation, Jewish Free Loan Association, JDub, IKAR, and PJA.

Another area of overlap involves different types of organizations learning from each other. For example, PJA's Jeremiah Fellowship took elements of the Federation's NLP in planning its programming (although, according to one PJA leader, the organization also looked at elements of the NLP as "what not to do"). More recently, the NLP has sought advice from Jeremiah staff members in order to implement some of PJA's innovative programs, such as bus tours exposing lack of resources in depressed areas. Another example is the Federation's new online newsletter, *The Wire*. In its early months, it used hip-hop music, edgy art (including the graffiti-esque font characteristic of JDub and PJA's promotional materials), engaging writing, and impressive applications of online tools, such as embedded videos, entertaining surveys, and blog discussions. For a while, *The Wire* even listed several "Friends of *The Wire*," none of which would be called mainstream: JDub, Jewcy, Jewlicious, Jewish TV Network, Reboot, *Tablet* magazine, The Righteous Persons Foundation, and Yiddishkayt. This listing of "friends" was clearly an attempt on the part of the Federation to appeal to a younger, less mainstream constituency.

A number of Jewish organizations and programs serve as bridges and unifiers, including Leaders of Young Leaders (LOYaL) and the Federation's NextGen Engagement Initiative. In addition, people who work for Birthright Israel Next say they refer Birthright alumni to all different types of organizations, including AIPAC, AJC, PJA, Aish HaTorah, Chabad, FIDF,

GesherCity, and various synagogues. Similarly, JConnect and the Federation partner with an array of organizations. In fact, a JConnect leader says:

> We're happy, it's a success for us if they come to our event and then they get connected, and then they go to the Federation, a shul, a *kiruv* (outreach) organization, an indie minyan, or some other kind of a thing, because from our point of view, our role is to get them connected. . . . We're able to help build the whole community of L.A. because we don't need to zealously guard our people and keep them away from other organizations, which is a self-preservation thing that many other organizations feel that they have to do.

JConnect has cosponsored events with many organizations, including the Happy Minyan, Orthodox outreach groups (Aish HaTorah and Chai Center), Zionist groups (Zionist Organization of America and Stand With Us), Persian groups (Ledorvador), social groups (JDate), and umbrella groups (Federation). It even cosponsored L.A.'s first Jewish "Tweet-Up" with the innovative Jumpstart, among other groups. Notwithstanding JConnect's partnerships, it is uncommon for Orthodox-run groups to partner with non-Orthodox organizations. Similarly, right-wing Israel groups rarely cosponsor programming with social justice and culture groups. This owes partly to the different ethos of the organizations but also to the lack of overlap in the social networks of those involved.

Another organization that has served as a bridge between spheres is Jumpstart. According to its website, "Jumpstart envisions a Jewish community that is a multi-generational partnership, committed to continuous and intentional self-renewal." Its mission is "to develop, strengthen, and learn from emerging nonprofit organizations that build community at the nexus of community, spirituality, learning, social activism, and culture."[19] Although Jumpstart positions itself as an advocate for the nonestablishment sphere, it has worked closely with the Los Angeles Federation and has even held several of its Jumpstart Innovation Forums—meetings with several nonestablishment organizations—in the Federation building.

The most "bridging" event I found was a conference organized by the Iranian American group 30 Years After in 2008. Cosponsors spanned the spectrum of Jewish life, including Aish HaTorah, AJC, ADL, the Federation, Zionist Organization of America (ZOA), Republican Jewish Coalition, and PJA. This unlikely list of cosponsors is due in large part to the work of one young man who is a leader of 30 Years After, the Federation, PJA, and other organizations. Bridging actions like this are rare, but they bring much-needed interaction to a fragmented community.

Based on this cursory analysis of event sponsorship, participation, leadership, and bridging actions, it is clear that there is a distinction between establishment and nonestablishment organizations but also a good deal of overlap. A Jumpstart report about Jewish innovation says:

> As with any ecosystem, the leaders and participants in the Jewish innovation sector are part of an interconnected web. New organizations feed each other ideas, people, and attention. At its best, the interaction of multiple organizations, each pursuing its own interests, supports the entire ecosystem. The network effect, in turn, strengthens each organization within it. (Jumpstart et al. 2009: 7)

Although this quote refers to the "innovation ecosystem" of "new organizations," I would argue that it also holds true for the "Jewish ecosystem" as a whole.[20]

Given both distinctiveness and overlap between the establishment and nonestablishment spheres, how do leaders of the two differ?" While there is not a one-to-one correspondence, I found that leaders of the different types of groups tend to differ in several ways, including their approach to conventionality, their views about Jewish issues, and their occupational/socioeconomic orientation. Establishment organizations tend to attract Jews who are part of or striving toward the upper class, those in for-profit networking-oriented occupations, those with a conventional orientation, and/or those with a survivalist approach to Jewish issues. Nonestablishment organizations tend to attract progressive Jews with an unconventional orientation and a more universalist approach to Jewish issues, especially people who work in the nonprofit world and are not striving toward the upper class (even if they come from wealthy families). In the sections to follow, I examine these dimensions.

Conventionality and Political Orientation

As we might expect, organizations seen as outside of the establishment tend to attract leaders who take an unconventional or anti-establishment approach to certain aspects of their lives. Many leaders of PJA, JQ International, and other nonestablishment organizations would prefer to patronize an independent coffee shop or bookstore over a Starbucks or a Borders (indeed, I met a few nonestablishment leaders at independent cafés and a few establishment leaders at major chains). They might attend a world music concert over Britney Spears or Beyoncé or even see a local, not-yet-famous hip-hop artist over Snoop Dogg or Kanye West. And when choosing a movie, they might first check the listings at the Laemmle—a family-owned chain of artsy movie theaters in L.A.—and then consider seeing the summer blockbuster at the AMC or Pacific. These preferences may stem from individual differences in aesthetics and progressive or liberal values, but they may also arise from a desire to distinguish themselves from the mainstream and align themselves with others in their peer networks.

This anti-establishment orientation extends to attitudes toward Jewish organizations. While groups like FIDF and Guardians attract leaders who were active in their college fraternities (especially Alpha Epsilon Pi), organizations like Reboot and Yiddishkayt attract leaders who would never step into a fraternity house. Some nonestablishment leaders see the Federation and other establishment groups as similar to the Greek system they disparaged in college. One man who is involved with a few start-ups says of the Federation, "I can't speak for anyone else in my generation, but there is almost nothing of that structure or organization that is appealing to me. In fact, it repulses me." A woman involved with several nonestablishment groups gives reasons why she does not contribute to the Federation, including its "narrow," "institutionalized" nature: "It's just not how I'm Jewish. I'm Jewish in a much more fluid, elastic, creative way."

One Federation professional says he knows the L.A. mind-set and does not believe that people here have a "'hate-the-man' view of the Federation or 'hate-the-institution' view. I think it's more, 'I'm just going to do what I'm going to do'; 'if the Federation's relevant to me or not' is the question." While a few of my interviewees did express an anti-establishment attitude toward the Federation, this professional's statement is for the most part supported by the stances I observed in my research.

Yet, this professional continues, the Federation takes a centrist approach to Israel and other political issues and, therefore, attracts centrist-leaning Jews like himself and might not appeal to people farther to the right and left:

> If you are a Stand With Us–type advocate for Israel, the Federation might be less right [wing] than you want it to be, . . . less of a hard-core advocacy organization, . . . too pareve for them. And on the other hand, if you're a PJA liberal, there may be things you would want us to do [so] that we may be too centrist, too right for them.

While I did not meet people who feel the Federation is too left-wing when it comes to Israel, I did meet a few Orthodox leaders who feel that the Federation does not concentrate enough on the Jewish community, as opposed to its outreach to Latinos and programs like Koreh L.A., a literacy program that benefits mostly non-Jews. I also met several progressive Jews who feel that the Federation is too right-wing. One PJA leader says that she and some of her group's participants feel that the Federation does not portray itself as open to multiple views on Israel. She acknowledges that the Federation "may not have an official statement," but "it's the unofficial things that they do that make it clear what their position is," like the language used in fundraising pitches and rallies. While she does consider it important for the Federation to focus on Israel and antisemitism, she also feels the Federation should focus more on economic issues: "If you're the central address for Jewish communal concern, then you take into consideration that the number-one thing that Jews care about according to the American Jewish Committee survey two years ago is the economy."

Certainly, political orientation plays a role in individuals' decisions regarding which organizations deserve their time and money. However, politics cannot be the only factor. While the right-wing leaders I talked to are involved with organizations that are seen as part of the establishment, a number of establishment leaders are centrist or liberal. Many Federation leaders are active in the Democratic Party. In fact, Steven Cohen's survey (this volume, chapter 2) found that 83 percent of nonestablishment leaders younger than forty identify their political orientation as "liberal," compared to 56 percent of establishment leaders under forty. In addition, some leaders of establishment groups are liberal on domestic issues and centrist or right-wing on international issues, especially Israel. Clearly, then, factors beside conventionality and political orientation influence young Jews' organizational engagement decisions.

Approaches to Jewish Issues

Research has found that young Jews tend to have weaker commitments than their parents to the Jewish people and the State of Israel (e.g., Cohen and Wertheimer 2006). As we might expect from young Jews who take on leadership positions in the Jewish community, the vast majority of leaders I interviewed expressed strong commitments to both the Jewish people and the State of Israel. However, I did find a continuum of positions on a cluster of issues related to the notion of "Jewish peoplehood," from leaders who are focused solely on Jewish concerns and take a survivalist approach to Jewish life to leaders who eschew survivalism and work toward a combination of bonding social capital and bridging social capital (Putnam 2001—that is, social ties among people similar to each other and people of diverse backgrounds). The majority of interviewees fall somewhere in the middle of this continuum, and a number expressed mixed or conflicted views. The issue of Jewish peoplehood is multifaceted and complex, and to understand it adequately, I examine four dimensions: pressing issues facing American Jewry, responsibility to Jews and others, intermarriage, and Israel.

Pressing Issues

I asked interviewees what they see as the most pressing issues facing American Jewry. A number of issues were mentioned by both establishment and nonestablishment leaders, including Jewish literacy, the financial crisis and the costs of Jewish living, the alienation of young Jews from Jewish life, and the lack of pluralistic thinking or the need to connect the "silos" of Jewish life. But a number of other issues came up almost solely in one sphere or the other. A few leaders of establishment organizations mentioned issues that have traditionally been part of the American Jewish communal agenda, including Israel, intermarriage, "continuity," and—for one young leader— antisemitism. In contrast, one nonestablishment leader expressed the view of many when he said he finds the "conservative narrative" of Jewish continuity "both alienating and offensive." Another said, "Maybe the most pressing issue for American Jews is to stop worrying about a decline and to embrace building something new." Some nonestablishment leaders demonstrated the tension between universalism and particularism when they mentioned issues like "the need to reconcile 'If I am not for myself' and 'If I am only for myself.'" Two leaders who are involved solely in nonestablishment organizations topped their list with "public school education," a pressing concern in Los Angeles, but one that most mainstream Jewish leaders would not consider a "Jewish issue."

Responsibility to Jews and Others

In my interviews I asked the leaders about their personal charitable giving. Interviewees varied widely on whether the organizations they give to benefit mostly Jews or non-Jews. Some—especially those involved with nonestablishment organizations and a few Federation professionals—are devotees of the American Jewish World Service and other Jewish organizations that benefit mostly non-Jews. A number of leaders of Israel advocacy and Orthodox organizations had never heard of AJWS and give mostly or solely to organizations that benefit Jews, including some in Israel.

A number of interviewees expressed a tension they felt between helping Jews and helping those in need, whether or not they are Jewish. One woman who works at a nonestablishment organization says, "If Jews don't feel responsibility for the Jewish community, then no one's going to." But she also feels a responsibility toward the most needy individuals, and her charitable giving reflects this tension. She gives to several local non-Jewish organizations (including Homeboy Industries and the Los Angeles Alliance for a New Economy) and Jewish organizations that benefit mostly non-Jews (AJWS,

Jewish Funds for Justice). She emphasizes that she gives to these groups because they work to strengthen Jewish identity and ensure continuity, in addition to their social justice and relief work. She also gives to the Solomon Schechter Jewish Day School she attended, as well as IKAR, and she gives to a few left-wing Israel groups (New Israel Fund, Just Vision). But during the Gaza war of 2008–2009, she gave money to Islamic Relief. She explains:

> I felt really bad for people in Sderot, like totally horrible, it was a lot of people living in terror, and like thirteen people who had actually experienced the terror. . . . [But] it was *hundreds* of Gazans. I personally feel responsibility for it. . . . In my mind I [was] like, "What if someone saw that I was giving my money to Islamic Relief and not to the Federation?" But I felt like that argument was really clear.

Many Jewish leaders, especially in the establishment sphere, would feel uncomfortable with this line of thinking. One Federation professional says, "As a fundraiser, one of the things that I talk about a lot is that only Jews are going to help Jews." Indeed, most establishment leaders I spoke to direct their charitable giving to Jewish organizations like the Federation and the other groups they lead, in addition to universities and cancer-related funds. The most extreme particularist position I encountered was the charitable giving of an Aish HaTorah professional. He gives to Aish HaTorah, two local Orthodox-run social service organizations (Tomchei Shabbos and Global Kindness), and a number of social service organizations in Israel, including Yad Eliezer and Efrat. When I asked another Orthodox outreach professional how he would divvy up a large sum of money, he said, "I'd give all the money to Jews," whom he described as "my blood." It bothers him that the Federation directs so much of its limited resources toward "helping Latinos." He says, "I do believe in *tikkun olam*, but we're in crisis mode. We only have a certain amount of money. . . . If we don't invest in ourselves, we can't invest in *tikkun olam*. We can't put all our marbles outside the basket." For him, the bonding social capital that flows from the work of Jewish-focused organizations is more important than the bridging social capital that derives from Jews helping non-Jews.

The desire to give charity to non-Jews can stem from either a general concern for humanity or an effort to improve the Jewish lot. One woman involved in a cultural organization says, "I feel like I'm responsible to leave the world in a better place than when I got into it, but I don't feel like I necessarily have to prioritize a Jew [above] everybody else." And a woman involved in a social justice organization says, "I feel like helping people who are poor or disenfranchised or whatever, it's just about helping your community, your human community." If she had a large sum of money to distribute, she would give it to those who were most in need, whether or not they were Jewish. Similarly, when I asked a man who is involved in the AJC and a few nonestablishment organizations whether Jews should help Jews alone or everyone, he responded, "I don't think Jews need that much help." These views are in line with Sylvia Barack Fishman's findings (this volume) about many young Jews' rejection of the notion of "us versus them."

In contrast, other leaders want to help non-Jews because they believe bridging social capital benefits the Jewish community. A lay leader involved with the Federation and AIPAC says, "I think it's in Jews' best interest to build alliances and to make friends outside of their own community, be- cause . . . it improves your culture to learn from other cultures, but also in times of need it's good to have friends." Similarly, a professional who works in Jewish community relations at the Federation says, "It takes a village, and you can't survive in this world as an insular community. Our health depends on the health of other communities; we thrive when they thrive. So, I want to see everybody be successful." Even among those leaders whose work and charitable contributions benefit non-Jews, a variety of motivations can be observed—from the more universalist (mostly nonestablishment groups) to the more survivalist (mostly establishment groups).

Intermarriage

Interviewees expressed diverse views and mixed feelings on intermarriage. But unlike the issues in the previous section, leaders' views on intermarriage did not correlate as strongly with the Jewish communal sphere they are in- volved in. Many leaders in both the establishment and the nonestablishment spheres said that intermarriage is a personal choice. A number of interview- ees who are single struggle with the issue for themselves, but they have no problem with Jewish relatives and friends who marry non-Jews. Some said that as long as they find someone who is willing to raise Jewish children, they are okay with marrying a non-Jew. A few interviewees are married to converts to Judaism, one is married to a Christian man who did not convert but participates in Jewish life, and two are dating non-Jews. One single woman in her early forties has given up on dating only Jews. She says she is looking for a man who is Jewish or "Jew-friendly," meaning willing to have a Jewish household. I observed these nontraditional stances on intermarriage from young leaders in both establishment and nonestablishment groups.

On the other hand, a number of the establishment organization leaders are opposed to intermarriage for various reasons. A common concern is the "numbers issue," the "continuity of the Jewish people." One Federation leader says, "I still think in terms of continuity, that it's always better for a

Jew to marry another Jew." (Her use of the word "still" indicates her understanding that many of her peers do not share her view.) Setting the issue in starker terms, an Orthodox outreach professional calls intermarriage "self-destruction" and "personal annihilation," an outlook that was certainly anomalous among my interviewees. Although views on intermarriage do differ in the establishment and nonestablishment spheres, this issue is not as bifurcating as others. This finding reflects changing views about intermarriage, especially in the younger generations.

Israel

The young Jewish leaders I interviewed expressed a vast range of opinions about Israel, as well as a vast range of knowledge. One leader of PJA is also involved with a number of left-wing Israel groups, including Jewish Voice for Peace, and another spent time working in the West Bank for a human rights organization. At the other end of the spectrum is a leader of Stand With Us who calls Israel "the most important thing ever." She says her views on U.S. politics revolve completely around Israel: "You've got my vote if you've got a good view on Israel, and if you don't, then I have no interest . . . [even] if it means that I'm going to have to—whether it's pay more taxes, suffer in some way . . . but [if] that politician has really great views on Israel or plans, then that's fine."

While most interviewees in both spheres expressed a special concern about Israel, a few leaders of nonestablishment organizations told me they do not follow Israel-related news any more than news about other countries. Even a few establishment leaders who are involved in Israel advocacy organizations said that they do not read any Israeli newspapers, although several are easily accessible in English online. One passionate supporter of Israel says, "I know almost nothing about the political parties in Israel," demonstrating this point by mentioning the main parties of several years ago: Likud and Labor. On the other hand, some leaders, especially those who are involved with the AJC, follow the news closely and have very sophisticated knowledge of the conflict and political situation.

The vast majority of interviewees have concerns about the settlements, and most—even some who are involved with Israel organizations—advocate stopping them. However, a few who are involved in Israel advocacy or Orthodox organizations support maintenance and expansion of the settlements. The most extreme view I heard was expressed by an Orthodox outreach professional, who said, "I don't think that they're settlements. I think that they are owned by the Jewish people because the right of conquest is a right recognized by international law." As with the other issues in this section, leaders expressed internal conflicts surrounding the topic of Israel. Those in both establishment and nonestablishment organizations have mixed feelings about the settlements, religious-secular tensions, American involvement in the peace process, and other issues. Even so, those with far-left views on Israel are leaders of nonestablishment groups, and those with far-right views are leaders of Orthodox or Israel advocacy groups.

Factors

While I did not conduct quantitative analysis, my research suggests that the most important factors in individuals' approaches to Jewish peoplehood are how many generations their family has been in the United States and whether they are Orthodox. Almost all the leaders who are involved in mainstream organizations and have a survivalist view about Israel, antisemitism, and assimilation are immigrants or children of immigrants from Iran, Israel, South Africa, and England. One leader who emigrated from Iran with his parents when he was a child comments that he loses sleep worrying about "whether or not my grandkids will be Jewish," as well as "the security of Israel and the strength and vitality of the Jewish community in Los Angeles." Another leader whose parents are from Israel is concerned about the security of the Jewish people in Israel and elsewhere. About the Holocaust, he says, "We can't just think that it won't ever happen again."

The other leaders who tended to have a more survivalist orientation are Orthodox Jews. My nonrandom sample of interviewees included only four Jews who consider themselves Orthodox. The two Modern Orthodox Jews I talked to are involved with Israel advocacy organizations and are concerned about intermarriage, but one takes a more universalist approach to Jewish life, as evidenced by her involvement with social justice issues. The two interviewees to the right of Modern Orthodoxy both work as Orthodox outreach professionals and have a strongly survivalist outlook. Aside from Jews who are close to the generation of immigration and/or Orthodox, the young Jews I spoke to, even several who are involved in the Federation, tend to be less concerned about survivalism and more universalist in orientation.

These qualitative findings are confirmed by the quantitative study conducted by Steven Cohen (this volume, chapters 2 and 3). The survey of professional and volunteer Jewish leaders found that compared to young leaders in establishment organizations, young leaders in nonestablishment organizations are much more likely to contribute to non-Jewish causes and much less likely to express concern about intermarriage, antisemitism, and threats to Israel (see table 4.1).

TABLE 4.1

Differences between Young Leaders (under 40) in Establishment and Nonestablishment Organizations

	Nonestablishment Leaders (%)	Establishment Leaders (%)
Average of individual charitable contributions directed toward Jews	30	54
Agree "It is important to encourage Jews to marry Jews"	18	41
Concerned about fighting antisemitism	23	49
Concerned about threats to Israel's security	23	43

Source: Wertheimer 2010

Clearly, young Jewish leaders in establishment and nonestablishment groups tend to differ in their approaches to issues surrounding Jewish peoplehood.

Socioeconomics and Occupation

As the event descriptions at the beginning of this chapter illustrate, young Jews involved with establishment and nonestablishment organizations tend to cluster in different occupations.[21] Through social and professional networks, individuals are targeted for particular organizations because of their occupation, and their participation in those organizations helps them accrue social and cultural capital (Bourdieu 1986) and advance in pursuit of their professional goals. The aesthetic differences between organizations relate to the socioeconomic and occupational concentrations of the leaders and participants. These differences are not surprising, given correlations between socioeconomic status/occupation and cultural practices/ideology found in previous research (e.g., Bourdieu 1984). In short, social and cultural capital are crucial to young Jews' communal engagements and the perpetuation of establishment and nonestablishment spheres.

Most of the lay leaders I met who are involved in establishment organizations are in the for-profit fields of law, business, and finance. This applies to leaders from Stand With Us, FIDF, Guardians, and several Federation lay leaders. In contrast, most of the lay leaders I met who are involved in nonestablishment organizations are public interest lawyers, educators, artists, professionals in other Jewish organizations, and other nonprofit workers. A former PJA professional described the organization's lay leaders as people who were involved in civil rights movements, including "a lot of lawyers and a lot of professors." The Reboot website describes its participants as "an eclectic and creative mix of people from the literature, entertainment, media, technology, politics, social action and academic realms."[22] Entertainment is a bridge field, as it includes people in business, the arts, and both. I met lay leaders in both establishment and nonestablishment organizations who work in the entertainment industry.

Related to the occupational split, I observed a discourse about mainstream organizations attracting Jews who are part of or striving toward the upper class. When I asked one leader of FIDF to describe the target group for his events, he said, "They like going out to nightclubs, to restaurants, and socializing. They are also either very successful in business or very upwardly mobile." Similarly, a lay leader of the Guardians describes his group as "very Hillcrest, very Brentwood Country Club," naming two prestigious and heavily Jewish country clubs in West Los Angeles. He says, "We see a lot of the old money. A lot of people get involved because their parents were involved." Even so, he says, many of the most active leaders are not from "old money" but are "upwardly mobile . . . young Jewish professionals."

Mainstream organizations plan events with such a crowd in mind, finding a "Malibu mansion," "private Bel Air residence," or "trendy club" as the venue, serving the highest quality cocktails and hors d'oeuvres, and, of course, offering valet parking. I learned about the importance of upscale events from leaders or promotional materials of the Guardians, FIDF, Stand With Us, the AJC, the Federation, 30 Years After, and JConnect. For example, the Federation's Real Estate and Construction Division has events like the "Summer Soirée Young Leadership Cocktail Party at the Gilmore Adobe" and "See and Be Scene Young Leadership Cocktail Party at MODAA [a gallery]." An AJC professional says that some young participants are attracted to "the upper-class nature of the receptions" at "the lovely Beverly Hills home of so-and-so." Some people, she says, "want to be in the room with . . . elegant and important people and drink champagne."

In contrast, I rarely heard about upscale cocktail parties or trendy club events from nonestablishment organizations.[23] When their leaders talk about the aesthetics of their events, words like "edgy" and "provocative" come up more than "sophisticated" and "glamorous." Others have described PJA as an organization that "combines a social justice orientation with a hip, contemporary aesthetic" (Chertok et al. 2009), a characterization in line with the annual dinner description at this chapter's outset. A leader of Yiddishkayt says, "If your idea of being Jewish is going to the big . . . club events that are put on by the Federation and the Israeli consulate, you know, somewhere in Pico Robertson [a heavily Jewish neighborhood] with, like, a crazy Israeli DJ and that sort of thing, that's not necessarily who we're reaching. We're reaching a very different crowd."

The contrasts between establishment and nonestablishment organizations extend beyond the events. One nonestablishment leader contrasts the newsletters of the Federation and her organization: "Their magazine is basically pictures of all their functions with all the wealthy people that give to them and real estate developers who they want to honor. . . . Ours is about the work that people are doing." This was the case, to some extent, until recently, when the Federation started its online newsletter, *The Wire* (discussed earlier), and even that still features profiles of Lions of Judah (women who give at least $5,000 annually) and other high-end donors.

Similarly, Kerri Steinberg (2002) examines fundraising materials for the American Jewish Joint Distribution Committee (JDC) and the New Israel Fund (NIF) and finds a comparable difference in emphasis and aesthetics. In the JDC report, the photos included several donors and board members, and the beneficiaries were depicted in an anonymous way. The NIF report highlighted the activists who lead the beneficiary organizations. In addition, the NIF photos were "more cutting-edge, conveying an artistic sensibility," as contrasted with the JDC's "more conservative, journalistic approach" (Steinberg 2002: 274–75). The aesthetic differences that I found between establishment and nonestablishment organizations are not limited to Los Angeles but can be seen as well in Jewish organizations at the national and international levels.

In line with the socioeconomic differences between the two spheres, some of the people I interviewed see establishment lay leaders as too materialistic or entitled. One public interest lawyer says he attended a few events with the young division of a support group for the Jewish Home for the Aging (similar to the Guardians), but decided not to continue his involvement because he thought the people he met there were "spoiled brats." For the professionals who work at fundraising organizations, socioeconomic differences are often crystal clear. One Federation professional says she sometimes feels a disconnect from her lay leaders, such as when someone in real estate tells her, "You guys should buy a house; it's a great time to get into the market." Even in the down economy, she and her nonprofit-working husband could afford to buy a house in their neighborhood only "if it was half the price."

The survey that was part of this book's larger study offers quantitative evidence for the occupational and socioeconomic split: vast differences in personal income. Among respondents under forty, only 29 percent of lay leaders in nonestablishment organizations report earning $60,000 or more, compared to 53 percent of lay leaders in establishment organizations. Median income for nonestablishment lay leaders was about $43,000, compared to $64,000 among establishment lay leaders. Seven percent of establishment lay leaders report income of $300,000 and up, compared to less than 1 percent of nonestablishment lay leaders.[24]

Factors

There are several factors perpetuating the socioeconomic and occupational differences I found between establishment and nonestablishment groups. First, many establishment organizations, including the Federation, FIDF, and Guardians, exist primarily to raise and distribute funds, and they do so partly by enabling social and professional networking. To meet their fundraising goals, these groups encourage participants with great financial capacity to take on leadership roles. This includes people in profit-oriented professions who have very high income, people who have inherited great wealth, and those serving as hubs of related social networks (often in the older generations, this means stay-at-home wives of wealthy lawyers, bankers, etc.). Among younger participants, this includes people who are currently working their way up the corporate ladder in business, real estate, finance, and law and have great financial potential.

In nonestablishment organizations, fundraising is important but mostly to help them meet their primary goals, which are to enable activism, cultural production and consumption, or religious, educational, or social engagement. While their boards do include wealthy and potentially wealthy people, these organizations encourage participation and leadership activity not just from the upper socioeconomic echelons. This difference in organizational goals leads to occupational clustering.

An outlier in the establishment/nonestablishment mapping is the American Jewish Committee, an organization that of course needs funding to operate but whose primary mission involves behind-the-scenes diplomacy. The AJC lay leaders I interviewed are very diverse in terms of profession and other Jewish involvements. Some are financial analysts and for-profit lawyers, and others are nonprofit lawyers and educators. Some are also involved with PJA, and others are also involved with the Federation. They come together over their shared interest in foreign policy.

Another reason people in different professions are attracted to different organizations relates to social networks. We can assume that people with similar views, values, and cultural practices tend to go into similar professional fields. People with a desire to become rich are more likely to go into professions that will help them attain that goal (or else they marry into wealth), and people dedicated to social justice and helping others are more likely to go into helping professions. Similarly, people with a right-wing political orientation tend to steer clear of social work, education, the arts, and nonprofit management, while people with a left-wing orientation often avoid corporate jobs. In addition, social networks play an important role in individuals' career choices. People tend to go into professions that their friends are in, and they often find jobs through friends or friends of friends.

The values-occupation relationship also works in reverse. We can assume that people in similar occupations tend to make similar decisions on how to spend their leisure time, how to vote, where to live, where to send their children to school, and so on. These decisions are based partly on what people can afford and how they think these decisions will affect their personal and professional well-being. But social networks also play an important role in these decisions. People spend time with their colleagues in and out of the workplace, and they make social and cultural decisions based partly on what their colleagues are doing.

These sociological trends play out in Jewish communal engagement. People in similar professions tend to get involved with similar Jewish organizations. These decisions are based partly on social networks—people hear about Jewish events and leadership opportunities from their friends, many of whom are also their colleagues. Individuals' decisions are also based partly on their interests and political leanings, which are related to their chosen professions. People in finance and business tend to be more conservative politically and would be less likely to be involved with the progressive work of PJA. And leaders of PJA and Yiddishkayt would be less likely to have an interest in soirées and mansions—they might even be offended that the precious dollars of their organizations were being spent on what they see as frills.

Finally, and crucially, Jewish communal involvements help individuals advance in their professions—both in the establishment and nonestablishment spheres. People in many fields thrive professionally because of their social capital. Realtors, mortgage brokers, and real estate lawyers rely on one another to connect to clients. Entertainment financiers, producers, directors, and casting agents succeed when they know and are known by many people in their field. Financial analysts and hedge fund managers need lawyers and doctors to be their clients, doctors need lawyers and businessmen to be their patients, and lawyers need large networks to recommend them when friends need legal help. It is no secret that the federation system taps into the professional need to network (e.g., Cohen 1978, Dashefsky and Lazerwitz 2009). In Los Angeles the three most prominent occupation-based divisions of the Federation are Legal, Entertainment, and Real Estate and Construction. People meet each other at the events, and their stature in their field grows as they take on Federation leadership roles, make large publicly acknowledged gifts, and earn accolades, all of which are interconnected.

The networking nature of many Federation events leads to profit-oriented professions being strongly represented in Federation leadership and participants. The same holds true for other philanthropic organizations, like FIDF and the Guardians. JConnect and Aish HaTorah have tapped into this phenomenon by offering business networking events. An Aish HaTorah professional even started an organization for business and law students in L.A. area universities, called the Jewish Graduate Student Initiative. Individuals' involvement in these organizations helps them expand their professional networks, make deals, land jobs, and advance professionally.

Clearly, the social capital that comes with involvement in mainstream organizations has potential benefits for professional networking and advancement. I also found similar benefits associated with involvement with nonestablishment organizations. For example, artists involved in the Jewish Artists Initiative may meet artists and art industry professionals and find more opportunities to exhibit their work. Musicians' involvement with JDub may help them meet collaborators and, if they are lucky, get signed to the JDub label. Reboot has facilitated several new collaborations and cultural products, helping their producers advance in their careers. Jewish Funds for Justice's Selah Fellowship has helped many Jews in the social justice world to expand their professional networks (and hone job-related skills). PJA has helped its lay leaders advance professionally through networking opportunities, not only through its Jeremiah Fellowship but also through its events and working groups. For example, one nonprofit worker says the skills she obtained and the people she met through the Jeremiah Fellowship will help her do her job more effectively and may even help her when she applies for graduate school or looks for other jobs. When individuals take on leadership roles in an organization, they are likely to strengthen their ties with other leaders—some of whom might be in similar occupations—and accrue the social capital that is so important for professional advancement.

Sociologists have devoted some attention to the relationship among social networks, professional activity, and voluntary involvement (see McPherson 1981, McPherson, Smith-Lovin, and Cook 2001). Galaskiewicz (1985) surveyed corporate contributions officers in Minnesota and their evaluations of prospective nonprofit organizations. He found that they were more likely to hold similar views to corporate colleagues who are more closely connected to them in professional networks. Similarly, Beggs and Hurlbert (1997) found that participation in voluntary organizations that attract both men and women helped job seekers foster social ties that enabled them to find higher status jobs. Active involvement in voluntary organizations was important because it allowed individuals to gain access to expert advice, financing, and other resources, as Davis and Aldrich (2000) found.

The benefits of Jewish communal engagement are not limited to making deals or finding jobs. They extend to one's personal position within various social networks and power structures (see, e.g., Cohen 1978, Odendahl 1990, Chiswick 1991, Ostrower 1995, Dashefsky and Lazerwitz 2009). As Ostrower found in her study of elite philanthropy in New York (including many Jews), "Philanthropy comes to function as a mark of class status that is connected to elite identity" (Ostrower 1995: 25), much like the musical and artistic preferences Bourdieu (1984) found in his study of class in France.

In an interview with one young Federation lay leader, he asked about my preliminary findings. One of the findings I mentioned was that many people involved in the Federation seem to be striving toward the upper class. He agreed but said he would re-phrase "upper class" as: "people involved in the power structure of the community." In fact, he told me that the aspiration for power in the upper echelons of the Los Angeles Jewish community was a major factor in his decision to take on leadership roles in the Federation. He had attended a few events but did not become hooked until he went on an Israel mission with some Federation board members and campaign chairs. Still in his mid-twenties, he was the youngest participant by several decades. But he enjoyed the company of his trip companions and was especially taken by stories one woman told him about her father-in-law, a major Jewish philanthropist. He liked the fact that this man wielded influence over his fellow country club members' philanthropic decisions. He said:

> And the way that she told that story, it sounded like, "Wow. That's how I would like to be." And then seeing the women that were on the trip, I thought, "You know what? This is, this is the kind of wife that I would want to have, and this is the kind of life I would want to have."

He tried out some other Jewish organizations, including the Guardians, but the Federation appealed to him most because of its centrality in Jewish organizational life. He relayed his thought process to me: "Here's the main mountain. If I get to the top of it, then I'm someone." Even in his early thirties, he has become "someone." He has made large gifts to the Federation, organized innovative programs that expand the Jewish learning component of leadership training, married a woman who is also a Federation leader, attained leadership positions, and won several awards, some of which are displayed prominently in his office. His position in the Federation power structure has also helped him in his business, commercial real estate.

Studies of Jewish communal involvement often highlight income but underestimate the importance of occupation. In Dashefsky and Lazerwitz's (2009) multivariate analysis of charitable giving using data from the National Jewish Population Survey (NJPS) 1990, they found that occupation does not have an independent effect on whether or not individuals gave to the UJA. However, in their analysis of 1980s interview data, they found major differences based on whether heads of households were self-employed. They also speculate about differences between doctors and lawyers on the one hand, who have practices tied to their ethnic community, and academics and scientists on the other hand, who do not (2009: 62). Even so, in the same book, they overlook what I see as occupation-based differences. In their qualitative analysis, they offer profiles of a few Jewish couples who are not affiliated with many Jewish organizations and do not donate to the Federation (2009: 76–81). They attribute these couples' desire not to donate primarily to their lack of childhood Jewish socialization experiences. While this factor certainly may play a role, I would point out that, according to the couples' profiles, they are all in education, research, and the arts. In addition, in line with my findings, some are involved with progressive political causes (Amnesty International, the "ban the bomb movement") and non-establishment Jewish life (a havurah, Yiddish culture) or have a countercultural stance in general. While it might be impossible to operationalize these occupation- and attitude-based dimensions for quantitative analysis, qualitative evidence points to their importance.

Another study of Jewish philanthropy highlights trends according to occupation. In Boston, Cohen (1978) found that big businesspeople and lawyers tended to give more to the Federation, while physicians tended to give much less than would be expected based on their income. Cohen's explanation is that businesspeople find great professional benefit from responding positively to their colleagues' solicitations and being seen as major donors, while physicians do not benefit from the same professional networking opportunities. He expresses concern that Jews' diminishing participation in business could lead to trouble for the organized Jewish community's fundraising numbers. Some might argue that this fear has already been realized. As a counterpoint, I would suggest that the Federation's professional divisions include high involvement from young leaders, the parties thrown by the young divisions of the FIDF and the Guardians are among the most popular events for wealthy young Jews in L.A., and all these young divisions raise many thousands of dollars for their organizations.

In addition, the increasing presence of Jews in the nonprofit and arts fields leads to more person power for new Jewish organizations, a cause for optimism within certain circles. These organizations need committed members who have financial capacity and can sustain the organizations when the grant monies dry up. But since the nonestablishment groups focus on culture and social justice and not primarily on fundraising, they do not need to worry as much as mainstream organizations about the financial capacity of their participants. Clearly, the relationship among occupation, social capital, and Jewish organizational engagement is alive and well, and I would argue that it is contributing to the diversity and vitality of the Jewish ecosystem.

Conclusion

Based on this analysis of several Jewish organizations in Los Angeles and their young leaders, we can discern two distinct but overlapping spheres of Jewish communal life: the mainstream or establishment sphere, focusing on philanthropy, social service, and Israel, and the unconventional or nonestablishment sphere, focusing on culture, social justice, and alternative engagement. These spheres are important in showing how young Jewish leaders—especially in nonestablishment groups—think about their work, and they fill important niches in the community. Different organizations attract Jews of different occupations, social and political orientations, and views about Jewish issues.

As this chapter found, social class plays an important role in the contemporary Jewish communal structure. Historically, Jews' synagogue and institutional affiliations were a key marker and constituter of socioeconomic status and advancement (e.g., Kramer and Leventman 1961, Epstein 1978, Diner 2004, Sarna 2004). Today, too, Jews continue to participate in Jewish organizations based partly on their occupation and social class. In line with recent work that has brought attention to the economics of American Jewish life (e.g., Chiswick 2008), this chapter suggests that further research on socioeconomic dynamics could increase our understanding of Jews' social networks and institutional engagement.

This chapter also increases our understanding of American Jews in their twenties and thirties. Much of the literature on young Jewish adults focuses on their negative attitudes toward Jewish communal organizations. Greenberg's (2006) study of Gen-Y Jews emphasizes their lack of knowledge or negative experiences with mainstream groups. Cohen and Kelman (2005) highlight young Jews who prefer attending cultural events to becoming members of Hadassah, the ADL, and other long-standing institutions. In advocating for start-ups, Jumpstart et al. (2009) even discuss mainstream organizations in the past tense:

> The Jewish communal infrastructure of the last century was built to unify, centralize, and coordinate the fragmented landscape of late nineteenth- and

early twentieth-century Jewish organizational life in America. Federations, defense organizations, and the denominational movements all were highly effective responses to this need for unity. These hierarchical and bureaucratic organizations drove the Jewish communal agenda and served as the primary addresses for involvement in American Jewish life throughout the last century. (4)

As I found in my research, these organizations are still serving as the primary addresses for involvement for many American Jews in their twenties and thirties (see also Wertheimer, this volume). For some of these young leaders, the Jewish communal agenda of the twentieth century is also the Jewish communal agenda of the early twenty-first century. Some, especially immigrants and their children, Orthodox Jews, and those in for-profit, networking-oriented professions, are the current and future leaders of the Jewish communal infrastructure founded in a previous era.

On the other hand, many young Jews are not interested in this agenda or these organizations and are founding and leading new organizations, constituting the nonestablishment sphere. These new groups share leaders and participants and cosponsor events together, but there is also some overlap with establishment groups. This diversity in the population of young Jewish leaders suggests that what has been seen merely as a generation gap is also a gap in social class and political orientation.

Some might argue that a glut of organizations caters to the young adult population, especially those with an emphasis on socializing and networking. At a Federation meeting geared toward leaders of new organizations, one speaker asked audience members why they were not part of existing Jewish organizations. Because it's not cool, was his joking reply: "Your Purim party is so much cooler than the other" (the force behind the alternative Purim party laughed good-heartedly at that). "You've got to leave your ego at the table. It doesn't always have to be new, and it doesn't necessitate a new organization." My research suggests that sometimes it does. While some redundancy may exist within the establishment sphere (certain young Jews see each other at multiple fundraising dinners each week), many groups are filling a niche, offering Jews opportunities to spend time and engage in common activities with like-minded Jews. Niche groups are serving populations of recent immigrants, queer Jews, and Jews who hold left-wing views about Israel. Even if these Jews do not feel marginalized by establishment Jewish organizations (and some certainly do), they derive great pleasure and social capital from interacting with other Jews like themselves in an institutional setting.

One nonestablishment leader highlights the importance of niche groups: "If there are a group of Jews who are interested in bocce ball, then as a Jewish community, we should think about bocce ball." Inspired by a Jumpstart report, this leader offers a metaphor from business. He says that in the twenty-first century, both business and Jewish life "will look like a forest, but a forest of bonsai trees, not a forest of redwoods. . . . There will be many small trees that all are separate identities serving separate populations with very small ecosystems that support them." An educator, writing about the "silos" of Jewish life, echoes these sentiments and the ecological metaphor: "The more diverse the Jewish community, the better we can adapt to different environmental conditions. Helping Jews develop diverse ways of connecting to Judaism is key to our ecosystem's survival" (Moskowitz 2007: 3).

In the 1980s and 1990s, there was a good deal of talk about interdenominational strife and its negative effects on Jewish communal life (e.g., Wertheimer 1997). While remnants of this friction persist today, especially between Orthodox and non-Orthodox Jews, we now see an emerging tension between establishment and nonestablishment organizations. In addition to competition for funding and for dates on the calendar, we see negative views based on lack of knowledge or stereotypes about participants. Through the current volume and similar research, groups can gain a better understanding of each other's values, motivations, and goals. And communal leaders can recognize that both establishment and nonestablishment groups are serving important niches, ultimately working to strengthen the Jewish people and the Jewish future.

APPENDIX
Organizations Included in This Study

Groups seen as establishment / mainstream / conventional:
1. American Israel Public Affairs Committee (AIPAC): A national organization that fosters relationships with U.S. elected officials in order to strengthen the U.S.-Israel relationship, AIPAC has branches on many college campuses, and several of my interviewees attended AIPAC national conferences as college students. Graduates can continue involvement through local events and programs.
2. American Jewish Committee (AJC): The AJC works behind the scenes through research, education, and diplomacy to help safeguard Jews in the United States, Israel, and elsewhere. The AJC's Access program allows young people not only to participate in their own group but also to gain access to seasoned AJC leaders and the high-level officials with whom they build relationships.
3. Birthright Israel Next: Under the auspices of local federations, this group offers Birthright Israel alumni opportunities for Jewish engagement in the cities where they live. The local chapter is run by two professionals who organize a variety of programs and guide alumni to Jewish events, synagogues, and classes of interest to them.

4. Friends of the Israel Defense Forces (FIDF): A national philanthropic organization, FIDF raises money for social and recreational programs for soldiers in the IDF and provides assistance to families of fallen soldiers. The L.A. chapter, one of the country's largest, has an active young leadership division that runs upscale social events and an annual mission to Israel.

5. GesherCity: An online portal for Jewish involvement for young adults, GesherCity includes local resources, a calendar of events, and participant-generated "cluster groups" for hiking, social action, and other activities. GesherCity is run by the Jewish Community Center Association and has been lauded for its success in Boston and elsewhere. The L.A. chapter remains small, due mostly to limited resources.

6. Jewish Federation: A "convener" for Jewish life in Los Angeles, the Federation raises and distributes funds locally and abroad. As part of a major restructuring effort led by board chairman Stanley Gold, the Federation has focused new attention on its Young Leadership Divisions and has reached out to young people to participate on the board, which has contracted greatly in recent years.

7. Jewish Free Loan Association: JFLA is a century-old microlending organization. Its young professionals group, Genesis, organizes social and educational events with the goal of increasing donor support and client volume.

8. Guardians of the Jewish Home for the Aging: A century-old Los Angeles Jewish institution, the Jewish Home is supported by a number of fundraising groups, including the Guardians (Westside) and the Executives (Valley). The young leadership divisions organize social and fundraising events such as mixers, comedy nights, the men's division's golf tournaments, and the women's division's "Shopping for a Cause."

9. Stand With Us: Founded in 2001, this group provides speakers and educational materials to ensure that "Israel's side of the story is told in communities, campuses, libraries, the media and churches."[25] The local L.A. branch recently started a young leadership division, which has social events to raise awareness about the organization and its cause.

Groups seen as outside the establishment / unconventional / innovative:

1. JDub: "Dedicated to innovative Jewish music, community, and cross cultural dialogue," JDub produces recordings and organizes concerts and parties geared toward young adults. Although JDub is based in New York, it has a growing presence in Los Angeles, including a staff member and local advisory council.

2. JQ International: A "safe space" for gay, lesbian, bisexual, and transgender (GLBT) Jews in their twenties and thirties "to reconnect to Judaism on their terms,"[26] JQ offers social networking programs, events surrounding most Jewish holidays, GLBT identity education, and consultation/training for Jewish organizations.

3. Progressive Jewish Alliance (PJA): From its founding in 1999, PJA has been led by a relatively young group of professional and volunteer leaders. PJA's Los Angeles regional council includes many Jews in their twenties and thirties, and two of its flagship programs are fellowships for those age groups: the Jeremiah Fellowship and New Ground: A Muslim-Jewish Partnership for Change.

4. Reboot: Founded by leaders of cutting-edge philanthropies, Reboot brings together young, influential Jews to talk about Jewishness at summits and salons. Because of the secretive way prospective participants are tapped, one Rebooter dubbed it "Jewish hipster skull and bones." A number of cultural products have emerged from Reboot networks, including several films, a quarterly magazine, and a record label.

5. Yiddishkayt L.A.: This group organizes festivals, concerts, "*kugl kuhk*-offs," and educational programming to bring Yiddish culture to the next generation. It recently started the Yiddishkayt Folks-Grupe, a three-month fellowship for young adults to learn about Yiddish culture.

Groups seen as neither establishment nor nonestablishment:

1. 30 Years After: A group of young Iranian American Jews recently founded this organization to encourage civic participation among Iranian Jews in the United States, especially surrounding the issue of Israel. They organize conferences, voter registration drives, letter-writing campaigns, and social events. Their upscale parties attract hundreds of Jews in their twenties and thirties, the vast majority of whom are Iranian.

2. Aish HaTorah: An Orthodox-run *kiruv* (outreach) organization, Aish HaTorah offers non-Orthodox Jews social and networking events, classes, religious services, Shabbat meals, and trips. The Los Angeles chapter has sections for young professionals ages eighteen to thirty-three, college students, young couples, and, through its quasi-independent subsidiary, the Jewish Graduate Student Initiative, law and business students on several L.A.-area campuses.

3. JConnectLA: A new organization started as an informal group of friends in its Orthodox founder's home, JConnect now has a mailing list of several thousand young Jews in L.A. JConnect fulfills its mission "to promote and inspire Jewish connectivity, community and identity" through diverse programs ranging from High Holiday services and meals to business networking events, from Bibliyoga and hikes to "sushi and sake."

This list is by no means exhaustive. By design, I did not include organizations that are primarily in the religious and educational spheres, as several have been analyzed in previous work (e.g., Cohen and Kelman 2007, Belzer and Miller 2007, Cohen et al. 2007). If I had included the religious/educational sphere, I would have looked at the all-volunteer educational group Limmud L.A.; new spiritual communities like IKAR; independent minyanim like Pico Egal, Shtibl, and Maley Shirah; several Orthodox congregations that attract large numbers of young adults, especially the Modern Orthodox synagogues B'nai David Judea and Beth Jacob; and long-standing Conservative and Reform synagogues that have vibrant young adult groups or Shabbat services, including Sinai Temple's Atid and Friday Night Live and Stephen S. Wise's W Group. Several of these religious groups, especially IKAR and Sinai Atid, came up repeatedly in my research because of their centrality in the establishment and nonestablishment spheres.

Even within the social, cultural, political, and philanthropic realms, there are several other organizations geared toward Jews in their twenties and thirties that are not analyzed in depth in this chapter, due to time constraints. These include Jumpstart, the Professional Leaders Project, Moishe House,[27] JCafeLA, Nextbook/Tablet, the Jewish Artists Initiative, the L.A. Jewish Film Festival, the Shalom Institute, Aaron's Tent, the Lev Foundation,

Ledorvador, Sababa Parties, Sephardic Tradition and Recreation (STAR), Israel 21C, several Orthodox outreach organizations (Chabad, Yachad Outreach Center, Isralight, Jewish Learning Exchange, Jewish Awareness Movement), young adult divisions/programs of the ADL, JDC, ZOA, Hebrew Immigrant Aid Society (HIAS), Women's International Zionist Organization (WIZO), ORT, Hadassah, the National Council of Jewish Women, New Israel Fund, and Magbit; Orthodox social service groups like Etta Israel, Tomchei Shabbos, Bikur Cholim, and Global Kindness; "friends of" various institutions in Israel; and educational institutions like Hebrew Union College–Jewish Institute of Religion and the American Jewish University. Even as I conducted research, a number of new organizations were started, including an L.A. chapter of Dor Chadash and Young Leaders of the American Friends of the Citizens' Empowerment Center in Israel. In fact, in 2009, Julie Childers (2009) estimated that at least seventy-five groups and organizations in Los Angeles reached Jews in their twenties and thirties. The young adult scene in Los Angeles is huge, multifaceted, and ever-changing, and it would be impossible to analyze every group in depth.

NOTES

This work is generously funded by the AVI CHAI Foundation. Thank you to the members of the research team for helping me conceptualize and realize the study—Jack Wertheimer, Steven M. Cohen, Sylvia Barack Fishman, Shaul Kelner, and Ari Y. Kelman—and to our consultants, Riv-Ellen Prell, Jack Ukeles, and J. Shawn Landres. Thank you also to my research assistants, Katie Light and Chaim Singer-Frankes, and to Mark Benor and Roberta Benor. Most important, thank you to the many Jewish leaders who were so generous with their time and thoughts. May this chapter help you in the valuable work you're doing.

1. Some might question the notion of including lay and professional leaders in the same study. After all, professionals are just doing their job; lay leaders are giving voluntarily of their time and often money. While I did encounter some professionals who see their work as a job rather than a passion, the vast majority of interviewees are ideologically committed to their work. A few federation employees, especially those who started their involvement as lay leaders, joked about "drinking the [Federation] Kool-Aid" and told me proudly that their largest charitable gift is to the federation. Another rationale for including lay and professional leaders in the same study is that the boundary between the two is permeable. A number of professionals, including at PJA and the Federation, started their involvement as lay leaders. A professional leader of JQ International began his involvement as a lay leader. And a lay leader with a few organizations says he can see himself dropping out of the corporate world and becoming a Jewish professional in the future. In addition, some of the professional leaders I interviewed are lay leaders at other organizations. For example, one woman who has worked at three Jewish organizations is currently a board member of two others. Organizers of the now-defunct Professional Leaders Project recognized the permeable boundaries between lay and professional leadership and included both categories in their programs (Landres 2009). Whether they are Jewish professionals, volunteers, or both, the young leaders I interviewed will likely have an impact on the Jewish world in years to come.

2. Jumpstart, http://jewishjumpstart.org, accessed March 2010.

3. The lower number is likely an underestimate, and the higher number includes outlying areas (personal communication, Bruce Phillips and Sergio DellaPergola, December 2009).

4. See Chichowolski de Jenik and Jenik 2005 on Latin American Jews, Golshan 2005 on Iranian Jews, and Schwarz 2009 on Israeli Jews.

5. But see Chiswick (2008: 14) on Jews' decreasing representations in some of these professions.

6. See the Los Angeles page of the GesherCity main website (www.geshercity.org).

7. See Moore (1994) on the historical basis for this fragmentation and individualism.

8. See, e.g., Rebecca Spence, "Leaders of Indie Prayer Groups Get Grants, Become Mainstream Darlings," *Forward*, October 8, 2008.

9. See, e.g., Claire Levenson, "Leading Blogger Joins Jewish Mainstream," *Forward*, August 15, 2007.

10. See, e.g., James D. Besser, "Jewish Groups Seek Distance From Peace Summit," *Jewish Week*, October 25, 2007; Amy Klein, "New Coalition Aims to Make Social Justice a Community Priority," October 25, 2009, JTA.

11. See, e.g., Marilyn H. Karfeld, "Chevrei Tikva to Close, Join Anshe Chesed," *Cleveland Jewish News*, June 2, 2005.

12. See, e.g., Rebecca Spence, "Think Tank Aims to Infuse Jewish Mainstream with Dashes of Color," *Forward*, May 8, 2008.

13. Joshua Avedon, "Where Would Darwin Daven?" *Forward*, December 4, 2008.

14. Ruth Messinger, "Making Service Fundamental to Jewish Life," *Jewish Currents*, September 2003.

15. Isaac Luria, "In Machers vs. Obama, the Youth Have Voted," *Forward*, July 24, 2009.

16. For more examples of this rhetoric, see Jumpstart et al. (2009).

17. Although they are not included in my research, left-wing Israel organizations, like the New Israel Fund, J Street, Brit Tzedek v'Shalom, and Americans for Peace Now, are discussed as part of the innovative sphere. During my fieldwork, these groups did not have young adult divisions and did not attract many young Jews in Los Angeles. In fact, the one event I observed that was cosponsored by a number of left-wing Israel groups was led and attended mostly by older Jews. I noted that only about eight of the fifty attendees were under forty-five, and most of these were active in IKAR, PJA, Shtibl, or other innovative organizations. The age of the crowd was explicitly referenced a few times. One speaker, when discussing the new J Street U college group, said ironically: "I'm assuming you all just graduated from college. . . . Okay, maybe you have a grandchild in college." In fact, one leader involved with the Los Angeles chapter of J Street, which was launched a year after my research, said, "I think that J Street was founded just as much to get out from under generationally stratified progressivism as to counter the right wing." In contrast, a few of the right-wing Israel groups have substantial young leadership divisions, including FIDF and Stand With Us. Others, including the Zionist Organization of America, cosponsor events with young groups like JConnect.

18. In some cases, cosponsorship merely indicates that the organizing group received a grant from the co-sponsoring group. Foundation grant recipients are required to include the Foundation's logo on promotional materials.

19. Jumpstart, http://jewishjumpstart.org/about, accessed March 2010.

20. As Moskowitz argues, "Applying the metaphor of an ecosystem to Jewish life offers a rich picture of the complexity of the dynamics between individual community members, between the multiplicity of institutions, and the integrated elements of Jewish life" (Moskowitz 2007: 3).

21. When we talk about occupation, we must focus on lay leaders, as professional leaders necessarily work in the Jewish nonprofit field.

22. Rebooters.net, "Reboot Summits," accessed March 2010.

23. An exception is Bet Tzedek's annual Justice Ball, an impressive club event that brings in thousands of young Jews.

24. Thank you to Steven Cohen for providing these data.

25. StandWithUs, www.standwithus.com/ABOUT/, accessed March 2010.

26. JQ International, www.jqinternational.org/programs-social.php, accessed March 2010.

27. During the time of my fieldwork, the Moishe House in Los Angeles had ceased to operate. But according to the remnant web presence, the people who ran the L.A. Moishe House before my fieldwork had relatively conventional fraternity-like social activities (parties, poker nights). The people running the new L.A. Moishe House after my fieldwork would be seen as unconventional: they include a black Jew, a lesbian Jew, and Jews of various levels of religious observance, some of whom are engaged in social justice and cultural activities with "unconventional" groups like IKAR and JQ International (Orit Arfa, 2009. "Moishe House's Creative, Communal Living," *Jewish Journal*, September 9, 2009.). The first iteration of Moishe House L.A. would likely be classified as conventional and the second as unconventional.

REFERENCES

Beggs, John J., and Jeanne S. Hurlbert. 1997. "The Social Context of Men's and Women's Job Search Ties: Voluntary Organizational Memberships, Social Resources, and Job Search Outcomes." *Sociological Perspectives* 40: 601–22.

Belzer, Tobin, and Donald Miller. 2007. "Synagogues That Get It: How Jewish Congregations Are Engaging Young Adults," *S3K Report*, Spring 2007.

Bourdieu, Pierre. 1984. *Distinction: A Social Critique of the Judgement of Taste.* Cambridge, MA: Harvard University Press.

Bourdieu, Pierre. 1986. "The Forms of Capital." In *Handbook for Theory and Research for the Sociology of Education*, edited by J. G. Richardson, 241–58. New York: Greenwood.

Bronznick, Shifra, and Didi Goldenhar. 2008. *Visioning Justice and the American Jewish Community.* New York: Nathan Cummings Foundation.

Chertok, Fern, Theodore Sasson, and Leonard Saxe. 2009. *Tourists, Travelers, and Citizens: Jewish Engagement of Young Adults in Four Centers of North American Jewish Life.* Waltham, MA: Maurice and Marilyn Cohen Center for Modern Jewish Studies, Brandeis University.

Chichowolski de Jenik, Judith, and Ariel Jenik. 2005. "Jewish Spanglish: The Latin American Jewish Community of Los Angeles." Master's thesis, Hebrew Union College–Jewish Institute of Religion, School of Jewish Communal Service.

Childers, Julie. 2009. "J-How: Organizational Strategies for Reaching Los Angeles Jews in Their Twenties and Thirties." Paper presented at the Association for Jewish Studies' Forty-first annual meeting, Los Angeles, December 21.

Chiswick, Barry R. 1991. "An Economic Analysis of Philanthropy." In *Contemporary Jewish Philanthropy in America*, edited by Barry A. Kosmin and Paul Ritterband, 3–15. Savage, MD: Rowman and Littlefield.

Chiswick, Carmel U. 2008. *The Economics of American Judaism*. New York: Routledge.

Cohen, Steven M. 1978. "Will Jews Keep Giving? Prospects for the Jewish Charitable Community." *Journal of Jewish Communal Service* 55/1: 59–71.

Cohen, Steven M., and Ari Y. Kelman. 2005. "Cultural Events & Jewish Identities: Young Adult Jews in New York." New York: National Foundation for Jewish Culture.

Cohen, Steven M., and Ari Y. Kelman. 2007. "The Continuity of Discontinuity: How Young Jews Are Connecting, Creating, and Organizing Their Jewish Lives." New York: Andrea and Charles Bronfman Philanthropies.

Cohen, Steven M., and Jack Wertheimer. 2006. "Whatever Happened to the Jewish People?" *Commentary*, June 2006: 33–37.

Cohen, Steven M., J. Shawn Landres, Elie Kaunfer, and Michelle Shain. 2007. "Emergent Jewish Communities and Their Participants: Preliminary Findings from the 2007 National Spiritual Communities Study." New York: S3K Synagogue Studies Institute and Mechon Hadar.

Dashefsky, Arnold, and Bernard Lazerwitz. 2009. *Charitable Choices: Philanthropic Decisions of Donors in the American Jewish Community*. Lanham, MD, Lexington Books.

Davis, Amy, and Howard Aldrich. 2000. "The Organizational Advantage? Social Capital, Gender, and Small Business Owners' Access to Resources." Paper presented at the American Sociological Association annual meeting, http://www.unc.edu/~healdric/Workpapers/WP132.pdf.

Dear, Michael J., and Steven Flusty. 2002. "The Resistible Rise of the L.A. School." In *From Chicago to L.A.: Making Sense of Urban Theory*, edited by Michael J. Dear, 3–16. Thousand Oaks, CA: Sage Publications.

DellaPergola, Sergio. 2007. "World Jewish Population, 2007." *American Jewish Yearbook* 107: 551–600. New York: American Jewish Committee.

Diner, Hasia. 2004. *The Jews of the United States: 1654–2000*. Berkeley: University of California Press.

Epstein, A. L. *Ethos and Identity: Three Studies in Ethnicity*. London: Tavistock Publications.

Galaskiewicz, Joseph. 1985. "Professional Networks and the Institutionalization of a Single Mindset." *American Sociological Review* 50: 639–58.

Golshan, Ziba. 2005. "Negotiating between the Hyphen: A Quantitative Study of Iranian Jews in Los Angeles." Master's thesis, Hebrew Union College–Jewish Institute of Religion, School of Jewish Communal Service.

Greenberg, Anna. 2006. *"Grande Soy Vanilla Latte with Cinnamon, No Foam . . ." Jewish Identity and Community in a Time of Unlimited Choices*. New York: Reboot. 3–33.

Herman, Pini. 1998. *Los Angeles Jewish Population Survey '97*. Los Angeles: Jewish Federation of Greater Los Angeles.

Jumpstart, the Natan Fund, and the Samuel Bronfman Foundation. 2009. *The Innovation Ecosystem: Emergence of a New Jewish Landscape*. Los Angeles and New York: Jumpstart, the Natan Fund, and the Samuel Bronfman Foundation.

Klein, Laurel. 2009. "Mitzvah Bar: A New Model for the Young Adult Jewish Community." Master's thesis, Hebrew Union College–Jewish Institute of Religion, School of Jewish Communal Service.

Kramer, Judith R., and Seymour Leventman. 1961. *Children of the Gilded Ghetto: Conflict Resolutions of Three Generations of American Jews*. New Haven: Yale University Press.

Landres, Shawn. 2009. "A Break in the Pipeline." *Jewish Journal*, August 26, 2009. Mc-Pherson, J. Miller. 1981. "A Dynamic Model of Voluntary Affiliation." *Social Forces* 59: 705–21.

McPherson, J. Miller, Lynn Smith-Lovin, and James M. Cook. 2001. "Birds of a Feather: Homophily in Social Networks." *Annual Review of Sociology* 27: 415–44.

Moore, Deborah Dash. 1994. *To the Golden Cities: Pursuing the American Jewish Dream in Miami and L.A.* New York: Free Press.

Moskowitz, Nachama Skolnick. 2007. "The Space between the Silos: Nurturing the Jewish Ecosystem." Coalition for Advancement of Jewish Education and Berman Jewish Policy Archive.

Odendahl, Teresa. 1990. *Charity Begins at Home: Generosity and Self-Interest among the Philanthropic Elite*. New York: Basic Books.

Ostrower, Francie. 1995. *Why the Wealthy Give: The Culture of Elite Philanthropy*. Princeton: Princeton University Press.

Phillips, Bruce. 2007. "Faultlines: The Seven Socio-Ecologies of Jewish Los Angeles." *The Jewish Role in American Life: An Annual Review* 5: 109–37.

Putnam, Robert D. 2001. *Bowling Alone: The Collapse and Revival of American Community*. New York: Simon & Schuster.

Sarna, Jonathan. 2004. *American Judaism: A History*. New Haven: Yale University Press.

Schwarz, Anna. 2009. "Is My Heart in the East if I Am in the West? A Study of Israelis Living in Los Angeles." Master's thesis, Hebrew Union College–Jewish Institute of Religion, School of Jewish Communal Service.

Steinberg, Kerri P. 2002. "Contesting Identities in Jewish Philanthropy." In *Diasporas and Exiles: Varieties of Jewish Identity*, edited by Howard Wettstein, 253–78. Berkeley: University of California Press.

Ukeles, Jacob B., Ron Miller, and Pearl Beck. 2006. *Young Jewish Adults in the United States Today*. New York: American Jewish Committee.

Wertheimer, Jack. 1997. *A People Divided: Judaism in Contemporary America*. Waltham: Brandeis University Press.

Wertheimer, Jack. 2010. "Generation of Change: How Leaders in Their Twenties and Thirties Are Reshaping American Jewish Life." New York: AVI CHAI Foundation.

SYLVIA BARACK FISHMAN,
WITH RACHEL S. BERNSTEIN
AND EMILY SIGALOW

5 Reimagining Jewishness

Younger American Jewish Leaders, Entrepreneurs, and Artists in Cultural Context

T HIS CHAPTER DISCUSSES the Jewish attitudes, ideas, norms, and values that animate the enterprises of young leaders and cultural figures. Innovative Jewish institutions created by entrepreneurial American Jews in their twenties and thirties have proliferated in recent years. Simultaneously, the cultural realm has seen a veritable explosion of literature, music, film, art, and electronic media drawing on Judaic cultural materials and exploring issues of pressing concern to younger Jews. These cultural expressions, institutions, and organizations created by young American Jews reflect and influence new understandings of Jewishness that, while quite diverse, differ strikingly from those of previous generations. Together, they indicate that younger American Jews inhabit a different Jewish world from that of their parents and grandparents.

Our discussion is based on interviews and focus group discussions with influential social justice advocates, rabbis, educators and scholars, writers, bloggers, musicians and impresarios, businesspersons, and artists.[1] We juxtapose these and other young leaders' revisionings of Jewishness and its role in their lives, and their perceptions of the wider culture and their relationship to it, with the entities they have created. We incorporate artistic expressions, especially recent literature and music, into our analysis because many of the attitudes, values, and behaviors manifested in our interviews are in conversation with those in literature, music, and other cultural materials. Artists are often trailblazers, drawing attention to emerging social developments. Not least, we study cultural Jewishness because our interviews reveal that for many young American Jews, culture—not "tribalism" that views the world divided into "us" and "them"—offers an important way to define their Jewish ethnicity and peoplehood.

Ethnicity as Cultural Jewishness

In recent decades, American Jewish identity has widely been understood as individualistic and personalized, and it is sometimes described as a series of rational choices in a marketplace of ideas. However, sociologists of religion such as Robert Wuthnow warn that "rational choice" theory pays too little attention to the profound impact of social and cultural norms on people's actual beliefs and actions—especially when looking at "the current patterns of religious belief and practice among young adults."[2] Journalist Malcolm Gladwell agrees, arguing that researchers miss critical dimensions of "an individual's personal choices or actions in isolation" without studying their community. To fully understand the outstanding individual, one must "look *beyond* the individual" and understand the culture to which she belongs, her friends and families, and her family's hometown. The values of the people we surround ourselves with have a profound effect on who we are.[3] Gladwell shows that even those characteristics that appear most idiosyncratic and individualistic are embedded in and often emanate from societal "structural dimensions."[4]

By looking at leaders, cultural creators and shapers, and the culture they produce, we have discovered a major paradigm shift: young American Jews define ethnicity in ways different from their predecessors and from many social scientists. Prior studies have often asserted that, while religion re-mains stable, a sense of ethnicity is declining among young American Jews.[5] However, our research shows that strong ethnic feeling is a central aspect of the attachment to Jewishness of many young Jews, but they perceive cul-tural expressions—rather than tribal identification—as the core of their eth-nic connections.

Some sociologists argue that ethnic identity is primarily about bound-aries, rather than cultural distinctiveness. That conception of ethnicity is accurate when describing many older American Jews, who, whether they themselves are secular or religiously observant, and whether attached to or alienated from communal institutions, often articulate a keen consciousness of Jewish peoplehood, highlighted by a clearly constructed "us" and "them." Where boundaries are important to ethnic identity, strong tribal taboos often exist against marital alliances with outsiders.

In contrast, other social scientists emphasize content or "nuclei," includ-ing ethnic languages, values, behavior, and cultural expressions—often grouped together as "social capital"—rather than the porous and shifting boundaries between ethnic groups.

Younger American Jews frequently embrace the particulars of Jewish cul-ture. Many of them have cherished networks of Jewish friends but still reject "us" and "them" constructions of ethnicity. In a marked change from the past, Jews in their twenties report a strong attachment to Jewish ethnicity but define Jewish music, food, books, comedy and cultural performance, family styles, and religious rituals as *primary* expressions of ethnicity. They are confused when they read assertions that emphasize ethnic boundaries, because those concepts do not match the way they think and talk about their Jewish ethnicity.

Culture relates directly to how our target population redefines and understands its own Jewishness—particularly in aspects of life involving religion and spirituality. This is common to the age group at large: as Wuthnow admonishes, it is a mistake to regard the role of art and music in young adults' lives "as little more than a form of entertainment." Instead, the arts "interact with their faith." He notes: "In qualitative interviews, young adults frequently point to art and music as sources of inspiration. When creeds and doctrines fail them, they turn to the more intuitive lessons of the arts."[6] Indeed, our interviews with young Jewish leaders and cultural figures ratify that some view artistic expressions as the most compelling and accurate reflection of their religious, spiritual, and/or ethnic connections.

We are especially interested in the conception of Jewishness—as an ethnicity, a religion, a moral system, and/or a culture—that characterizes these young leaders and culture shapers, and the ways in which those expressions of Jewishness play out within their institutional and cultural creations. We begin our analysis with the cultural landscape—the field—that sets the context for contemporary Jewish leadership and cultural expression. The scene is international, global, and eclectic ("Picturing Multicultural Jews around the World"). We next discuss a ubiquitous emphasis on social justice, as expressed not only by young Jewish advocates and their organizations but also by a broad range of young Jewish leaders and culture shapers ("Pursuing Justice Globally—No Special Cases"). We consider conceptions of Jewish peoplehood, which Jews have traditionally regarded as a kinship or family-like relationship, along with attitudes toward the State of Israel and the Jewish diaspora experience, both as related in the interviews and cultural expressions by younger American Jews ("Israel and Jewish Peoplehood"). We look at the focus of an important minority on rigorous Jewish spiritual and intellectual enterprises ("Entrepreneurs Realigning Spiritual Boundaries"). We note that young leaders characteristically describe themselves as being both "inside" and "outside" conventional American Jewish institutional systems ("Challenging Problems from the Inside Out). Our attention then turns to attitudes and behaviors in regard to social groupings, such as the Jewish family, which has often been considered the building block of Jewish societies ("The Personal Is—Still—Political"). Regarding the cultural context, we present music utilizing Jewish materials and targeting younger American Jews as a case study of the centrality of cultural expression ("Jewish Arts Both Particularistic and Universal"). Finally, we consider the implications of these developments for Jewishness today ("Conclusion: 'Scholar-Warriors' Reimagining Jewishness").

Picturing Multicultural Jews around the World

Novels that "claim the world as an extension of their homes" are prevalent among American fiction generally—"all the world's stories are America's stories now," as the travel writer Pico Iyer beautifully articulates the phenomenon.[7] In particular, a fascination with Jews and Jewish societies in far-flung corners of the world—the "planet of the Jews"—characterizes much recent American Jewish fiction. However, planet of the Jews fiction has resonance distinct from non-Jewish fiction and from much of the American Jewish fiction that preceded it.

During the twentieth century, American Jewish fiction primarily told an American story, as Jews developed unique, hybrid forms of Jewishness, blending the values, experiences, and concerns of America with those of historical Jewish communities.[8] Jewish authors were read and celebrated by non-Jewish as well as Jewish readers not only because of their literary excellence but also because their dual vision as Jews and Americans provided insights into American history, culture, and life. Today, when younger Jewish authors fuse international, transhistorical materials, they leave the well-established comfort of self-reflexive American Judaism and cross imaginative boundaries to explore new ways of thinking about Jews and Jewishness. Both tribalism and assimilationalism are replaced in these novels by very individualistic and frequently spiritual yearnings toward personal, rather than national, redemption.

When, in the early 1990s, the nonfiction writer Rodger Kamenetz wrote of a Jewish journey to Tibet to learn from the Dalai Lama and to discover *The Jew in the Lotus* (subtitled *A Poet's Rediscovery of Jewish Identity in Buddhist India*), such boundary crossings seemed edgy and unusual. The encounter Kamenetz described was innovative because it brought knowledgeable Jews into interaction with a non-Western religious ethos,[9] unlike the tendency in the 1970s for Jewish spiritual seekers, who were often ignorant of Judaism, to abandon it in favor of Eastern religions.

The Jewish planet has expanded not only externally but also internally and thematically, with an ethos of cultural fusion, or Jewish multiculturalism. Today, Jewish fiction mainstreams the merging of religious and cultural traditions, like contemporary Jewish music that features the fusion of diverse

ethnic musical traditions—for example, Aharit HaYamim, a band performing in New York for Jewlicious is billed as "Israeli reggae, dub and ska"[10]—
or innovative Jewish fusion cuisine that blends several ethnic culinary traditions. In novels that incorporate cultural fusion, protagonists frequently are
Jews of mixed racial or cultural background, or they fall in love across racial or cultural boundaries. Protagonists identify with ideas and experiences
from diverse sources with an intensity that goes beyond what I have called
"coalescence."[11]

Young American Jews produce novels and music that reflect the ethos of
what Micah Sachs calls "Planet Obama" in discussing the film *Rachel Getting Married*, in which a white woman and a black man are joined by a
"cultural mishmash of a wedding" that is "heavy on Indian influences . . .
Irish music, hip hop dancing, belly dancing, marching band, American bar-
becue." Most telling, Sachs notes, "not one reference is made to the jumble
of races, religions, and ethnicities on display" and "only the most positive
aspects of multiculturalism are apparent."[12]

Rather than portraying Jews in big American cities like New York, for
example, or Jews in Israel—long the staples of American Jewish novelistic
settings—many recent novels offer settings less familiar to American readers:
Argentina, Alaska, Asia, North Africa. The striking relocation of American
Jewish fiction to international destinations has emerged partially because
assimilation is now a stale story, and partially because there is little to struggle against in the familiar American urban setting, producing a paucity of
ready-made dramatic tension. In planet of the Jews novels, Jews travel the
world, which is in many ways unfamiliar. In this world, the Jewish characters encountered by readers often seem unfamiliar as well. In many cases,
the protagonists hurtle from pogroms to pain to unconventional passions,
through a grotesque Jewish picaresque.

By placing the performance of Jewishness in a setting unfamiliar to the
writer and many of his or her readers, the novelist decenters the reader and
creates fresh insights and analysis. Novels about Jews in unfamiliar places
and times stretch the imaginative capacities of the reader as they illuminate
contemporary Jewish existence.

Planet of the Jews novels include such very different works as Nathan
Englander's *The Ministry of Special Cases* (2007), Judith Katz's *The Escape
Artist* (1997), and Rivka Galchen's *Atmospheric Disturbances* (2008), each
of which brings its Jews to Argentina. Jews shiver in Siberia in Anya Ulinich's
Petropolis (2007) and end up in Alaska in Michael Chabon's *The Yiddish
Policemen's Union* (2008) and Amy Bloom's *Away* (2008). Sephardic Jewish
culture and the dislocation of Jews in Muslim, Arab, or North African lands
are depicted in novels such as Dalia Sofer's *The Septembers of Shiraz* (2007)

and Gina Nahai's *Cry of the Peacock* (1991), echoing celebrated pieces of memoir literature portraying similar subject matter and societies. Other novels, such as Gary Shteyngart's *Absurdistan* (2006) and Jonathan Safran Foer's *Everything Is Illuminated* (2002), and Allen Hoffman's strange *Small Worlds* (1996) and *Big League Dreams* (1997), tell unfamiliar stories about European Jews, recounting eerie travels that, whether they proceed through familiar or unfamiliar countries of origin, are painted with grotesque details distant in every way from the warm hominess of *Fiddler on the Roof.* These Jews are not in Kansas—or Kasrilevka—anymore!

Pursuing Justice Globally—No "Special Cases"

The one overriding theme in our interviews with young American Jewish leaders and cultural figures was dedication to global and local social justice through vigorous efforts that transcend ethnic, geographic, and socioeconomic boundaries. That commitment to world justice was articulated by most of the creators of intellectual and religious "start-ups," as well as the young founders of social justice organizations. Cultural signposts and reflections are found in the emphasis on social justice in recent novels such as Englander's powerful *The Ministry of Special Cases*, situated in the nightmare world of 1970s Argentina, where "kidnappings and extortions . . . murders and disappearances" occurred "on all sides."[13] Englander's working-class, everyman protagonist, Kaddish Poznan, illegitimate son of a prostitute and married to an ex-prostitute, Lillian, mistakenly believes that he can protect himself and his family by ignoring growing evidence of Argentine fascism and brutality. "It's a tragedy for someone, but it's not ours," he says to his son Pato when they discover a murdered gentile boy lying between graves in the Jewish cemetery. Rationalizing that the strange boy must have been guilty of some crime or else he would not have been punished, Kaddish asserts, "The government is cleaning up and when they're done things can only improve."

But young Pato—the moral touchstone of Englander's novel—refuses to rationalize evil or make himself unknowing about social injustice. He rejects Poznan's division of the moral world into insiders who deserve a principled fight for justice and outsiders who do not. "It was another kid," the clear-eyed Pato declares. "Innocents shot dead."[14] Pato insists—and the plot concurs—that when witnesses do not protest against evil, they themselves may be the next victims. Surrounded by evil, Englander argues, even people disadvantaged by lower socioeconomic status and discriminatory prejudice cannot reject the responsibility of speaking out against injustice. Soon enough, the outsider's tragedy becomes entirely personal. Although Lillian purchases a massive door with a putatively invincible lock, Pato is seized by government thugs before his father's eyes at home, disappearing into some horrific, unknown fate.

Unlike older Jewish examples who often predicated universalistic social justice on eradicating Jewish exceptionalism, Englander, emblematic of a younger revisioning of Jewishness, insists on Jewish particularism. Pato angrily refuses rhinoplastic surgery to alter the nose provided by Jewish destiny, remarking, "The nose stays. It's enough what this government forces on us already; we don't need to volunteer to make ourselves look the same" (72). Pato's individualism underscores Jewish difference: Is it ugly? Can Jews assimilate and still have personal integrity? Why do Jews keep sticking their big noses into other people's business? Politically active in protests against the government, Pato courageously epitomizes the Jewish tendency to poke around and to discover and combat injustice.

Jewish Identity *Is* the Fight for Justice

The pursuit of social justice as the most worthwhile Jewish characteristic is echoed by many informants, such as one young rabbi who is a veteran of a variety of chaplaincy, rabbinic, and educational positions and a participant in Project Otzma (a ten-month Israel volunteer program for American Jews in their early twenties), the American Jewish World Service, Hazon, and Jumpstart. She sees fighting for justice as the only nonnegotiable, quintessential, core Jewish activity. "Don't keep kosher, that's fine, don't keep Shabbat, that's fine, marry a non-Jew—whatever. But understand that it will take away your Jewish identity if you don't fight for justice," she says.

Many of our informants—with backgrounds in all wings of Judaism— discussed social justice in language virtually identical to classical Reform Jewish conceptions of the universalistic mission of Judaism to be an *ohr lagoyim* (a light unto the nations). Several recalled previous Jewish work for social justice causes, such as activism on behalf of the Civil Rights movement: "Jews were on the right (ethical) side of history then. Jews were on the right side of history in the gay rights movement. We should try more often to be on the right side of history."

The passion for social justice crosses vocational and denominational lines, and was advocated by artists, intellectuals, and various types of Jewish communal professionals. A few examples: Rabbi Sarah Chandler, a veteran of the leadership program ROI—a global community of young Jewish leaders created by Lynn Schusterman (and a play on the economics phrase "return on investment")—who supports the work of organizations like Teva, Adamah, and the AVODAH programs and who supports activities that make so-called quotidian Judaism accessible (such as blogs and other Internet sites like jewityourself.com), urges the integration of moral and Judaic values into daily behavior to give a wide spectrum of young Jewish Americans the cultural literacy to imbue their social justice lives with Judaic knowledge. Shmuly Yanklowitz, in his late twenties, founded the Orthodox social justice enterprise Uri L'Tzedek and studied rabbinics at the open Orthodox seminary Yeshivat Chovevei Torah (YCT).

Why not just make the old organizations work for younger Jews? The proliferation of social justice organizations for young American Jews reflects a community that is "fragmented," not united around one great international or national social justice mission, says Yanklowitz. Young Jews are attracted to diverse causes, and even a single individual may be attracted to many different causes. Rather than carrying a "holistic" sense of mission, they have multiple missions, "because they belong to many different communities," Yanklowitz continues. "They don't expect one community to fulfill all their needs—or to absorb all their social justice energy." Rather than "a life of faith or a life of meaning," they seek "moments of faith or moments of meaning." Spiritual leaders must "bring all these things into a conversation in a complex way: social community, text, lived experience, activism, and spirituality."

Uri L'Tzedek, with local, national, and international projects, has three main targets: "education for day school students, teenagers, college students, young professionals and synagogue goers; leadership development, which is empowerment for lay people, giving them mentors and tools; and what we call actions." One recent "action" in which Yanklowitz takes pride is the *Tav HaYosher*, an Orthodox version of the ethical kashrut certification first initiated by the Conservative movement (*Hechsher Tzedek*) and a progressive Israeli group (*B'maglei Tzedek*). Yanklowitz describes *Tav HaYosher* as transforming the Manhattan kosher restaurant scene: "We're now empowering people. We have armies of people running around Manhattan kosher restaurants trying to get restaurants signed on to this, where we go in a compliance team and verify that they're meeting these standards. [We're training] customers in New York in terms of people saying, 'Oh, yes, it's kosher; but does it have the seal?'" Such advocacy requires activists to become savvy about economics and financial realities as well as social justice issues.

Rabbi Dara Frimmer shares similarly strong feelings about the importance of social justice. Young Jews, says Frimmer, have a commitment to make the world "less broken" and must stand up and fight for justice as part of their Jewish inheritance. Within Temple Isaiah, in Los Angeles, Frimmer's fight for social justice plays out through community organizing, a "new approach to mainstream Jewish communities to look at issues around who we are within a larger city and sustainable change long term." Frimmer and her community are involved in a huge campaign "to strengthen Westside schools in L.A., because most Jews pulled out [of the school system] thirty years ago, and it feels like this is the perfect time to use Isaiah's powers to positively affect significant numbers of schools if we can get our parents back into the public school system." Frimmer strives to make Temple Isaiah "a place to be innovative," such that it can "move in a responsive, flexible way to whatever is happening in our world, instead of a large institution that moves very slowly and dissolves into the status quo."

Economics also influence the rejection of "parochialism" and promote an emphasis on universalistic social justice. Among those discussing the impact of affluence on renewed commitments to social justice, Benjamin Samuels, a Modern Orthodox rabbi in Newton, Massachusetts, who supports intra-denominational dialogue and Orthodox feminism, notes that the current preoccupation with "global" social justice may be "the luxury of children" raised with high expectations. "I see a greater interest in travel or exotic locales, a greater humanistic pluralism amongst the next generation." Rather than the "backpacking trip through Western Europe" that was his generation's adventure, he sees American Jews in their early twenties drawn to "spending a summer learning Spanish in Mexico or observing at a medical clinic in rural India or attending a roommate's wedding in Paris or visiting China." While these actions are influenced by insulation from genuine poverty for most such Jews, the net effect is broadening, Samuels says, leading to a "passion for new vistas, new approaches, not being narrow or provincial in whom you interact with."

Young leaders assert that social justice causes have genuine religious authority even when their confidence in conventional sources of Jewish authority declines to affirm them. As Yehuda Kurtzer, a young academic active in the Washington Square minyan in Brookline, Massachusetts, explains, the liberal Jewish rejection of the concept of "commandedness" or a condition of religious obligatedness—*mitzvah*—assumes "that mitzvah is somehow derived from the truth of the commander, so if you no longer believe in the commander, you're not commanded anymore." In contrast, Kurtzer says, the religious commitments of younger, non-Orthodox Jews arise from "what we see as our responsibility toward the world." Being obliged to better the world even if one does not believe in a "commander" is the essence "of what it is to be a Jew." This trumps "the other overarching sense that we're completely autonomous." In other words, Jews are people who are obligated to make the world a better place with or without a belief in God.

To many baby boomers, this existential challenge to repair the world has a familiar ring. Internet innovator, blogger and writer, and social justice advocate Dan Sieradski, who has handed numerous projects over to new leaders, only to create new projects, agrees that he and his cohort are building on the principles of *tikkun olam* and social justice emphasized by the havurah movement in the 1970s and the Reform movement before that. Other young leaders, however, insist that their generation differs in method and message from the preceding generations.

Israel and Jewish Peoplehood

For many young American Jewish leaders, social justice concerns become especially poignant in critical examinations of Israel's policies. This is particularly true for a constellation of individuals and institutions that one leader calls the "New Israel Fund, J-Street, pro-peace, pro-Israel, pro-Palestinian, progressive, post-Zionist elite," as we discuss in a section to follow on Israel connections. It should be emphasized that other voices are prominent among young leaders, including many who are strongly "pro-Israel" in the conventional sense. However, these leaders are far more likely to locate themselves in conventional leadership positions with the major wings of American Judaism or within the Jewish communal network.

American Jewish writing by younger authors reflects the continuum of attitudes toward Israel and Jewish peoplehood, including exemplars of diasporism at one pole and Zionism—a form of protective traditionalism—at the other. Some writers portray intrepid wandering Jews and Jewesses who pursue personal existential salvation in remote diasporic locations despite daunting odds. Others—equally feisty—are traditionalists. There is a new emphasis on female players: some protagonists are literally Jewish mothers. Others—like the biblical Deborah—are virtual "mothers in Israel."

Creative Traditionalists

In her interview, novelist Dara Horn explained that her deep attachment to survivalist ethnic Jewishness was forged through the 9/11 terrorist attacks, which were "tremendously devastating" to her emotionally and "alienated me from university life, university culture." Returning to Harvard, she found an overtly anti-Israel environment, which "felt like a different planet" to her after being in New York. Horn was strengthened by her thesis advisor, Yiddish scholar Ruth Wisse, "herself of course alienated from university culture." In absorbing Wisse's combination of deep commitment to Jewish ethnic survival and love of literature, Horn was encouraged to continue believing in "the value and importance of literature, at a time in my life when I did not see it." Horn soon discovered that it was politically incorrect to be pro-Israel on the Harvard campus at the height of the second Palestinian intifada, and that her overt pro-Israel stance brought students into her class "almost as a refuge from campus culture, who were very afraid of their peers." Even today, Horn says "the terrorist attack was tremendously formative in my adult life."

Horn's *The World to Come* (2009) legitimates tribalism by capturing the vulnerability of contemporary Jewish communities to terrorist threats, while at the same time emphasizing the immanence of spirituality in various un-likely persons and places. Horn grew up in a Conservative home and today maintains Conservative Jewish connections and activities, relating to Jews and Judaism in intellectual, literary, emotional, and strongly traditionalist ways. She earned a PhD in comparative literature at Harvard, learning Yid-dish to help her understand nineteenth century Hebrew writing: "I realized they were thinking in Yiddish," she says of the master Hebrew stylists of the time.

Other writers also have strong connections to traditional Jewish com-munities—and strong arguments with them—and utilize both their insider knowledge and their outsider critiques in their fiction. Allegra Goodman's *Kaaterskill Falls* (1999) masterfully captures the gradations of accommoda-tion and rebellion within stringently Orthodox summer colonies in the Cat-skill mountains, while the sociological jockeying of religious in-groups and out-groups animates Tova Mirvis' *Ladies' Auxiliary* (2000) and *The Out-side World* (2004), which depict inbred Southern Jewish communities inter-acting with outsiders from the North. Both Goodman and Mirvis take a special interest in the enterprising Orthodox woman who has a head for business but is thwarted by the patriarchy in which she has located her life. Goodman's book is a particularly sophisticated presentation of the unno-ticed multiculturalism of some putatively monolithic communities—"young and old mix together, and their languages mix: English and German, a little Hebrew, a little Yiddish"—and of the pull of outside cultures even upon inwardly focused Haredi (ultra-Orthodox) communities that carefully main-tain intellectual and social boundaries. Indeed, Goodman's characters, situ-ated in a clearly defined, particularistic religious community, carry within them simmering, conflicting passions, embedded in and surrounded by work-ing class non-Jews.

Whether they are musicians, artists, and authors or they work within religious, communal, or social justice organizations, creative traditionalists listen well and reflect today's complex multicultural ethos. Being both cre-ative and a traditionalist can even give one a competitive edge, a case that applies palpably for Tamar Snyder, an award-winning reporter. Snyder, a staff writer at the *Jewish Week*, where she covers entrepreneurship, personal finance, and philanthropy, has written for the *Wall Street Journal*, Inc.com, Edutopia, America Online, MSN, and the *Staten Island Advance*. She is also the founder of Pazit.org, a nonprofit dedicated to empowering Jewish women to take control of their finances. Snyder grew up quite Orthodox, and attended the "Centrist Orthodox" Touro College. She is proud to defy stereotypes as part of a group of innovators with diverse Jewish backgrounds— "People who are Orthodox, Conservative, Reform, people who are post-denominational, people who even consider themselves kind of unaffiliated, like Jewishly motivated and proud to be Jewish but unaffiliated"—and goals—"Their motivations are different. For some people it comes from a religious motivation, for some people it's more of this broader *tikkun olam*, you know." Snyder includes herself as one holding this social justice motivation: "I know that I have to do something, my role is to help people. I have to use my talents to improve the world."

Seeking Existential Salvation in the Diaspora

In contrast to works by the traditionalists, novels by other American Jewish writers argue with the concept of Jewish peoplehood, and articulate a deeply ambivalent, critical approach to the State of Israel. Some of their work is accompanied by a celebration of the diaspora as the home of multicultural Jewishness, a view that is also expressed in a revival of interest in Yiddish language, literature, and culture—as opposed to Hebrew. Recent American Jewish novels as well describe diaspora experiences around the world rather than gravitating to the Israeli Jewish experience. Revealing examples of diasporism are two recent novels by American Jews that reject conventional Jewish expectations and place their Jewish protagonists in Alaska—what location could be more the incarnation of *galut* (exile) than Alaska?—Michael Chabon's *The Yiddish Policemen's Union* (2007) and Amy Bloom's *Away* (2008). Although these books do not soft-pedal the episodic horrors of diaspora history, they almost defiantly declare that the Jewish future is in the diaspora, both personally and collectively. *Away*, for example, propels the protagonist, Lillian, out of a bloody pogrom through a series of bruising experiences in one city after another; nevertheless, Lillian reflects that diaspora Jews have lived through journeys as incredible as all the fantastic voyages of Greek myth—and Jews belong in the diaspora, with all its flaws: "Surely, somewhere in the back of Bulfinch, in a part Lillian had not gotten to, there is an obscure (abstruse, arcane, shadowy, and even hidden) version of Proserpine in the Underworld in which a tired Jewish Ceres schleps through the outskirts of Tartarus." In this Jewish version of the mother's quest for her kidnapped daughter, Lillian realizes, "Proserpine does not eat pomegranate seeds by mistake." Instead, she serves her mother "cups of sweetened tea" and *"politely tells her that here, in this new (under) world with Pluto, she has made her home"*[15] (our emphasis).

The Yiddish Policemen's Union portrays the battle of Jewish individuals against the dual evils of sweeping antisemitic historical movements and powerful, wicked Jewish leaders. Chabon locates the struggle in an historical fantasy, a "what if" world. What if Israel didn't survive its War of Independence in 1948? As he puts it, "Jews have been tossed out of the joint three times now—in 586 BCE, in 70 CE and with savage finality in 1948."[16] What if there was no State of Israel, and all the Jewish survivors of the Holocaust were sent to Sitka, Alaska, where they created their own Jewish society? Monitored so that they cannot easily come or go, the sequestered Jews in Chabon's fantasy have their own government, their own language— Yiddish, the language most familiar to most of them—and their own police force. The survivors and their children have now lived in this Jewish reservation for sixty years, and very soon their world will be voted out of existence by the United States government—"reversion" to the way things used to be. Except things cannot go back to the way they used to be. There is no final solution. Where will these Jews go?

These questions are only the backdrop of the novel's action. *The Yiddish Policemen's Union* is a detective story, and contains the literary protocols of that good-against-evil genre. Meyer Landsman, the "everyman" policeman protagonist, has lost his moral direction. When Landsman finds the murdered body of a young man who turns out to be the rebbe's son, a saintly drug addict and chess prodigy, Landsman and his estranged wife, Bina Gelbfish, the redheaded, freckled senior police inspector, are thrown back together to solve the murder mystery. They uncover ever-darker layers of corruption in this little planet of the Jews, much of it emanating from the religious establishment, headed by an obese ultra-Orthodox rabbi. Like *Hamlet*'s Denmark, the Jewish state stinks from the top.

Bina Gelbfish is revealed as the very model of an efficient *aishet hayyil*, woman of valor, anticipating every need with the same foresight that she would prepare a picnic, and also the exemplar of the resourceful, resilient diaspora Jew:

> You have to look to Jews like Bina Gelbfish, Landsman thinks, to explain the wide range and persistence of the race. Jews who carry their homes in an old cowhide bag, on the back of a camel, in the bubble of air at the center of their brains. Jews who land on their feet, hit the ground running, ride out the vicissitudes, and make the best of what falls to hand, from Egypt to Babylonia, from Minsk Gubernya to the District of Sitka. Methodical, organized, persistent,

resourceful, prepared . . . Bina would flourish in any precinct house in the world. A mere redrawing of borders, a change in governments, those things can never faze a Jewess with a good supply of hand wipes in her bag. (155)

What Landsman and the reader discover is that Bina is not only the practical *aishet hayyil* of Proverbs 30, she is also *Bina*, discernment and understanding, the divine consort of earlier passages of Proverbs as well (16:16, for example). Chabon's Bina is not only tough, calm, clever, funny, and a terrific policewoman, she is also the key to Landsman's salvation. Chabon ends his novel with a redemptive and hopeful vision—but one that utterly rejects Jewish tribal peoplehood or Judaic religion as sources of redemption. In this dark, grotesque, alternative Jewish universe, Landsman's and Bina's personal integrity and their loyalty to each other can give them the courage to fly over the abyss of existence, like a cartoon character who continues moving forward even after stepping over a cliff:

> There is no Messiah of Sitka. Landsman has no home, no future, no fate but Bina. The land that he and she were promised was bounded only by the fringes of their wedding canopy, by the dog-eared corners of their cards of membership in an international fraternity whose members carry their patrimony in a tote bag, their world on the tip of the tongue.[17]

To Chabon, like the biblical prophets, societal integrity and loyalty are symbolized by the relationship of husband and wife, *ve-erastikh li le-olam*, eternally betrothed. However, the prophets saw the Jews as a national entity betrothed eternally to the universal God, whereas Chabon's novel argues subversively that nationalistic historical Jewish understandings are fundamentally unworkable and dangerous. In Chabon's vision, land will not save the Jews, and religion will not save the Jews. Unchecked Jewish governmental power transforms religious autonomy into a stinking morass of Jewish corruption. Genuine Jewish values triumph only if individuals confront evil and take a chance on integrity, their dearest held truths, and each other.

Chabon, cochair of Americans for Peace Now, and his wife, novelist Ayelet Waldman, reject conventional "pro-Israel" policy, declaring in the November 2008 Peace Now newsletter, "As Jews and Jewish novelists, we devote our lives to envisioning and imagining the world as we have inherited it and as we wish it might be. But all of that history and all those imaginings are endangered, *now*, by those who are committed to ensuring future bloodshed, violence and fear." Some readers feel that the couple's critiques of Israel permeate *The Yiddish Policemen's Union* and have thus reached and influenced a broader audience. Ruth Wisse, renowned Harvard scholar of Yiddish literature—the mentor who helped Dara Horn through her Jewish existential crisis—describes Chabon as a dangerous charlatan who uses "Jewish-sounding surnames, plus a smattering of low Yiddish expressions" to "impart an air of cozy, chuckling intimacy"—but also to soften his dangerous message. In Chabon's novel, both religious and government authorities in an Alaskan Yiddish-speaking Jewish state become corrupted by the quest for power in many of the same ways that Israel's rabbinate and government—according to their accusers—have done. Wisse calls this depiction "the Arab alternative version of Jewish history, which erases Israel from the map of the world while simultaneously fantasizing a gigantic Zionist-American anti-Arab crusade," a vision characteristic of the "progressive circles to which Chabon belongs." Chabon, she says, "as a supplier of mass culture, dutifully supplies" what his readers crave.[18]

Critiques of Israeli Policies

Many young American Jews have high standards for moral national behavior. They expect the countries they feel attached to—like the United States and Israel—to live up to those moral standards. Their criticisms of Israel reflect not so much a lack of interest in Israel as a redefinition of their relationship and involvement with Israel. As a result, repeated trips to Israel, in a pattern that may differ from the past, are related not only to attachments but also to knowledge of and critical attitudes toward a broad range of Israeli policies. For example, a young rabbi describes at length problems in Israeli life, such as "trafficking sex workers, foreign workers who are oppressed, Bedouins who don't have water."

Critiques of Israeli policies sometimes take a toll on liturgical expressions of support for Israel—some congregations will not recite the Prayer for the State of Israel, for example, because they object to the "messianic" tone of the phrase "the beginning of the flowering of our redemption." In contrast, a celebration of Israeli cultural materials like literature, food, films, and especially music is noncontroversial and seems to cross political lines. Musical entrepreneur Aaron Bisman notes, "All the individuals whom I can think of who are non-Zionist are very connected to Israel. Some of them work for Israeli organizations. All of them have spent significant time in Israel. There is a whole range of liberal Israeli feelings." As the young rabbi cited in the previous paragraph puts it, "My Israel activism is not primarily coming from a place of Zionism, it is coming from a place of caring about modern, liberal Jews' ability to stay connected to Jewish life." She combats Israeli injustice, she says, because if it goes unchallenged, "that type of attitude undermines the ability of people in my age cohort not only to have a relationship with Israel, but to have a relationship with Judaism as a whole."

Young Jews reject dichotomous "us" and "them" thinking and Jewish tribal alliances, and want to be able to move fluidly between the Jewish and non-Jewish worlds. They do not relate to the "particularism, of like—six million died, we need to protect ourselves; we need to get to Israel; we have to stick by our own," as another young rabbi explains. The world, in general, "doesn't seem that threatening," so she doesn't understand why Jews are "so closed-off." Many young Jews, echoes a third rabbi, "are very resentful of a Jewish life and a Jewish experience that is insular, that's only worried about Israel or that's only worried about the Jewish community or Jews in need." Young adults are looking for "some more broad articulation of what it means to be a Jew and a human being in the world," seeking engagement with "not only the Jewish community, and not only the Jews in Israel, but far beyond the Jewish community as well." This push-back against Jewish particularism and tribalism also translates to a more nuanced and complicated relationship between young Jews and Israel, and a discomfort with the view that "you can't say anything bad about Israel." Many insist they are critical along with being deep in relationship with Israel: "It's important to have the conversation. We have to celebrate Israeli Independence Day. It's just like—I'm not a perfect person, you should still celebrate my birthday, but, you know, you should help me work on it the rest of the year. Same thing with Israel. We should support it, and be supportive of it, but we can also call our friends on their stuff."

An outgrowth of this evolving, visceral relationship between young Jews and Israel is new organizations that promote measured and critical engagement with the Jewish state. Rabbi Melissa Weintraub, for example, founded Encounter, an educational organization dedicated to exposing Jewish diaspora leaders to the realities of Palestinian life. She explains that the mission of her work is "to cultivate an awareness in the Jewish community of Palestinian narratives and realities in order to foster more complex and constructive engagement with the situation as a whole." Weintraub envisions building "a community founded on listening, learning, and loving."

Musician Alicia Jo Rabins articulates ambivalent feelings typical of many of her generation: While she is "very grateful for Jerusalem being the place where I studied Torah—it's really moving and incredible," she feels "sad and worried" when she thinks about Israel's behavior and positions in the world. "I feel ashamed about what's being done in the name of Jews," she says. "When you see people doing things in the name of Judaism that you don't really believe in, it's very hard as a Jew." At the same time, she says she's aware that "no one's an angel in this situation" and "there's a lot of knee-jerk, pro-Palestinian" rhetoric "that is not thought through and is antisemitic." Rabins points out that she—like most of her age group—is a second-generation leftist-liberal with regard to attitudes toward Israel. Although she has moved far closer to Jewish connections than her parents in text study, rituals, worship, and spiritual and cultural expression, in her political attitudes she is very much like her baby boomer parents. As Rabins says, "Politically, the dominant kind of progressive, leftist American position on Palestine and Israel and stuff is what we grew up with." The attitudes of many young American Jewish leaders today reflect not so much a lack of interest in Israel as a redefinition of their relationship and involvement with Israel.

The New Zionists

Passionate protectionists of Israel are also represented among young Jewish leaders, including innovators like The David Project's Rachel Fish, a Brandeis doctoral candidate in Israeli studies who served as the point person for combating anti-Israel divestment campaigns. Coming from an isolated southern Jewish community, Fish believes in Jewish vulnerability on a deep level. She trains college students in strategies for defending Israel on campuses, and is happily parenting while writing her dissertation. Similarly, recent Brandeis graduate Avi Bass did a study of factors encouraging immigration to Israel. Bass had the original idea to create an organization called Impact Aliya, and worked with two friends to make it a reality. He has now immigrated and works to make aliya transitions easier for new North American *olim* (immigrants to Israel).

Orthodox rabbi and teacher Seth Farber embodies the "love-hate" relationship of many innovative contemporary Zionists, saying, "I love the idea of Israel, having lived here for fourteen years, but I'm very frustrated by the immaturity of this country in terms of, and I say that as someone who kind of works on the front lines, the difficult religious culture and ethos of this country." Farber calls the modern State of Israel "the greatest Jewish experiment in two thousand years," a country that "never ceases to amaze me and enamor me and challenge me." Farber descends from prominent Orthodox leaders who dreamed of coming to Israel, and he is constantly aware of his privileged status: "It always amazes me that I can just hop on a plane and come over for a day or two and come back. Whenever I fly, there's always a thrill." At the same time, quotidian existence in Israel "presents a lot of challenges which I wish didn't exist." Farber recognizes that being "an outsider" in Israel makes his life more difficult—but it also gives him insights and strength to challenge the status quo.

Entrepreneurs Realigning Spiritual Boundaries

Just as young Jewish artists and entrepreneurs use musical media to explore Judaism and push against conventional boundaries, young Jewish religious leaders express their religious identities and spiritual goals and challenge conventional models in worship environments. This "realigning of the boundaries" is a primary characteristic of young Jewish leaders, says Rabbi Elie Kaunfer, cofounder and executive director of the Mechon Hadar Institute, an independent minyan and study environment, described in more detail below, especially when compared to earlier generations of American Jewish leaders who tended to locate themselves within denominational affiliations. The categories Orthodox, Conservative, Reconstructionist, and Reform convey networks of meaning, particular religious attitudes, and styles. They explicitly signify not only (or even primarily) theological convictions but also lived styles of Jewish practice and belief. In today's American Jewish communities, however, as rabbis and lay leaders within the different wings of Judaism battle to assert their boundaries and strengthen their denominational identities, young American religious leaders often reject these labels with their prepackaged meanings and redefine religious affiliations in their own terms, creatively shaping their Jewish practices to make them relevant to and resonant with their own visions and values.

Both denominational fluidity and post-denominationalism were influenced, many informants say, by the trans-denominational environments and institutions that many of them experienced in their teen and young adult years: BBYO in high school, Israel travel with the Nesiyah high school program (for example), summer programs at Brandeis University's Genesis or Bima, college Hillel—all of which entailed friendships crossing denominational boundaries. Rabbi Sharon Brous, founder of the spiritual community IKAR, was ordained through the Conservative movement and says that although the Conservative movement best approximates who she is, she does not "feel connected officially or identified officially as a Conservative Jew or any other kind of Jew, really." Instead, "progressive, traditional, egalitarian, radical, you know, foundational, covenantal" are much more resonant for her than any particular denominational affiliation. Rabbi and author Danya Ruttenberg observes that "part of the move away from denominationalism is a move toward pluralism." Young Jews do not want to be branded or divided by denominational affiliations. They want a content-rich, pluralistic Jewish life in which, as Elie Kaunfer notes, their "self-identity is not of denominations."

At one level, Ruttenberg says, "I feel that logically and theoretically I am a Conservative Jew. I really do believe that halakha (rabbinic law) is meant to be embedded in tradition and that there's room for change. I really do believe in the God that [Abraham Joshua] Heschel describes. I don't know that Heschel himself would describe himself as a Conservative Jew, but the Conservatives claim him anyway." At another level, however, she explains that she lives in a cultural milieu focused on post-denominationalism and nondenominationalism in which "identity politics have sort of ebbed away." She no longer feels like she has "to wave around the flag of Conservative Judaism. Like—I'm a Jew—I'm this flavor, this is the movement that best approximates the flavor Jew that I am." Ruttenberg and the others make evident the discomfort and annoyance they feel from being forced to fit their Judaism into a seemingly contrived box.

Independent Minyanim

An important segment of young Jewish religious leaders is breaking with the mold and providing alternatives to denominationalism. These leaders have transformed the American Jewish landscape by creating independent minyanim, worship and study communities that are independent of denominational movements. The concept of independent worship communities has a strong precedent in the 1960s and 1970s, when rebellious young Jewish leaders founded experimental worship communities called havurot in reaction to what they saw as an unspiritual, overly materialistic, and pro-forma institutional Jewish world. Havurot, much like the independent minyanim, emphasized an egalitarianism that included women, and urged innovative approaches to achieve passionate prayer in a noninstitutional structure with lay-led services. Yet today, most independent minyan leaders are eager to distinguish between the havurot and independent minyanim, arguing that havurot did not emphasize rigorous mastery of liturgical and textual materials, and "did not produce the next generation of minyan founders, even if some of the goals of these minyanim and the havurot were the same." This is according to Elie Kaunfer's new book, which depicts the creation of and rationale for Mechon Hadar.[19]

Independent minyanim can be divided into two types: (1) those similar to Orthodox environments and (2) those with more in common with Reconstructionist or Reform values and practice. Although different experiences motivate the leaders of the independent minyanim movement, many perform traditional—some of them virtually Orthodox—services according to egalitarian principles. Indeed, Kaunfer explicitly says that his group's *davening* (prayer chanting) sounds "just like Orthodox if your eyes are closed," with the firm proviso that egalitarianism is a sacred principle in the independent minyanim movement. Rabbi Ethan Tucker, cofounder of the Mechon

Hadar institute, explains, "There are any number of people who, by all rights, would just be in a Modern Orthodox synagogue if certain trends with women or interactions with the larger Jewish and non-Jewish society had played out in a different direction than they did." Tucker then adds, "If the gender nut were really cracked in Orthodoxy such that you wouldn't join or not join an Orthodox synagogue because of gender—if that could be taken off the table, I think you'd have a lot of people would say, 'Great, I'm signing up for this.'" Tucker continues, "I think it boils down to gender, nothing more, nothing less."

Partnership Minyanim

A specialized, Modern Orthodox subset of the independent minyanim phenomenon is represented in twenty-two partnership minyanim in the United States, Israel, and Australia. Men and women are separated, usually by a halakhic *mekhitzah* (divider), but girls and women are allowed to lead all parts of the service and Torah reading except for the Amidah and other prayers for which women's leadership is explicitly proscribed by rabbinic law. Partnership minyanim are reported to provide intense worship experiences. Allie Alperovich, board member of the Jewish Orthodox Feminist Alliance (JOFA) and a member of Darkhei Noam, on Manhattan's Upper West Side, observes that participants say "they want to be inspired. . . . People really have this thirst for inspiration, and not in a new age-y way but really in a deep spiritual way." She and other young leaders are committed to halakha and Orthodoxy, and are also committed to enabling women to experience prayer deeply and intimately.

Rich Environments for Spiritual Intensity

Of great importance to many emergent congregation leaders is creating vibrant yet traditional worship services unlike the bourgeois services typical of their parents' synagogues. Kaunfer explains that praying in the independent minyan such as Manhattan's Mechon Hadar "awoke a sense of passion, mystery, and awe I didn't know I could ever feel."[20] Significantly, Mechon Hadar's service follows the traditional structure of Jewish prayer services and according to participants is infused with passion and spirituality. Brous describes her parents' generation as unquestioning affiliates of synagogues or federations, even though these institutions did not resonate with their lives. Now, however, "there is this sense that 'If it's not going to be what I want it to be, I'm going to go somewhere else.' I'll go to a movie. I'll go spend time with my friends. I'll go to an art gallery. I don't think there is the same sense of guilt and obligation that there used to be." In lieu of guilt and obligation, Brous thinks there is "a deep yearning for some kind of communal connection, some very strong sense of identity and the need to have a meaningful and authentic connection to the Jewish tradition," which is coupled with this "unwillingness to engage in convention in the ways that our parents' generation did, meaning going to support an institution or a conventional synagogue just out of guilt or out of some sense of responsibility that this is just what Jews do." For Brous and others, the "unwillingness to sit through Jewish ritual experiences that are not meaningful in some way," and the "unwillingness to engage in Jewish communal experiences that are not pushing, that are not at least striving, for some kind of deep and meaningful and purposeful engagement in the world," and "the real reluctance to engage in something that is for the sake of the edifice and not for the sake of the soul and the community and some larger purpose" are defining characteristics of younger Jews.

Meaning and purposeful engagement are rooted in connecting to Jewish traditions that feel genuine and salient. Thus, *spiritual intensity is married to independent judgment and religious autonomy*. Ethan Tucker recognizes "a fierce sense of people feeling like they are going to buy in to what they decide they want to buy in to." The determination of young Jews to accept only the traditions that resonate parallels the trend in the non-Jewish world of "pick and choose" religiosity.[21] Generally, young Americans do not want to feel bound to rituals or practices that do not mirror their worldviews; they want instead to select among different observances from those they find most relevant and stimulating. "What people are looking for," says Alperovich, "is to have options Jewishly, to not be boxed in. They want to have Jewish experiences on their own terms." As a result, these young Jews cultivate a bricolage of religious practices. This independent construction of religious environments, says Ethan Tucker, does not come from a sense of, "I don't want to be a part of any existing Jewish institution" but rather from a space like, "I have a dream. I have a vision. I don't really want to let an existing Jewish institution stand in the way of that vision, but to the extent that there can be partnerships of existing institutions and still stay true to the mission, that's great."

Elie Kaunfer believes that the "group experience of prayer" and the "shared trust that everybody in the room is striving for that meaningful experience" ultimately translates to "the permission to have—to be open to a meaningful experience. It is individual, but it's only actualized by the group." Danya Ruttenberg elaborates on the importance of the community over the individual: "I think how we are together as a community is a really big part of it." Nevertheless, existing communal institutions are often rejected. No longer are Jewish leaders seeking out synagogues, federations, or JCCs for services and support, but rather new types of communal connections outside of conventional institutions. It is probable that denominational plausibility structures have been weakened. Sociologist of religion Peter Berger famously coined the concept of "plausibility structures" in his foundational study, *The Sacred Canopy*, applying the concept to interfaith settings. When a person is always surrounded by coreligionists, that religion's belief structure seems plausible; however, interaction with persons of other faiths and their alternative narratives can undermine the plausibility of one's original religious dogmas.[22] Today, the plausibility structures of Orthodox, Conservative, and Reform Judaism may be undermined by exposure to Jews from other wings of Judaism.

Unconventional Worship with Universalistic Goals

Many young Jews are not looking for the liturgical rigor and prayerful intensity of independent minyanim and partnership minyanim, and, in turn, other young Jewish leaders create extremely nonconventional forms of Jewish spiritual expression. For example, Rabbi Jamie Korngold, founder of the Adventure Rabbi Program, intends to meet young Jews exactly where they are: on the ski slopes, climbing mountains, or relaxing around a campfire. Korngold's motto is, "OK, so you are going skiing on Shabbat? Let me come with you and I will show you how to make it Jewish" (website). Korngold bases her spiritual entrepreneurialism on the fact that 70 percent of young Jews are not affiliated with congregations. "Who's going to reach a hand out to them?" she asks. Once when in the desert, Korngold realized, "I have this really unique gift, based on my combination of skills, as a rabbi and as a mountain guide. Today many people are really, really busy and if being Jewish means going to synagogue, and they have to pick on the weekend between going skiing and being Jewish, Judaism is going to lose." Wanting to make Judaism accessible and relevant to young Jews, Korngold started hosting Shabbat services on skis or during hikes, incorporating Judaism into nonsectarian and often unconventional settings. She replaced the traditional model of synagogue dues with a fee-for-service program, explaining: "Young Jews look for value for their dollars. They are not willing to pay a $2,000 membership [fee] if they are only going to use it once a year. They want to know they are getting their money's worth." Korngold's program appeals to young Jews who like the idea that "this is what I'm getting, and this is what I am giving." Korngold says that partly as a result of free trips like Birthright Israel or other heavily subsidized travel programs, some young Jews feel they do not need to pay for religion.

Social Justice in Worship Communities

Other young Jewish leaders are building new models of Jewish engagement around the pursuit of social justice. Sharon Brous founded IKAR because she felt "we needed to organize and have a voice, and Judaism has something to say about what's going on in the world." Brous wanted to build a community to be "an incubator to experiment with the redefinition of Jewish community: rich and resourceful and healing and deeply challenging, integrating social justice and spiritual practice." Leaders like Brous seek to be catalysts for a conversation in the broader Jewish community about the connection between Jewish ritual and spiritual practice and Jewish social justice.

These young leaders are, in essence, boundary breakers. They are challenging the boundaries between Jewish denominations in a move toward greater Jewish pluralism. They push against traditional gender roles and blur the lines between lay and professional Jewish life, exchanging the bourgeois prayer of their parents' generation for worship practices they find most inspirational, relevant, and stimulating. They seek to move seamlessly between the Jewish and non-Jewish worlds, championing universality and global allegiance. As they blaze trails for the future of Jewish life, they also face a number of real challenges. Some leaders struggle with ways to introduce new members to their communities of traditional religious practice in which the bar for participation and engagement is set very high. Brous explains that this challenge is complicated by the fact that an individual sometimes has to "engage very deeply for many years before you can even get a moment of magic." In a generation focused on "instant gratification," pulling in Jews from the outside for an endeavor requiring great patience can be an especially difficult task.

A yearning for more structure may develop with time. As Kurtzer, of Brookline's Washington Square minyan, explains, "They [young adults] want to have a place where they send the check. They want to have a shul directory, and they want to make meals for others." These young leaders also face the larger, fundamental questions of "Why be Jewish?" and "How do I make Judaism meaningful?" In terms of motivating a desire for Jewish continuity, Encounter founder Weintraub asserts, "Jewish survivalism, concerns about intermarriage, and baby-making don't really speak to this generation." Jewish identity is only worthwhile "if it means something or if it adds to my life and helps me serve the world, makes me a better person, makes me kind, makes me happy, and allows me to give." Creating a Judaism rich in meaning and purpose is a requirement—yet it also means that younger leaders set ambitious and often daunting standards to achieve.

Challenging Problems from the Inside Out

Many of our interviewees explain that creating positive change requires having an insider's knowledge but an outsider's willingness to think independently and take risks. They describe maturation narratives that put them both inside and outside the framework of the established American Jewish communal structure. Some grew up as "insiders" and some as "outsiders," but they almost universally position themselves outside of the framework of conventional Jewish institutional leadership, which some have accused of being self-serving and self-aggrandizing, committed to the status quo that serves them well but does not necessarily serve the needs of the American Jewish community or international goals of social justice.

Despite dramatic differences in the backgrounds of our "bloomed" and "groomed" young leaders, many have been affected by what Wuthnow calls the "geographic mobility and general unsettledness of our society." Wuthnow says young American adults have "opportunities to make choices that are unprecedented," and engage in "seeking" and "tinkering" behaviors. His description uncannily reflects many of the spiritual narratives of our Jewish leaders, artists, and entrepreneurs:

> Many have been reared by parents who encouraged them to think for themselves and to make such choices. . . . Seeking is also conditioned by living in a society that often does not supply a single best answer to our questions or needs. This is why seeking results in tinkering. It becomes not only possible but also necessary to cobble together one's faith from the options at hand.[23]

Paradoxically, both critics and defenders of Israeli policies often describe themselves as "outsiders"—which they are, but in differing ways. Thus, novelist Ayelet Waldman, an articulate post-Zionist who co-heads American Friends of Peace Now grew up in an Israeli household, while the passionately Zionist Rachel Fish of The David Project grew up in Wheeling, West Virginia. Both say their political leadership and particular sensitivities are informed by their experiences as "outsiders" vis-à-vis the established Jewish community.

When "Orthodox Feminist" Is Not an Oxymoron

Perhaps nowhere is the insider/outsider conundrum more evident than in Orthodox feminism, where much creative ferment is generated both in Israel and in the United States. While older generations of Orthodox feminists created JOFA, spread Women's Tefilla Groups (WTG) internationally, and made intensive higher Jewish education for women commonplace, younger generations build on that foundation and are involved in more revolutionary changes. In Israel, Orthodox young women create films at the Ma'aleh Film School and theater projects that explore explosive issues in contemporary Jewish life. The motherships of partnership minyanim, Shira Hadasha in Jerusalem and Darkhei Noam in Mod'in, have proliferated in twenty-two locales. In the United States, Rabba Sarah Hurwitz, a young American Orthodox woman, was ordained in 2009 under the supervision of Rabbi Avi Weiss with the title Maharat and renamed Rabba in 2010. Hurwitz, who heads a seminary for women called Yeshivat Maharat, explains that she learned activism from her parents in South Africa, who battled the country's racist policies before Nelson Mandela ended apartheid. "I'm a product of my parents, who imbued me with a sense of openness and tolerance and, really, activism," she reflects. Hurwitz defines this activism as getting up and disrupting your whole life because you morally don't agree with what's going on in the place you live. The message was brought to me at a very early age of righting a right."

Devorah Zlochower, a rabbinical scholar who served for years as the first female member of the "Scholars Circle" at the Drisha Institute in New York City, also sees her innovative attitudes as deriving from the outside culture, "coming from a very American kind of place." Now in her forties, Zlochower says she would have become an Orthodox rabbi today if she were a bit younger. She notes, "Ten years either way, and my life would have been very different." As an American woman, she says she and her peers assume "we are entitled to make our mark and have a place. That sense of being entitled to it and feeling that that is just and right is incredibly important." She is very conscious of "balancing the conflict and tensions between the American piece and the Jewish piece," a process that is "very different depending on where in the Jewish community you're identifying." Zlochower reflects that the battle fought by Orthodox feminists has been not just to achieve access to the rabbinate but "about how the rabbinate needs to be a more democratic institution and a less hierarchical institution."

Breaking down that hierarchy will be the challenge faced by young women like Rabba Hurwitz. Like many innovators, Hurwitz does not rest on her laurels. She is currently involved in expanding horizons for Orthodox women who have not received "thinking outside the box" as their birthright, as she has. Apologizing for "speaking in generalities," Hurwitz says that women who marry early often lack life experience, and she does "quite a bit of work in sexuality," counseling women whose married relationships are dysfunctional or unsatisfying. She elaborates: "These women and men have very little sense of adventure, very little self-knowledge, and sexuality is not as central and key to a relationship as the kids and the emphasis on family."

Such women are often ignorant of "how to name their body parts," and misunderstand the breadth of halakhic tolerance. Hurwitz sees her goal in this work as to help women "think creatively, whether it's their relationship or halakha or tradition."

Looking at Jewishness from Both Sides

Insider-outsider change agents abound both across and outside the denominational spectrum. Rabbi Sarah Chandler, founder of the *JewSchool* blog, which helps put young people in touch with a plethora of educational and cultural activities, describes "a very countercultural enterprise." She describes herself as "a thousand percent a product of the system. It's funny to think that the result of an extremely successful [Reform] family education and Hillel leadership development and all these things that I'm a product of has resulted in my shunning Jewish institutional life, to a certain extent."

More than a decade ago, a Wexner Foundation–funded study of then-young American Jewish communal leaders found that they arrived at their leaderly roles via two basic routes: Those who had been raised in intensively Jewish environments, often by parents who were themselves scholars, teachers, or communal leaders, were said to have been "groomed" for leadership. Those who, in contrast, had grown up in Judaically impoverished surroundings, but had experienced some kind of personal Jewish epiphany—precipitated by a teacher, a book, a spiritual experience, a trip to Israel—were described as having "bloomed" into leadership.

Our interviews with today's young American Jewish leaders divided into these two paradigms as well. However, even those young leaders who were "groomed" in the bosom of Jewish leadership perceive themselves as simultaneously inside and outside conventional Jewish norms. For example, Rabbi Ethan Tucker describes himself as having been trained for Jewish communal leadership from early childhood onward. When asked about his greatest religious influence, Tucker speaks with respect and deep emotion about his father, Rabbi Gordon Tucker, who has played leadership roles within the Conservative movement. Nevertheless, Tucker himself chose to pursue Orthodox rabbinical ordination and has been a leader of the trans-denominational movement. Similarly, Yehuda Kurtzer grew up within centers of Jewish political learning and power in the Middle East and the United States. Nevertheless, he describes his journey as one of insider-outsider status, which he found suited him well, since he flourished "in environments that would test my own capacity to withstand them."

Other young leaders feel like insiders and outsiders at the same time because of geographical, social, and to some extent ethnoreligious mobility. Innovator Dan Sieradski describes a childhood that incorporated a 180-degree turn religiously, giving him a perennial outsider's vision. When he was about ten years old, his parents had a "falling out" with their Orthodox day school in Teaneck, New Jersey. As a result, he says, he went "cold turkey" educationally, "from being in yeshiva to being in public school in a day. I was thrust from a very insular Jewish background into being 'the Jew' among non-Jews." Sieradski says that, to some degree, he "never fully recovered" from that "culture shock," but paradoxically it "shaped my entire relationship to Judaism and secular culture." Having fallen "off the *derekh* (pathway)," he explored Buddhism and Eastern mysticism, "learning meditation and other kinds of techniques for refining one's consciousness." It was only when his guru told him, "So go be Jewish. It's the same thing. It's just a different set of symbols," that he began rediscovering Judaism and exploring creative approaches.

Iris Bahr, most publicized for her one-woman show, *Dai* (enough), depicting numerous characters involved in a suicide bombing in Israel, describes herself as "a little kid with a double existence." References to divisions echo repeatedly in her narrative, as she attended an Orthodox American school and came home to secular Israeli parents. She "lived a splintered existence," which was exacerbated when her parents divorced and she and her mother moved back to Israel. Thrust repeatedly into situations where she was a knowledgeable outsider influences her work: "I play eleven different people, because I feel I have that splintered identity."

Splintered Jewish Identities

Thus, American Jewish leaders respond not only to "ethnic options," as Mary Waters has argued,[24] but also to religious or spiritual Judaic options—a kind of Jewish multiculturalism. This sense of open choices and options leads many young American Jews—like their non-Jewish counterparts—to both extensive "denominational switching" and what Wuthnow calls "church shopping"—looking for an institution in which they will feel comfortable and attend regularly—or "church hopping"—moving back and forth between institutions with the assumption that no one environment will perfectly match the ideal spiritual profile.[25] For Jews, as for non-Jews, this "spiritual tinkering is a reflection of the pluralistic religious society in which we live, the freedom we permit ourselves in making choices about faith, and the necessity of making those choices in the face of the uprootedness and change that most young adults experience."

Not long ago, Robert Putnam made sociological headlines when he asserted that Americans had lost interest in organizations and communal institutions, an avoidance of social responsibilities symbolized by "bowling alone."[26] Putnam argued that a willingness to trust others and to assume civic obligations had both diminished, impoverishing American public life.[27] This decline in civic involvement emerged during a period when concepts of patriotism and nationalistic pride had also faded in many young liberal cultures around the world, including the United States and Israel. Zionism, specifically, had come under fire in academic circles, and seemed to some vocal critics hopelessly naïve, out of touch, and even dangerous, the raison d'être for what was sometimes referred to as Israel's colonialist policies. This combination of general American social mistrust and the academic and journalistic rhetoric of post-Zionism set the stage for the apparent retreat of many young adult American Jewish leaders from conventional Jewish communal institutions, accompanied by a reevaluation of concepts of Jewish peoplehood and Israel's role for young American Jews. However, the reality is neither so simple nor so negative. Rather than retreating from organizational life, young American Jewish leaders are creating new Jewish organizations—which are often supported by established Jewish organizations—and flocking to participate in those that express their values and concerns.

The Personal Is—Still—Political

When Jennifer Met Brad—a True Story

Ten years ago, three different dating services recommended that Jennifer Walzer and Brad Berkowitz get together—and so did many of their friends. So Brad and Jennifer dated twice. Brad liked Jennifer a lot: "She was great, beautiful, bright," he said, "a great catch." And Jennifer liked Brad, too, declaring she "had a blast." But Jennifer refused to date Brad again, because of "the little matter of her list: Like so many New York singles, Ms. Walzer kept a precise mental inventory of what she wanted in a mate. He should be entrepreneurial, like her; he should be Jewish, as she is; and they should share goals and values, including a devotion to family." Unlike the actress Meg Ryan, who rejected Billy Crystal for a decade in the celebrated film *When Harry Met Sally* because she thought she didn't like him, Jennifer was immediately attracted to Brad, who passed most of the criteria on Jennifer's list, but failed in one. Jennifer had stipulated, "I didn't want him to be more than three or four years older than me," but Brad was "nine years older than she was." So Jennifer refused to date Brad after their second date. She dated—and complained about—men she found utterly unsuitable but wouldn't compromise when it came to her list. Then, eleven years later, Brad's persistence finally paid off, when they dated again, fell in love, "were married on January 9, 2010, by Rabbi Anthony Fratello at the Polo Club of Boca Raton in Florida," and their wedding was featured in the "Vows–Sunday Styles" section of the *New York Times*.

The story of Jennifer and Brad is just one true-life illustration of the ways in which the personal expectations of young Jewish Americans—especially the highly educated—differ dramatically from those of previous generations in regard to romantic liaisons and marriage. The commodification of human relationships through personal lists of "deal-breaking" qualifications that each potential romantic partner must demonstrate, the rigidity of adhering to those lists rather than allowing relationships to develop at their own pace, and the aversion to making romantic commitments—or even looking seriously for appropriate partners—before one reaches one's thirties are all typical today of well-educated American Jews and non-Jews alike. These phenomena are widespread, as Wuthnow describes:

> Married couples in their twenties were a majority—i.e., were typical—of their peers in the 1970s, but were atypical by 2000. For people in their twenties, it has become the norm to remain unmarried. And for people in their thirties and early forties, the change means that a much more sizable minority (a third) are now single or divorced, whereas that proportion had been no more than a fifth of their age group in 1970.

Moreover, as Wuthnow emphasizes, "Because many other aspects of young adult life are affected by marital status—including children, and the timing of children, housing needs, jobs and economic demands, and relationships with parents and friends—the importance of this shift in marital patterns can hardly be overstated."[28] The ramifications of this shift for Jews may be even more dramatic.

The lived Jewishness of young American Jews has been transformed by effective sweeping postponement of marriage and childbearing, even among some American Jewish leaders, a trend related to high levels of educational and occupational achievement, to the ubiquitousness of contraception, and to widespread sexual activity before marriage. These tendencies, of course, are not limited to Jews. Jews, however, are distinguished by their liberalism on views of premarital sexual activity. According to a recent General Social Survey of respondents ages twenty-one through forty-five, "very few" Jews and Mainline Protestants disapprove of premarital sex, and 95 percent of unmarried Jews in the sample reported that they were sexually active. (Mainline Protestants came in second, at 78 percent.)

Statistical studies show that late marriage often diminishes Jewish connections, as Jews typically engage with communal institutions when they are married and have school-age children. Conversely, highly identified Jews have been most likely to marry and start their families in their twenties, a pattern still true of a minority of American Jews, especially those who have grown up within the Orthodox community. However, for a majority of young American Jews (including some who are Orthodox), marriage and children are "simply not talked about." Social activist entrepreneur Jesse Sage comments: "We're very afraid to talk about these issues with each other." Talking about marriage and children has become a transgressive behavior. As Sage notes, "People are worried about seeming judgmental."

A female rabbi in her thirties, for example, articulates one prevalent view when she talks about the resentment single women, as well as single men, feel at the perceived pressure to get married and have children "as soon as possible." While some expect Jewish communal functions to provide singles with opportunities to advance romantic goals, some singles don't want activities to overtly push them toward pairings and matrimony, she says, with "pressure that is so eighteenth-century." Instead, singles "want to be able to walk into any sort of organization or group and just be who you are and enjoy for what it is and not worry if there are people you might marry." Activities planned simply as singles mixers may actually keep singles away. Much preferred are wholesome opportunities to socialize and network with diverse participants, like going "hiking and backpacking and cooking, and all these things that I enjoy doing."

One psychological factor in postponed marriage and childrearing seems to be a profound unease with the idea of tying oneself down and giving up potentially better opportunities when one remains unsure of one's own preferred path in life. As Wuthnow notes, "Marriage is a significant form of settling down. It means making a commitment to another person, it may mean settling into a community and taking one's financial responsibilities more seriously, and for most couples it means at least starting to think about having children." This constellation can, for many young people, "imply conformity to mainstream social values." Conversely, Wuthnow comments, not being married and not having children are ways of being "unsettled."[29]

A number of the men and women interviewed strongly expressed the view that adults should achieve self-understanding—colloquially, "find themselves"—before they commit to a sustained relationship with someone else. A male rabbi says he only felt settled enough and ready to make a commitment when he was well into his early thirties. He asserted that among his circle, there is little or no "peer pressure to get married" in college, and most of his cohort assume they have "permission to take some time to find out who they are *before they lock themselves into a life partner*" (authors' emphasis). Thus, serious dating and marriage had the connotation not of romance but rather of closing off options.

Many young American Jewish leaders and cultural figures see the formation of conventional marriages as a nonissue and are much more concerned
with legitimating alternative family styles, such as gay marriage. Typical is
musician Dan Saks, who, when asked a general question about marriage
and family mores, responded: "I think, speaking at least from my community and my friends, gay marriage is okay." When pressed to talk about the
broader issue of marriage, he said he had married recently: "We're just getting older as a whole in this country before getting married, or opting not to
get married."

Performance artist Iris Bahr comments from the multiple inside-outside
lenses of gender, artist-versus-conventional lifestyles, and American and Israeli social norms: "Artistic men in their forties act like twelve-year-olds,
and nobody wants kids." She sees this as a particularly American phenomenon: "Everything in America is about choice. And there's always a bazillion
choices. That's what Americans are used to, whether it's food or shul or
online dating, there's millions to choose from." In contrast, Bahr reflects,
"Israelis tend to gravitate toward forming families. It's very important."

Delayed Marriage across the Denominational Spectrum

Long years of noncommitment—frequently accompanied by an active sexual life—are an interesting phenomenon, particularly for religiously observant
young Jews. Jewish tradition historically promoted earlier marriage to manage and domesticate sexual impulses. For those Orthodox young adults who
postpone marriage, a bimodal approach to sexuality seems to have developed, with some becoming sexually active in nonmarital settings and others
trying to maintain traditional Jewish standards of premarital chastity.

For example, one young rabbinical candidate in his late twenties says his
generation "has a different attitude toward intimacy. . . . We don't feel the
need to know someone for a long time, or have the promise of a sustained
relationship over the years, to feel very close to someone. We develop a kind
of instant intimacy." On the other hand, at a 2005 Orthodox Forum (Yeshiva University) panel discussion on relationships between men and women
inside and outside of marriage, participants discussed an Orthodox singles
culture that fostered very serious observance of *shomer negiyah*—the pro-
hibition against touching anyone of the opposite sex to whom one is not
married. The panelists presented a scenario in which strictly observing Orthodox couples have broken up because they feel sexual attraction to each
other and they are afraid they will not be able to maintain their no-touching
rule. Not ready to commit to marriage, they break up rather than continuing
the relationship.

Convinced that Orthodox conversations around sexuality were routinely silenced by lack of language and concepts as well as religious and social discomfort, two Orthodox Forum participants, Jennie Rosenfeld and Coby Frances, subsequently cofounded and directed Tzelem (a reference to the phrase "in the image of God"), a special project of Yeshiva University's Center for the Jewish Future. Established to open up a conversation about sexuality within the Orthodox world, Tzelem provides educational resources and classes, curricula, and conferences. Rosenfeld, who graduated from the Program in Advanced Talmudic Studies for Women at Stern College, and pursued a PhD in English literature as a Wexner Fellow, notes both adults and children face conflicts between the realities of modern life and the laws they believe they must uphold as Orthodox Jews. After writing powerfully about the emotional pressures experienced by Orthodox singles, Rosenfeld married, had a daughter, and moved to Israel, where she continues her work. A similar educational goal is advocated by Naomi Marmon Grumet, also a young American academic living in Israel, who has written on women's experiences of Jewish modesty and family law and hopes to use her research to create programming to open up conversations about sexuality within the Orthodox community.

In a controversial response to these sexual challenges, Israeli rabbi Noam Zohar tried to establish a way for Orthodox singles to be sexually active and halakhically observant. The attempt, Ethan Tucker remembers ruefully, "caused a firestorm in the yeshiva world," partially because it acknowledged the "reality in Israel" of "a whole group of people living in cities, particularly Jerusalem and Tel Aviv, basically unmarried until they were thirty, and, you know, clandestinely this way or that way having various kinds of sexual relationships." The response of the community has been "just turning a blind eye to it or condemning it." Tucker notes that Orthodox readers argued over whether or not it was appropriate for a rabbinic leader to publicly acknowledge the sociological reality that a substantial proportion of observant singles in their late twenties, thirties, and forties are sexually active. The very controversy, he points out, is an eloquent testimonial to the way in which Jewish young adults today "grapple with a new chapter."

The Case for Abandoning Lists

Lori Gottlieb, who has now written a book expanding on her controversial and much-discussed article, "Marry Him: The Case for Settling for Mr. Good Enough,"[30] asserts that women are as likely as men are to evaluate potential spouses as commodities and to demand what they perceive as perfection, rather than to develop multifaceted human relationships with potential partners—to give them a chance—and then see where the relationships take them. Gottlieb's assertion was borne out by many of our interviews. Gottlieb argues that popular culture encourages both men and women to cling to unrealistic romantic expectations. Today Gottlieb, who became a single mother by choice in her late thirties, reflects, "It's not that I've become jaded to the point that I don't believe in, or even crave, romantic connection. It's that my understanding of it has changed. . . . What I long for in a marriage is that sense of having a partner. . . . As your priorities change . . . the so-called deal breakers change."[31]

Cultural perspective is added by Ethan Tucker. He and his wife had their second child at age thirty-one, when they were living at Kibbutz Maaleh Gilboa and Tucker was studying for rabbinical ordination with the Orthodox kibbutz rabbinate. In that setting, Tucker says they felt like "laggards" and spoiled "bourgeois" because other kibbutz couples their age were already giving birth to their third or fourth child. However, back in the United States they suffered severe culture shock, where they were made to feel like they had participated in a "child marriage." They found: "None of our friends even had one kid, basically, and many were still not even married." The "alpha" marriage story was marriage in the late twenties or early thirties, followed by several years of waiting before starting a family. This postponement of familial responsibility affects personal development as well, Tucker asserts:

> People in their most formative years of life are not also grappling with that component. In that reading, having kids, to the extent it happens at all, becomes almost a postscript. But here's the thing: *if you wait until you have found yourself before you take on responsibilities, you find a different self than if you have responsibilities.* (authors' emphasis)

Some signs indicate these trends may have turned a corner. Aliza Klein, executive director of greater Boston's progressive mikveh and educational institution, Mayyim Hayyim (the brainchild of author Anita Diamant), and the daughter of a Reform rabbi, has been startled to see women she works with getting married earlier. While Klein finds their comfort with earlier marriage and parenting "a little bit backward," she also appreciates their positive energy regarding the balancing of parenting and careers. After all, she says, "I am in the business of sanctifying sex."

Jewish Arts both Particularistic and Universal

"Music is always at the forefront of social development," says musicologist Edwin Suissa. "One person can transform a culture by bringing music that crosses cultural borders into a new setting,"[32] one can easily watch social transformations by tracing the relationship of Jewish artists to their Jewish and host cultures. Music has long been a telling indicator of the relationship of American Jewish artists and other cultural figures to their Jewishness. During the first half of the twentieth century, artists like Irving Berlin, Aaron Copland, the Gershwin brothers, and the great Jewish creators of American musical theater articulated the voice of America—and arguably helped shape American values—but kept any connections to their Jewish musical roots private and out of the public eye. In the 1960s and 1970s, as in literature, film, theater, and other art forms, ethnicity became newly attractive in music, and overtly Jewish references became popular on every brow level. Over time, Theodore Bikel and Harry Belafonte gave way to Yitzhak Perlman playing klezmer music in the streets of Warsaw and Israeli rock stars giving concerts at Masada on public television fundraisers. Adam Sandler sang endless variations on "The Hanukkah Song." *Fiddler on the Roof*'s "Sunrise, Sunset" became a staple of lounges, elevator Muzak sequences, and National Public Radio musical interludes. Jewish music became mainstream, at least in some geographical locations.

Today, young American Jewish artists and entrepreneurial leaders fuse global Jewish musical motifs with many different ethnic and cultural musical expressions. A young musician named Mathew Miller experimented with LSD with the band Phish on its visit to Israel, eventually found his way to Hasidic Orthodox Judaism, and burst onto the pop music charts with wildly popular sets blending reggae music with devotional Jewish words and themes. Today, Matisyahu reports that he is "still Orthodox, still high level kosher, still keep *shabbes*, and just like I warm up my musical skills in the morning I warm up my spiritual skills" through prayer and music. His new album goes even farther both into the fusion of global musical styles and themes and into overt and often tender religious expression.[33] On a highbrow level, the celebrated young Argentine Jewish composer Oswaldo Golojov brilliantly illustrates his own eclecticism and musical cultural fusion in his opera *Ainadamar—Fountain of Tears*, in which he blends Sephardic musical motifs into a libretto about the martyrdom of Federico Garcia Lorca, a Spanish poet and cultural hero. In the popular musical world, Jewish elements have become so mainstream that some groups have put Hebrew refrains into rock songs that otherwise have no relationship to anything Jewish.

Many young American Jews searching for entry points into Judaism find culture a gateway providing significant opportunities, and yearning for the kind of spirituality sought by others in prayer or a deep connection not felt in other aspects of Jewishness. Music, in particular, has emerged as a cultural expression of Jewishness with exceedingly broad appeal. Jewish playwright and actor Dan Wolf, who adapted Adam Mansbach's 2005 novel *Angry Black White Boy* for the stage, calls music "another way into something that feels very foreign and feels very distant." Whether its expression consists of lyrics about biblical figures, old Hasidic melodies, or songs in Yiddish, Ladino, Hebrew, perhaps intermixed with English, music is for many a portal to Jewish identification and connection. Robert Wuthnow, writing about the phenomenon of music and art in American religion in his book *All in Sync*, finds that "Music and art are closely wedded with spiritual experience. They draw people closer to God, often by expressing what cannot be put into words. They spark the religious imagination and enrich personal experiences of the sacred."[34]

Conversations with young Jewish musicians corroborate Wuthnow's findings. "Music is definitely one of the deepest ways to connect to one's culture," says Daniel Zwillenberg, drummer for the kippah-sporting rock band Blue Fringe. Zwillenberg insists "there's kind of a sacredness to music that doesn't necessarily have to be religious." Music is especially valuable, he adds, for being "emotionally provocative and powerful." More than "just a series of sounds," music can "be the basis of one's faith." On one end of the spectrum of Jewish connection through music and art is Sean Altman, the comedic singer behind the *Jewmongous* stage act. "Music, as opposed to spirituality," Altman states, "is definitely my vehicle for involvement." This cultural connection is forged through his "naughty ditties that both celebrate and lovingly skewer the trials and tribulations of the tribe," as well as through his work with the Jewish a cappella group Kol Zimra, even though he professes to know "squat about Judaism." Lou Cove, executive director of Reboot, views culture in a similar way, especially for Reboot, which Cove describes as having a "special niche in working with young, unaffiliated, disconnected Jews on the margins." For Cove, culture "was a very important entry point for understanding [his] own identity and for understanding in a much greater way what the full Jewish experience is all about." Golem bandleader Annette Ezekiel Kogan connects to Judaism through culture as well, mainly through Yiddish, which she feels "very passionate about" in lieu of regular synagogue attendance.

Jewish culture producers and entrepreneurs across the denominational spectrum are passionate about the critical role played by cultural expression. For example, Dan Saks grew up in a Conservative Jewish home listening to cantorial music, especially the Sephardic and Ladino sounds of cantor Ramón Tasat.[35] Now Saks fronts the Sephardic rock band DeLeon. Jewish Chicks Rock creator Naomi Less enjoyed a close relationship with the cantor at the synagogue in which she grew up and says this cantor encouraged her to go to cantorial school. The musical influences were cross-cultural. Alongside stories of connection to liturgical synagogue songs and close ties to rabbis and cantors when growing up, many of the artists listed such artists as folk-singer Pete Seeger, the Beatles, and even rapper Tupac Shakur as personal favorites and influential mentors. Now, as adults in a Jewish community with a wide range of ritual observance and affiliation, these artists insist that music remains a very important way—for some the most important way—that they connect to Judaism.

You Don't Have to Be Jewish to Love Jewish Music

Much music by Jewishly connected young artists sounds like other indie-folk rock on college hit charts or rap hits on the radio—and it attracts similarly wide audiences. Reggae artist Matisyahu is a prominent figure in the music scene at large. Alternative rock singer-songwriter Regina Spektor enjoys sold-out live shows. In books such as *The Heebie-Jeebies at CBGB's*, Steven Lee Beeber investigates the Jewishness of punk rock's early heroes such as Lou Reed, Tommy and Joey Ramone, and CBGB OMFUG founder Hilly Kristal. Likewise, Michael Billig's *Rock n' Roll Jews* and Guy Oseary's *Jews Who Rock* analyze Jewish rock stars, songwriters, and musicians in the past decade.[36]

However, very much unlike in the past, when, as Beeber reveals, many punk rockers tried to deny or hide their Jewishness,[37] our interviewees, and the examples of Matisyahu and Regina Spektor, illustrate an open embrace of and engagement with Jewishness and Jewish materials in a spectrum ranging from liturgical music and Hanukkah songs to every musical style imaginable informed by Jewish religious and cultural materials, all enjoyed by diverse audiences of Jews and non-Jews alike. Young Jewish adults enjoy being part of these multicultural audiences. They appreciate the incorporation of Jewish musical motifs into contemporary rock, pop, rap, or punk while the music also speaks to their Jewishness. In contrast, when they suspect that the music is being manipulated to interest them alone, they lose interest. As Dan Wolf puts it, "It's when we limit our abilities, and limit our fights, and limit our horizons to a certain type of box or a certain type of expression, that's when people get turned off and say, 'Oh, there's nothing in it for me, I'll see ya later.'" Musicians—and their audiences—want their music to express their human range, not to confine them within cubby-holes.

Art that fuses Jewish and international cultures gives young Jewish cultural leaders a way to express their Judaism. Most of the musicians we interviewed first explored musical expression in folk music, rap, a cappella, and alternative rock and released CDs with non-Jewish bands before form-ing their own Jewish bands or creating Jewish-themed records. Not only for performers but for audiences as well, cultural venues from rock clubs to book clubs serve as refreshingly open alternatives to what they view as the contrived feel of the conventional Jewish singles scene. These venues form a unique opportunity in the spiritual lives of these young professionals—and their audiences—who may shy away from synagogues and other Jewish in-stitutions. Dan Wolf describes this new arena as "sacred space," elaborating that young people are "able to define sacred space as anything that we hold important in our lives and give weight and value to." Redefinitions of sacred, Jewish space, according to Wolf, include "Purim parties in clubs," "[reading] the same novel, Jewish or not, and using it as a sacred text," and "five hun-dred people or a thousand people dancing, sweaty, to a DJ from Tel Aviv in San Francisco, or Balkan Beat Box on tour."

Beyond Chopped Liver—Niche, but Not Kitsch

Above all else, our interviewees want their cultural enterprises and products to be *relevant* and *contemporary*, while at the same time in dialogue with historical Jewish cultural materials, as exemplified by materials involving the Torah, ancient Jewish history, and stories of the Holocaust. For example, it was important for *Kosher by Design* author Susie Fishbein to produce kosher recipes for a "modern palate" that "[look] elegant." Susie Fishbein de-clares that in her cookbooks, "You're not gonna find your bubbe's brisket. . . . I try to look at international flavor profiles." Seth Galena created a website where Jews could connect, but also where anybody can search for an apart-ment on the Upper West Side of Manhattan. Alicia Jo Rabins says she can imagine writing a song cycle about the rest stops along the New Jersey Turn-pike. Dan Saks worked as a sound technician for folksinger Pete Seeger. These artists are rediscovering the sacred in Judaism and redefining it for them-selves. They are wary of Jewish music and cultural production becoming kitsch and "dorky," so they gear their sound and performance toward a more universal audience with open-minded, yet modern, tastes.

The fusion of universally appealing cultural expression with Jewish mo-tifs is thus a shared goal of young Jewish cultural producers and performers on many levels, and from many religious and cultural backgrounds. This fusion reflects their own musical tastes. For example, the Orthodox Blue Fringe member Avi Hoffman has always been a fan of secular, contemporary rock music, and says, "I guess, for me, what I really found beautiful about playing the type of Jewish music that Blue Fringe has come to play is that it sounds the way we sound, and the way we grew up."

Alicia Jo Rabins "played a lot in Israel and then came back and became a part of a band called The Mammals [with relatives of folk legends Pete Seeger and Jay Ungar]." Later she "found out about klezmer fiddling," took lessons with Alicia Svigals of the Klezmatics, "and got a job with Golem, a band which is 'very secular'—is half non-Jewish"—but celebrates the "gorgeous" klezmer musical tradition at both "Jewish venues and regular rock clubs." Rabins describes Aaron Bisman as "definitely the Jewish cultural leader for our generation" and, in his own way, a patron of the Jewish musical arts. When her band, Girls in Trouble, which she started for her thesis at the Jewish Theological Seminary, played her songs for Bisman, he encouraged her to write a three-album song cycle about "women from the Torah or Apocrypha," which constitutes "a different form of text study." Rabins says she is inspired by the vividness of her "midrash research in the process of writing the songs." Rabins and others insist that Jewish music should appeal to Jewish and non-Jewish audiences. Young Jewish musical cultural leaders do not compartmentalize their artistic worlds. At the same time, at noted before, they are confident and unself-conscious about using Jewish subjects and musical motifs within their multicultural mix.

Most of these young artists not only aim to produce universal music—they also see their music as universally appealing. They strive to reach a population that has not experienced anything Jewish before and say, likewise, that appealing solely to Jewish audiences is futile. Much as writers do, these musicians believe that their work comments on humanity, and thus is accessible for all audiences. Limiting themselves to one community is neither personally nor creatively desirable. As Dan Saks comments jokingly, "We can't just be aiming for the Sephardic rock enthusiasts 'cause that's an uphill battle." For his own part, Saks speaks eloquently about experiencing transcendence through his love of Brazilian music. So, despite producing the very specific musical genre of Sephardic rock—and "a lot of the songs are in Ladino"—he still sees its success through the diverse demography of his audiences, who see no "language barrier" and connect to the "visceral level of the booty-shaking and rock-and-roll-ifying."

The young musicians and culture shapers seek not only to express themselves in ways that combine their personal sense of Jewishness with contemporary media but also with whatever they define as "authenticity." Alicia Jo Rabins, for example, condemns deliberate musical indoctrination—manipulatively using music to "sneak around teaching people about Torah"— even though she states that one of her ultimate goals is to share the biblical stories that inspire her so that the audience might connect with Torah as well. Naomi Less reflects on this conundrum as well, by way of addressing her peers: "So my challenge to us as artists, and my challenge to us as cultural conveners, is: let's have quality and authenticity as a part of that, too, and then still push the forward button and be proud of it."

Even an Orthodox performer like Avi Hoffman of Blue Fringe states he is "not a big fan" of forming Jewish bands with a particular mission. Hoffman riffs on how such groups might be imagined: "Let's purposefully make a Jewish band and through that we'll reach the kids." The musicians generally approve of expressing oneself through Jewish music and presenting one's own Jewishness through cultural production; however, the motivation behind this work must be sincere, authentic, and transparent. Many of these artists speak of rigorously eschewing what Naomi Less calls "taking advantage of the commercial appeal of the Jew as kitsch." Dan Saks describes this undesirable behavior as "celebrating the Jewfro." The Jewish music produced by such bands as Girls in Trouble, DeLeon, Blue Fringe, and Jewish Chicks Rock is in some ways niche music; it appeals to certain audiences because of the lyrics, or the sound, or because of each band's select venues and tour schedule, but the artists insist that "niche" does not mean "kitsch." Again and again, they speak about how they would not "[throw] a Hebrew word in there just for fun,"[38] but are, in contrast, deeply interested in using Jewish materials meaningfully. For example, Daniel Zwillenberg admires the way his group, Blue Fringe, wrote a song that had "a melody that was used in the *Beit HaMikdash* [ancient temple in Jerusalem] thousands of years ago." He feels that it "was incredibly powerful to be taking this tune and reinterpreting it for the present," a kind of musical Judaism for the modern palate, just as Fishbein rejects brisket and instead offers kosher chicken *negimaki* with red pepper chutney.[39] Dan Wolf calls such combinations "the purest . . . cross-pollination of arts, culture, and tradition," expressing the particular universalism or universal particularism of this generation of American Jews.

Hear O' Israel—Culture That Conveys a Torah Message

For Matt Bar, the impetus to combine rap music and Torah passages comes from a long-held appreciation of hip-hop. Other than rap music's ability to "turn sentences into spells," he sees a "certain depth of spirit" in the artists' voices. The spirit in rap creates a "more profound type of authenticity [that] people are turned on to." Bar, along with Bible Raps musical partner Ori Salzberg, harnesses just this spirit and authenticity to engage Jewish youth in text study.

Naomi Less and Clare Burson came to Jewish music after working for a number of years as musicians without incorporating Jewish themes. Less did attend Camp Ramah, work at the Foundation for Jewish Camp, and later was a founding member of Storahtelling, but before she formed her Jewish

Chicks Rock band and educational program, she fronted the "general rock band" Less Nessman. In this role, Less realized, "I was playing clubs, all clubs that many New Yorkers know, mainstream clubs, and I would play my music there and it would be pretty clear liturgically based music." In her current project, Jewish Chicks Rock, Less faces such challenges as how to incorporate Hebrew lines such as "*da lifnei mi atah omed*" ("know before whom you stand") into a rock song when it does not "roll off the tongue" and does not translate to the feminine form as easily as this self-professed feminist would like. Less' musical journey illustrates the shift from "general music" to music that sounds equally contemporary but is consciously informed by the musician's Judaism, especially through the incorporation of biblical passages.

The pervasive power of culture and music for this young generation of American Jews is especially important for those who have rejected "old guard, institutional Jewish life" and say, "Okay, temple on Friday night's not my way." These Jews may find a different way to experience those connections to Judaism through "hearing a Jewish novelist speak," says Dan Wolf. Some assert that "Vanessa Hidary spinning a poem on *Def Poetry* about being Jewish" is "as valid as this week's Torah portion."[40] Dan Saks finds almost a transcendent power in music that does not translate to synagogue worship. Saks comments that sometimes while reading through the prayers he thinks, "I can't really get into this. There's certain language here that's kind of . . . keeping me from really losing myself in this prayer." Music, on the other hand, gives Saks the entryway he needs. "When I'm singing these songs," he says, "I can lose myself in them." For deeply musical young Jews, "there must be a benevolent God if something so seemingly insignificant makes someone feel something so strong." In other words, if there is music, there must be a God.

Fresh Articulations of Holocaust Themes

Clare Burson decided to make a Jewish record. She had already received critical acclaim for her indie rock albums,[41] but as one of twelve New York–based artists awarded the Six Points Fellowship, a two-year fellowship established through the alliance of Avoda Arts, JDub records, and the Foundation for Jewish Culture to support emerging Jewish artists, Burson found the opportunity to explore her Jewish identity and her family's past through music.[42] Burson embarked on a new project, *Silver and Ash*, with the goal of combining contemporary music and Jewish themes. Burson says, "I thought it would be really cool for me to make an album that could stand on its own as a piece of art . . . that resonates with people regardless of what religion they practice or what country they're from, but that also can be inherently Jewish." The result is a melodic, folk- and country-influenced song cycle about Burson's grandmother's life in Germany before World War II. Burson's gentle strumming matches that on her earlier indie rock CDs, but the lyrics describe such bleak prewar situations as "Everything's gone but we're all still here"[43] and "There's a hole in the house where my baby boy lay."[44]

As the younger generation faces a future without Holocaust survivors, Burson's musical exploration of Holocaust-related topics through contemporary indie-folk music opens up the subject in a way that is attractive to younger Jews. By singing in the first person in such lines as "And I can see you standing with your suitcase in the lamplight there without me,"[45] Burson creates a Holocaust narrative, despite being generations removed from World War II. She reflects on the tension inherent within cultural production by non-Holocaust survivors: "And [I] was a little worried that, you know, [in] some of my songs, I put myself in the shoes of my grandmother when she was living in Germany and I had this fear that I was going to be seen as a fraud because I wasn't really there and who am I to be singing about these experiences that I didn't have and I can't even fathom." Unfortunately, soon cultural production by Holocaust survivors will no longer be a reality, but with younger Jews like Clare Burson engaging the topic in new ways, stories and memories of prewar Europe and the Holocaust will be transformed but not lost. Burson's work represents an unconventional and, for some listeners, startling way of examining and internalizing the Holocaust, as well as a way for young Jews in the iPod generation to explore these themes through a familiar medium.[46]

"Honest" Culture That Touches Alienated Jews

Unaffiliated Jews and non-Jews are very important to most artists we interviewed. Alicia Jo Rabins muses, "People who wouldn't go to anything Jewish, but see that there's this Jewish thing happening at a rock club and are intrigued by that, are often not involved in the Jewish community, which is why they come." For some artists, music is one of the ways, but for others it is *the only way*, that they currently experience their Judaism. As Matt Bar, Naomi Less, and Clare Burson are enacting their Jewishness onstage and through their educational programming, they serve as leaders to a whole population of Jewishly involved students or peers through synagogues, schools, and community centers; yet they also influence the nonaffiliated Jews and non-Jews when they appear at rock clubs and concerts. This Jewish music and these Jewish musicians, with contemporary sounds that sometimes nearly mask the Jewishness of the lyrics, are attractive not only to unaffiliated young

Jews but also to young Jews who are looking for rich new platforms for Jewish expression.

About half of the Jewish musical-cultural creators we interviewed state explicitly that they appreciate having non-Jews in the audience. Alicia Jo Rabins explains that to reach a Jewish audience is "only part of my hopes." Iris Bahr, who has performed her one-woman show, *Dai*, across the country for a wide range of audiences, says that while "it's been gratifying to perform for Jewish communities, it's been even more gratifying to perform for non-Jewish communities." This allows both to be moved "on a universal level," to connect to Israeli characters, and to gain "insight into a kind of complex Israeli psyche that they wouldn't have experienced."

Aaron Bisman, founder of both JDub records and Altshul, in Park Slope, Brooklyn, together with his wife, is very much aware that the music he produces and promotes attracts hundreds or even thousands at some concerts, from the Jewishly knowledgeable to the almost completely unconnected to non-Jews, from ex–day school students to "bikers in Portland." However, he says, his audience does have one common denominator, musical passion: "We're dealing with bands which aren't on mainstream radio. We deal with music, and with people who actually care about music." The Jewishness of the music he promotes is often "very blatant," so he expects that some in his audience are attracted by this Jewishness whereas others "presumably are not turned off by the Jewish piece." The musical excellence that he insists upon in JDub's rock concerts brings in large, mixed-religion audiences, and the music's appeal to non-Jews as well as Jews—even though it contains overtly Jewish material—actually attracts alienated or underengaged young Jewish adults. Bisman considers alienated Jews one of his "core audiences," and he considers attracting them a significant function he can provide for the larger Jewish community. He sees alienated young Jewish Americans like this even among his staff.

Artists who comment frequently on sincerity (or lack of it) within the music also prefer "transparent" venues. For example, Annette Ezekiel Kogan, leader for the Eastern European punk band Golem, finds the neutral space of a rock club to be ideal for presenting Jewish music authentically without expecting anything of the audience. Kogan first mentioned that she remembers the "Jewish young scene" not long ago focusing on "singles events," but now there is much more of a "hip, Jewish scene." With this move away from singles events, Kogan notes, "I think it's become a much richer environment with music and all kinds of events that are not necessarily about getting married, but cultural experiences." The music is not preaching, and neither is the venue. Many artists are heartened that they now have the option of listening to klezmer punk or indie rock music that is not trying to force a message on the audience. Nor are the organizers working to pair everyone off—the experience is solely about the music, expressing oneself, and exploring one's identity. These creative spaces provide an outlet for artists to express themselves and their Jewishness, and also supply an arena for other young Jews to explore their Judaism *without pressure, without artifice, with no strings attached.*

Conclusion: "Scholar-Warriors" Reimagining Jewishness

The young American Jewish leaders, entrepreneurs, and culture shapers this chapter has described are a diverse group representing a broad range of personal, political, and religious attitudes and behaviors. Nevertheless, they have significant commonalities. They are disproportionately well-educated, both in the secular and Jewish worlds. They are well connected to Israel, many having spent substantial time in the Jewish state. While some were raised in weakly Jewish or even non-Jewish environments, a large number were the children of rabbis and Jewish educators or participated in intensely Jewish environments.

Almost across the board, these leaders are the inheritors of the sweeping social movements of the 1950s through the 1980s. To varying degrees, they are post-assimilation, post-tribal, post-nationalist, post-Zionist, post-feminist, post-modernist, post-establishment. Most have been raised in middle or upper-middle class households where a range of talents has been nurtured. Many are consequently polymaths committed to supporting various aspects of their personhood instead of throwing all their energies into a single fierce vocational effort; they are, one might even say, post-professionalist. Not least, many are post-denominational. Each of these characteristics of our "post-er" generation affects its members' relationship to Jewishness, and can be seen as the foundation for policy implications.

Post-assimilationist: One may say that the battle for *Giving Up America*, as Pearl Abraham (1999) titled her second novel, is over for most of today's third-, fourth-, fifth-generation, and higher young Jewish leaders and artists. Today, all but gone in American Jewish fiction and the lives of younger American Jews is that excruciating awareness of "us" and "them" and the hunger for assimilation that goes with it. Even first- and second-generation Jews from the former Soviet Union, like Gary Shteyngart, who bemoans that he must "rehash the old immigrant narrative," say they are "the last immigrant Jews in this country who have a foot in both worlds." Today's younger American Jewish leaders are not attracted to middle American blandness and do not measure success by their ability to disappear into the smooth, sweet world that Philip Roth would later subversively call the "American pastoral."[47] In Jewish literature and music, as in Jewish life, multiculturalism has overflowed the "threshold" and become a Gladwellian "epidemic."[48]

Some have worried that Jewish cultural distinctiveness may be swamped by multiculturalism, and cultural fusion may lead to cultural confusion. Indeed, the revisioning of Jewishness by young American Jews has much in common with the construction of *post-modernist* art. As for Jewish post-modernist narratives, they create new ways of looking at and thinking about Jewish history, experience, culture, and identity.[49] Within narratives that are fluid and openly constructed, the realities that protagonists and readers perceive are only one version of the "real" story that might be posed. Even when set in what might be construed as a familiar environment, historical transmutations make events unfamiliar, thus facilitating the revisioning of Jewishness. Perhaps most disturbing, attitudes toward Jewish peoplehood share in this ethos of competing narratives.

Post-tribal, post-nationalist, post-Zionist: Younger leaders sit comfortably in their American Jewish skin, partially because Jewish cultural references have become part of the American context. Some are critical of both Jewish tribalism and American nationalism. Many associate primarily with other young Americans who see the world through at least partially post-nationalist, global eyes. Except for isolationist political right-wingers, these leaders are likely to be sensitive to moral weaknesses and political mistakes associated with the American government. They are eager for Judaism to be a force for good in the world. As Dan Saks says: "Judaism has more than once in history really been on the right side of things, been on the wrong side of things too." They were on the "right side during Civil Rights." Contemporary challenges, he says, give Jews "a good chance to get it right again. And some Jews are getting it right and I think some Jews are getting it wrong."

Not only are many young Jewish leaders post-nationalist in regard to America, some are also post-tribal in their Jewish lives, and post-Zionist. Like their Israeli peers, many agonize about the perils of Israeli military and political power. Some are far more worried about Israeli militarism than about Jewish survivability. For most of the young Jewish leaders we interviewed, ideals of tolerance and inclusivity were compelling and seem to have become the new dogma. Where their parents or grandparents may have sought Jewish environments that enabled them to build social capital by "bonding" with like-minded individuals, today's young American Jewish leaders, to borrow Putnam's useful phrase, privilege "bridging" forms of social capital instead.[50] Almost to a person, they see international social justice as a critical core of Judaism. They tend to cherish the concept of peoplehood not in terms of tribal ethnicity or for its own sake but as a context for building community and searching for meaning.

Post-feminist: Younger American Jewish leaders share assumptions about their personal lives that are profoundly influenced by second wave feminism, assumptions that have become so mainstream among the educated classes that they can be described as post-feminist. Both men and women assume that their levels of secular educational and occupational achievement will be equal. They also assume that men's and women's roles in the household, including child-care responsibilities and domestic chores, will be roughly parallel. A substantial proportion of leaders, like their nonleader peers, have postponed marriage and parenthood significantly, both to maintain their personal options and to achieve other life goals. Any articulation of conventional family expectations by the Jewish establishment is deeply resented and often described as "anti-woman." Those leaders who have chosen to marry and have children in their early to mid-twenties regard themselves as atypical and going against demographic trends; on the other hand, the newest statistics indicate that such trends may be in the process of reversal. Once children are born, both male and female parents are often deeply invested in "managing" their children's secular and Jewish lives. Some aspects of the post-feminist ethos have given rise to unintended consequences, as this chapter has discussed.

Post-professional: Very few of the younger American Jewish leaders we interviewed were driven or single-minded or felt the deep urgency about professional achievement that was true even a generation or two ago among many young American Jews. (It will be interesting to observe the impact of the current economic climate on this characteristic.) Instead, most assumed that their life journeys would take interesting twists and turns and were committed to creating balance. They were very conscious of their diverse musical, artistic, and intellectual talents, and did not wish to sacrifice these dimensions of themselves by throwing all their energy into one vocational enterprise. Much of this equanimity concerning the financial consequences of career twists and turns has surely resulted from the generosity of the established Jewish community toward "nonestablishment" enterprises, as well as relative financial comfort in their families of origin. The financial aspect of professional decision-making was, perhaps ironically, discussed by the musicians interviewed, all of whom mentioned financial vulnerabilities and the role of seeking money in their professional and personal lives. Comments ranged from Alicia Jo Rabins' wishes that she could "focus more on doing my art and a little less on working to make money" to Aaron Bisman's reflections on the role of money in making his creativity and cultural leadership possible. There was also his accusation that the field of Jewish studies tends to assume "middle and upper-middle class" financial capacity in the people it studies, and thus to ignore the powerful effect of money on people's lives and behaviors. Financial issues also arose at the AVI CHAI focus group discussion with the New York *Jewish Week*'s "36 Under 36" winners, when Daniel Kestin, a computer science professional who does pro bono work for Mazon, B'nai Jeshurun, and other Jewish causes, emphasized, "Cost is a huge challenge facing the Jewish community. I'm a Jewish professional and I won't be able to send my children to day school." "It costs money to innovate, significant money," Bisman emphasized, as he traced the various grants and other types of aid he had received from the organized Jewish community and other sources, beginning with his parents, who took on his college loans. He explained, "If I stopped getting support from the Jewish community, I couldn't do the creative work I'm doing."

Similarly, many were *post–ivy tower*. They rejected the idea, common in earlier generations, that one must choose between political advocacy and intellectual or artistic excellence. Young American Jewish leaders on opposite sides of the political spectrum like The David Project's Rachel Fish and Americans for Peace Now's Michael Chabon and Ayelet Waldman joyously affirmed their right to exercise their intellectual and literary crafts and also to engage in political activism and social commentary. "We are scholar-warriors," said Rachel Fish—one of her few sentiments that Chabon and Waldman would agree with—"and we don't want to give up any part of ourselves."

Post-denominational: In significant ways, particularly those related to intellectual and spiritual intensity and an emphasis on knowledge, fluency, and accessibility, many of today's independent congregations—from Orthodox partnership minyanim to traditional liturgical independent minyanim and trans-denominational egalitarian worship-and-study congregations to more leftist, new-age groups—have characteristics seemingly distinct from past enterprises. In our interviews, leaders expressed the overt goal of creating a worship and study environment that is distinctive and different from conventional congregations. As leadership cadres considered decisions such as whether to stay within the synagogue building where they had been renting space or whether to institute certain liturgies, rituals, or activities, our informants reported that minyan members often worried about whether certain moves would make them seem "like a regular congregation"—a direction they clearly wanted to avoid. In some interviews, this anxiety began to sound like a liturgical refrain: "But we're really not a regular shul."

The tension between elitism, openness, and the desire for excellence frequently articulated by the creators of today's post-denominational Jewish movements evokes the havurah movement before it—arguably its role model and parent—and the Reconstructionist movement before that. But it is not only left-leaning Jewish movements that have taken a nonestablishment stance.

The rebellions of Hasidic Judaism in the eighteenth century and the youthful Orthodox Young Israel movement in the twentieth century are just two examples of prior movements that have prompted significant changes in the Jewish scene, including some permanent transformations. After some time, however, many aspects of rebellious movements are eventually subsumed into more conventional formats as their practitioners move on to other concerns.

Many creators of nonestablishment Jewish expressions are keenly aware of how much their enterprises have gained from the supportive embrace of the establishment Jewish community. Adam Gaynor, executive director at the Curriculum Initiative, which enhances Jewish culture and identity in non-Jewish independent high schools, and a "36 Under 36" member, talks about the "huge turn-on" of a "wildly successful" cornucopia of Jewish cultural materials, including films, fiction and nonfiction, and performance personalities, all of which have worked together to bring "Jewishness [into the] mainstream." Similarly, "36 Under 36" awardee Jacob Strumwasser, who arranges microloans for Argentine Jews, points out that young American Jews have been active in a plethora of start-up activities, "adapting new technology, using it to help explore Jewish life . . . professions, arts, fashion, film." They "want to use their energy in a positive way," he continues, "and being Jewish appeals to them." Given the appropriate funding, says Strumwasser, "young people now are very innovative, and they will work to find a way to make it [Judaism] meaningful to them. And I'm not sure traditionalists will be happy with that, but it will continue to happen as long as they have the resources to do that."

Creative Traditionalists Who Negotiate Both Sides of the Hyphen

The devotion of young Jewish leaders, artists, and entrepreneurs to their causes is on one level a testament to their seriousness of purpose: they are truly regarding their Jewish connections as a personal commitment, as though they themselves "had come out of Egypt." On the other hand, some of the individualistic and idiosyncratic creative spiritual expressions this chapter has discussed are a form of assimilation into a peer culture that prizes and nurtures individualism and freedom of choice, often at the expense of familial and communal values.

The characteristics we have focused on in this essay emphasize rupture with the past. It is important to note, however, that a significant number of young, very innovative Jewish leaders have strong ties to Jewish traditionalism. These young leaders have incorporated the values of their generation into a deeply Jewish framework. These creative traditionalists themselves are doing many of the things that Strumwasser talks about, engaged in projects of making Judaism meaningful to diverse audiences. Creative traditionalists among the young artists, musicians, and writers offer less knowledgeable young American Jews access to their own cultural heritage. Creative traditionalists in institutional settings—both innovative and conventional—also work to create gateways for Jewish experience and connections.

Very consciously and deliberately, young creative traditionalist leaders negotiate between the values of the surrounding culture and the values of historical Judaism. Many—but not all—locate themselves within conventional Jewish structures, where their work can influence a broad spectrum of people. So, for example, Rabbi Benjamin Samuels, who leads a Modern Orthodox congregation in Newton Centre, Massachusetts, articulates ideas very similar to those of Mechon Hadar's Rabbi Ethan Tucker. Samuels, who was ordained at Yeshiva University, jokes that like many younger people he enjoys all kinds of music: "I used to like everything but country—but now I even like country." However, like other creative traditionalists, he offers a critique of his generation's cavalier attitude toward sexuality and family formation, which he believes has "a great negative effect on people, particularly men willing to make marriage commitments."

Young leaders like Mayyim Hayyim executive Aliza Klein combine conventional and unconventional approaches to Judaism. Klein balances a fierce, longtime love for Israel and Hebrew with an awareness that she depends on American openness and freedom. As a child, Klein thought that her father's vocation as a Reform rabbi interfered with the family's Sabbath rest. Today, Klein cherishes the ritualized peace of Shabbat in her dual-career family, but she constructs Shabbat in a very personal way, with more emphasis on chocolate and playground time than on synagogue attendance with her very young children. Young creative traditionalist writers like Tova Mirvis send in drafts of a third novel on the way to the hospital to deliver a third child. The daughter of Modern Orthodox, artistic parents, Mirvis still worships at a Modern Orthodox congregation—and writes feminist novels that contain wicked satires of the intricacies of the shades of Orthodoxy. Brandeis master's student Jason Lustig, who started the student journal D'vash and worked with Avi Bass to initiate Impact Aliya, worries, "There's been a shift toward subsidizing so much of young, independent Jewish life." His cohort, he says, is accustomed to receiving "free" music and richly privileged educational experiences and needs training to understand that adulthood means philanthropic responsibilities as well as creative opportunities.

Rabbi Shmuel Herzfeld of Congregation Ohev Shalom in Washington, D.C., incorporates hospitality to developmentally disabled adults through the area's nonsectarian Jewish Foundation for Group Homes. He specializes in creative ways to design the National Synagogue's Purim and Yom

Ha'Atzmaut festivities. Herzfeld reflects on the challenges of running a high-energy, innovative, open—and Orthodox—synagogue center. To deepen the awareness among his young and very diverse congregation of Israel's complex concerns, he brings speakers from the feminist "Women of the Wall" as well as Israeli Jewish survivors of terrorist attacks. He runs a strictly Sabbath-observant congregation—and has drumming sessions on Saturday night.

Supporting an Open Multivocal Dialogue

Today's younger Jewish leaders and culture shapers—both the traditionalists and nontraditionalists described in this chapter—have revitalized American Jewish life with their passions for global social responsibility, for intensity and traditional skills in prayer, for communities that support halakhic behaviors along with egalitarianism, for artistic expressions that bring Jewish culture to new audiences without ghettoizing or trivializing. Leaders of the veteran Jewish establishment groups would do well to celebrate these accomplishments—and to borrow successful strategies. They would also benefit from creating and nurturing dialogue with the many different types of American Jews in their twenties and thirties: artists and writers, social activists and rabbis, individuals both passionate and apathetic about Jewish practice itself.

Clearly, different strategies will be effective for diverse segments of the younger American Jewish population. It is urgent for multivocal dialogues to go in both directions. Perhaps the most hopeful news of all is that in many quarters, such dialogue is already happening. A poster boy for creative traditionalism, Modern Orthodox historian and Rabbi Seth Farber, now living in Israel, is especially concerned about promoting in Israel the "values of tolerance" he learned in America. "In my generation I think a lot of the young American Jewish intellectual leadership, religious leadership, has exceptional tolerance and respect for one another." That tolerance is a new development, says Farber, "which didn't really exist 25 years ago." Farber presents evidence for his claim, talking about innovators who span the gamut from religion and spirituality to social justice and activism:

> Elie Kaunfer is a student of mine—Elie Mechon Hadar, right? And a guy like Shmuly Yanklowitz, you know the guy that started Uri L'Tzedek. They're willing to share ideas, they're willing to work together. They might not see eye to eye with the guys in PresenTense, but they still like to share ideas and sit around the same table and schmooze and joke.

The model for "respect, openness, and sharing" of ideas among the innovators extends to some of the pioneers, like AVODAH: The Jewish Service

Corps' David Rosenn. Rosenn says about himself, "I'm motivated to live out Jewish values." According to Farber, "David's the kind of guy [who] if he has a problem, he'll walk up to someone like me and say, 'Hey, I've read about you, let's sit down and have a cup of coffee.'"

Maybe there's something I can learn from you, maybe there's something you can learn from me."

APPENDIX
Informant List with Grant Awards

	Name	Grant/Award/Fellowship
1	Allie Alperovich	Bronfman Fellow
2	Sean Altman	
3	Iris Bahr	
4	Matt Bar	PresenTense Fellow 2007, ROI
5	Ariel Beery	36 Under 36 2008, [cofounder, director PresenTense], ROI, Jewish Jumpstart (Presen-Tense Group), Schusterman (PresenTense Magazine), Natan
6	Aaron Bisman	*Forward 50 2006, Slingshot Guide* (JDub Records) [see website for grants] Includes: Joshua Venture, Schusterman (JDub), Natan
7	Rabbi Sharon Brous	*Forward 50 2006, Slingshot Guide* (IKAR)
8	Clare Burson	Six Points Fellowship
9	Rabbi Sarah Chandler	36 Under 36 2008, ROI
10	Edoe Cohen	36 Under 36 2008, ROI
11	Lou Cove	[executive director Reboot] Reboot Network supporting Jewish cultural innovation (i.e., magazine *Guilt & Pleasure*, film *The Tribe*), Andrea and Charles Bronfman, Jim Joseph (Reboot)
12	Ray Ellin	
13	Seth Farber	
14	Rachel Fish	
15	Susie Fishbein	*Forward 50 2008*
16	Jen Taylor Friedman	*Forward 50 2007*
17	Rabbi Dara Frimmer	
18	Seth Galena	36 Under 36 2009, KolDor
19	Shmuel Hertzfeld	(Ohev Sholom: The National Synagogue)
20	Avi Hoffman	
21	Dara Horn	*Forward 50 2009*, Bronfman Fellow

	Name	Grant/Award/Fellowship
22	Aharon Horwitz	[cofounder, director PresenTense], ROI, KolDor, Jewish Jumpstart (PresenTense Group), Schusterman (PresenTense Magazine), Natan
23	Sarah Hurwitz	36 Under 36 2009, *Forward 50 2009*
24	Jill Jacobs	
25	Rabbi Elie Kaunfer	36 Under 36 2008, *Forward 50 2008*, Wexner Fellow, Bronfman Fellow, two Bikkurim grants (Mechon Hadar, Kehilat Hadar), Natan grant (Mechon Hadar), Jim Joseph (Kehilat Hadar), Samuel Bronfman (Mechon Hadar)
26	Max Klau	KolDor
27	Aliza Klein	
28	Annette Ezekiel Kogan	
29	Rabbi Jamie Korngold	Natan grant (Adventure Rabbi: Synagogue without Walls)
30	Yehuda Kurtzer	Wexner Fellow, Bronfman Fellow
31	Esther Kustanowitz	ROI, ROI staff, KolDor
32	Naomi Less	36 Under 36 2008, ROI staff 2009
33	Jason Lustig	
34	Tova Mirvis	
35	Jared Polis	
36	Alicia Jo Rabins	Girls in Trouble honored/performed at Museum of Jewish Heritage for "Fourth Annual New York's Best Emerging Jewish Artists" 2009
37	David Rosenn	
38	Rabbi Danya Ruttenberg	
39	Jesse Sage	
40	Dan Saks	DeLeon honored/performed at Museum of Jewish Heritage for "Fourth Annual New York's Best Emerging Jewish Artists" 2009
41	Rabbi Benjamin Samuels	Wexner Fellow (Shaarei Tefillah Congregation)
42	Yehuda Sarna	36 Under 36 2009
43	Ronit Sherwin	ROI, Jewish Jumpstart (Nishmah)
44	Dan Sieradski	36 Under 36 2008, ROI, Schusterman and Jim Joseph (Jewish Coalition for Service)
45	Tamar Snyder	ROI

(*continued*)

	Name	Grant/Award/Fellowship
46	Alana Suskin	
47	Rabbi Ethan Tucker	36 Under 36 2009, Wexner Fellow, two Bikkurim grants (Mechon Hadar, Kehilat Hadar), Natan grant (Mechon Hadar), Samuel Bronfman (Mechon Hadar), Jim Joseph (Kehilat Hadar)
48	Ayelet Waldman	*Forward 50* 2009 *(shared with Lenore Skenazy)*
49	Rabbi Melissa Weintraub	36 Under 36 2008, Wexner Fellow, Bikkurim grant (Encounter), *Slingshot Guide* (Encounter)
50	Dan Wolf	2008 "New Jewish Theatre Projects" grant from the Foundation for Jewish Culture for *Angry Black White Boy* ($4,000 according to http://www.jewish-theatre.com)
51	Shmuly Yanklowitz	36 Under 36 2008, Bikkurim (Uri L'Tzedek)
52	Devorah Zlochower	
53	Daniel Zwillenberg	

NOTES

1. Sylvia Barack Fishman, Emily Sigalow, and Rachel Shaina Bernstein conducted fifty-three in-depth personal and telephone interviews, and Fishman facilitated two focus group discussions with fourteen awardees of the "36 under 36" designation, sponsored by the New York *Jewish Week*, for young, innovative American Jewish leaders at the AVI CHAI headquarters in New York, all during 2009. Interviews and focus group discussions were recorded and professionally transcribed before analysis. Unless otherwise cited, all direct quotes are drawn from the interviews and focus groups, with the permission of participants. ·

2. Robert Wuthnow, *After the Baby Boomers: How Twenty- and Thirty-Somethings Are Shaping the Future of American Religion* (Princeton: Princeton University Press, 2007), 157.

3. Malcolm Gladwell, *Outliers: The Story of Success* (London: Penguin Books, 2008), 10–11.

4. Malcolm Gladwell, "The Courthouse Ring: Atticus Finch and the Limits of Southern Liberalism," *The New Yorker*, August 10–11, 2009, 26–32, 28.

5. Steven M. Cohen, *Religious Stability and Ethnic Decline: Emerging Patterns of Jewish Identity in the United States* (New York: Jewish Community Centers Association, 1998).

6. Wuthnow, *After the Baby Boomers*, 47–48.

7. Pico Iyer, "Crimes of Innocence," review of *The Vagrants*, by Yiun Li, *The New York Times Book Review*, March 8, 2009, 1.

8. Sylvia Barack Fishman, *The Way into the Varieties of Jewishness* (Woodstock: Jewish Lights Publishing, 2007), 213–215.

9. Rodger Kamenetz, *The Jew in the Lotus: A Poet's Rediscovery of Jewish Identity in Buddhist India* (San Francisco: HarperSanFrancisco, 1994). In one particularly telling vignette, the historian Paul Mendes-Flohr states "that what really moved him in his encounter with the Tibetans was living in a community that so absolutely abhorred anger. He had worked for peace for years at the political level, and he was painfully conscious of the effect of constant war and conflict on the Israeli psyche" (104).

10. An e-flyer, "Jewishlicious Music Spotlight: Aharit Hayamim," on Tuesday February 17 advertised the concert in the following way: "Aharit Hayamim is Israel's #1 Festival Band. Aharit's Israeli reggae, dub and ska groove and sensibility is rooted in a longing for peace and love of Zion they share with their Rastafarian Brethren. . . . They embody the Grateful Dead and Bob Marley rolled into one" (Adam S., Music Director).

11. Sylvia Barack Fishman, *Jewish Life and American Culture* (Albany: SUNY Press, 2000), 11.

12. Micah Sachs, "A Wedding on Planet Obama," InterfaithFamily.com. Network Blog, February 3, 2009.

13. Ted Solotaroff, "Jacobo Timerman as Prophet," in *A Few Good Voices in My Head: Occasional Pieces on Writing, Editing, and Reading My Contemporaries* (New York: Harper & Row, 1987), reviewing Jacobo Timerman's memoirs, aptly describes Argentina as "a kind of Hobbesian state of nature" in which "kidnappings and extortions . . . murders and disappearances" occurred "on all sides" (119–127, 122).

14. Nathan Englander, *The Ministry of Special Cases* (New York: Alfred A. Knopf, 2007).

15. Amy Bloom, *Away* (New York: Random House, 2008), 212–213.

16. Michael Chabon, *The Yiddish Policemen's Union* (New York: HarperCollins Publishers, 2007), p. 17. Further parenthetical citations of this novel refer to this edition.

17. Ibid., 411.

18. Ruth Wisse, "Slap Shtick: The Yiddish Policemen's Union," *Commentary* 124, no. 1 (July/August 2007): 73–77.

19. Elie Kaunfer, *Empowered Judaism: What Independent Minyanim Can Teach Us* (Woodstock: Jewish Lights Publishing, 2010), 95.

20. Ibid, 3–4.

21. Wuthnow, *After the Baby Boomers.*

22. Peter L. Berger, *The Sacred Canopy: Elements of a Sociological Theory of Religion* (New York: Doubleday, 1967).

23. Wuthnow, *After the Baby Boomers,* 114.

24. Mary C. Waters, *Ethnic Options: Choosing Identities in America* (Berkeley: University of California Press, 1990).

25. Wuthnow, *After the Baby Boomers,* 114.

26. Putnam, *Bowling Alone.*

27. Ibid.

28. Wuthnow, *After the Baby Boomers,* 23.

29. Ibid., 54, 86.

30. Lori Gottlieb, "Marry Him! The Case for Settling for Mr. Good Enough," *The Atlantic.com,* March 2008.

31. Ibid.

32. Brandeis, Schusterman Center for Israel Studies Graduate Seminars, Oct. 4, 2009. Indeed

33. "Singer Matisyahu, Keeping It Kosher," National Public Radio, Washington, D.C., September 1, 2005.

34. Robert Wuthnow, *All in Sync* (Los Angeles: University of California Press, 2003), xiv.

35. Ramon Tasat (website), www.ramontasat.com, accessed November 16, 2009.

36. Steven Lee Beeber, *The Heebie-Jeebies at CBGB's* (Chicago: Chicago Review Press, 2006); Michael Billig, *Rock n' Roll Jews* (Syracuse: Syracuse University Press, 2000); Guy Oseary, *Jews Who Rock* (New York: St. Martin's Griffin, 2000).

37. Beeber, 40, 41, 100.

38. Naomi Less, interview by author, July 14, 2009.

39. Susie Fishbein, *Kosher by Design* (New York: Artscroll/Shaar Press, 2003).

40. Dan Wolf, interview by author, July 9, 2009.

41. The term "indie rock" used in this article typically connotes music with a pared down sound, but it originally defined the way the album was produced. This term is also sometimes used in reference to the genres of singer-songwriter and acoustic rock.

42. See the "About Us" page on the Six Points Fellowship website, www.sixpoints fellowship.org.

43. Clare Burson, "Everything's Gone," *Silver and Ash,* Rounder Records, Spring/Summer 2010.

44. Ibid.

45. Ibid.

46. For an interesting article on the idea of the "iPod generation," see R. Sedricke Lapuz, "The Generation That Auto-Shuffles," *Philippine Online Chronicles*, September 18, 2008, http://www.thepoc.net.

47. Paul Zakrewski, *Lost Tribe: Jewish Fiction from the Edge* (New York: HarperCollins/Perennial, 2003), 49–55.

48. Malcolm Gladwell, *The Tipping Point: How Little Things Can Make a Big Difference* (New York: Little Brown, 2000), 33.

49. Among many additional relevant examples of recent post-modernist narratives are Michael Chabon's *The Amazing Adventures of Kavalier and Clay* (2000) as well as his *Yiddish Policemen's Union* (2007); Judith Katz's *The Escape Artist* (1997); Myla Goldberg's *Bee Season* (2001); Dara Horn's *In the Image* (2005) and *The World to Come* (2006); Nicole Krauss' *The History of Love* (2005) and *Man Walks into a Room* (2002); and Rivka Galchen's *Atmospheric Disturbances* (2008). A striking number of these post-modernist novels take readers on dark journeys back into imagined homelands.

50. Putnam, *Bowling Alone*.

ARI Y. KELMAN

6 The Reality of the Virtual
Looking for Jewish Leadership Online

I N September 2009, MASA, a partnership between the Jewish Agency and American communal organizations that provides a "gateway to long term Israel programs," launched a public relations campaign on Israeli television and the Internet. A central feature of the $800,000 effort was a commercial, shot with a vague MTV aesthetic, that featured mocked-up missing persons posters of American Jews. The advertisement's female narrator urged her Israeli audience to connect their American acquaintances with MASA in order to encourage them to travel to Israel in order to save the "more than 50% of diaspora youth [who] assimilate and are lost to us."[1]

Though intended for an Israeli audience, the advertisement quickly caught the attention of Jewish bloggers and journalists in the United States, many of whom objected vociferously to the commercial and its implicit message. Most expressed outrage at the use of the term "lost" and questioned an outreach strategy that insulted its target population.[2] Some bloggers questioned the cost of such an effort, and a handful of print publications, including the *Jerusalem Post*, published their own critical responses online.[3] In response to the broad and loud chorus of blog-based objections, MASA removed the commercial and issued a public apology, explaining the event as a "misunderstanding."[4]

The MASA incident highlights three critical ways in which the Internet is changing the landscape of Jewish life. First, the Internet made the objections possible by bringing the commercial to American viewers. Were it not for the Internet and its ability to facilitate the rapid sharing of information, the commercial likely would have run its course on Israeli television without comment from American Jews. However, the "viral" nature of media on the

The sociograms discussed in this chapter are too large-scale to reproduce effectively on the book page. They are described in the text, and figures are available for download on the *New Jewish Leaders* book detail page at UPNE.com.

Internet, and the ability of people to share information quickly, cheaply, and transnationally meant that an Israeli cultural product quickly became part of a global Jewish conversation.

Second, the incident highlights the power of the Internet as a new forum for debate and conversation about contemporary Jewish issues. The chorus of voices raised in objection to the MASA commercial resulted in a short-term change in the organization's media strategy, but more important, the event showed that established, mainstream Jewish organizations no longer have sole proprietorship over the content of communal Jewish debate, nor do they control the venues in which those debates take place. Before the Internet opened up these new spaces for communal debate, it would have been unimaginable that a collection of relatively independent writers could force the Jewish Agency to change its policies and shelve a costly advertising campaign.

Third, the MASA incident revealed the diversity of Jewish voices eager to participate in communal discussion. From the left and the right, the religious and the secular, from established newspapers and solo-authored blogs, the MASA commercial generated responses from almost every corner of the Jewish world. One could read the variety of responses as indicative of the fragmentation of the Jewish people, or one could understand it as a reflection of diverse opinions within a single, unifying conversation. Either way, it is clear that the Internet enabled participants from a variety of Jewish communities to join the debate without having to channel their participation through established communal organizations, news sources, or congregations.

Episodes like this one are as mythical as they are myriad in the literature about the Internet. Both journalists and scholars have argued that the Internet will radically reshape the commercial marketplace, alter how we regard knowledge and education, challenge our understandings of marketing, shift our conceptions of power, and even change our relationship to democracy.[5] One need only look to the role of Twitter in the social upheaval in Iran during the summer of 2009 for one small example of how these changes are playing out globally, or the significance of Facebook in the uprisings in Egypt, Yemen, and Tunisia in early 2011.[6] What these changes mean, however, remains the subject of active and ongoing debate.

Why Study the Internet?

Of course, the changes initiated and enabled by the Internet are affecting Jews as they are everyone else. Abundant anecdotal examples aside, we know almost nothing about how the Internet is changing the arrangements of power and order in Jewish communities worldwide, or how it is informing conceptions of Jewish collectivity, education, and leadership. What does it mean for Jewish communal organizations when individual bloggers can challenge the Jewish Agency over its characterizations of diaspora Jews? How is the diverse chorus of voices on the Internet changing the qualities of Jewish communities? What do dynamics like these mean for a global sense of Jewish communal membership? Who is leading these conversations? Are we seeing new expressions and modes of leadership or merely new venues for older forms of leadership? How is the Internet challenging some of the established structures of Jewish life, and how is it reinforcing others? Where are new loci of power emerging in the Jewish community as it takes shape online? How does what happens online inform what happens offline?

As a response to these questions, this chapter will focus primarily on the Internet as a representation of communal life, one that is connected to offline realities but that operates according to a slightly different set of rules and norms. Focusing on the Internet means exploring the ways in which Jewish websites and blogs interact with one another to create a network, but it also means never losing sight of the fact that the Internet functions, effectively, as a representation of offline Jewish communal dynamics. Jewish communal organizations, activists, advertisers, resources, and services all contribute to the online network of Jewish websites and blogs. Insofar as every website has a person or people behind it, they are all representations of something offline, and their online relationships capture and produce communal dynamics that cannot appear through surveys, interviews, or other social scientific tools of investigation with which Jewish communal professionals are more familiar. Focusing on the network of Jewish websites and blogs as a representation of Jewish communities and communal dynamics offers another window into questions of community, influence, information, and leadership.

As an increasingly necessary sphere of Jewish life, the Internet offers an illuminating case study in the changing dynamics of the American Jewish community. The Internet has made information far more accessible, enabled new venues for communal debate, discussion, and engagement, and allowed more voices into the Jewish communal conversation. The organizations and institutions of the organized Jewish world, built primarily in the thick of the twentieth century, have found themselves working in a world where communication is much more multifarious, and in which information (and the curation of that information) plays an ever-increasingly important role.

Jewish organizations are discovering what record companies, television networks, advertisers, and PR firms are all learning: the old broadcast model does not work as well as it used to. As a result, the ways in which organizations imagine and engage their audiences have to change as well. Just claiming to be the "central address of the Jewish community" no longer packs the punch it once did, especially because we can measure whether or not a particular website's address (or URL) actually is central within a given network. (Spoiler alert: Jewishfederations.org is not the "central address" of the network. Not by a long shot.)

Online, the centrality of a URL can be measured, in part, by documenting its relationships to other sites. The more sites with which it is connected, the more deeply embedded the site is in the overall network. Consider an offline analogue. Jewish institutions like synagogues, museums, and federations are typically housed in freestanding buildings and work relatively independently. Relationships between these organizations are not always clear— sometimes they cosponsor, sometimes they don't, and an individual can belong to one or more organizations and have little or no contact with others, even within one's local Jewish community.

Similarly, the Internet is built out of relatively freestanding sites, but it is fueled by the relationships between sites. We call these relationships links. A site with no links will, in all likelihood, not attract much traffic because people navigate the Internet by following links between sites. Without links, the Internet would be almost impossible to navigate and quite cumbersome to use. Links turn freestanding websites into a network. Usually, the more links a website has, the more traffic gets driven to the site and the more the site benefits. Links concretize relationships online that can be quite ethereal offline, and they represent some ways in which sites interact and direct visitors. Mapping and measuring those links will provide important insights into the dynamics of community organization, leadership, and influence within the network of Jewish websites and blogs.

To date, much research and popular wisdom have shown that technology is dominated by young people.[7] Thus, the significance of sites written by and for younger audiences might not come as a surprise. This assessment is generally accurate, but it reveals only part of the overall story. Although it currently favors the young, its importance is not an effect of age; the current generation of people in their twenties and thirties will not "age out" of using the Internet. Therefore, the Internet is crucial for examining current communal dynamics that will likely shape the future, not despite but because of the prevalence of young people in shaping it. The picture of the Internet presented in this chapter, then, is important for the specifics it reveals about contemporary Jewish life online, but it is more important for the general trends it emphasizes about the Internet in Jewish life both online and off.

This chapter is in conversation with other social scientific investigations of online and offline studies of religion and technology. Specifically, it is an attempt to engage two other research projects helping to deepen and develop our understanding of religion online. The first paper, "Mapping the Arabic

Blogosphere," is a project of Harvard's Berkman Center for Internet and Society's Internet and Democracy Project.[8] It explored six thousand of the "most connected" Arabic-language blogs and mapped them both geographically and in relation to one another, in an attempt to find correlations between blogging and emergent democratic movements. The second paper, "The New Landscape of the Religion Blogosphere," is a project of the Social Science Research Council (SSRC), and it explores the dynamics among English-language blogs that focus on religion in an effort to "foster a more self-reflective, collaborative and mutually-aware religion blogosphere."[9] This project both builds on and extends the findings of these two others, and attempts to account for the particulars of Jewish websites and blogs as crucial voices in online discussions of politics and religion.

This chapter takes a systematic look at a network of Jewish websites and blogs. Examining websites and blogs as nodes in a network allows us to assess the significance of each and the role each plays in the overall network. Moreover, it allows us to read the overall dynamics for the ways in which Jewish activity online is informing Jewish life offline. Employing methods of social network analysis, we will map relationships among websites, creating a detailed depiction of Jewish communal relations among Jewish blogs and websites. First, we will apply this analysis to 148 popular Jewish websites. Then, we will recalculate and recalibrate our measurements to account for nearly 300 Jewish blogs. Finally, we will turn our attention to two particular communities, Los Angeles and San Francisco, in an effort to account for differences of scale in the virtual sector.

Methodology and Social Network Analysis

Defining Websites and Blogs

This chapter is concerned first and foremost with evaluating relationships among blogs and websites as indicators of leadership. It takes, as its primary data set, blogs and websites that account for the network of Jewish individuals and organizations that contribute to and share in the collective production of a Jewish conversation online.[10] Because of the dynamic nature of the web, this definition is necessarily flexible and partial. It is also a broad one that leaves the determination of the "Jewishness" of a particular site or blog up to its authors.

As a result, this chapter does not focus on the content of particular sites, nor does it focus on audience size, beyond some basic considerations. This chapter is not an examination of "best practices," and it does not explore how to optimize search engine capabilities or generate advertising revenue.

Similarly, it does not focus on any of the three most popular social networking platforms: Facebook, Myspace, and Twitter.[11] Instead, this chapter examines how dynamics shape the network of Jewish websites and blogs emerging loci of influence and leadership within discussions and performances of Jewish communal life.

This chapter distinguishes between websites and blogs, so a word about that distinction will be helpful. In truth, the distinction between the two is blurry, and visitors may either not care or know about the finer points of the difference. A 2008 survey from the Pew Internet and American Life Project reported that one third of Internet users read blogs and that 42 percent believe they never have done so.[12] These numbers, however, may better reflect the reality that many websites have blogs embedded in them, or that many bloggers consider their efforts to "count" as websites. In terms of visitor behavior, there is little difference between blogs and websites.

However, for the purposes of this project, which is concerned with identifying the ways in which leadership is exerted online, the difference between blogs and websites is both important and instructive, as will be explained in greater detail shortly. Despite the potential power of individual voices, as evidenced by the MASA incident, there remain important differences between individuals and organizations. This is not to say that one is more important than the other, and it should go without saying that the latter would not exist without the former. Yet, as social actors, individuals and organizations behave in different ways, and while no correlation exists between one or the other and leadership, those differences must be recognized, if only to highlight how their roles are changing. Pretending that the Internet has so fully leveled the Jewish communal playing field ignores both the ongoing importance of organizations, and the changes that individuals have been empowered to effect. As a result, I define a "Jewish website" or a "Jewish blog" as any site that regularly contains overt Jewish content, targets a Jewish audience, and self-identifies as Jewish. More broadly considered, Jewish websites and blogs engage in a larger, evolving, and common conversation about Jewish issues. According to this definition, websites like *Haaretz*, JDate, and Jewlicious all count as Jewish websites, but the Wikipedia entry on "Jews" does not. Neither does Jewatch, an antisemitic site dedicated to tracking Jews and their influence (both real and fictional). For the purposes of this chapter, Shamash, the self-proclaimed "Jewish search engine," is a Jewish website, but Google, even though it can find the most sites with information about Jews, is not.[13]

Included in the study of websites are those that either represent or have come to represent either an offline organization or a collective editorial perspective. In some cases, these institutions have walls, buildings, and a professional staff. This applies to the websites of the Orthodox Union and the Anti-Defamation League, as well as those of J-Dub records and Jewcy.[14] These websites serve largely as portals for connecting an organization with its audience or membership, and they play important roles in distributing information or engaging in online debate. News outlets like JTA and Haaretz are included here, as well, and although they often have blogs embedded in their websites, I treat these blogs as elements of the larger website, not as stand-alone sites. I also include in this category the handful of group-authored blogs like Jewschool, Jewlicious, and Jcarrot. Although they may have begun as individual or group-authored blogs and do not necessarily pay their writers for content, they maintain a robust and regular presence, and they either have editorial boards or operate like a kind of collective, which makes them function much like online magazines or newspapers with which they are in conversation (and competition). Thus, the operational definition is that a website represents an entity of some kind, even when that entity is a loosely organized editorial board.

Blogs, by contrast, are solo-authored websites that reflect or represent the voice of a single author, and in the study that follows, I treat them as a different category from websites because they represent a different kind of relationship between an individual and his or her Jewish community. They are cheap to maintain, because of free blogging platforms like Blogger or Word-Press, and although some blogs sell advertising and generate a little income, most do not. Typically, blogs have much smaller audiences than websites and most do not reach more than a few people. (This does not necessarily mean they are not influential—if read by the "right" five people, a blog with only five readers could be quite powerful.) Because of their typically small readerships, blogs are more interesting in their aggregate impact on the overall network than they are for their individual content. As we will see in the passages to follow, accounting for blogs within the larger social network of Jewish websites reveals a significant force as well as new loci of leadership within the Jewish online world.

What We Counted and What We Didn't (and What We Couldn't)

From the outset, two items bear repeating. First, our primary data set for this project is not a comprehensive ranking of popular websites from top to bottom. Traffic only matters as a baseline for inclusion. It is not the ultimate measurement of a site's significance. Second, the Internet is dynamic, which means that links are constantly updated, added, deleted, and changed. It also means that the ways in which people use, access, navigate, and otherwise engage with the Internet are changing. We completed data collection for this project before Mark Zuckerberg was named *Time* magazine's 2010 "Man of the Year," an honor that he earned as Facebook overtook Google as the most popular site on the Internet. The increasing popularity of Facebook and Twitter evidence the increasing significance of personal networks for providing references and links, as a complement to Google's more scientific approach to search and navigation. When we began this project, links remained the most valuable and reliable indicator of connections between websites, and thus offered a novel way of assessing Jewish communal ties online, and for identifying emerging loci of leadership.

We well understand that this chapter enters into a conversation about a moving target in which we are moving, as well. Nevertheless, we thought it even more shortsighted to investigate the dynamics of Jewish leadership and neglect to attend to the Internet and what it might reveal. The data presented here provide a useful snapshot of the network of Jewish blogs and websites during the middle of 2009. The analysis that follows is instructive but not definitive, and if we were to analyze this same set of sites in a year or two, the data would reveal an entirely different set of relationships and dynamics, some of which we cannot even imagine yet (who could have predicted Twitter six or seven years ago? Or the changes in communication that Smartphones or cloud computing have initiated?). Thus, this chapter should be understood as a first attempt to explore relationships among Jewish entities online and what those relationships might tell us about patterns of leadership in Jewish communities. The trends observed and discussed here should be understood within the larger framework of the broader, well-documented changes that are reshaping Jewish communities at the outset of the twenty-first century.

In order to assess the network of Jewish websites and blogs, we began by surveying available literature on measuring the "significance" of websites. Quickly, we discovered that there was no single method or unit of measurement. Within the industry that has developed around calculating the significance of websites, no gold standard can be found with respect to what makes a blog or website influential, significant, or otherwise important. Any number of programs, metrics, and companies exist to undertake this work, and none is perfect. There is no Nielsen-type rating system for Internet use. "Page views" are one measure of the gross number of visitors and thus an indicator of popularity, but then the number of visitors merely raises the question of how long people stayed on the site, how many times they came back, and whether or not they clicked on one of the advertisements. Similarly, blogs can track the number of visitors, but bloggers also count numbers of followers, comments, and the number of times a particular post is quoted elsewhere, as evidence of a blog's significance. Though each of these matters in some respect, there is no standard measure for the popularity, significance, or influence of a single website.

Moreover, these measurements are even less instructive with respect to evaluating a site's place in the network of Jewish blogs and websites. Audience measurement services do not calculate what percentage of visitors are Jewish, so the difference in traffic between Haaretz (which attracted more than 300,000 unique visitors in January 2010) and My Jewish Learning (which drew only 81,000 during that same month) indicates a difference in general popularity, but not necessarily definitive popularity among Jewish visitors.[15] Additionally, most of the metrics and tools designed to measure significance or influence online are calibrated to much larger scales than those appropriate for measuring the relatively miniscule number of Jewish websites and blogs.

Given these limits in our ability to assess the significance of blogs and websites that participate in the relatively small conversation about Jewish issues, and accounting for this chapter's primary interest in leadership within the Jewish community, broadly defined, this chapter focuses on the relationships between websites as a key indicator of a site's significance within the overall network. This chapter focuses on links for two reasons—one sociological and one technical.

Both leadership and community require relationships with people. Clumsily paraphrasing Rabbi Hillel from *Pirke Avot* (2:5), one cannot be a community of one, and neither can one lead without followers. By this reasoning, both leadership and community can only be measured by social relationships. Social scientists have a wide vocabulary for talking about these relationships. Robert Putnam calls them "social capital"; Mark Granovetter calls them "ties"; social network analysts call them "edges."[16] What is important for our purposes is that these relationships are central to defining and determining the strength and importance of both communities and leaders. Consequently, they occupy a central place in this chapter.

The technical reason derives from the general agreement that popularity (as measured by total number of visitors) and "links in" (links from other websites) are two of the most important measures of a site's significance. Because of the way the Internet works, it is difficult to imagine either a site with high traffic and a low number of links or a site with low traffic and a high number of links. More influential sites attract large numbers of visitors, but perhaps more important, they are also connected to other sites. Links both direct traffic and serve as indicators of reliable content, much like references in an academic paper or a news source. According to one oft-recited saying, "Links are the currency of the Internet."[17] Indeed, much of the value of Facebook and Twitter in the past few years derives from their respective abilities to provide links to other sites outside their otherwise closed networks. Therefore, this chapter focuses on how websites and blogs connect to one another, as indicators of how they facilitate exchanges of information and build relationships that can represent and lead the Jewish community.

In calculating links, then, we counted only mutual links, which indicate the strongest possible connection between two sites. The presence of a mutual link, in which site A links to site B, and site B links back, indicates a reciprocal relationship between two sites in which each considers the other reliable or worthy of linking to. If site A links to site B but site B does not link back, then this indicates a weaker relationship than if that link is reciprocated. Any site can embed nearly infinite "links out" (links to other sites) with minimum effort. However, the presence of large lists of links does not indicate much beyond the industriousness of the creator of the list. Trying to account for the sheer number of links out or links in would have produced abundant interesting data, but it would not have shed much light on the ways in which the relationships between Jewish websites help us understand Jewish communal life more broadly.[18]

Focusing on links allows us to emphasize this quality of the online community and discuss in detail the emergence of leadership that is cultivated through developing relationships. However, this focus also means that we downplay two important aspects of websites and how visitors interact with them. First, focusing on links means looking for connections that are *potential* passages for visitors; we were not tracking individual users or how they actually moved from site to site. Second, our approach flattens the differences between kinds of links, effectively treating a page with a list of links the same as a link that appears in the middle of a paragraph of text (as long as both links were reciprocated). Visitors are much more likely to follow links that appear within the flow of a webpage's text than they are to navigate to another page with a list of links. As a result, our method does not account for the ways in which visitors actually navigate sites. Instead, it focuses on the actions of a webmaster or blogger to cultivate links as an indicator of an attempt to lead, influence, or shape Jewish conversations online.

Sampling

We collected data on 148 websites and 257 blogs between May and November of 2009, using a combination of readily available online services and custom-authored script. We determined both popularity and demographics through an aggregate analysis of existing rankings from four well-known sources: SEOmoz.com, Compete.com, Google pagerank, and Alexa.com.[19] Although each of the four sources provided different assessments of a site's significance, they all basically agreed on which sites constituted the most popular Jewish sites. Yet, because the traffic to Jewish websites is so small in the context of the broader Internet, the sources we used, which are calibrated to measure much larger traffic patterns, may have excluded some sites that should have been included. Though we did our best to include all the relevant sites, our tools may have excluded some sites that could have been included.

Based on our accounting of these four traffic measurement tools, we generated a list of the 99 most popular Jewish websites. Because this project is explicitly interested in the generational dimension of leadership as it is represented online, we also included the 49 most popular Jewish websites that attracted audiences between ages twenty-one and thirty-five. To assess the top 49 sites that catered to audiences between ages twenty-one and thirty-five, we examined reports by Compete.com, Alexa.com, and SEOmoz.com, each of which provided a breakdown of audience by age. The calculation of age is, at best, approximate, and obviously a great deal of crossover exists between which people visit which sites.[20]

This baseline measurement of popularity generated the list of 148 websites that constitutes the primary data set of the analysis that follows (see Appendix A for the list of 99 sites and Appendix B for the list of 49). We followed this with a deeper analysis of each site's links, digging five pages deep within each site. We chose to stop after five pages for two reasons. First, we concluded that five pages would provide enough depth to gather a significant amount of data, but not too much that it would prejudice our findings toward older sites, which necessarily accrue many more links. This would balance our findings between older and newer sites. Second, the number of visitors declines rapidly the deeper one looks into a site, so links embedded deeper than five pages within a given site likely fail to generate enough traffic to be sufficiently significant for our purpose.

These measures generated a profile of each site and identified mutual links between each site and the other 147 sites. In this way, we created a kind of "closed network," because we counted only mutual links among the primary set of 148 sites. Although this kind of assessment goes against much conventional wisdom about the power of the Internet (i.e., that it can connect disparate communities and opinions), we found it necessary to limit our network in order to focus on the particular dynamics within a general Jewish conversation. The analysis of Jewish websites and blogs produced here depicts a closed community when, in truth, the network is far more porous.

In addition to the list of 148 websites, we generated a list of 257 blogs by following the listings included on two major Jewish blog aggregators: Jrants and Jewishblogging. Of the more than 800 blogs listed on the aggregators, we included only those updated within three months of our investigation.[21] We also pursued a snowball sampling method, following links from within the blogs themselves to other blogs. Because most blogs, as noted, have very small readerships, we could not create a traffic baseline for inclusion, so we included all the active Jewish blogs we found. Part of the story here is the prevalence of blogs (particularly among the Orthodox), so their sheer number is, itself, significant. Moreover, they are not easily categorized according to topic or viewpoint, and they are not exclusively the domain of either the old or the young. Thus, they represent a powerful and unique forum for expression and potential organizing that is only made possible because of the Internet.

Once we generated these two lists, we began a detailed and systematic social network analysis of the relationships between these sites, in an effort to better understand these relationships and how they inform our understanding of influence and the emergence of Jewish leadership online.

An Overview of the Network

The network of Jewish websites and blogs constitutes, as network analysts explain, a "small world," a dense cluster of nodes situated within and connected to a much larger network that generally accrues through shared affinities or interests.[22] The dynamics of this particular small world serve to both amplify and mitigate certain ways in which the Internet is changing. For example, at the time of this writing Facebook had recently surpassed Google for users' time online, and Facebook, Twitter, and Google are all contending to direct the most online traffic.[23] This trend has continued, as social networking sites continue to play a more active role in "leading" people than either links or search engines do. Tshift curtails the importance of links in locating leadership; if people are making their way to websites via Facebook or Twitter and not through embedded links, then Facebook or Twitter becomes a more important venue for exerting and identifying leadership within this small world. Yet, Facebook and Twitter work because recommendations are not random; they are offered by someone either "trustworthy" or interesting and thus strengthen the possibility that leadership will emerge from outside of traditional seats of communal leadership.

Given that this small world exhibits certain qualities unique to small worlds, let's turn to a more finely tuned analysis of the websites that constitute it. Despite the general density of this network and the homophily among sites relative to the rest of the Internet, the sites display significant differences worth exploring. In other words, though the world is small and relatively homogeneous, it is quite diverse internally. To begin, we can categorize the 148 sites into nine different affinity areas that represent various aspects of Jewish life. Figure 6.1 (online) shows the percentage of the total represented by each affinity area.

Three important facts emerge from this first level of analysis. (For a list-based breakdown of these nine interest areas, see Appendix C.) First, given the large number of Jewish service organizations, it should be no surprise that they account for a significant proportion of Jewish websites. By that measure alone, one could conclude that the virtual sector is but a reflection of the public sector. However, the equally significant presence of reference sites committed to making information about Jews and Jewish life available to their visitors indicates that the Internet is a fertile place for the production and distribution of information. Indeed, seen alongside media sites, news sites, and group blogs and magazines, information rather than community organizing appears to be one of the leading sectors of the networks of Jewish websites.

The second notable aspect of the affinity area breakdown is the presence of sites that cater to the interests and needs of Orthodox Jews. In fact, the percentage of such sites is even larger than the 11 percent calculated here because dating sites like Frumster or Sawyouatsinai are counted as "singles" sites, even though they cater almost exclusively to religiously observant Jews. Likewise, the majority of the commerce sites also likely serve a predominantly Orthodox audience who are looking for kosher food products, ritual items, or other goods that serve the needs of religiously engaged Orthodox Jews. Far from technophobic, Orthodox Jews, we see here (and will see again later when we account for blogs), are active in Jewish life online, and as such play a disproportionate role in the overall shape of the network of Jewish websites.

The third finding speaks directly to questions of leadership and influence. Traditional news outlets and group blogs/magazines account for equivalent percentages of the total. I am counting group blogs (like Jewlicious) and magazines (like Jewcy) together here because they operate a long a spectrum of organization and style. Some (like Tabletmag) are more journalistic, but they trade in similar content and unlike JPost (the *Jerusalem Post*'s website), they do not have an offline component. More important than their parallel presence, however, is that the group blogs/magazines tilt heavily toward a younger demographic. This is not to say that group blogs/magazines are as popular or powerful as traditional news outlets; generally speaking, the two most popular Jewish websites by far belong to the Jerusalem Post and Haaretz (with Jdate holding steady in third place). However, the prominence and popularity of blogs/magazines among younger readers indicates that younger visitors are likely to be visiting them instead of or in addition to traditional news sources.

Clay Shirkey, in his book *Here Comes Everybody*, explains that the low cost of starting and maintaining a website (as opposed to the relatively high start-up costs for a newspaper or print magazine) has made it possible for anyone to seek an audience online.[24] Within the network of Jewish websites, this situation has created an environment in which a handful of group-authored blogs have successfully moved into important positions within the world of Jewish information sharing, becoming valuable sites for news, culture, and community on their own merit (consider Jewlicious, which began as a blog and now hosts a large annual festival of Jewish culture in Southern California). The rise of group blogs/magazines with younger editorial boards and younger audiences than those reached by traditional news outlets reinforces the prominent ways in which the Jewish virtual sector is changing the structure of Jewish communities by altering not only what "counts" as part of a larger Jewish communal conversation but also by engaging audiences that otherwise might not find their way to more traditional news sites.

Group blogs/magazines represent a variety of voices and perspectives. Some focus on humor, others on popular culture, and still others on providing alternative news or commentary within the Jewish community. Some group blogs/magazines see themselves as a kind of free-form op-ed addendum to traditional news sources either through alternative reporting or through parody and humor. Most offer a little of everything. Over the past few years, they have also played a significant role in breaking and exploring important news stories, including the MASA incident, the revelations of health and labor practices at the Rubashkin's meat processing plant, and revelations of sexual misconduct at Brooklyn yeshivot.

This accounting provides some general data about the breadth of Jewish websites, but in order to understand them as a network, we must consider the relationships between the sites themselves. To do this, we will need to move from a list to a sociogram. Sociograms map networks of relationships, with each "ego" or "node" in the network represented by a dot, and each relationship, mutual link, or "edge" (all synonyms) represented by a line. In our sociogram, each node will represent a website, and each edge represents the presence of mutual links between nodes.

We generated this sociogram using the Fruchterman-Reingold "physics model" algorithm, which operates according to the following principle: Imagine a general force that is trying to move each node away from each of the others, as in models of the expanding universe following the Big Bang. But counteracting this general force is a secondary force (like a spring) that works between nodes that share links in common. The dynamic tension between the general force of repulsion among all nodes and the specific force of attraction among particular nodes eventually creates an equilibrium in the network as a whole.

Using this algorithm, we generated a map that highlights two aspects of the Jewish virtual sector. First, a node's size indicates the number of mutual links it possesses; the larger the node, the more mutual links it has. Second, the node's location within the sociogram indicates the presence of common links among neighboring sites. JPost and Haaretz don't link to one another, but they share many links in common, so they appear close to one another in the sociogram.

In order to understand the figures that follow, it is important to remember that specific pairs of linked nodes cannot reach equilibrium on their own within a complex network because of the other forces working upon them. Instead, they only reach equilibrium through a clustering of linked nodes, whose mutually attractive forces work in combination to stabilize the network as a whole. The colors correspond to the affinity areas described in Figure 6.1.

Three general observations: First, and consistent with small worlds generally, this network is fairly dense and very well-connected. The greatest distance between two sites is only 4 links, and the average distance between two sites is 1.93 links. That means that it is possible to traverse the entire network in only four "clicks," and that many sites are less than two clicks away from many others. Moreover, this measurement does not include linked advertisements that one site might purchase on another. So, for example, though Chabad might advertise on Jewlicious, thus allowing visitors to click directly from the latter to the former, this measure does not account for such options. This means that if we account for the prevalence of advertisements on one Jewish website for another Jewish website, the network is likely even more easily traversed than the current measures suggest.

Second, the largest nodes, indicating the sites with the most links in the network, belong to sites dedicated to sharing information. Specifically, they represent Myjewishlearning, a "trans-denominational" resource for information about Jewish life, Shamash, a "Jewish search engine," the Jewish Virtual Library (Jewishvirtuallibrary), which describes itself as "the most comprehensive online Jewish encyclopedia in the word," and the Israel News Agency (Israelnewsagency), an Israeli news source. All four of these sites are information sites, and none has an offline component. Since we collected this data, Myjewishlearning purchased Shamash, and the Israelnewsagency has apparently ceased posting regular updates. These changes in the network offer further evidence that the Internet will continue to evolve and that some seemingly vital sites will fade away, creating opportunities for new sites to emerge. Despite these changes to the network, the data we captured in 2009 provide evidence of the significance of information in the distribution of collective Jewish leadership online.

It is possible that, by focusing on links, we have weighted our findings toward these reference sites, because many sites will link to them for basic information. Jewishvirtuallibrary, for example, has thousands of pages with reliable information about a vast array of topics, and many sites will link to it, meaning it has a lot of "links in." Our emphasis on links might put these sites at a methodological advantage, as reference sites contain information whose content and value do not change that much over time. They will continue to attract links regardless of changes in fashion or season; people are still going to be looking for information about holidays or historical figures. That is precisely the point, however. Unlike business, sports or entertainment websites, where up-to-date information is crucial to success, the network of Jewish websites trades in information according to a different logic. The relative significance of these sites suggests that people looking online for information about Jewish life are very likely to find their way to one of these sites very quickly, no matter where they begin.

Additionally, these nodes are notable, given both their size and position in the sociogram, not just because they absorb lots of incoming links but also because they reciprocate—capitalizing not only on their reputations for providing information but also playing an active role in developing the network of Jewish websites and blogs. These sites are therefore not only references that contain information and attract visitors, but they also channel potential visitors to other sites, as well. These sites lead both by providing information and by influencing how visitors might navigate from site to site, suggesting that leadership online takes a different form than leadership offline.

Third, this network appears to be relatively healthy. The overall "health" of a network can be measured by the chance that it could be crippled by the disappearance of a single node. A network as depicted in a sociogram that resembles spokes radiating outward from a single hub is highly centralized but not terribly healthy, as it relies entirely on the single, central node for its survival. Healthier networks are characterized not by a single, strongly linked node, but by many nodes that distribute power throughout the network.[25] From this perspective, the network of Jewish websites appears to be relatively healthy because it does not have a single, dominant, central node, although a few claim significantly more links than the rest. Although some sites play more influential roles than others, the network overall benefits from a more or less even distribution of links.

The four sites discussed earlier play a powerful role in organizing the network. By sharing a large number of links with other sites, they appear not only as trusted references but also reciprocate trust and become important hubs in the small world. More important, because links provide visitors with a virtual roadmap for traversing the network, these sites are more likely than many others to turn up when visitors attempt to move throughout the network, should they follow available links. In this way, they can exert far more influence over the network than any communal institution, any traditional news source, or any representation of a religious body or single community. Online, information plays a key role in convening community, and our findings indicate that both visitors and other sites are seeking reliable sources of information about Jewish life.

Accounting for Links (Not Just Counting Them)

Counting links tells us a part of the story, but only one part. To get a fuller picture of the dynamics of the network, we want to measure not only how many links a node has but what kind of role it plays in brokering relationships and what kinds of other sites it links to. If a site has lots of links to other fairly weak sites, it might be less significant to the network than one with fewer links with more significant sites. To help evaluate these dimensions of the network, we can turn to social network analysis.

First, we want to evaluate the ability of a site to broker relationships between other sites. In the language of social network analysis, this means measuring "betweenness centrality" or, the "capacity to broker contacts among other actors—to extract 'service charges' and to isolate actors or prevent contacts."[26] In other words, betweenness is not a gross measurement of the number of links but rather an attempt to account for the active participation of a particular node within the overall network.

The measurement of one site's ability to connect other sites is important because people can traverse the Internet by "clicking through" one site to the next. Even if Facebook, Twitter, and Google direct more traffic than embedded links do, sites still labor to link themselves to other sites, and links remain an important indicator in a site's influence over a network. Since we are examining the small world of Jewish websites as a discrete network, we are more interested in how the sites interact with one another than in how visitors to the sites actually behave. Mapping this network, we can infer that a site with high betweenness centrality can play a valuable role in facilitating movement through the overall network. The results of these calculations are presented in Table 6.1, which presents the ten sites with the highest betweenness centrality scores. To keep this in perspective, these measurements do not capture actual "click-throughs" by website visitors, but instead, they calculate the number of possible relationships that a particular node helps to broker within this representation of the Jewish world.

TABLE 6.1
Betweenness Centrality

Rank	Betweenness Centrality	Site Name
1	1317.231	Myjewishlearning.com
2	328.1	Shamash.org
3	302.784	Jewishvirtuallibrary.org
4	237.196	Jpost.com
5	231.13	Jewcy.com
6	167.507	Urj.org
7	163.053	Israelnationalnews.com
8	161.52	Israelnewsagency.com
9	152.396	Headcoverings-by-devorah.com
10	137.067	Juf.org

The four sites represented by the large nodes in the first sociogram are all represented in this table, but Myjewishlearning has a betweenness centrality score approximately four times as large as its closest counterpart. This means that Myjewishlearning potentially plays a far more active role in brokering relationships and directing traffic than its closest counterparts. Although Jpost may have more overall traffic than Myjewishlearning, the latter occupies a more central role than the former within this small Jewish world, and can be said to exert more influence over the network. By comparison, the low score of Israelnationalnews indicates that it plays a much more marginal role in the overall network, despite the presence of numerous links. Given its younger audience, Myjewishlearning is just one example of an endeavor that is taking advantage of the Internet to supersede more traditional Jewish communal institutions in shaping Jewish experiences online.

Perhaps even more important for the larger discussion of leadership, the website Jewcy has a higher degree of betweenness centrality than every other established news source except Jpost. Even with a much smaller audience than its more established competitors, Jewcy is nearly as successful as Jpost at brokering relationships within the small Jewish world, and thus exerts even greater potential influence within the network. Compounded by the possibility that Jpost, a well-established and well-respected authority, may not feel compelled to link back to sites that link to it, Jewcy's score suggests a greater investment in building linked relationships within the network than its better known counterpart. In terms of leadership, Jpost may possess a greater aura of authority, but Jewcy might be playing a more active role in attending to relationships that constitute the online Jewish communal conversation.

Again, betweenness centrality does not account for how visitors actually move from site to site but rather measures the relative value of each node within the network in terms of its ability to direct visitors as they move from site to site. Taking stock of the top ten sites reveals the clear significance of information-brokering sites, which account for seven of the ten. Clearly, Jewish people and websites share a desire for reliable information, and the former rely on these reference sites to provide corroborating data or extended explanations of aspects of Jewish history, culture, and politics.

Taken together, Myjewishlearning and Jewcy, which both have editorial staffs largely between ages twenty-one and forty and cater to an audience from that same demographic, are employing strategies to become powerful players in the network of Jewish websites. The influence they exert may or may not translate to sheer numbers of unique visitors, and their links may not mean that visitors actually follow them, but their results suggest a conscious attempt to build connections among Jewish websites, an endeavor in which they are outpacing most traditional news sources and establishment Jewish organizations.

By comparison, Jewish communal organizations have been less successful at building relationships online, as they are represented in Table 6.1 by only two websites: The URJ (Union for Reform Judaism) and JUF (Jewish United Fund/Jewish Federation of Metropolitan Chicago). The relatively thin showing of communal organizations illustrates a great disparity between their ability to convene community and build relationships online and off. Compared to news and reference sources, establishment communal organizations hold weaker positions within the network of Jewish websites and thus lag in their ability to either lead or build relationships online.

Yet measuring betweenness only tells us how many short paths a particular node sits on. It does not tell us if those paths connect otherwise important sites. If a site connects other sites that are unpopular, then we might say that, despite its high betweenness centrality, it is less significant than a site that connects other sites with greater prestige. When we account not only for betweenness but also for the prestige of the sites to which each node connects (according to what social network analysis calls the Bonacich centrality measure), we find slight adjustments in the bottom four of the top ten from Table 6.1. JTA appears and Headcoverings by Devorah (Headcoverings-by-devorah) disappears, but little else changes.

Headcoverings-by-devorah may have appeared on the earlier chart because of its unique product and because of the prevalence of sites that cater to Orthodox visitors. Once we account for prestige, however, it drops far off

TABLE 6.2
Bonacich Centrality Measure

Rank	Bonacich Centrality Measure	Site Name
1	88	Myjewishlearning.com
2	61	Shamash.org
3	59	Jewishvirtuallibrary.org
4	50	Jpost.com
5	49	Jewcy.com
6	49	Israelnewsagency.com
7	45	Forward.com
8	43	Urj.org
9	39	Juf.org
10	38	Jta.org

the list because it does not broker relationships with other prominent sites, even though it brokers a significant number of relationships on its own.

Viewed through the lens of prestige, we find a few sites with younger audiences and editorial staffs asserting significant influence and competing with established outlets for influence not only over the structure of Jewish conversations but also over those conversations' content. The ability of sites like Myjewishlearning and Jewcy to amplify certain voices within the broader Jewish community makes them both significant and influential, and their connectivity with other sites in this small Jewish world makes them important and active nodes in the network. Particularly when we take into account the very real possibility that many visitors to these two sites are younger (between twenty-one and forty, generally speaking) and thus rather unlikely to belong to synagogues or Jewish Community Centers (JCCs), these sites are positioned to exert significant influence not only within the network online but also among visitors who are likely to live largely outside the Jewish institutional world.[27]

Having mapped the network of Jewish websites, we can see a complex image of American Jewish leadership coming into focus. It includes organizations and individuals who have not, historically, been close to centers of Jewish communal power. It emphasizes the importance of information in sustaining and shaping conversations about Jewish communities and Jewish life. It is an image that features younger Jews who not only direct the flow of information but generate it as well. Finally, it runs counter to the more conventional notion of the "Jewish community" as represented primarily by establishment organizations.[28] What emerges is a very densely connected small world of websites, the most valuable of which, from the perspective of social network analysis, are not establishment communal organizations but rather sites that trade primarily in information.

Given the prominence of information over communal service organizations in this network, it is clear that the Internet is not simply a reflection of Jewish life offline. Instead, it is a relatively independent sphere of Jewish communal engagement and involvement, representing certain qualities of Jewish life more broadly considered. The preceding analysis revealed the growth and development of a network of Jewish websites in which younger voices compete with and often outperform traditional organizations, newer voices occupy central positions within the overall landscape of Jewish websites, and leadership emerges through the ability to contribute to and shape common, if internally varied, Jewish communal conversations.

Neighborhood Networks

Having laid out this overview of the network and its emerging loci of influence, we will now turn our attention to the internal organization of the network as a small world. Therefore, it is instructive here to return to a brief discussion of the algorithms employed to produce the sociogram, with the goal of revealing further insights into the nodes, the links between them, and what they tell us about the network. Because the Fruchterman-Reingold algorithm uses common links to create equilibrium among all nodes in the sociogram, it necessarily produces certain groupings or "clusters" of websites based on commonly held links. In order to emphasize the appearance of clustering, we employed another algorithm that we hoped would produce a clearer representation of those clusters. Instead, as figure 6.3 (online) demonstrates, this second algorithm revealed an even more densely connected map featuring two not terribly distinct clusters.[29]

This second algorithm failed to reveal a more nuanced clustering pattern, in part, because we are already dealing with a densely connected small world. Therefore, the differences between clusters might not appear as vividly as they would if we were analyzing a more diverse or diffuse network. In any event, this second mapping revealed two scarcely discernible clusters: one, in the upper left-hand corner, that caters largely to the Orthodox, and another, spanning the middle, that does not. This clustering reinforces the earlier finding about the significance of Orthodox Jews in the Jewish virtual sector, and the impression that the large number of such sites share more in common with one another than they do with other Jewish sites. However, the proximity of the two clusters suggests that these differences are easily transgressed online, as one can move from one cluster to the next with a simple click.

The other cluster, comprising the rest of the sites (with a few far-flung exceptions), is large and densely connected, with the Jewish Women's Archive (JWA) sitting just to the right of the main cluster and the Jewish Agency (Jewishagency) just to the left. Slight openings emerge between the large mass in the middle and the two clusters immediately below it, but they are so close to the main cluster that they hardly qualify as independent clusters.[30] If any clustering logic could be applied here, it might be that the smaller cluster at the bottom of the sociogram represents sites with an overtly transnational focus, given the inclusion of Haaretz from Israel and the *Jewish Chronicle* (TheJC) from England.

The failure of the clustering algorithm to produce significant distinctions reinforces the earlier observation that the network is relatively small and well-connected. So, in order to observe any clustering at all, we must return to figure 6.2 (online) and take a closer look at a few subtle but significant groupings. Strictly speaking, these are not clusters, so instead I will refer to them as "neighborhood networks," a term that suggests some similarities between the sites but does not denote the same mathematical standard as clustering.

At the center of figure 6.4 (online, showing neighborhood networks within the Jewish online network) are the four large nodes representing the Reference Section. The large, relatively dispersed network across the top of the sociogram constitutes the Orthodox Archipelago. On the far right sit two neighborhood networks that constitute the Start-Up Sector, both of which primarily include sites by and for Jews between the ages of twenty-one and forty. The upper grouping includes three sites that are actively engaged in a Zionist conversation, while the lower one features sites for which Israel features among a broader array of other issues. Below the lower grouping lies the Establishment Bloc, which includes most of the sites belonging to the major communal service organizations. It is worth noting that within the Reference Section, Shamash sits slightly further toward the top of the sociogram, suggesting slightly more shared links with those sites falling within the broadly dispersed neighborhood network catering primarily to Orthodox communities. Religiously observant users might favor Shamash over search engines like Google or Yahoo! because it would be more likely to return results that address their particular needs and less likely to yield pages that lead them astray. By contrast, less religiously observant users might not even know that Shamash exists, as they would sooner turn to Google or Yahoo.

The Orthodox Archipelago (see figure 6.6, online) includes news sources as well as dating sites, reference sites, and commercial portals, all of which show evidence of dimensions religious life. Thus, the sites tend to link with one another, as visitors who would be interested in Vosizneias, a news service dedicated to meeting "the demanding needs of the Orthodox Jewish community," might also be interested in Oukosher, or any of the number of Orthodox dating sites. The Orthodox Archipelago is not, however, exclusively Orthodox, and it includes sites of interest to Jews of all ages. In fact, a handful of sites in this region, including Frumsatire and Bangitout, are written by and cater to younger Jews, and both feature humorous takes on religious life from the perspective of people within the religious world. In terms of the overall shape of the network of Jewish websites, this large neighborhood network indicates that the internet has become an important aspect of contemporary Orthodox Jewish life.

Although none of these sites score very highly in terms of betweenness or prestige, the sheer number of sites that cater to the needs and interests of Orthodox Jews is worth our attention. However, the absence of a single site that dominates the Orthodox Archipelago indicates that the community it represents remains rather diffuse, diverse, and decentralized, despite its significant presence online.

Because Orthodox Jews tend to be deeply embedded in Jewish social networks offline, the preponderance of online sources that cater to them makes sense; people interested in Jewish issues offline are more likely to seek out Jewish websites than those who are not. The Orthodox Archipelago comprises sites—like Headcoverings-by-devorah—that cater almost exclusively to Orthodox Jews, whose needs are particular to their Jewish interests, practices, and communities. The relatively small size of most of these nodes is not of much consequence, as none seems to seek a position of broad communal prominence as much as to serve the particular needs of its communal niche. Thus, the Orthodox Archipelago illustrates the prevalence of Orthodox Jews who have expanded their search horizons to include the Internet, which has become a powerful alternative to offline sources.

The same is not quite true of the Establishment Bloc (see figure 6.7, online), which sits almost directly opposite the sociogram of the Orthodox Archipelago. The Establishment Bloc includes leading cultural and educational organizations like the 92nd Street Y (92Y) and Hillel, as well as the sites of important communal organizations like the American Jewish Committee (AJC) and the website of the United Jewish Communities (UJC, now Jewishfederations). Unlike the diversity of nodes that constitutes the Orthodox Archipelago, the Establishment Bloc consists primarily of large, well-established educational and communal service organizations. The generally small size of the nodes in the Establishment Bloc indicates that these sites do not share many mutual links with other sites in the network. However, the sites represented here likely do share similar links in common, which means that the establishment organizations are, in some measure, talking to one another, even if they share fewer links in common with other websites.

In other words, the emergence of this neighborhood network might represent high bonding social capital, as in the case of Nextbook (now Tabletmag), which appears close to the 92Y because the two cosponsored programs during our period of data collection, but weak bridging social capital, as they are generally not very successful in establishing mutual links with sites across the larger network.[31] The Establishment Bloc represents the shortcomings of many communal organizations in building the links necessary to connect with other websites and either contribute to or influence Jewish conversations and relationships online. By way of comparison, if Myjewishlearning were to be deleted, it would have an impact on but not cripple the overall network, but if JewishFederations.org were to be deleted, it would have almost no impact at all because it does not occupy a central place within the network. Insofar as the network of Jewish websites represents broader Jewish communal dynamics, the emergence of new loci of leadership online effectively challenges establishment organizations to develop new strategies for cultivating influence by developing relationships with other sites in the network and by engaging other segments of their Jewish communities in active, engaged conversation.

By contrast, the final neighborhood network, the Start-Up Sector, consists of two different groupings, both of which comprise sites that largely cater to and are authored by Jews between ages twenty-one and forty. None of the sites in these two subneighborhoods has proven particularly adept at leveraging its role in the network, although they do tend to be better connected than their more established counterparts. The primary distinction between the two subneighborhoods corresponds to the centrality of Israel in each. The first subneighborhood includes sites that foreground a connection to Israel, while the second subneighborhood locates Israel alongside a host of other contemporary Jewish issues.

The first subneighborhood consists of three nodes representing very different entities, though each is committed to a shared conversation about Israel and Zionism. These three organizations—one long-standing institution and two others established within the past ten years—represent three different approaches to contemporary conversations about Zionism. Jewlicious, as noted earlier, began as a blog and now hosts annual Jewish cultural festivals, PresenTense (Presentense) is an incubator for Jewish social entrepreneurs, and the Jewishagency oversees MASA and coordinates thousands of Israel trips for young Americans annually. Of these three sites, two are run by younger Jews but all three appeal to an audience age forty and younger. Additionally, all three of these organizations articulate a strong Zionist sensibility and a connection to Israel, and thus end up sharing many similar links that correspond to the emergence of this neighborhood network.

By contrast, the other subneighborhood in the Start-Up Sector includes many nonestablishment organizations for which Israel and Zionism are not primary concerns. The sites included here generally cater to younger audiences and represent a variety of efforts to reinvigorate Jewish culture, primarily for American Jews. Both Birthrightisrael and Roicommunity serve Jews roughly between the ages of eighteen and thirty-five. Likewise, Jdubrecords and Heebmagazine both cater to similar audiences of young Jews who are seeking routes of connection to Jewish life, culture, and community that are not explicitly centered on Israel.

Birthrightisrael, much like the Jewishagency, centers on trips to Israel but, unlike its counterpart, does not necessarily advocate aliya (emigration to Israel), nor does it raise money for Israeli causes. In this way, Birthrightisrael is dedicated to deepening connections between American Jews and Israel, not to helping American Jews become Israelis, which differentiates it from Jewishagency and partially explains its appearance in this subnetwork as opposed to its counterpart. As is the case with the neighboring cluster, what accounts for the particular grouping is less a matter of explicit politics and more one of shared sensibility and audience, as evidenced by the links they have in common.

In terms of leadership, the emergence of this neighborhood network within the more general network suggests that these sites are playing a role in cultivating a distinctly youthful Jewish presence with an emphasis on American Jews. And, like their counterparts in the Establishment Bloc, they are better at cultivating a conversation amongst themselves than they are at leveraging mutual links to transgress the network. The significant exception to this trend is Jewcy, which bridges the Start-Up Sector and the not-quite-a-neighborhood consisting of news sites that falls just to the right of the reference sites.

The presence of Jewcy among these other news sources, all of which have large offline readerships, reinforces the contention that the Internet has opened up opportunities for engagement in public discourse in ways that significantly weaken the positions of traditional media outlets. Certainly, Jewcy's relatively large number of links, high betweenness score, and presence in the stretch of nodes belonging to traditional news sources indicates that the news arena is making room for voices and audiences that would likely have been excluded from the conversation prior to the advent of the Internet.

The network of Jewish websites illustrates changes like these and can be seen, partially, as a representation of larger Jewish communal dynamics. Yet the network explored here is not merely a representation. Rather, it is produced discursively alongside the emergence of new communal agendas, trends, opportunities, and forces. Examining the shape and structure of the network reveals just how the network of Jewish websites both represents and points to new directions in Jewish leadership. Online, we find a more level playing field between new and old, establishment and nonestablishment, organizations. The MASA example is but a small one of how an establishment organization changed its communications strategy in response to a chorus of criticism. But the fact that some of the most influential sites in the network do not represent offline organizations and the most powerful offline organizations tend to take less influential positions within this small Jewish world indicate that the Internet is enabling a new array of dynamics of Jewish life. The prominence of Myjewishlearning, the emergence of Jewcy, the sheer size of the Orthodox Archipelago, and the relative marginality of the Jewish-federations illustrate that any conversation about the "Jewish community" must begin to account for these new realities of virtual life.

As discussed earlier, one quality of this new reality is the prominence of information and the influence wielded by sites that broker information. Whether focusing on news or reference, sites that trade in information are among the best connected and most valuable to the overall network. Insofar as the web excels at making information widely and readily accessible, we should not be surprised that the network of Jewish websites follows this pattern. However, what is striking here is that these sites both provide information to their visitors and potentially shape the ways in which people navigate between and among Jewish websites. In this way, the reference sites provide both information *and* links for their visitors to follow. Information, then, is more than mere facts; it literally shapes how people engage in Jewish life online and off.

Attending to the virtual dimension of Jewish life also reveals that most establishment organizations exert only a modest force upon the overall network. Not significant in terms of centrality, betweenness, or prestige, the majority of these nodes, representing the majority of establishment organizations, they do not represent the offline prominence of their parent organizations. Though well funded and quite powerful in the public sector, these organizations show only modest success at establishing relationships with other websites and building online relationships suited for a more tightly knit small world.

As a venue for investigating the exertion of leadership in Jewish communal matters, the network of Jewish websites reveals emerging dynamics in the structure of American Jewry. Information plays a crucial role in the network, and sites that facilitate the sharing of information are better positioned to lead and influence the network. The leading sites in this conversation do not come from establishment organizations, and the Orthodox represent a significant percentage of Jewish websites in general. As a representation of the American Jewish community, the online network captures a very different image in which there is no central address, and within which leadership and influence are more diffuse, derive from a greater diversity of sources, and ultimately take very different forms than they have in the past.

Accounting for Blogs

As we expand the Jewish virtual sector to include blogs, the picture becomes both clearer and murkier. Blogging technology has made entering the Jewish communal conversation easy and nearly free; both Jewschool and Jewlicious began as blogs authored by one person or small groups of people, and each has since grown into a significant source of information for younger Jews. Moreover, blogging platforms like WordPress or Blogger provide all the hosting, search-engine placement, and widgets that one could need to create a fairly robust and comprehensive web presence, all without having to learn a single line of programming code. Indeed, blogs are so easy to start and so many blogs are created that something like 95 percent of all blogs are essentially abandoned.[32]

Nevertheless, as an often unfiltered, varied, and popular vehicle for personal expression, blogs represent the voices of individuals who are motivated enough to put their own thoughts online for anyone to read. Still more important, they are not just independent journals, but linked to other blogs, they become a loosely affiliated cacophony of voices that contribute to and shape a collective conversation. Moreover, because of the "comments" feature and the protocol that bloggers respond to comments left for them, blogs are more than virtual soapboxes (although they are that, too) but often opportunities for connection and conversation within a larger social network.

The reports of both the Berkman Center and the SSRC focus explicitly on blogs as indicative of larger phenomena. Their focus on blogs reflects the projects' respective interest in democracy and academic publishing, and both reports argue that blogs offer an alternative platform for the expression, publication, and circulation of ideas that might not otherwise find an appropriate venue. In mapping the Arabic and religion blogospheres, respectively, these two reports reach insightful conclusions about the function and meaning of blogs within their larger communities and conversations. In those two reports, blogs emerged as a crucial platform for expanding available venues for the discussion and circulation of ideas. This is true for Jewish blogs, as well, whose authors often seek venues for the free expression and exchange of ideas outside of traditional communal institutions or news vehicles. Blogs represent a crucial aspect of this small Jewish world not because they exemplify leadership in any traditional sense or because any one blog has the ear of the "right" readers, but because they represent a network of individuals in conversation. Traffic, again, proves less important than the presence and value of links between sites because those links represent relationships and those relationships constitute and traverse a broad and varied population of Jews.

Although it would be impossible to categorize most blogs because of their varied content, our survey of nearly eight hundred Jewish blogs makes clear that many writers either identify as Orthodox Jews or indicate that they were raised in Orthodox families. Some identify themselves as having left that community, while others regularly post lengthy exegeses about Torah portions or politics, the lives of single people looking for partners or the daily experience of young mothers. Given the sheer dominance of Orthodox bloggers over non-Orthodox bloggers overall, it appears that for Orthodox Jews, blogging has become both a popular pastime and a powerful vehicle for expressing dissent or differentiation within that community, and their presence shadows the large, dispersed network of websites that cater to those same communities.

The preponderance of Orthodox blogs lends itself to many possible explanations. One is that a *non*-Orthodox Jewish blogger might not identify her blog as "Jewish" and, as such, post about any number of issues, only some of them easily identifiable as Jewish. Orthodox bloggers, given their relatively deep investment in Jewish issues, might be more prepared than their non-Orthodox counterparts to engage primarily in those conversations. In other words, this project might identify more Orthodox bloggers because more Orthodox bloggers identify themselves and their blogs as Jewish.

Other reasons for the high number of Orthodox blogs might be that blogs provide an outlet for sharing stories and information beyond the grasp of traditional communal authority. The distance and potential anonymity of the blog format provide a safer space for people to raise issues and questions that might be otherwise taboo. For those questioning their relationship to Orthodoxy, the web might provide a safer space for doing so than their synagogues, families, or schools. Similarly, those who have left the Orthodox world may use blogs as a way to remain in contact with friends and family, but from a safe distance. Still others use their blogs as forums for sharing Torah or teachings, as a form of outreach to those who might be seeking a way into Orthodox Judaism.[33]

Whatever the explanation for their predominance, Orthodox blogs are worth noting for their sheer numbers, and accounting for them all dramatically shifts the overall map of the network. Figure 6.10 (online) represents the overall network, including both websites and blogs, mapped out according to the same algorithm used to produce the sociogram of Jewish websites, so as to emphasize the pull of common links. In order to highlight its general dynamics, we have omitted the names of the sites represented.[34] Blogs are represented in light green and websites appear in purple.

In terms of the effect on the overall size of the network, accounting for blogs increases to 6 the greatest number of links between nodes (versus 4, when calculated for websites), and increases the average distance between nodes to 2.622 links (it had been 1.93). Thus, the presence of 279 additional websites expands the size of the small Jewish world, but only slightly, maintaining its earlier characterization as a fairly well-connected and easily traversed network.

The sociogram, even without the sites' names, shows clearly that despite the pronounced number of Jewish blogs and the sizable links accrued by a handful, the map divides fairly neatly in half, with the majority of websites on one side and blogs on the other. This split indicates that most blogs, while certainly capable of generating lots of links, do not generally garner the reciprocal attention of Jewish websites, which limits the ability of the former to exert influence over the network as a whole. Nevertheless, a significant number of blogs are well connected to one another, and the location of a smaller number within the sociogram indicates that they have successfully attracted the attention and trust of some more prominent websites.

At the center of the map is a collection of very active and very well-connected blogs, as evidenced by the cluster of large, overlapping nodes. The size of these nodes indicates the large number of links, and their placement shows that they share many links in common. Yet the balance of blogs are sprinkled around the bottom half of the sociogram, suggesting that most blogs are small, not terribly well-connected, and without discernible patterns with respect to links held in common.

The few blogs at the center of the sociogram reveal a committed core of bloggers whose collective efforts indicate the emergence of a Jewish blogosphere. Perhaps more important, its impact on the network of websites and blogs is substantial. In order to highlight this phenomenon, we can take a closer look at the core of the sociogram. Figure 6.11 (online) gives a close-up view of the center of Figure 6.10, capturing the contact zone between blogs and websites. The graphic features only a handful of site names, for the sake of legibility.

In this zone, we find some of the usual suspects, including Myjewish-learning and Jewishvirtuallibrary (both located in the upper right-hand quadrant). But we also find the websites Frumsatire, Frumster, Aish, Israel-nationalnews, and Jewcy, each of which has relocated to the center because of its their relationships with both websites and blogs. The dense, overlapping center suggests a common conversation among these sites, even if it does not indicate how visitors interact or move between them. Looking at the size of the nodes in this dense center reveals a handful of sites and blogs with lots and lots of links. Additionally, accounting for links between blogs and websites changes the size and location of a few notable sites. The node representing Tabletmag basically does not change size once we account for blogs, although it moves closer to the center of the network because of its shared links with other blogs and websites. Jewcy expands and relocates, dwarfing Israelnationalnews and emerging as a central source of connection within this expanded small world. Meanwhile, nodes representing a few other sites, like Frumsatire, expand dramatically and emerge as particularly influential forces within the overall network.

The shifts evidenced here—toward the young and the Orthodox—indicate the emergence of new loci of leadership in Jewish life online. An outlet like Jewcy or Jewlicious (accidentally appearing in green here) might be more prepared to share links with an Orthodox blog than Haaretz or the Jewish-federations would be. Differences in approaches to sharing links between websites and blogs, and commonalities in those links, position some sites far more advantageously than others to lead online. Calculating for between-ness centrality affirms this trend. See Table 6.3 for a list of the ten blogs and websites with the highest betweenness centrality.

Accounting for blogs considerably alters the Jewish virtual landscape, favoring those that are willing to share links broadly. Myjewishlearning and Jewishvirtuallibrary retain their strong positions within the network, as do Jewcy, Jpost, and Haaretz. Yet we also see the emergence of two single-authored blogs and one website, Frumsatire. This site is the work of one Heshy Fried, which apparently receives no funding beyond what it makes in advertising (which, according to Mr. Fried, is not much). In terms of betweenness, Fried is more important than every other website save the Myjewishlearning and including Jpost, Jewcy, and Haaretz, and he brokers far more relationships than the websites of any of the establishment Jewish organizations. Fried owes his success to his mixture of Jewish insider knowledge and his ironic, humorous attitude, which allows him to attract attention (and links) from the Orthodox world while simultaneously transcending it. Fried's influence derives from his location on the margins of the Orthodox

TABLE 6.3
Betweenness Centrality for Blogs and Websites

Rank	Betweenness Centrality	Site Name
1	117	Myjewishlearning.com
2	112	Cj-heretic.blogspot.com
3	101	Frumsatire.net
4	100	Jpost.com
5	91	Jewcy.com
6	89	Forward.com
7	88	Jewishvirtuallibrary.org
8	85	Jewishjournal.com
9	77	agmk.blogspot.com
10	76	Haaretz.com

Calculating for Bonacich power reproduced this list almost exactly. The only change was that in the new calculation, Haaretz dropped off and was replaced by JTA.

world and his ability and desire to engage in conversations about current Jewish issues that intentionally transgress the offline boundaries that structure Jewish communities.

In an interview with Fried, who is both young and Orthodox, he explains that his efforts with Frumsatire are intended to engage the very large Orthodox audience in conversations and debates over contemporary Jewish life. "Blogger is still a dirty word in some Orthodox communities," he says, adding that sites like his and Failedmessiah are attempts to foster dialogue and transparency. Fried attributes his success to two factors. First, he talks openly about subjects that Orthodox people are not "supposed" to talk about, including sex, dating, and interfaith relationships. Second, he regularly includes opposing viewpoints on his blog. "And I mean really opposing. I push people's buttons." He explains, "When you go to Myjewishlearning, people are expecting to find [opposing views]. When you go to Aish, you're not going to find it." This strategy enables him to host a dialogue among the religious, the nonreligious, and the ultra-Orthodox in ways that are rare in the offline world.[35] Further, he explains that he is not interested in the "Manischewitz Judaism" that he sees Jewcy and Heebmagazine peddling. "There's only so many times you can talk about the hole in the sheet," he says.

Fried's betweenness centrality score indicates that he practices what he preaches, gives evidence of his ability to create and sustain mutual links with bloggers and websites. Indeed, much of his cache derives from his connections to other bloggers; recall that Frumsatire did not appear terribly central within the Orthodox Archipelago or in the network of Jewish websites more generally.

If leadership can be measured in terms of one's ability to exert influence, then the network of Jewish websites and blogs clearly demonstrates the influence of younger, Orthodox voices on the overall network. For their efforts to build relationships between sites, occupy positions in every neighborhood network, and bridge the gap between blogs and websites constituting the Jewish virtual sector, younger voices overall are leading their older, more established counterparts by virtually every measure. They are making inroads into every sector of Jewish life online, they are more skilled at establishing mutual links between blogs and websites, and they are more deftly leveraging the potential for community organizing online. As a relatively independent arena of Jewish communal engagement, the network of Jewish websites and blogs is clearly taking shape around a younger cadre of leaders who are both contributing to and reconfiguring Jewish communal conversations.

Two Local Case Studies

The preceding analysis is instructive for what it reveals about information-sharing and relationship-building as qualities of leadership online. Additionally, it demonstrates the ways in which the network of Jewish websites and blogs has enabled the emergence of new modes and expressions of leadership from outside the traditional halls of communal or institutional power. Examining the network at this scale assumes that websites like Jpost, Myjewishlearning, Jewcy, and Frumsatire all participate in and shape a transnational exchange of information that is by, for, and largely concerning Jews. In this way, the preceding assessment of the Jewish virtual sector primarily focuses on the large and often abstract notion of Jewish collectivity on a global scale.

Yet Jewish life is always lived locally. Regardless of mobility and resettlement patterns, people can only live in one place at a time, and while the previous analysis reveals some important dynamics regarding leadership and influence in global Jewish collectivity, we cannot neglect the ways in which people build and live Jewish lives locally. Internet use reflects these two scales as well. People search for answers to questions or buy books from Amazon.com, but they also use the Internet to find restaurants, local services, movie times, synagogues, schools, and more. So, in order to better understand the role of the Internet in the actual Jewish communities in which people live, we will turn to representations of Jewish life online in two case studies: those of Los Angeles and the San Francisco Bay Area.

These two communities exhibit a few important qualities that make them well suited for analysis within this larger conversation about influence, innovation, and leadership. The San Francisco Bay Area is home to one of the largest Jewish communities in the United States, and it has one of the highest rates of interfaith families and some of the lowest rates of synagogue membership in the country. Given the region's role in the high tech boom and its history of political radicalism, the Bay Area has the reputation of being an innovative, risk-taking community that is only loosely bound by tradition.

Los Angeles, as the second largest Jewish community in the United States, provides another rich site for analysis. Sarah Benor's essay in this volume offers a deep qualitative portrait of its organizations and leadership, and this analysis offers a different perspective on that community in order to understand the relationship between online and offline organizing, influence, and leadership. Comparing offline and online representations of the L.A. community will complement Benor's ethnographic analysis.

To examine our two communities, we gathered lists of local websites and applied the same algorithms and formulae as we did to the data in the earlier part of the paper. The sociogram of the San Francisco Bay Area appears in Figure 6.12 (online).

Unlike the fairly well-distributed sociogram of the network of Jewish websites depicted in Figure 6.2, the Bay Area's map resembles the spokes of a wheel radiating out from a central hub, more or less resembling the geographic layout of the community. Nodes representing organizations in the East Bay largely sit to the right of the map, and organizations based in San Francisco and the Peninsula sit to the left. The large node in the upper left belongs to BayJews, a kind of bulletin board that promotes itself as "your portal to Bay Area Jewish life." The size of its node indicates many mutual links, although its location shows that it shares many more common links with East Bay sites than with those focused on San Francisco or the Peninsula. In other words, BayJews has high-degree centrality (lots of links) but markedly lower betweenness centrality, as it plays a less significant role in brokering relationships among sites across the network.

At the center of the sociogram we find two overlapping nodes, one representing the San Francisco Jewish Community Foundation (SFJCF) and the other, Jewishsf (now Jweekly), representing the "J," the Jewish newspaper of northern California. The node representing the SFJCF dwarfs that of Jewishsf, indicating a departure from the earlier pattern emphasizing information-brokering sites in the broader network. Calculating for betweenness and prestige reinforces this pattern. The dominance of SFJCF in the network thus indicates yet another significant difference between global and local map-pings. Here, SFJCF appears to hold a powerful place online, as the site with the greatest number of links, the highest degree centrality, and the highest betweenness centrality.

Yet, such a highly centralized network indicates an overall weakness, as it is forced to rely too heavily on this single node to maintain the overall network. Were we to remove this site from the sociogram, the network would be deeply compromised, and the coordination of information within the network would become far more difficult. Without the central role of SFJCF, links between the organizations of the East Bay, San Francisco, and the Pen-insula would become quite strained. Though this assessment speaks to the centrality of the SFJCF website, it also indicates the overall weakness of the network as a whole. Healthier, more balanced networks are typically more diffuse, featuring a number of well-connected sites that do not rely on a single hub to sustain the entire network.

The sociogram of the San Francisco Bay Area therefore reveals a rather old-fashioned distribution of local power and leadership, one that is highly centralized amid an otherwise weakly connected population. This represen-tation of the community raises significant questions about the nature and style of leadership and influence exerted in this context. Online, the SFJCF is leading and leading strongly, but little evidence suggests it is successful in building coalitions among constituents or relationships among communities, as illustrated by the relative paucity of mutual links between synagogues, JCCs, museums, and other local agencies. Additionally, the SFJCF is not closely clustered with other sites, indicating that although it has many links, it does not share many links in common with other sites representing orga-nizations or agencies in its community.

It would be a mistake to simply read this sociogram as a representation of the Bay Area's demographic profile, which features a large but fairly dis-connected Jewish population, because the sociogram does not map individ-uals.[36] Instead, it maps representations of relationships between organiza-tions that are, by definition, committed to building Jewish life. If the most committed organizations are represented here, and they appear as relatively weakly linked, then the actual offline population of Jews might be even more weakly connected to one another than this representation indicates. In this way, the centrality of the SFJCF does not indicate overall communal health but rather, perhaps, just the opposite.

Los Angeles, by comparison, looks quite different. (See figure 6.13, online.)

The online network of Jewish Los Angeles appears to be more evenly distributed and not dominated by a single node. Like San Francisco's map, Los Angeles's roughly resembles a wheel, but unlike its counterpart to the north, Los Angeles is not dominated by a single node. Rather, the center is occupied by a cluster of nodes, with none claiming mutual links with a majority of sites and instead demonstrating close proximity that suggests quite a bit of similarity between the links they share.

Before focusing on the center, though, we will turn to some clusters, which, owing to the size of the overall map, emerge with some clarity. Across the upper right-hand corner is a string of nodes representing organizations that cater primarily, but not exclusively, to Los Angeles' younger Persian Jewish community: Nessah (a Persian Education and Cultural Center), 30yearsafter, and Ledorvador. (See figure 6.14, online.)

It makes sense that the nodes representing organizations that cater to young Persian Jews would all appear in a cluster, owing to the greater likelihood of their common interests and the presence of other links in common. In addition, it is worth noting the presence of Jconnectla nearby, an orientation owes in part to a number of cosponsored events during the data collection period and the increased likelihood of common ties.

The same dynamics of cosponsorship and common interests inform the emergence of a small cluster of nodes to the lower left of the center, which represent organizations that appear, as well, in Benor's paper (highlighted in figure 6.15, online). These clustered organizations share similar visions of their roles within the social and generational landscape of Los Angeles, and they represent some of the most active and interesting organizing efforts by and for younger Jews in the area. The largest node of these four belongs to the Progressive Jewish Alliance (PJA), which, while not the oldest, is clearly the most successful of these organizations at building relationships, as evidenced by mutual links between itself and other Los Angeles–based organizations. The presence of the 110-year-old Workmen's Circle (Circlesocal) in this group can be explained both by its generally progressive political commitments, which ally it with PJA, and by its relationship to the Shtibl Minyan, an independent prayer group that meets at the Workmen's Circle building. Shtibl's node lies further toward the margin of the sociogram, close to that of IKAR, another "spiritual community" that attracts some members of the same demographic as PJA and Reboot, a national organization with a strong presence in Los Angeles.

Turning to the center of the sociogram, we find a diverse collection of sites, none of which dominate either in either centrality or links. But their cluster indicates the presence of a common pattern of linking. (See figure 6.16, online.)

A quick look at the center reveals a few larger nodes belonging to one locally based philanthropy (Righteouspersons), Uclahillel, and Jewishfoundationla, the last being the city's central Jewish philanthropic organization.

TABLE 6.4
Betweenness Centrality in Los Angeles

Rank	Betweenness Centrality	Site Name
1	1015.25	jconnectla.com
2	806.234	30yearsafter.org
3	714.231	righteouspersons.org
4	712.231	laguardians.org
5	696.677	jdubrecords.org
6	686.779	jewlicious.com
7	668.992	jewishfoundationla.org
8	471.978	jewishla.org
9	469.024	16hazon.org
10	456.301	jcpsocal.org

Also present is Jewishjournal, which, despite its central role in the larger network of blogs and websites, plays a much smaller role here, suggesting that much of its local influence is exerted through its weekly paper publication.

In order to reveal differences among the roles these sites play, we can calculate for betweenness and prestige as well.

Calculating for betweenness centrality reveals the centrality of jconnectla and 30yearsafter, which, despite their marginal presence in the sociogram, occupy important roles in brokering relationships in the network. We also find Jewishla, the website of the Jewish Federation of Greater Los Angeles, and Jewlicious, which emerged as an influential site in our earlier discussion and also has a strong connection to Southern California. Jconnectla, a relatively new organization that caters mainly to Jews between twenty-one and thirty-five years old, echoes earlier findings that sites representing nonestablishment organizations have been much more successful at leveraging their position online than establishment organizations. Indeed, on its website, Jconnectla expresses exactly this sensibility with regard to community building. As the self-described "premier Jewish experience organization for young professionals in Los Angeles," the organization also emphasizes its independence, boasting that it is "an independent, grass-roots organization, not affiliated with any movement or parent organizations."[37] The absence of affiliation or "parent" organizations seems to empower Jconnectla to establish relationships across different social realms, much like we observed earlier with Frumsatire and other similar sites.

TABLE 6.5
Bonacich Centrality

Rank	Bonacich Centrality	Site Name
1	19	righteouspersons.org
2	14	pjalliance.org
3	14	uclahillel.org
4	11	jconnectla.org
5	11	30yearsafter.org
6	10	birthrightisrael.com
7	10	jdubrecords.org
8	8	jewishjustice.org
9	8	jewlicious.com
10	8	yiddishkaytla.org

However, looking at the Bonacich centrality measure reveals a slightly different account of the sites, as illustrated in table 6.5.

When we calculate which sites are connected to others with high prestige, Righteouspersons emerges as the most significant and influential site in Jewish Los Angeles, in terms of the links it maintains. As the website of a powerful foundation, it follows that Righteouspersons not only has high betweenness, but that it is connected to other sites with high prestige. Hardly a start-up, Righteouspersons supports a few of the organizations represented in this sociogram, including Jdubrecords and Reboot. More important for the question of influence and emerging leadership, this recalculation finds both Jewishla and Jewishfoundationla—the nodes representing the city's most established communal organizations—missing.

Overall, this list of centrally influential sites in Los Angeles consists almost exclusively of those representing organizations either run by or catering to Jews between ages twenty-one and forty. This finding speaks volumes about the ways in which the Internet is changing the definitions, dimensions, and articulations of influence in the larger Jewish world on the local level. The Los Angeles sociogram reveals a diffuse and stable network that is being led by a handful of organizations headed by and catering to younger Jews. Calculating for centrality reveals the powerful role of nonestablishment organizations in creating a well-connected and stable network that manages to cross social boundaries that often divide ethnic and religious communities from one another. In comparison to San Francisco, for which the sociogram is dominated by a single node representing an establishment organization,

Los Angeles reveals the vital power of nonestablishment organizations to build healthier, more diverse Jewish communities both online and off.

A closer look at these two local studies both reaffirms and refines what we observed in the study of the network of Jewish blogs and websites more generally. Most significant, we find that online, older models of leadership, such as that revealed by the San Francisco Bay Area sociogram, are not effectively fostering healthy networks. And as the analysis of Los Angeles reveals, new modes of influence, leadership, and community building are being driven in large measure by organizations led by or catering to younger Jews. As illustrated by the difference between Myjewishlearning and UJC, or by the difference between Righteouspersons and Jewishla, this discovery reinforces our earlier finding that nonestablishment organizations are more deftly able to mobilize mutual links on the Internet than their establishment counterparts.

Conclusion

This chapter is a first attempt to assess the role of the Internet in Jewish life by examining relationships and dynamics between Jewish websites and blogs, with the broader goal of better understanding how Jewish life online represents and informs Jewish life offline. This chapter reveals evidence of a well-established trend in Jewish communal life, namely that community, politics, leadership, and influence are both virtual and real. They exist and are created both online and off, and, increasingly, the virtual and the real are mutually constitutive of Jewish life. In terms of community, communication, and leadership in the twenty-first century, the virtual and the real are not opposites, they are collaborators.

Yet websites, blogs, and sociograms only matter if they help us understand the shifting landscape of contemporary Jewish life. This essay argues that they do. The blogs and online newspapers that ultimately forced MASA to rethink its public relations strategy exerted influence over a large establishment organization. Because of its strategy of investing in mutual links, Myjewishlearning exerts influence over the network of websites, and once we account for blogs, Frumsatire appears to do the same. In Los Angeles, Jconnectla works on a similar principle, and as a result youthful organizations dominate the virtual sector. Each of these cases represents one way in which websites that are authored by or cater to a younger audience are putting themselves into influential positions within the online network that represents the Jewish community.

Part of what makes Myjewishlearning, Jewcy, Jewlicious, Frumsatire, and Jconnectla so influential in this analysis are their respective abilities to cultivate mutual links that cross offline social distinctions and, in this way, build relationships that circumvent some of the older social and cultural differences (though sometimes creating others). Working largely outside the establishment Jewish organizations (though sometimes funded by them), the websites of these organizations (and Mr. Fried) prove far more capable of creating and sustaining mutual links than their establishment counterparts.

This dynamic is brought into sharp relief by the comparison of the San Francisco and Los Angeles sociograms. San Francisco, dominated by the SFJCF, presents a strongly centralized but weakly connected network in which nonestablishment organizations play a marginal role. Los Angeles, by contrast, reveals a well-connected and diffuse network in which sites representing nonestablishment organizations emerge as the most significant and influential presences.

Additionally, clusters or neighborhood networks within the small Jewish world indicate common links, even in the absence of direct links between specific sites. These clusters illustrate the existence of a common conversation, or at least a common set of concerns among sites, and suggest areas of shared interest. Looking closely at the sites that participate in these common conversations opens up ways of understanding new modes and expressions of leadership that do not fit more traditional models.

In this way, we can observe the creation of new venues for Jewish communal leadership. But even more important, we can understand that the Internet is modeling a different kind of communal structure, one that is decentralized, multidimensional, diverse, and conducive to leadership being exerted in a variety of forms. Blogs are but one artifact of this environment, and their inclusion is crucial here not only because they reshape the overall network but because they also provide a forum for voices from outside established Jewish organizational structures. The conversations in which bloggers share and the uncoordinated relationships they create make for a healthy, relatively decentralized network, and this uncoordination itself helps fosters the network's overall dynamism. It also supplies a crucial factor in the emergence of new leadership within the community generally.

Whereas the "Jewish community" used to be shorthand for the organizations that claimed to represent the concerns and needs of Jews, the map of the small Jewish world online captures a much more variegated and diverse community, sustained across social divisions. The Internet has given both younger and more marginal voices a platform for speaking about, broadcasting, organizing, and creating their own communities while still participating in larger communal conversations. Online technologies have opened up the possibilities for new forms and formulations of leadership, and, in turn, these voices are spurring the Jewish virtual sector to vie for prominence alongside its public and private counterparts. The leaders are those who have most successfully taken advantage of this new technology and who continue to activate their social networks both online and off.

APPENDIX
APPENDIX TABLE 6.A
Top 99 Jewish Websites by Traffic for the Period of May–November 2009 (in alphabetical order)

adl.org	jccmanhattan.org	luach.org
ahuva.com	jccsf.org	maven.co.il
aipac.org	jcpa.org	mechon-mamre.org
aish.com	jewfaq.org	my-hebrew-name.
ajc.org	jewishagency.org	com
ajudaica.com	jewishaz.com	nmajh.org
ajws.org	jewishblogging.com	ohr.edu
akhlah.com	jewishencyclopedia.com	oorah.org
anshe.org	jewishfamily.com	ort.org
artscroll.com	jewishgen.org	ou.org
askmoses.com	jewishjournal.com	oukosher.org
babaganewz.com	jewishmag.com	remember.org
beingjewish.org	jewishpress.com	seraphicpress.com
chabad.org	jewishrecipes.org	shamash.org
cjh.org	jewishsoftware.com	shemayisrael.co.il
cjnews.com	jewishvirtuallibrary.org	shlager.net
crownheights.info	jewishworldreview.com	shmais.com
debka.com	jnf.org	templeinstitute.org
feldheim.com	jpost.com	thejc.com
forward.com	jrants.com	thejewishmuseum.org
haaretz.com	jsingles.com	thejewishweek.com
hareshima.com	jta.org	torah.org
hebcal.com	jtf.org	torahmedia.com
hebrewbooks.org	jtsa.edu	tzadik.com
hebrewsongs.com	judaicawebstore.com	ujc.org
holocaust-history.org	judaism.com	urj.org
holocaustresearchproject.org	juf.org	uscj.org
huc.edu	jwa.org	ushmm.org
huji.ac.il	k12.il	virtualjerusalem.com
iranjewish.com	kashrut.com	vosizneias.com
israelnationalnews.com	kkl.org.il	wiesenthal.org
israelnewsagency.com	kosher.com	yadvashem.org
jbooks.com	kosherdelight.com	ynetnews.com

Top 49 Jewish Websites with Significant Audiences between Ages 21 and 35 by Traffic for the Period May–November 2009 (in alphabetical order)

92y.org	jewishclub.com
atime.org	jewishfriendfinder.com
bangitout.com	jewlicious.com
bbyo.org	jewssip.com
birthrightisrael.com	jewssip.com
brandeis.edu	jewtube.com
calmkallahs.com	jlove.com
chossonandkallah.com	jpeoplemeet.com
frumchat.com	jvoices.com
frumsatire.net	mostlymusic.com
frumster.com	myjewishlearning.com
g-dcast.com	ncsy.org
geshercity.org	nextbook.org
headcoverings-by-devorah.com	nfty.org
hebrewcollege.edu	presentense.org
heebmagazine.com	roicommunity.org
hillel.org	sawyouatsinai.com
israel-music.com	shabot6000
israelfree.com	theknish.com
isreallycool.com	theyeshivaworld.com
jcarrot.org	tznius.com
jdate.com	usy.org
jdubrecords.org	wejew.com
jewcy.com	yu.edu
jewishcafe.com	

Sector Breakdown of Websites

News	Singles	Blogs, Magazines
jpost.com	jdate.com	theyeshivaworld.com
haaretz.com	jpeoplemeet.com	jewcy.com
jewishworldreview.com	frumster.com	bangitout.com
ynetnews.com	jewishfriendfinder.com	Jewlicious.com
israelnationalnews.com	jewishcafe.com	nextbook.org
debka.com	sawyouatsinai.com	heebmagazine.com
jta.org	jsingles.com	seraphicpress.com
jewishjournal.com	jewishclub.com	jewishblogging.com
forward.com	jlove.com	frumsatire.net
vosizneias.com		jewschool.com
jewishmag.com		jewssip.com
thejewishweek.com		jbooks.com
jewishaz.com		jrants.com
israelnewsagency.com		jcarrot.org
jewishpress.com		jvoices.com
thejc.com		theknish.com
cjnews.com		babaganewz.com

APPENDIX 6.C (CON'T.)

Orthodox	Service Organizations	Museums, Schools
aish.com	adl.org	ushmm.org
chabad.org	jewishgen.org	brandeis.edu
ou.org	urj.org	yu.edu
torah.org	ujc.org	92Y.org
crownheights.info	uscj.org	yadvashem.org
oukosher.org	hillel.org	thejewishmuseum.org
akhlah.com	ort.org	jtsa.edu
ohr.edu	birthrightisrael.com	jccmanhattan.org
shmais.com	jnf.org	huc.edu
shemayisrael.co.il	juf.org	jccsf.org
oorah.org	jewishagency.org	cjh.org
torahmedia.com	ajws.org	nmajh.org
anshe.org	ajc.org	huji.ac.il
frumchat.com	israelfree.com	hebrewcollege.edu
atime.org	jtf.org	
calmkallahs.com	aipac.org	
	bbyo.org	
	nfty.org	
	usy.org	
	wiesenthal.org	
	ncsy.org	
	jcpa.org	
	kkl.org.il	
	iranjewish.com	
	geshercity.org	
	roicommunity.org	
	presentense.org	

NOTES

The author would like to extend his deep gratitude and appreciation for the insight and assistance of the following people: Steven M. Cohen, Sarah Bunin Benor, Shaul Kelner, Sylvia Barack Fishman, and Jack Wertheimer. These are some of the finest collaborators, thinkers, colleagues, and friends with whom I've had the pleasure to work. At various points Riv-Ellen Prell, Jack Ukeles, and J. Shawn Landres provided valuable insight into some of the issues discussed here. Ted Sasson and Charles Kadushin offered vital criticism and assistance at exactly the right times, and without their help, this project would have been much impoverished and the paper significantly less interesting. Eli Kannai provided some very thoughtful and instructive critiques on a later draft that have changed my thinking and challenged my findings. Robert Swirsky wrote the custom script used to gather the data for this project, and he also mapped the networks that appear here. Without Robert, this project could never have happened, and I'm deeply grateful to him for his help, patience, curiosity, and interest in the project. Finally, I want to express my gratitude to the AVI CHAI Foundation, which helped usher an idea into a research project and a research project into this chapter.

1. "Advert for Saving Jewish Yourth [sic] From "Getting Lost." A thirty-five-second commercial posted on YouTube by auc1 on September 2, 2009, accessed December 10, 2009.

2. Kung Fu Jew's *Jewschool* post of September 3, 2009. "MASA TV commercial: Intermarried Jews are Lost" is one of the most widely cited and circulated of these (http://jewschool.com), accessed December 10, 2009. Other objections came from bloggers like Esther Kustanowitz, "Lost: Not the TV Show, the Intermarried Jews" (http://esther kustanowitz.typepad.com), accessed December 10, 2009, and Ed Case, CEO of interfaithfamily.com (www.interfaithfamily.com/smf/index.php?article=3373), accessed December 10, 2009, who bluntly titled his post "A Stupid, Ill-Conceived Approach from Israel."

3. J. J. Goldberg, "'Lost' in Plain Sight: An Israeli Plan to Rescue American Jews," blog section, *Forward*, September 6, 2009 (http://blogs.forward.com/jj-goldberg), accessed December 10, 2009. It should also be noted that anecdotal evidence exists of conversations between American Jews and leaders at the Jewish Agency that helped foment the organization's change of heart, but nevertheless, the conversation online demonstrated the widespread concern over the advertisement and its overtones.

4. The Jewish Agency posted its response on its website on September 6, 2009 (http://www.jewishagency.org), accessed December 10, 2009. The full text of the letter explaining the response appeared in a number of blogs and a host of online Jewish news sources, including ejewishphilanthropy.com (http://ejewishphilanthropy.com/masa-officially-pulls-the-plug-on-lost-campaign/), posted September 8, 2009, accessed December 10, 2009; and *The Fundermentalist* blog on JTA.org (http://blogs.jta.org), posted September 8, 2009, accessed December 10, 2009.

5. For examples of each, see Chris Anderson, *The Long Tail* (New York: Hyperion, 2008); James Surowiecki, *The Wisdom of Crowds* (New York: Anchor Books, 2005); Charlene Li and Josh Bernoff, *Groundswell* (Boston: Harvard Business Press, 2008); Clay Shirkey, *Here Comes Everybody* (New York: Penguin, 2009); and Yochai Benkler, *The Wealth of Networks* (New Haven: Yale University Press, 2006).

6. Malcolm Gladwell's thoughtful critique of this event notwithstanding, the global dimension of local political events is an undeniable effect of online communication platforms. See Malcolm Gladwell, "Small Change: Why the Revolution Will Not Be Tweeted," *The New Yorker*, October 4, 2010 (www.newyorker.com). For the response of Twitter's founders to Gladwell, see Liz Gannes, "Twitter Founders: Gladwell Got It Wrong," GigaOM, October 11, 2010 (http://gigaom.com), accessed November 28, 2010.

7. The Pew Research Center's Internet and American Life Project routinely releases data on gaps (generational, class, race, region, and otherwise) in Internet use. The most recent data still shows a significant lag in people sixty-five and older, when compared to their younger counterparts, although it also shows that 79 percent of all adults eighteen and older are online.

8. Both an executive summary and the full report are available online at http://cyber
.law.harvard.edu/publications/2009/Mapping_the_Arabic_Blogosphere.

9. Social Science Research Council (SSRC), *The New Landscape of the Religion
Blogosphere* (New York: Social Science Research Council, March, 2010), 3. The full report is available as of press time online at http://blogs.ssrc.org/tif/religion-blogosphere.

10. This is an adaptation and a paraphrase from Technorati's definition of its 2008
State of the Blogosphere report, which describes the blogosphere as "the ecosystem of
interconnected communities of bloggers and readers at the convergence of journalism and
conversation." Technorati's definition is also employed in the SSRC *Religion Blogosphere*
paper, page 18. For Technorati's report, see Technorati's 2008 installment of its annual
State of the Blogosphere report, which it has been issuing since 2004. For access to every
State of the Blogosphere report Technorati has released, see its complete listing as of press
time here: http://technorati.com/blogging/state-of-the-blogosphere.

11. Certainly, these social networking platforms are changing the ways in which people are engaging online. They are changing how websites and blogs interact, and they are
changing the ways in which people discover and experience new websites. These platforms are continually evolving, and their use continues to expand. They are, undoubtedly
and along with mobility, the trend of the future. However, measuring or assessing the
impact of these tools lies beyond the scope of this chapter. Facebook, famously, does not
share its data, and Twitter is still not deeply infused throughout the Jewish community,
though it's impact and import are growing. So, this chapter focuses on websites and blogs,
excluding social networking platforms. As a first investigation into Jewish communal
dynamics online, this chapter hopes to begin a conversation that will reveal additional
insights about technology, community, leadership, and Jewish life well into the future.

12. Aaron Smith, "New Numbers for Blogging and Blog Readership," Pew Internet
and American Life Project (www.pewinternet.org/Commentary/2008/July/New-numbers
-for-blogging-and-blog-readership.aspx). As quoted in Social Science Research Council, 9.

13. A note on nomenclature: when referring to websites, I will be excluding the .com
or .org suffixes throughout the body of this chapter, for the sake of readability. A full list
of websites included in this chapter, complete with their suffixes, is included in Appendix
A and Appendix B.

14. During the primary data collection period for this project, Jewcy and JDub records
were independent organizations. Since that time, they have joined together and, though
they maintain separate web presences, are effectively different branches of a single organization. This marks but one of many significant changes online in the relatively short
period between our initial data collection period and this writing. Undoubtedly, others
will occur between this writing and the final publication of this report.

15. See www.compete.com, accessed February 5, 2010.

16. Mark Granovetter, "The Strength of Weak Ties: A Network Theory Revisited," *Sociological Theory* 1 (1983) 201–233; Robert Putnam, *Bowling Alone: The Collapse and
Revival of American Community* (New York: Simon & Schuster, 2001)

17. This aphorism is repeated countless times around the net to summarize how sites
interact. One of the best explanations I've read recently belongs to Pete Cashmore, the
editor and founder of the social networking site Mashable.com. In an article he wrote for
CNN.com, he embedded his definition in an explanation of his objections to the *New
York Times'* announcement of a fee-for-service model for access to its online content. See

Cashmore, "Why the NYTimes.com Fee Is a Step Back," CNN.com, January 21, 2010 (www.cnn.com), accessed February 8, 2010.

18. To be sure, some sites expend a great deal of energy and attention on building a rich network of other sites to which they are linked, and certain companies will, for a fee, consult with an organization looking to optimize its placement in Google searches and so on. Services like these might give some sites an advantage over others in terms of their ability to position themselves both within general searches and within networks of other sites. This, however, is a strategy for enhancing the position of one's site online, and ought to be considered as one dimension of the Internet, generally. That is, if using a search engine optimizer (SEO) helps position a site within the network, then that is a strategy worth exploring for sites wishing to enhance their position within the network. That said, we did not ask webmasters if they employ these SEO tools.

19. The SSRC report on the religion blogosphere used Alexa and Compete in addition to Technorati (SSRC, p. 20). I opted to exclude Technorati because so few of the Jewish sites used it during our data collection period. Because Jewish sites did not rely on Technorati, it seemed unlikely to produce an accurate measure of a site's significance.

20. This list was never intended to be a definitive compilation of a site's popularity or significance, and although we attempted to be as conclusive as possible during our data collection period, we likely missed a site or two that could have qualified for inclusion. As with all social scientific sampling methods, there is no perfect sample. Additionally, the distinction between websites and blogs might have played a role in this, as I might have counted a site as a blog, while its author may consider it to be a website. However, given the number of websites and blogs for which we do account, and the qualities of the network we discovered in this analysis, I am confident in the sample, its size, and its ability to represent the broader dynamics of this network.

21. Jewish blogs, like all blogs, have a very low survival rate. The vast majority of blogs have a life span of less than one month. Because they are free to maintain, they are rarely taken down, and most are simply abandoned by their authors after a few posts.

22. Duncan Watts, *Small Worlds: The Dynamics of Networks between Order and Randomness* (Princeton: Princeton University Press, 1999). See also Duncan Watts and Steven Strogatz, "Collective Dynamics of 'Small-World' Networks," *Nature* 393 (June 1998), 440–442.

23. Nick Clark "Facebook overtakes Google" March, 18, 2010 (www.independent .co.uk), accessed March 22, 2011.

24. Clay Shirkey, *Here Comes Everybody: The Power of Organizing without Organizations* (New York: Penguin, 2009).

25. The distribution of links as the sign of a healthy network is well documented. See Albert-Laszlo Barbasi, *Linked: How Everything is Connected to Everything Else and What It Means* (New York: Plume, 2003); Mark Buchanan, *Nexus: Small Worlds and the Groundbreaking Theory of Networks* (New York: Norton, 2002); Watts, *Small Worlds*.

26. This definition of betweenness is provided in the online version of Robert A. Hanneman and Mark Riddle's *Introduction to Social Network Methods, an online textbook* (Riverside, CA: University of California, Riverside, 2005), www.faculty.ucr.edu/ ~hanneman, accessed February 5, 2010.

27. The literature on Jews ages twenty to forty is now fairly substantial. For some examples, see Steven M. Cohen and Ari Y. Kelman, *Uncoupled: How Our Singles Are*

Reshaping Jewish Engagement (Andrea and Charles Bronfman Philanthropies, 2008). See also Pearl Beck, Ron Miller, and Jack Ukeles, *Young Jewish Adults in the United States Today* (New York :American Jewish Committee, 2006); Leonard Saxe, *Tourists, Travelers, and Citizens: Jewish Engagement of Young Adults in Four Centers of North American Jewish Life* (Waltham, MA: Steinhardt Social Research Institute, 2009).

28. Jerome Chanes, *A Primer on the American Jewish Community* (New York: American Jewish Committee, 2008), http://www.ajc.org.

29. To produce this sociogram, we used the LinLog energy model, a different algorithm that typically produces a more pronounced clustering pattern than Fruchterman-Rheingold.

30. This pattern of clustering was reproduced when run through two different algorithms.

31. Putnam, *Bowling Alone*.

32. Douglas Quenqua, "Blogs Falling in an Empty Forest," *New York Times*, June 5, 2009 (www.nytimes.com), accessed September 4, 2009.

33. These are speculations as to the preponderance of Orthodox bloggers, and additional research into the writers and their blogs would be necessary to properly account for this phenomenon.

34. To include the names of all the websites and blogs would have made the map entirely unreadable.

35. Heshy Fried, interview by author, Berkeley, CA. February 10, 2009.

36. Bruce Phillips, *2004 Jewish Community Study* (San Francisco: Jewish Community Federation of San Francisco, 2004).

37. The full description, currently posted on the right side of the JConnectLA homepage, reads like this: "JConnectLA is the premier Jewish experience organization for young professionals in Los Angeles. We are an independent, grass-roots organization, not affiliated with any movement or parent organizations. Dedicated to promoting community, unity and Jewish connectivity, find out more about us today!"; accessed March, 13, 2010.

7 In Its Own Image

Independent Philanthropy and the Cultivation of Young Jewish Leadership

IN MARCH 2009, the graphic artist Eli Valley published a comic in the *Forward* entitled "Social Entrepreneurs Lost in Space." The piece satirizes the Jewish communal discourse about young leadership that is embodied in the present volume. In the comic, an asteroid is about to smash into Earth, and NASA decides to save a remnant of the human race by sending a select group of individuals to colonize another planet. Deciding that Jews are "the smartest people in the world," NASA dispatches an expert to identify "the top tier of the Jewish people." The expert returns, waving research reports with titles that parody those of studies like the one you are reading now. "Apparently, the entire Jewish community is entranced by 'social entrepreneurs,'" he announces. When the NASA official responds dismissively, the expert reprimands him: "You fool! How can you expect to comprehend Jewish intelligence?"[1]

Valley's satire maps the contours of late twentieth and early twenty-first century American Jewish discourse about youth, leadership, and change. The past decades have seen substantial resources devoted to advancing the notion that a vibrant American Jewish future depends primarily on empowering young leaders and innovators to reshape Jewish life for changing times. In this essay, I offer an institutional analysis of the emergence and evolution of this understanding, as it has manifested itself through a now-thriving field of Jewish leadership and change initiatives located outside the degree-granting institutions of professional training.

Forty years ago, one would have been hard-pressed to speak of a trans-institutional, transdenominational field of Jewish leadership development. Leadership development, such as it was, was bounded and tracked by career area, denomination, and institution. Movement-specific seminaries ordained rabbis and invested cantors to work in the synagogues of the sponsoring denomination. Teachers' colleges trained educators to work in schools. Grad-

The comic "Social Entrepreneurs Lost in Space" was originally published in *Forward* March 27, 2009. Copyright © 2009 by Eli Valley (www.evcomics.com). All rights reserved. Reprinted with permission of the artist.

uate programs in social work and Jewish communal service prepared professionals for employment in federations and federation-supported agencies. Jewish civic organizations independently ran their own donor-development, volunteer-engagement, and continuing professional education programs. Even for children and teenagers, initiatives in youth leadership were typically movement-specific and even summer camp–specific.

Contrast this to the present state of affairs: Today, neither seminaries nor graduate programs in Jewish education and nonprofit management have monopolies on the professional training of their students. Through independent leadership development programs such as the Wexner Graduate Fellowship, the Schusterman Rabbinical Fellowship, and, from 2006 until 2009, the Professional Leaders Project (PLP), large numbers of those studying to earn Jewish-sector professional degrees have also been receiving professional socialization alongside colleagues from other seminaries and graduate schools. Early- and midcareer professionals can continue this type of transinstitutional, transdenominational leadership development in programs like the Center for Leadership Initiatives' Tzimtzum program, Jewish Funds for Justice's Selah initiative, and (until recently) Synagogue Transformation and Renewal's Professional Education for Excellence in Rabbis program (STAR PEER). Volunteer activists and donors are taking part in equivalent programs such as Reboot, Grand Street, ROI,[2] and the Wexner Heritage Program, all of which are independent of the particular Jewish organizations in which their participants exercise their leadership. Teenagers and college students are being cultivated as future leaders by nondenominational foundation-based programs such as the Bronfman Youth Fellowships in Israel, the Dorot Fellowship in Israel, and Denver's Rose Youth Foundation. In addition, activists, leaders, and social entrepreneurs can find support to create new initiatives and institutions through change-cultivation programs with names like Jumpstart, Upstart, PresenTense, and Bikkurim (lit., "first fruits").

In short, a new institutional field flourishes that did not exist in the 1970s. Its hallmark is the cultivation of individual leadership and innovation through transinstitutional and transdenominational non-degree-granting programs that complement or supplement the professional training provided by seminaries and graduate schools. No umbrella organization or professional association formalizes this field of Jewish leadership and change initiatives (hereafter, JLCIs). In spite of this, the professionals involved in the various ventures intuitively recognize one another as being engaged in a common enterprise, and easily converge on a similar set of names when asked to identify the other players in the field. Programs tend to be organized and funded along similar lines, mostly as initiatives of independent Jewish foundations or as stand-alone operating foundations. Their work usually shares common structural elements: typically, a committee draws upon stringent admissions criteria to select among individual applicants, who are grouped into cohorts and provided retreat-based learning and networking opportunities for a specified period, and then cultivated afterward through alumni engagement efforts. The programs often look to the same literatures and vocabularies to conceptualize their work. They draw on overlapping sets of consultants and researchers to aid in this process (including the authors in the present volume). The programs also regularly select many of the same recipients (although not necessarily at the same stage in the recipients' career life-cycles.) Additionally, their professionals interact with one another formally and informally in a variety of Jewish communal convenings.

Because the JLCI field's boundaries are amorphous, it is impossible to give a precise count, but we are speaking of a network of perhaps fifty or more initiatives whose budgets (including staff and overhead) mostly range from hundreds of thousands of dollars a year to between five and ten million dollars. The institutional core of this network consists of philanthropic foundations supported by third-party knowledge producers, including contracted researchers, academy-based scholars of leadership, and leadership consultants. The Jewish federation system maintains a degree of involvement, even as it struggles to define its role in the enterprise. In the current decade, the JLCI network has expanded to include a small number of independent nonprofit organizations, typically founded by people with existing ties to the network.

Although the field is commonly thought of as being engaged in the cultivation of leaders and leadership, in fact, some of its most important work is conceptual. If it seems self-evident to the reader that the Jewish community needs innovation to thrive, that individual leaders hold the keys to American Jewry's collective well-being, and that young leaders—more than their elders—hold the best promise for building the Jewish future, this is at least in part because for almost three decades, these ideas have been systematically developed and advanced through the JLCI field's programming, research, and advocacy.

Research has been and remains central to this field's work. Indeed, researchers have often provided the very language that practitioners use to understand their efforts (e.g., historian Jonathan Sarna's distinction between "the bloomed" and "the groomed," coined for a 1995 Wexner Foundation study, and Joshua Avedon and Shawn Landres' field-defining appellation, "the innovation ecosystem," coined for a 2009 Jumpstart, Natan Fund, and Samuel Bronfman Foundation study). Because research has not stood apart from the JLCI field but has helped to shape it, the present chapter will treat research on Jewish leadership as a vital dimension of the JLCI field itself, part of what needs to be analyzed and understood. To do otherwise would misrepresent the JLCI field. "Young Jewish leadership" should not be thought of as an opaque phenomenon "out there" for foundation-funded researchers to make sense of. Such an approach wrongly implies that young Jewish leadership is primarily about individuals, that the meaning of the concept is cut-and-dry, and that a radical divide separates the people being studied, the people doing the studies, and the people sponsoring and using the studies. Better instead to think of young Jewish leadership as a holistic and unfolding enterprise in which foundations and other organizations are developing processes for talking about, investing in, and supporting certain groups of individuals, informed by an evolving conversation that is continually being shaped and reshaped by researchers, practitioners, and funders alike.

Yet even this distinction between funders, recipients, researchers, and practitioners is misleading. One can get a sense of how fluid the boundaries actually are simply by considering how deeply the authors in the current volume have been enmeshed in the field as both its products and producers. To take myself as an example, I am an alumnus of the Wexner Graduate Fellowship and the Jewish federation system's Project Otzma, as well as a former participant in The Conversation, a collaborative project of the Center for Leadership Initiatives and the *Jewish Week*. I have taught in all three Wexner Foundation leadership programs (Graduate Fellowship, Israel Fellowship, and Heritage Program), in the Mandel Foundation's Jerusalem Fellows program, in the STAR Schusterman Rabbinic Fellowship, and in the alumni program of the Bronfman Youth Fellowships in Israel. In addition to the present research, conducted under the auspices of the AVI CHAI Foundation (which sponsors a leadership fellowship of its own), I have conducted applied research commissioned by the Professional Leaders Project. Similarly, my cocontributors to this volume have played diverse roles in the JLCI field as fellows, faculty, observers, and advisors.

The present research is but one moment in a conversation in a thriving JLCI field. Indeed, such research is imaginable only in the context of the field and its conversation—a conversation that we have been shaped by and that we are continuing to help shape. How did the JLCI field, with its particular conversation, begin? How has it developed over the years? In this chapter, I trace the evolution of the JLCI field by drawing on oral history interviews with thirty-seven professionals working in or consulting for more than thirty Jewish leadership and change initiatives.[3] I focus attention primarily on the field's grounding in the world of private philanthropic foundations, which, I will argue, is the most significant factor shaping the development of the programs and the way that the intersection of youth, leadership, and change is now understood, discussed, practiced, developed, and studied within the Jewish not-for-profit sector.

Many readers may wonder whether the plethora of Jewish leadership and change initiatives have made a difference in Jewish life. On whether the programs have succeeded in creating effective leaders who later made an impact, I will have little to say. That is better left to individual program evaluations. My interest, in any case, is not with the individuals in whom these programs invest, but rather with the programs themselves as actors in an institutional field. In this regard, the question of outcomes is already clear: irrespective of any direct effects that the programs may have on the individual "leaders" or "innovators," and irrespective of any secondary effects we may find through the subsequent efforts of these individuals to influence Jewish life, the Jewish leadership and change enterprise itself has already been transformative. Within the space of three decades, it has institutionalized a robust new system of Jewish sector human resource development, both professional and volunteer. There is an irony in this, for although the JLCIs espouse a person-centered model of change, the creation of this field of Jewish endeavor was not the result of stronger individual leaders but rather of a new *institutional* mechanism, the independent foundation.

Roots of the JLCI Field

Today's vibrant network of independent Jewish leadership and change initiatives emerged as part of a redistribution of power in the American Jewish community that began in the 1980s. For most of the Cold War period, the American Jewish "polity"[4] was dominated by a centralized philanthropic system that concentrated power in the Jewish federations, on one hand, and a system of religious-cultural production that concentrated power within three large but competing denominational umbrella groups, on the other. Each of these systems had its own mechanisms of internal leadership development in place: for the federations, programs like the Young Leadership Cabinet to cultivate its lay leaders and the Federation Executive Recruitment and Education Program (FEREP) to cultivate its professional leaders. The denominations each had religious seminaries for preparing rabbis, cantors, and Jewish educators to serve in the movements' congregations and institutions.

For all its advantages and strengths, this federation- and denomination-centered model of governance had weaknesses and a host of internal contradictions that would ultimately serve as engines of change. At the height of its power in the mid-1970s, the federation system's centralized philanthropy was effective at proclaiming and enacting the central value of Jewish unity. Yet the consensus politics of its big tent made the large bureaucracy a less than nimble agent of change. Moreover, its vision of a single community united in common cause clashed with the resurgent particularisms of the large denominational movements, Reform, Orthodoxy, and Conservatism.[5] As efforts to ensure Jewish survival turned inward to focus on issues of culture and education, activists found the two main power centers incapable of forging an agenda for coordinated action.[6] The federation system's decades-long policy of Jewish communal "church-state" separation—in which the federation, in the role of the "state," deemed the potentially divisive matters of religion, culture, and education outside its purview—had created as its legacy an organizational culture marked by secularism, a certain Judaic illiteracy, and sometimes fraught relations with the synagogue movements. Meanwhile, the notion that American Jewish survival would depend on a deeper engagement with Jewish meaning raised the stakes for the denominations, whose theological disputes over the proper relationship to the Jewish past broadened (yet again) into sociological disputes over the best model for ensuring a vibrant Jewish future.

Of the three major transorganizational, interdenominational leadership and change initiatives launched in the 1970s, two can be seen as attempts to contend with the weaknesses of the communal system of their day, and the other has already been written of as a case study in these very weaknesses.[7] The Center for Learning and Leadership (CLAL, established 1974) pioneered conceptual frameworks and programmatic paradigms for leadership development, and forged networks of key influential figures who would go on to carry its model forward. Yet in spite of its successes, the organization was in many ways hamstrung in the 1970s and 1980s by the very systems it was attempting to change. CLAL's offshoot, the Radius Institute (1977–1986), anticipated trends in venture philanthropy and social entrepreneurship that would independently emerge from other sources a decade and a half later. It was beset, however, by problems of sustainability that it could not overcome. As for the Council of Jewish Federations' Institute for Jewish Life (IJL) (1972–1976), in retrospect, it appears to have been doomed from the outset, premised as it was on the notion that a centralized, consensus-based governance institution might serve as an effective mechanism for empowering innovators to present challenges to this very model of communal organization. A brief consideration of each of these cases will not only help situate the contemporary Jewish leadership and change initiatives as part of a historical continuum, but will also highlight the crucial importance of the broader philanthropic/ organizational context to the rise of the JLCI field. The contrast between what CLAL, Radius, and the IJL were unable to realize in the 1970s and early 1980s versus what their foundation-backed successors did achieve just a few years later bespeaks the dramatic shift of power away from the federations and denominations at the national level over the past quarter-century.

Stream 1: Developing Leaders—The Center for Learning and Leadership (CLAL)

Founded at City College of New York (CCNY) in 1973–1974 by Rabbi Irving (Yitz) Greenberg, future Nobel Peace Prize winner Elie Wiesel, and Rabbi

Steven Shaw, the Center for Learning and Leadership is among the oldest programs in the JLCI field today. Known by its acronym, CLAL, a Hebrew term suggesting a diverse Jewish people united across lines of division, the center helped pioneer the practice of engaging select groups of communal elites in cross-denominational Jewish learning and leadership retreats. This model, whose deeper origins might be traced to the United Jewish Appeal's (UJA's) Young Leadership Cabinet established in the early 1960s, was emulated by the designers of subsequent leadership programs—people who often knew CLAL's work firsthand, and who sought Greenberg's input when planning their new initiatives.

Unlike the majority of its successors, CLAL was not the creation of an independent foundation. Yet the very prominence of foundations in the JLCI field today can be better understood in light of the financial and organizational travails CLAL faced in its first decade. The challenges of realizing CLAL's vision within the institutional constraints of the American Jewish polity circa 1970–1980 highlight some of the very issues that have led to the field's constitution today as something that largely stands apart from the federation system and the denominational movements.

In its initial conception, CLAL was to be a retreat center that would undertake interdenominational leadership education, focusing in particular on equipping philanthropists and rabbis to grapple in Judaically informed ways with what Greenberg saw as the two major challenges of the era: an impending "catastrophic rise in assimilation" and "religious complacency" in the face of the theological challenge posed by the Shoah. To Greenberg, both of these challenges demanded solutions that were interdenominational and cross-institutional. CLAL would therefore "teach across all existing lines."[8]

Greenberg, a yeshiva-trained Orthodox rabbi, had himself been introduced to interdenominational rabbinic study in a Montreal-based group organized by Rabbi David Hartman in the mid-1960s. The group would influence the subsequent development of CLAL not only philosophically but also organizationally. Rabbi Eugene Borowitz (Reform), whom Greenberg first met in the study group, made the initial match in 1970–1971 between Greenberg and CCNY, which would become CLAL's first home.

The choice to house CLAL outside a denominational context was deliberate, but the choice had not been self-evident at first. Initially, Greenberg had tried to establish his center through the Modern Orthodox congregation where he held a pulpit:

> Only, I wasn't successful in convincing them to do it. . . . They were uncomfortable with the idea of Orthodox-Conservative-Reform, et cetera. And they would say, if I would have made it an Orthodox outreach, they were willing to

do it. But I felt that [educating about] the Shoah couldn't be Orthodox outreach. Everyone had to be on the same level, same equality. So I gave up on the shul as a vehicle, and decided to go back to the university. . . . I felt I'm not going to succeed in creating a center but at least I can go to a place where I can spend more time writing about the Shoah and how . . . Jewish history has to be transformed. And writing about the coming Americanization and why we're not ready for it.

A legacy gift to CCNY from a donor who specified that the money be used for Jewish purposes provided the seed money for Greenberg and Wiesel (also lecturing at CCNY at the time) to hire Conservative rabbi, Hillel director, and former student activist Steven Shaw, and to establish what would eventually become known as CLAL. As Greenberg explains:

We called it originally "National Jewish Conference Center," because both Steve and I were convinced that a conference center would be a major new institution in a way of getting people, influencing them powerfully. . . . Total environment, strong bonding, total experiences, programmatic, intellectual as well as emotional, so on.

The dream of a conference center was never realized. Instead, the organization rented venues in which it conducted leadership retreats for federation volunteers, rabbis, and academics. CLAL also ran classes throughout the year and organized Shabbat programming for the federation leaders gathered at the Council of Jewish Federations' (CJF) annual General Assembly (GA). Religious programming at the GA was an innovation in its day. Shaw, who had helped lead a student protest at the 1969 GA,[9] speaks of CLAL's work with the CJF as a "much more civilized . . . takeover, in a different way, of the GA." He continues:

These people needed to be Judaized. . . . Yitz, single-handedly, I think, more than any other person, Judaized the organized American Jewish community. He made it respectable to have a Shabbes at the GA. Unbelievably, before that, they'd never done a thing like that, and they were uncomfortable with overt expressions of Jewishness.

In spite of tensions with the CJF, CLAL's GA Shabbat programs were crucial for the young organization. Save for a small grant from the CJF's Institute for Jewish Life, CLAL received no funding from the national philanthropic clearinghouse. Nor did program fees cover much beyond a small portion of the organization's budget. Financially, CLAL was dependent on donations by participants who, in Greenberg's words, "would be turned on and . . . would become a supporter of CLAL." The GA offered CLAL exposure to people active in Jewish philanthropy who might then become donors or bring the organization to their communities to run retreats and classes. "We started . . . with the federation," Greenberg says, "because that's where the money is—meaning, we thought they could support their own education . . . and then hopefully once you do that, you can broaden it to rabbis and to groups that could not pay."

This model proved successful enough that CLAL also was able to run conferences that brought rabbis and thought-leaders together across denominational, institutional, and sectoral lines. By 1980, the organization was known for its efforts "to link the new generation of Jewish academics, rabbis and communal professionals with their lay counterparts."[10] Its focus on a young generation; on retreats; on bridging denominational, town-gown, federation-synagogue, and lay-professional divides; on high-level Jewish learning; on the power of ideas; and on influencing elite opinion would set patterns that to this day characterize the JLCI field. CLAL's focus on fostering conversations among emerging leaders would also bear fruit, as those touched by the center would later assume positions of influence in communal organizations. Reflecting on the model and on the network, Bethamie Horowitz, a consultant for the Mandel Foundation's leadership programs, recalls:

> I worked with Yitz Greenberg right when I came out of college, and you know, they—he and Steve Shaw . . . —had a notion of how to affect the American Jewish community by working with elites. They wanted to work with the scholars, they wanted to work with the interesting organizational people. . . . I helped work on this conference in 1979 that was a legendary conference in its time. It had David Ellenson, Arnie Eisen, Deborah Lipstadt[11]. . . . It was actually quite an extraordinary list, because it was an academic conference, but it led to names of a lot of people that . . . ultimately became leaders in a lot of the institutions we see now. But my point was that Yitz and Steve Shaw had this idea that you've got to reach the key elites to make anything happen in the Jewish world.[12]

Yet with no secure source of funding, CLAL weathered several financial crises in its first decade and, as alluded to before, never realized its founders' dream of creating a retreat center. Its relationship with the CJF, although not with local federation activists, was often fraught. Issues of church-state separation complicated CLAL's relationship with CCNY and ultimately led to the loss of this institutional home. Mergers with other organizations were contemplated as a means of providing greater financial stability, but these efforts did not yield a long-term source of funding. In spite of this, the organization has managed to survive, later reinventing itself under different leadership.

Greenberg's own assessment of CLAL's success in its first decades is mixed. CLAL realized its vision of a center for Holocaust education after Jimmy Carter, at the suggestion of his domestic affairs advisor, CLAL alumnus Stuart Eizenstat, established the President's Commission on the Holocaust, and appointed CLAL cofounder Elie Wiesel as chairperson, who in turn brought Greenberg on as director. With regard to the changes CLAL sought to effect, Greenberg says:

> It was a paradox. I felt [that], on the classes and the teaching, the ideology, it was a huge success. On the unity and cross-denominational lines, it was a huge failure. . . .
>
> The idea of learning and enrichment of Jewish leadership, that became a huge success. Leadership through learning, and leadership becoming more Jewish, as the key to the future. And therefore, that leadership, in turn, developing more investment in Jewish education and developing more investment in the internal agenda of the Jewish people. That part was hugely successful. We weren't the only player, but it was a time when the community and the laity were open to this idea and moving toward it. . . .
>
> Whereas the idea of cross-denominational lines and unity of Jewish people in light of this new era—that is where we got shellacked, because the real forces were the other way . . . the rabbis and institutional leaders of the religion were moving in the other direction, and then the laypeople were moving with them. . . . When CLAL started, because of my background, we had a very strong Orthodox rabbinic participation and Orthodox lay participation. . . . But, as the situation polarized, the percentage of Orthodox rabbis and the willingness to come went down. . . . As the situation polarized, we were less and less able to get the establishment, or the religious leadership, the institutional leadership, to come, even though laypeople came, and even though younger rabbis—not just younger, some highly qualified, qualified rabbis. But they were the minority and they didn't call the shots. The main activity went the other way.

Both Greenberg's and Shaw's work after they separately left CLAL tells as much about the subsequent evolution of the JLCI field as the story of their joint efforts tells about the field's origins. For Greenberg, the desire to create an institutional vehicle capable of effecting large-scale communal change led him down the path of working through an independent philanthropic foundation—the institutional framework that would soon become the driving force in the JLCI field:

> I took a sabbatical in '92–'93. After the 1990 [National Jewish] Population Study,[13] I was convinced that my life was a total failure. . . . I knew this was

coming. I mean, that's why we set up CLAL in the first place. But I felt that, in effect, I had been doing all kinds of small things retail, while wholesale assimilation was spreading rapidly and there was a catastrophic outcome. I felt I and every other Jewish leader should resign and admit we failed. I went to Israel for a year to cool off and think about what I wanted to do with my life. And when I came back from that sabbatical, I met Michael [Steinhardt][14] . . . and he brought up the idea, which turned into—we talked together and work[ed] together to create the Steinhardt Foundation/Jewish Life Network.

As for Shaw, who departed CLAL in the mid-1970s, his work establishing the Radius Institute anticipated the JLCI field's second major stream: the stream focused not on leadership from within existing institutions but rather on the seeding of innovation and change by empowering what are now called social and cultural entrepreneurs. An earlier effort in this area, the Institute for Jewish Life, had closed its doors a year before Shaw's Radius Institute got under way. Its failure sheds light on the direction that the Radius efforts would take.

Stream 2: Fostering Innovation—The Institute for Jewish Life and the Radius Institute

It was known as the Institute for Jewish Life, and if you have never heard of it you are not alone. Few today remember it. But when it was born . . . it was perceived by many as the panacea for all the ills of American Jewish life . . . an organization to "develop, guide and commission innovative projects . . . that would serve as new models of enrichment to the Jewish community."[15]

So begins Gary Rosenblatt's 1980 cover feature for the *Baltimore Jewish Times (BJT)*, "The Life and Death of a Dream," which details in fourteen pages the brief and troubled history of the Institute for Jewish Life. As Rosenblatt, then editor of the *BJT*, describes it, the Institute traces its origins to the 1969 CJF General Assembly—the same GA that had been stormed by the student activists demanding greater investment in Jewish education. Delegates to the GA ended up voting to establish a task force that would plan the creation of a National Foundation for Developing Jewish Identity. Reflecting the big-tent politics of the federation system, the task force was composed of an unwieldy forty-five members, including federation professionals and lay leaders, several of the student protestors, academics, and representatives from a variety of American Jewish organizations. The inclusion of the last was especially consequential in that it immediately embroiled the task force in battles over organizational turf. As the situation played out, leaders of organizations like the American Association for Jewish Education and the National Foundation for Jewish Culture argued that funds should be directed toward strengthening their own existing agencies rather than establishing competing bodies with an overlapping mission. Similarly, student activists and academics squared off against federation leaders over whether the new mechanism should be autonomous or governed by the federation. After two years of wrangling, the task force presented its recommendations to the CJF's board, which responded with a counterproposal far more limited in budget, time, and autonomy. Ultimately, the task force and the CJF agreed to establish an Institute for Jewish Life as a division of the CJF. The IJL would have funding of $1.3 million spread over three years, with the possibility of an additional $750,000 for a fourth year depending on the results of a program evaluation. It was to use these funds as seed money for "making possible innovative experiments and demonstrations, and developing new models."[16]

The IJL lasted four years, from May 1972 to June 1976, during which time it allocated $688,000 of its own funds and an additional $1.27 million in local matching funds across forty-four different programs dealing with Jewish education, family life, leadership development, Israel, the arts, and media. Three quarters of these initiatives were sponsored by local organizations such as federations, Jewish Community Centers (JCCs), and individual Jewish schools, and also by national agencies like the congregational unions of the major synagogue movements, professional associations for educators and communal workers, and the large fraternal and Zionist organizations. The remaining quarter comprised initiatives under IJL sponsorship, sometimes in partnership with the CJF. Among the ventures in leadership development receiving IJL funding were Greenberg, Wiesel, and Shaw's National Jewish Conference Center, which received $20,000, and an IJL-sponsored Fellowship in Jewish Educational Leadership, which received $150,000 over three years. Under the heading of "miscellaneous" projects, the IJL also gave small grants to ventures in do-it-yourself Judaism, including the highly popular *Jewish Catalog* ($4,500) and the long-forgotten *Shiloah: Discovering Jewish Identity through Oral/Folk History* ($10,000).[17]

Rosenblatt's recounting of the institute's history suggests that it was probably doomed from the outset. He tells of a seventy-three-person board rife with conflicts of interest, and of tensions between a Boston-based staff committed to maintaining the little autonomy it had and a much stronger New York–based CJF leadership committed to reasserting its control. These problems were symptomatic. Rosenblatt approvingly cites a 1974 evaluation that called attention to the contradiction at the core of the enterprise: "The very establishment of the Institute involved an implied criticism of the present functioning of various Jewish organizations—indeed, of the Jewish community as a whole."[18] Yet the very targets of reform were placed in charge of the change agent. Unwieldy and lacking an independent power base, the IJL had little chance of sustaining a focused, vigorous program of innovation and reform.

The closing of the Institute for Jewish Life in 1976 effectively signaled that the national federation system would not be taking an activist role in coordinating efforts to seed innovation. With no possibility of a centralized effort, and with the model of centralization itself seemingly called into question, the resultant vacuum was filled piecemeal by independent efforts. Private funders such as Henry and Edith Everett, Micha Taubman's Emet Foundation, and the Max and Anna Levinson Foundation took a lead in the late 1970s in supporting new, often progressive ventures such as *Lilith* and *Moment* magazines, the Coalition for Alternatives in Jewish Education, and Zalman Schachter's B'nai Or Community. Both the donors' modes of giving (directly, not through federations) and their choices of recipients were unconventional enough at the time to be deemed newsworthy: "Alternative Jewish philanthropy, an outgrowth of the 1960's counter-cultural movement," *BJT* editor Rosenblatt wrote in a 1979 profile of the Everett, Taubman, and Levinson funding, "is still too small-scale to be labeled a 'movement.'" Yet small in scale though it was, this "alternative" still challenged prevailing norms enough to generate controversy:

> To some, the philanthropists who support this sub-group of New Jews are considered fools, squandering their money on faddish experiments; to others in the Establishment, they are viewed with contempt for siphoning off funds from the mainstay charities like Federation or UJA; to still others, they are seen as heroes, Robin Hoods, the vanguard of a new age of Jewish creativity.[19]

Between the independent philanthropists and the new initiatives emerged a mediating institution whose work constituted one of the first moves toward a systemic (though not systematic) approach to cultivating sustainable American Jewish innovation. The Radius Institute, founded by Steven Shaw in 1977 after he had left CLAL, began as a convener of public conversations among intellectuals.[20] It made forays into a variety of areas, however, and soon was consulting for independent philanthropies, providing technical assistance to new Jewish projects, and informally matching donors and grantees. The work was ad hoc in many ways, and strongly centered on "Shaw's interests and enthusiasms at a particular time,"[21] a tendency that generated criticism among Radius' supporters and detractors alike.[22] Yet in its efforts, one can discern a consistent attempt to link innovation in Jewish programming with innovation in Jewish philanthropy.

On the programming side, Radius functioned as a capacity-building organization, making small grants, providing technical assistance, and running skill-building workshops on fundraising, grant writing, public relations, and the like for that generation's start-ups. Although the work was neither systematic nor sustained, it managed to provide some level of support to new ventures like the Abraham Joshua Heschel School, the Ansche Chesed Project, the Coalition for Alternatives in Jewish Education, Interns for Peace, the Jewish Student Press Service, the National Havurah Movement, *Lilith* magazine, the New Israel Fund, New Jewish Agenda, and the Jewish Women's Resource Center.[23]

In retrospect, a striking component of the workshops was their attempt to bring the skill sets and vocabularies of the management world into the Jewish communal sector. A trend was thus heralded that would transform Jewish communal work and professional training over the next decades. In the early 1980s, however, the idea was still novel. At a time when the appropriate graduate degree for Jewish communal service work was still almost universally considered to be rabbinic ordination or a Master of Social Work, Shaw's decision to supplement his own rabbinic *smicha* (ordination) with graduate studies at the Columbia University Business School's Institute for Not-for-Profit Management was itself an innovation. Describing the rationale for the organizational development workshops in a 1983 interview, Shaw said:

> Money is a highly charged issue in the new Jewish culture. . . . These people had rejected the UJA ethos, but had nothing to put in its place in terms of how to finance themselves. . . . What the technical workshops were about . . . were [Radius Institute executive director] David Szonyi and Steve Shaw training themselves and then disseminating what they'd learned.[24]

In addition to providing technical assistance to new projects and organizations, Radius sought to support emerging leaders associated with the new Jewish culture and facilitate their networking. Writing about Shaw's work in a 1982 *Baltimore Jewish Times* cover article, Gary Rosenblatt put it this way: "If you don't know [Shaw]—or worse, if he doesn't know *you*—you're obviously not among the elite. If you *do* know him and you're involved in an innovative Jewish project, chances are you may be asked to join the Radius Fellowship."[25] The fellowship convened approximately two dozen Jewish activists, communal professionals, and academics ("many of whom were featured in *Moment* magazine's article 'Some Jews to Watch in the Eighties'"[26]) monthly for informal conversations about matters of professional and personal interest. It included executives from organizations like the New Israel Fund, National Havurah Coordinating Committee, Jewish Museum, 92nd

Street Y, National Foundation for Jewish Culture, and Jewish federations of New York, Philadelphia, and Washington. Among its fellows were names already well known in Jewish communal circles and even better known since: Stephen P. Cohen, Rachel Cowan, Arthur Green, Malcolm Hoenlein, Paula Hyman, Sam Norich, and John Ruskay, among others.[27]

On the philanthropic side, Radius sought to cultivate private giving outside the federation system. It did so at a time when the number of private foundations in the United States was about to mushroom,[28] but when few people had any inkling that this "alternative" avenue for giving would within two decades supplant the federation system as the key agenda-setting force in the American Jewish polity.[29] Working at the cusp of a sea change in the organization of American Jewish philanthropy, Radius was among the first institutions to treat Jewish foundations as a distinctive field of organizational endeavor and to develop programming with them in mind.[30] Radius's work with foundations and individual donors involved "small group and private consultations . . . on 'strategic philanthropy,' including evaluating project proposals, leveraging gifts, becoming involved with funding coalitions and assessing project effectiveness."[31] At wider intervals, it also gathered donors, foundation executives, and communal professionals for daylong consultations on matters philanthropic. Its October 1984 fifty-person consultation on "Giving Wisely: Creative and Effective Philanthropy" brought together the heads of the Revson Foundation, New York Foundation, and YIVO Institute for a morning panel discussion on philosophies of giving, an afternoon panel on "New Directions for Involvement and Funding" in Israel, and a closing simulation, "A Million Dollars to Give Away."[32]

Foreshadowing later ventures such as the Andrea and Charles Bronfman Philanthropies' Grand Street initiative, Radius also engaged philanthropic families in cross-generational conversations about inherited wealth, the transmission of philanthropic values, and generational differences in philanthropic priorities. In addition to working directly with families, Radius used its various conferences to open the conversation about philanthropic goals and strategies. For example, the October 1984 consultation included a panel on the issue, and a June 1982 "Consultation on Jews and Inherited Wealth" was devoted entirely to the topic.[33]

Through its work with foundations, on one hand, and new program initiatives, on the other, Radius became a broker connecting funders to grantees and vice versa. Both contemporaneous and retrospective journalistic accounts of Radius' work highlight Shaw's informal and idiosyncratic matchmaking efforts as the signature feature of the organization's work.[34]

Whereas the Institute for Jewish Life can be read as a late chapter in the history of a federation-dominated polity, the Radius Institute fits as an early chapter in the history of the multipolar, foundation-dominated system of communal philanthropy that became prominent by the mid-1990s. Radius anticipated dynamics that would soon blossom independently in American Jewish life, and that were local aspects of the broad global transformations set in motion during the Reagan-Thatcher-Gorbachev era: the shift from centralization to decentralization, from collective planning to private entre-preneurship, from regulated to deregulated economies, and from structured organizations to flexible networks.[35]

Although the innovative ideas in Jewish religious life, culture, and educa-tion largely emerged from the experience of participants in 1970s counter-culture, these individuals' ability to successfully institutionalize these inno-vations owed at least something (although how much remains an open question) to the rise in the 1980s of a more business-minded ethos among both donors and grantees. I am tempted to refer here to the much bally-hooed "yippie to yuppie" phenomenon that was a core trope of *People* magazine–style cultural analysis in the Reagan era, but it does not really capture the dynamic at work in the Jewish nonprofit sector. By the late 1990s, a postboomer generation of Jewish activists would rush to embrace dot-com-era private sector models and language as templates for Jewish in-novation. This enthusiastic relationship to the business world has been iden-tified as a key element differentiating this generation's work from seemingly similar innovations led by the Jewish counterculture a quarter century ear-lier. I recall hearing an observer of the independent minyan scene say that whereas the havurah of the 1970s looked to the commune, the independent minyan of the 2000s looked to the start-up. What the consideration of Ra-dius' work suggests, however, is that the generation gap is not as sharply defined as one may think. We can see in the 1980s a period of transition in which the innovators of the boomer generation continued to adapt and revise their organizational and conceptual models. By the mid-1980s, the havurah may not have been looking to the start-up, but it was no longer looking to the commune. When a new generation of innovators entered the scene in the late 1990s, they would find support from older figures who had themselves already begun drawing on private sector models to inform their own work.

The Rise of the Foundation Model

The absence of a robust Jewish leadership and change field in the 1970s does not indicate lack of effort in these areas. Rather, as the examples of CLAL, Radius, and the IJL highlight, the Jewish philanthropic system of that era was structured in a way that proved generally inhospitable to those attempts that were made. To draw on Avedon and Landres' ecological metaphor,[36] it was an "innovation ecosystem" that did not allow new growth to easily take root. The dearth of financing outside the federation system undermined independent initiatives like CLAL and Radius, while political constraints inside it thwarted reform efforts like those of IJL. The second round of leadership and change initiatives, begun mostly in the 1980s, would avoid these problems by situating themselves within a more financially secure and politically independent institutional base.

If this analysis has one unifying theme, it is that today's JLCI field is thoroughly a creature of independent philanthropy. The field's rise is part and parcel of the shift from a philanthropic system structured around one central community campaign to a system in which a large number of private foundations operate as multiple, independent centers of power. Recognizing the JLCI programs' grounding in the foundation world will explain much about why the field looks the way it does, and why the terms of the conversation about leadership and innovation have been set in the particular ways they have been.

The marriage of leadership development to private philanthropy began in the 1980s, with the establishment of initiatives like the Jerusalem Fellows Program (1982, later renamed the Mandel Jerusalem Fellows program),[37] the Bronfman Youth Fellowship in Israel (BYFI, 1987), the Dorot Fellowship (1990–91), the Wexner Heritage Program (1985), and the Wexner Foundation's Graduate Fellowship (1988) and Israel Fellowship (1989). The six programs targeted different populations, had different goals, and to an extent, applied different models of leadership cultivation. First, consider the four Israel-connected programs:

> The *Bronfman Youth Fellowship in Israel* selected approximately two dozen high-achieving high school students for an intensive experience in pluralism that combined travel and education in Israel, led by a "faculty of rabbis and educators . . . associated with various movements and perspectives within Judaism."[38]

> The *Dorot Fellowship*, as originally conceived, selected an elite group of postcollege young adults for individually tailored yearlong learning and volunteer programs in Israel, with the expectation that the experience and knowledge gained would qualitatively enhance their future volunteer leadership efforts. Steve Jacobson, the program's current director, describes it in these terms: "It was common to hear people speak of the Dorot Fellowship—perhaps aspirationally, but nonetheless—as the Jewish Fulbright. And it really was largely an academic experience for academic super-achievers. It's no longer that."

The *Jerusalem Fellows Program* sought to enhance Jewish education by recruiting early-career educators from around the world for a one- to three-year training program in Jerusalem, after which time they were expected to take on leadership positions in Jewish educational institutions in the diaspora.

The *Wexner Israel Fellowship* sought to improve the effectiveness of Israel's public and not-for-profit sectors by annually enrolling a cohort of carefully selected midcareer governmental, military, and nonprofit professionals in the Master of Public Administration program at Harvard University's Kennedy School of Government.

As to the programs in North America for North American Jews:

The *Wexner Heritage Program* worked on a city-by-city basis to forge select groups of lay leaders into learning communities engaged in adult Jewish education, via weekly classes and retreatlike institutes. Developed by the architect of the UJA's Young Leadership Cabinet, Rabbi Herbert Friedman, and drawing on models introduced in the 1960s by the Cabinet program and refined in the 1970s by CLAL, the Heritage Program centered its efforts on Jewish learning as a basis from which vision-driven Jewish leadership could be built.

The *Wexner Graduate Fellowship Program* supported the graduate training of students preparing at a variety of institutions of higher learning for careers as rabbis, cantors, Jewish educators, communal service professionals, and later, Jewish studies professors. Each year it selected a cohort of up to twenty such individuals for a four-year program that included generous financial support (covering tuition, living expenses, health insurance, and dependent care) and two annual institutes—one focused on leadership skills training and the other on a thematic issue of Jewish importance.

In spite of their different target populations and programmatic strategies, the programs (all of which are still operating today) shared in common a model of cohort-based leadership training for a carefully selected group of elites who demonstrated what the selection committees deemed to be either a *record* of leadership or a *potential* for future leadership. The speedy convergence on a common model resulted, in part, from interorganizational learning, as program professionals exchanged ideas, discussed best practices, and looked to one another for benchmarks. (Prior to instituting new programs, foundation professionals commonly sought guidance from colleagues running similar programs, sometimes individually and sometimes by convening them together.)

The convergence on a selective cohort-based model for leadership training was also rooted in the programs' funding structure. Contrast the foundation-based programs with CLAL, for instance. CLAL had demonstrated great flexibility in its approach to the question of selectivity. Some of its conferences were by invitation, but its Shabbat programming at the GA was far more open. Because it had to generate its own funding, CLAL sought to continually expand its client and donor base. Economic logic led it to cast a wide net. Selectivity emerged as a norm when JLCIs became the projects of private foundations. With financing secured, the foundation-based programs could literally *afford* to be selective.

A closer examination of the different institutional histories of the 1980s-era leadership programs further illuminates the structuring of the field. At the initiative of educator Seymour Fox, the Jerusalem Fellows Program began in 1982 under the sponsorship of the Jewish Agency for Israel (JAFI), with funding from Bank Leumi. Fox was the respected founder of the Hebrew University's Melton Centre for Jewish Education, in which context he also created its Senior Educator Program, whose mission of fostering educational leadership for the diaspora was similar to that of the Jerusalem Fellows. His decision to work through JAFI to create the Jerusalem Fellows had the important consequence of investing JAFI's American Jewish federation lay leaders with funding and oversight responsibilities for the program. JAFI, a state-supported nongovernmental organization (NGO), was the primary recipient of the UJA–Federation system's allocations to Israel, and had a governance structure that reflected this function. In the mid-1980s, a Cleveland-based federation leader, the philanthropist Morton L. Mandel, chaired the JAFI education committee that funded the Jerusalem Fellows. He and Fox established a partnership that would last until Fox's death in 2006, and that would involve them together in the creation of the Commission for Jewish Education in North America, which evolved into the Council for Initiatives in Jewish Education before being absorbed into the Mandel Foundation. In the 1990s, responsibility for the Jerusalem Fellows Program was transferred from JAFI to the Mandel Foundation, which subsequently operated the program through its Mandel Leadership Institute.[39]

Jerusalem Fellows is exceptional in that it began not as the creation of an independent foundation but rather as a project of the older system of federated philanthropy. Yet, within a decade, responsibility for it had been transferred from JAFI to the family foundation of the federation donor who, by virtue of his board role at JAFI, had been most closely associated with the program. Contrast this with the case of the Wexner Graduate Fellowship (WGF), Israel Fellowship (WIF), and Heritage Program (WHP), which are solely creations of the Wexner Foundation and Wexner Heritage Foundation (now merged). Leslie Wexner had held senior board positions in the CJF and other Jewish communal organizations, and had initially thought to develop a leadership program through the federation system. Although he decided instead to pursue the efforts through two new independent foundations, he brought the ethos and experience of the federation system to the enterprise by engaging as his lead professionals two rabbis who had risen through the ranks of communal organizations. Working on two tracks, the former CEO of the UJA and creator of its Young Leadership Program, Rabbi Herbert Friedman, developed a program for American Jewish volunteer leaders (WHP), while the former director of development for B'nai B'rith International and a onetime Jewish Community Relations Council staffer, Rabbi Maurice Corson, began developing programs for professional leadership in the United States and Israel (WGF and WIF). The two rabbis populated their staffs with other professionals who had also held senior positions in communal organizations.

The wave of JLCI creation in the 1980s marks a turning point in American Jewish organizational life. It is one of the first indications that an independent base of philanthropic agenda-setting was arising to challenge the heretofore hegemonic federation system. In their efforts to foster lay and professional leadership for communal institutions, key philanthropic players on the American Jewish scene concluded independently that their efforts would be best advanced through the vehicle of private foundations.

Three important caveats are in order. First, federations were not irrelevant to the efforts of the new JLCIs. In the case of Wexner Heritage, for example, the foundation began partnering with community federations to select and fund its cohorts.

Second, even though the JLCIs of the Dorot, Mandel, Wexner, and Samuel Bronfman foundations can be seen, structurally, as representing a general break with the federation system, they can also be seen, thematically, as rooted in its ethos and worldview. With their language of "leadership" rather than change, their emphasis on peoplehood and often Israel, their goals of cultivating individuals to fill lay and professional positions in existing communal organizations, and their commitment to conducting their work across denominational boundaries, the foundation-run JLCIs of the 1980s carried federation ideals forward into a national Jewish philanthropic landscape in which the federation was no longer the hegemon. Their model would be further elaborated in initiatives of the mid-2000s, such as the Synagogue Transformation and Renewal's Professional Education for Excellence in Rabbis program (STAR PEER) and STAR Schusterman Rabbinic Fellowship, as well as by the Professional Leaders Project, which was funded by a consortium of foundations.

Third, federations have continued to envision a role for themselves in the JLCI field, particularly (but not exclusively) at the local level, where they retain a strong ability to orchestrate network-wide programming to support organizational development. Two cases in point—representing different ends of a spectrum, in terms of impetus and implementation—are the UJA–Federation of New York's Muehlstein Institute and the Berrie Fellows Leadership Program of the UJA–Federation of Northern New Jersey. Muehlstein can be seen as a newer iteration of the federation system's long tradition of investing in the recruitment, retention, and professional development of its workforce. (Among the flagship programs at the national level are, for recruitment, the Federation Executive Recruitment and Education Program, established by the CJF in the 1970s and still running today; and for retention and executive development, the Mandel Executive Development Program, established with foundation support in the 1990s and recently renewed after more than a decade's hiatus.) Born of the Jewish communal sector's perennial fear of facing a personnel crisis,[40] the Muehlstein program was initially conceived as a workforce retention initiative that would provide continuing professional education (CPE) to UJA–Federation of New York employees. As the idea was developed, however, the target population was expanded to include professionals of grantee organizations and then, in a significant move, to professionals of any New York–based Jewish not-for-profit organization.

The Berrie fellowship, by contrast, stemmed not from the workforce retention tradition of federation-based CPE, but from the volunteer-focused, community-embracing, leadership-as-vision tradition of CLAL and the Wexner Heritage Foundation. Initiated by the Berrie Foundation and led by the Jewish Federation of Northern New Jersey, this local leadership development program was designed by Wexner Heritage alumnus Stuart Himmelfarb and by former executive director of the Wexner Heritage Foundation Rae Janvey (now a leadership consultant). The two have used the Wexner Heritage template as a springboard to craft an approach to local leadership development that is simultaneously tailored to local needs and intended to suggest broadly applicable paradigms for leadership development theory and practice. The initiative represents a synthesis of the foundation, federation, and consulting worlds, demonstrating how the JLCI system itself generates flows of personnel and ideas and the mixing of national and local currents.

From "Leadership" to "Innovation"

During the dot-com boom of the 1990s, the image of hordes of twenty-five-year-old latte- and venture-capital-fueled entrepreneurs sitting blue-jeaned in exposed-brick workspaces, spinning e-gold, and revolutionizing the world had restored a glamour to youth unknown since the days of Woodstock.[41] There was a difference, though. Playing to deep strains in the American psyche, the unbridled optimism of the Giddy Nineties lashed its faith in young people to a corresponding (but decidedly un-Woodstocklike) faith in technology, capitalism, progress, and the future. In addition to celebrating the postboomer generations as agents of social progress, the dot-com boom's model of using venture capital to incubate risky entrepreneurial start-ups popularized new ways of thinking about progress itself.

The current wave of JLCI creation, which began in the year 2000, has embodied these broader trends—both the exuberant celebration of youth and the embrace of models, metaphors, and language drawn from the high-tech and business sectors. With their emphasis on using "venture philanthropy" to create "incubators" where "social entrepreneurs" can bring their "start-ups" to "sustainability," the initiatives of the new millennium are rooted in a vocabulary that hardly existed when the JLCI field began coalescing in the mid-1980s.[42] Embedded in this new language are novel understandings of the JLCI enterprise as a whole. Particularly telling is the way in which even the word "leadership" is often eschewed. Mission statements for incubator programs like Bikkurim and PresenTense choose their words deliberately when they speak not of "leaders" but of "visionaries," "promoters of new ideas," "social entrepreneurs," "innovators," and "pioneers." When I asked PresenTense founders Ariel Beery and Aharon Horwitz about their work in the field of "leadership development," I was immediately rebuked: "Yeah, we don't do leadership development," Beery told me. "What we've always said is, 'Not leaders, but doers.'"

The new language of innovation and entrepreneurship draws attention to the fact that the phenomenon sometimes spoken of as "leadership" is intimately bound up with issues of change. Indeed, this is a central axiom of many of the theories of leadership that have informed JLCI curricula since the Wexner Foundation first engaged Harvard's Ronald Heifetz, creator of the Adaptive Leadership model, to teach the Graduate Fellowship's inaugural cohort in 1988. The foundation's president, Larry Moses, describes the Adaptive Leadership model in these terms:

> It's a leadership framework which thinks about leadership as fundamentally bringing about change . . . leadership is centrally about change. And there is a certain dynamic at work. On the one hand, change is inevitable and constant. On the other hand, individuals and organizations and communities invariably resist change. And therefore the goal or the role of the leader tends to be to manage and orchestrate change. . . . And in those very simple propositions, I

think we have something that is at the core of our understanding of what leadership is about: leadership is the dynamic through which . . . individuals, organizations, and communities remain dynamic, open, relevant, and capable of adapting to a constantly changing environment.

Recognition of the centrality of change to the field's work was expressed explicitly by many of those interviewed for this chapter. Yet despite a shared emphasis on supporting and cultivating effective agents of social change, the innovation-focused initiatives of the 2000s and, before them, the leadership-focused fellowships of the 1980s arose from different visions of where and how change occurs. Whereas the earlier wave of initiatives assumed at first that young leaders would effect change by steering existing Jewish organizations in new directions, the newer wave challenged this assumption and specifically sought to help innovators cultivate independent organizational bases from which to conduct their work. In essence, and without any explicit recognition of the fact, the post-2000 efforts to foster social entrepreneurship have sought to replicate in miniature among a younger generation of resource-poor culture-workers the same innovation that the older generation of resource-rich philanthropists had themselves already effected in the 1980s and 1990s. Just as the foundations' principals had shifted their major efforts out of the federation system by launching their own private philanthropic start-ups, so too they were helping their grantees establish the institutional independence that would enable them to make change from the outside.[43]

Foundation Imperatives

Venture philanthropy's efforts to create a world in its own image are exemplified in the original Joshua Venture, founded in 1998 as a partnership between the San Francisco–based Walter and Elise Haas Fund, the New York–based Nathan Cummings Foundation, and director Steven Spielberg's Los Angeles–based Righteous Persons Foundation; and in the work of the Andrea and Charles Bronfman Philanthropies' (ACBP's) symbiotic initiatives, Reboot (2002), Grand Street (2002), Slingshot (2005), and Slingshot Fund (2007).

One way of telling the story of Joshua Venture (revived and renamed in 2010 as the Joshua Venture Group) is to note that it emerged from conversations among four foundation professionals attending a conference of the Jewish Funders Network (JFN), an organization for Jewish grant makers giving away at least $25,000 annually. The JFN's annual members-only convening can be said to represent today what the CJF's open General Assembly had represented in 1969, when Steve Shaw led the students in protest: the primary gathering of American Jewish philanthropy's decision-making elite. In the JFN conference conversations that sparked the Joshua Venture initiative, Rabbi Rachel Cowan and her assistant Liz Greenstein (both of Cummings), Rachel Levin (of Righteous Persons), and Robyn Lieberman (of Haas) were discussing the empowerment of younger Jews, and the notion that, as Cowan puts it, "There should really be a fund for young people to fund the projects that they really believe in," and the idea that "this is the 'Joshua generation.' . . . The power in leadership had been passed on to them . . . how were they going to shape it?"

The project's development ended up being based in San Francisco, where the Haas Fund was headquartered and to which its grant-giving was restricted. "We looked at awards, we looked at big grants, block grants, incentive grants," Lieberman recalls. "We found the Echoing Green[44] fellowship model to be the best way to go. . . . They were an inspiration and one of the few successful fellowships for young nonprofit entrepreneurs we found." From 2000 through 2005, the resulting program, known as the Joshua Venture fellowship, provided funding, mentoring, and technical consulting for two years apiece to two cohorts of eight social entrepreneurs chosen on the basis of their project ideas and their personal potential to bring these ideas to fruition. Among the projects supported by the fellowship were Ronit Avni's Just Vision, which promotes grassroots Israeli-Palestinian peace efforts; Aaron Bisman's JDub record label; Idit Klein's Keshet, a Jewish gay, lesbian, bisexual, and transgender (GLBT) advocacy group; and Rochelle Shoretz's Sharsheret organization for Jewish women facing breast cancer.[45] As to whether the program was funding the fellow as an individual or the project as an organization, Lieberman says, "That was always the big dilemma we had. . . . This was a question we never really resolved." In 2005, facing a budget deficit and governance problems, the program suspended operation, restarting under new governance in 2010.

A different way of telling the story of the original Joshua Venture would explain the program as a product of institutional imperatives within the sponsoring foundations. A brief account of how the Haas fund came to Joshua Venture offers a window onto the ways in which grounding in the foundation world shapes the JLCI field's character.

The Haas fund is a family foundation whose board consists of descendants of the fund's founders, the late Walter and Elise Haas. There was an agreement that to honor the founders' giving patterns, the fund would allocate 30 percent of its philanthropy to Jewish causes. Among the board members in the 1990s, however, Jewish interests, passions, and commitments were not uniformly shared. A lack of consensus over the fund's Jewish priorities was reflected in a marked difference in the way the fund approached its giving to Jewish versus non-Jewish causes. As Lieberman, the fund's former program officer for Jewish giving, describes it:

> They continued to give that 30 percent, but mostly as a block grant to the federation and also to a couple of organizations that had approached them. . . . It was not strategic, as opposed to the $12 million that they were giving away in education and human services and the arts, which was highly sophisticated, very thoughtful, strategic philanthropy.

Lieberman was hired in 1996 to bring a more strategic approach to the fund's Jewish philanthropy. Returning to San Francisco from Washington, D.C., where she had been involved in foreign policy work in the United States Senate and in Jewish as well as non-Jewish NGOs, Lieberman, with her political skills and a life experience that straddled Jewish and non-Jewish professional worlds, seemed a good fit for a position that required helping the board negotiate the delicate questions of the fund's Jewish identity and mission.

The challenge that Lieberman immediately faced would be echoed by other foundation professionals I interviewed:

> We were running out of things to fund. We had a Bay Area–only restriction and we had $3 million to spend. We just couldn't find enough things to fund that fit into our progressive agenda. [A further challenge] was that since [many] on my board [were] interfaith married, if an organization didn't accept interfaith families, I couldn't recommend the fund put its money there. . . .
>
> I was running out of creative approaches, and I was thinking, "We are just going to have to create something . . . that we can fund. Or we're going to have to put more money into creating ideas."

A similar phenomenon in which donors' search for grantees prompted investment in social entrepreneurship can be seen in the Andrea and Charles Bronfman Philanthropies' creation of *Slingshot: A Resource Guide to Jewish Innovation*. Even more than demonstrating a similar model, however, the creation of the *Slingshot* guide highlights the extent to which the present-day JLCI field rests on a symbiotic relationship in which foundations and grantees each create opportunities for the other to push the field forward. Moreover, the story of the *Slingshot* guide, insofar as it is also a story about a network of ACBP initiatives, including Birthright Israel, Reboot, Grand Street, and the Slingshot Fund, points to another way in which the JLCI field is shaped by its grounding in independent foundations: in the coevolution of ACBP's network of initiatives, we can see how a foundation dynamically develops its programs by creating institutional knowledge, by transferring this knowledge across program domains, and by establishing feedback mechanisms that shape how the foundation branches out into new areas of work.

As ACBP senior vice president Roger Bennett recounts it, "The origin of all of the programs here [at ACBP] are somewhat similar. They're all rooted in Birthright Israel." ACBP had helped launch the Birthright program in 1999, spending more than $10 million of its own money as part of a venture philanthropy–driven effort to strengthen Jewish identity among young adults by providing them with free ten-day educational tours of Israel.[46] Following up on its investment, the foundation, in 2000, began exploring modes of engaging program alumni upon their return. Bennett describes the challenge they faced:

> Thousands of Birthright participants were coming back . . . and it was as if they [the American Jewish organizations involved in Birthright Israel] were getting them all excited via Birthright and then serving up that same old stuff they couldn't stand before they went. . . .
>
> It was thought that kids would go on Birthright and it would be like a lobotomy—that they'd come back and say good-bye to their non-Jewish friends, say goodbye to their non-Jewish girlfriends or boyfriends, and start to live in a very 1950s communal Jewish fashion. . . . And there was an attitude, a sense, that Birthright would just make kids rain from the sky and all they [the Jewish organizations] had to do is put out the barrels for young leadership programs and kids would just fall into them. And I think they learned pretty quickly that that was not the case.

Within ACBP, the challenge of engaging Birthright alumni was seen as one piece of a broader puzzle of how to strengthen Jewish identity among American Jewish young adults more generally. The foundation hired Bennett, a young British immigrant, "to look into these generational changes in identity and community and meaning." To do this, he "spent a year 'wombling' around America":

> It was a very odd year. I phoned people up out of the blue—they had all been nominated by people who I had met previously. I'd phone them up and I'd say, "Hi, I'd love to talk to you about your Jewishness." And if this is in England, people would put the phone down immediately, but because this is America and thankfully Americans love to talk about things . . . almost everybody said, "Sure. . . ."
>
> I'd sit down and interview them. . . . I always let them set the place. . . . Most often they chose very quiet, incredibly dull places where we'd almost

exclusively be the only people in the restaurant or bar. And I'd always say to them, "You're the president of MTV blah, blah, blah, and one of the founders of Google or the self-professed leaders of the anti-globalization movement, you know. What the hell are we meeting here for?!" And again and again and again . . . people would say, "I thought you'd be some seventy-five-year-old rabbi who was here to solicit me for a gift, and I didn't want anyone to see us together."

And once we got over that hurdle . . . they'd say, "You know, I am fascinated"—these conversations were so rutted, incredibly rutted, repetitive, over and over—they said, "I am fascinated by my identity. I love it and I hate it. It's incredibly complex. It throws up a lot of questions, but when I've tried to answer those questions," . . . they said it was as if their question was ignored and . . . the answer was always the same, "You must love Israel, Jerusalem is the undivided capital of the Jewish world, and for God's sake marry a Jew now!" . . .

They all finished by saying, "If the opposite was true [i.e., if their questions were not ignored], if it [the conversation about these questions] was a smart cast of characters in a cultural setting, I'd feel okay. I'd be there in a heartbeat. But until it is, then 'Sog it!'"

And while I was traveling around I spent time with Rachel Levin [of Steven Spielberg's Righteous Persons Foundation]. . . . She gave me [historian] Jonathan Sarna's little pamphlet, *The Great Awakening*, which says that Jewish history is one of challenge and response.[47] That identity is actually incredibly flexible. That's its strength. It changes generation to generation. And he says it changes as the young rather than the old, outsiders rather than insiders, come together in small groups, to question without assumption. He says when that occurs, just good stuff naturally happens. . . .

So [Rachel and I] called the bluff of forty of the people who I had interviewed and just put together an eclectic set of characters. . . . We invited them to a place, Utah, where none of them felt comfortable. . . . Everybody came. We used a methodology called Open Space. . . . It lets participants' own questions frame the agenda. We did it with the values of, "There is no right, no wrong." They had to really bring their questions.

Since the first Reboot "summit" in 2002, the program has recruited new cohorts each year and has brought them together in Open Space gatherings. Reboot does not define its mission in terms of "leadership." Instead, it seeks to serve as a catalyst for cultural innovation by fostering open-ended conversations about Jewishness among handpicked elite chosen from outside the circles of Jewish organizations. In Bennett's words,

I identified a young audience who were *craving* conversation. My role is to convene that conversation, provide an opportunity for that conversation to see what, if anything, happens, and then to foster it. . . . It's not alchemy. It's really quite simple.

Among the creations Reboot has helped inspire are books like A. J. Jacobs' *The Year of Living Biblically*, films like Tiffany Shlain's *The Tribe*, and projects like Ben Greenman's 10Q (an online tool that helps guide reflection during the High Holidays), and Dan Rollman's Sabbath Manifesto.[48]

It took several years and a number of intermediate institutional steps before Reboot's influence would extend to helping philanthropists identify and cultivate innovative grantee organizations. The foundation took the model that Reboot had developed—open-ended conversation designed to raise questions about Jewish and generational identities without providing prefabricated answers—and adapted it to engage a different population: young heirs to family wealth who would soon be seated on the boards of their family foundations. ACBP had been interested in grooming a new generation of philanthropists, and had hired to lead these efforts Sharna Goldseker, a Joshua Venture board member who herself hailed from a Baltimore family with a prominent foundation. At first Goldseker's work focused on the creation of a giving circle, the Natan Fund, as "a vehicle to engage the next generation in philanthropy." Soon, she and Bennett were developing a new initiative called Grand Street. As she tells it,

> While we were working on Natan, a fourth-generation member of the Nathan Cummings Foundation came to us and said, "I can't put money on the table at this point, but I know at twenty-five I'll be eligible for the board of the foundation, and I'm really interested in talking to my peers. We don't often have friends who are in a situation of family philanthropy; can you help me connect with people?"

In Bennett's version of the Grand Street origin narrative, Reboot figures more centrally:

> I described Reboot to them and one of them said to me, "I am not your Reboot kind of character. I am fascinated by these conversations of identity and community because they are playing their way out in my family in terms of how we do our philanthropy, and the only place I can actually talk about them—because I don't tell any of my friends that I'm a Cummings—and the only place I can actually talk about them is with my family, and frankly, that's part of the problem. I need a place to start to discuss this stuff. . . . " [This person]

wanted to talk about identity, philanthropic strategy, and family dynamics. It's a different conversation. [This person] said, "Can you get together twelve to fourteen of my peers and do a Reboot-style conversation and then we'll see what happens?"

Goldseker describes ACBP's response:

[Along with several of the eventual participants], we organized a weekend. Roger and I facilitated. We brought our tools that we had started to develop to be catalysts for conversation, and we invited twelve participants to bring all of their questions. And they did [in] full force, about what does their Jewish identity look like, especially if their parents and grandparents were very involved in the Jewish community and were expecting that the next generation would fund the Jewish community; what did that look like and how could they evolve their own identity, honoring their parents' and grandparents' tradition, but . . . responsive to where their generation was. . . .

We realized that the space was effective for them and asked them if they wanted to continue meeting, and that really became Grand Street. Each year since then, we've added a cohort of twelve individuals, same criteria, between the ages of eighteen and twenty-eight, Jewish identity, family philanthropy, and desire to explore questions. And at the end of each of those weekends, we asked them what would be your individual next step and collective next step, and how could we help you in realizing those.

As Grand Street's conversation evolved, the issue of what projects younger philanthropists could fund was put on the table, and ACBP responded by helping Grand Street to create *Slingshot: A Resource Guide to Jewish Innovation*, a "compilation of the 50 most inspiring and innovative organizations, projects, and programs in the North American Jewish community today." Per Bennett:

We got them back the next year and had a second class . . . and they said, "You know, we're ready to start funding now." Not all of them were at the funding table yet . . . but one of them said, "I am ready [slams fist on table] to start funding. What I don't know is what I should start funding? We have thousands of proposals, and I can't tell the wheat from the chaff. Can you do a *Zagat*-style guide that can narrow it down?" We argued around a framework and all that stuff. Boom! *Slingshot* is born.

And to cut a long story short, the next year we did the *Slingshot* guide, and I went out for a drink with an amazing guy [from the Grand Street network], Scott Belsky . . . he's now [the chair] of Reboot, [a trustee of the Rita and Stanley] Kaplan Foundation. He is an unbelievable gentleman. And he took me out for a drink and he's laughing with a *Slingshot* guide and he threw it on the table. And he goes [slyly], "I know what you're thinking, aren't you?"

And I was like [suspiciously], "Yeah, yeah, yeah, what are you talking about?"

And he goes, "You want us now to start a fund, don't you, based on the [list of programs in the] back of the [*Slingshot*] book?"

And I was like, "Honestly, I had never thought of that."

He goes, "Rubbish! That was your plan all along, right?"

I said, "I honestly—all of this—there's no desired outcomes."

And he said, "I would like to start a fund."

His idea was like an index fund, based on the back of the *Slingshot* book. And we executed it. To this day, I think he thinks it was always my long-term plan . . . [and] to this day I'm always like, "Dude! You are a genius. Claim the idea."

At each stage in ACBP's work, the initiatives launched by the foundation created a dynamic that propelled the creation of new ventures. The investment in Birthright Israel created pressures to engage the tens of thousands of program alumni, which led not to programs for the masses but to "summits" for an elite group of cultural leaders (most of whom had no connection with Birthright). The Reboot summits created a model that was adapted for young philanthropists, who, as a result of Grand Street, sought ACBP's involvement in identifying innovative Jewish programs to which they could steer philanthropic dollars. When this *Slingshot* guide found its way back into the hands of members of the Grand Street network, they proposed the creation of a philanthropic fund to support the initiatives in the book and worked with ACBP to bring the idea to fruition. The foundation had created a network of initiatives, in which knowledge and information flowed easily across programmatic lines, informing the work of each and generating new ideas through the interchange—a replication on the organizational level of the Sarna model that Bennett and Levin had used to design Reboot: in Bennett's words, "Get these people together, don't force an agenda, and good things will naturally occur."

The original Joshua Venture and the ACBP efforts exemplify key aspects of the shift from leadership-focused initiatives to innovation-focused ones. What especially marks them as ideal types is their near complete disconnect—in origin, evolution, and outcome—from mass-membership communal structures such as the federations, denominational movements, community centers, and communal defense and welfare agencies. In this regard, they can be seen as having completed the break that the first foundation-based JLCIs began making in the 1980s.

Integrative Models

Even as Haas, Cummings, Righteous Persons, and ACBP (along with others) were helping to cement the independent foundations' dominant position in the new American Jewish communal power structure, other leadership and change initiatives emerging in the first decade of the new millennium were demonstrating the continued feasibility of other models.

Since 2000, Bikkurim—an independent operating foundation that began as a partnership among the Kaminer Family Foundation, the United Jewish Communities (UJC; successor to the CJF and precursor to the Jewish Federations of North America, or JFNA), and the Jewish Education Service of North America (JESNA)—has functioned as an incubator for New York–based Jewish nonprofit start-ups. Bikkurim provides up to four years of support that includes free office space, capacity-building consulting, start-up capital, a community of fellow social entrepreneurs, and access to local and national networks. As with most of the other innovation-oriented JLCIs, the impetus for Bikkurim came from an independent foundation (Kaminer). In contrast to the others, however, the foundation did not pursue the venture on its own or with other foundations but rather sought a partnership with the federation system, through UJC and JESNA. Kaminer provides the bulk of the funding, UJC/JFNA provides the office space, and JESNA, in the initial years, provided the back office support.

For the federation system at the national level, Bikkurim represents a reentry into the field of change incubation, albeit in a much more circumscribed role than it played two decades prior, when the CJF exercised a primary governance role over the Institute for Jewish Life. On one hand, the foundation-federation partnership that gave birth to Bikkurim ratifies the new agenda-setting power of private foundations vis-à-vis the federations. On the other hand, it highlights that the federations are engaged in efforts to define a role for themselves within a decentralized Jewish philanthropic polity.[49]

How far this "public-private" partnership between communally representative federations and autonomous foundations can go remains an open question. Bikkurim offers evidence of both the advantages and the challenges of such a partnership. JFNA, as a national network with broad communal involvement, offers a platform that gives Bikkurim's social entrepreneurs exposure and a degree of legitimacy (what Bikkurim's executive director, Nina Bruder, calls the "seal of approval" or, colloquially, the "*hechsher*"[50]). "It's just been a tremendous benefit to us to be able to bring a delegation to the GA every year," she says appreciatively. "We're on panels. . . . [we get] visibility by virtue of being here."

At the same time, Bikkurim is on the front lines of a clash of organizational cultures dividing the brand-new start-ups from the century-old federation system. The federations have long based their fundraising campaigns on appeals to serve Jews in material distress and to further the cause of Jewish unity. The JLCI field's start-ups, by contrast, tend not to emphasize these themes. As Bruder relates:

> [There was] a really talented marketing person [who] worked for UJC. . . . She did this beautiful photo shoot with [Bikkurim residents] Nigel Savage from Hazon [an organization sponsoring environmental bicycle rides], Rochelle Shoretz from Sharsheret [an organization for women facing breast cancer], and Aaron Bisman from JDub Records [a Jewish music label]. And she did these great posters of . . . "Your federation dollars at work." . . . "Hitch a ride" for Hazon, and "Launch a rock star" . . . for JDub Records. . . . It was edgy, and it was catchy, and it was great. . . . UJC does these marketing packages that federations can buy and the work's all done for them. I don't think anyone bought it.

Long-established patterns of funding place other constraints on the federation system's ability to act on its interest in supporting the work of the start-ups. A good example of institutionalized constraints is evident in the UJA–Federation of New York, which has been active in funding Bikkurim-backed projects, but only in particular ways. As Bruder explains:

> I give . . . credit to New York UJA–Federation. . . . Most Bikkurim groups get some grant money [from the organization]. . . . [But] the conversation I want us to have soon is, even in the federation, there's the Network, which is the year-in, year-out, annual core operating funding, which is all the human services agencies. It's like the old-world federation structure. And then, there's the whole Commission, which are grants. They run out. . . . You work for a few years to get one, you get it for a few years, and then it's gone. I want to know how [a Commission-funded start-up like] Hazon can get into the Network and get unofficially guaranteed funding every year. What would it take for a Hazon . . . to become like FEGS [the Network-funded Federation Employment and Guidance Service]?

Another integrative model is that of the Center for Leadership Initiatives (CLI), run out of Vancouver. Now independent, CLI began as a creation of the Charles and Lynn Schusterman Foundation. Like the original Joshua Venture and the ACBP programs, the center was created to serve needs generated by internal processes within the foundation itself. Executive Director Yonatan (Yoni) Gordis explains:

When Charlie [Schusterman] died in the end of December 2000, the unveiling
of his tombstone was a few months later. At his unveiling, two gentlemen . . .
each executive directors of organizations funded by the Schustermans, working two blocks from each other in Washington—they met in Tulsa at Charlie's
unveiling. They had never met before. Lynn said, "This is kind of crazy. It
doesn't make a wise sense with our investment. If we were investing in companies and the two CEOs were a block away from each other and in the same
field, we would make sure that they met." So they started to form a series of
gatherings. The first one was called Tzimtzum from the kabbalistic term of "creating space," "vacating space." It was a gathering of executive directors of their
major grantees. A forty-eight-hour gathering. That started a model which eventually evolved into the creation of CLI.

CLI absorbed many of the Schusterman Foundation's existing leadership
development programs, created new programs, and also worked on a fee-
for-service basis to provide leadership development programming to other
organizations. It has relied primarily on a strategy of "crafted gatherings"
and has sought explicitly to articulate and refine this model of leadership
development. Although the emphasis on generating conversations (one of its
programs, created in association with the New York *Jewish Week*, is in fact
called The Conversation) places it in a similar methodological camp with
the ACBP programs, the inclusion in its target populations of both executive
and early-career professionals in Jewish communal organizations roots it
more clearly in the tradition of earlier JLCIs such as the Wexner Graduate
Fellowship Program. So, too, does its unapologetic embrace of the term
"leadership." (A similar pattern was evident in the Schusterman-funded
Synagogue Transformation and Renewal fellowship programs for rabbis
and rabbinic students, and in the Professional Leaders Project, supported by
a consortium of foundations including Schusterman.)
   A third institutional model to emerge among the innovation-focused programs revives the original approach adopted by CLAL in the prefoundation
era: incorporation as stand-alone entities. UpStart Bay Area, which provides
support services akin to those offered by Bikkurim, was established in 2006
with a Haas Fund grant as a project of the San Francisco Board of Jewish
Education (BJE), and left the BJE two years later to incorporate as an independent, foundation grant–supported entity. The Jerusalem-based PresenTense
Group (established 2006) relies on a combination of grant money and fee-
for-service programming to provide training institutes that assist selected
social entrepreneurs in creating their own business plans. The Los Angeles–
based Jumpstart, founded in 2008, works with similar start-ups at a later
stage in their life cycle, serving as a fiscal sponsor that alleviates certain costs

of doing business. In return for Jumpstart's fiscal and technical support, organizations on its "platform" pay a fixed percentage of the grant moneys they receive.

Field Building

If developing leadership and cultivating innovation constitute the two ends of the loom holding tense the warp of the JLCI enterprise's fabric, then the woof woven through this is the desire to advance specific changes in particular issue areas. In their work with rabbis, for instance, CLAL and the Institute for Jewish Spirituality are not efforts to simply enhance rabbinic leadership in a generic sense. Rather, each puts forward an understanding of rabbinic leadership that is inseparable from its organizers' broader notions of where American Jewish religious life should be headed. For Yitz Greenberg at CLAL in the 1970s and 1980s, this meant confronting the enormity of the theological challenged posed by the Shoah.

> [Elie Wiesel and I] began to have these conversations. Of course, we both [felt that] the Shoah is a turning point, but the American Jewish community doesn't understand that. They're business as usual. The shuls are denominational as usual. It's just outrageous. Denominationalism in the face of [the] Shoah is just an embarrassment—a spiritual, moral embarrassment.

Engaging rabbis across denominational boundaries, therefore, was not merely a strategic or pedagogic or methodological choice for CLAL, it was the manifestation of a moral commitment and a prefigurative modeling of the direction in which CLAL wanted rabbis to lead.

The post-Shoah peoplehood theology (my term, not Greenberg's) that CLAL sought to embody and advance under Greenberg is less prominent in the organization's current work on rabbinic leadership. Today's orientation envisions Judaism as an ancient wisdom tradition with teachings of universal value, and seeks to bring this wisdom beyond the boundaries of American Jewish communal life. CLAL's current copresident, Rabbi Bradley Hirschfield, explains:

> Jewish leadership, for me, is about the exercise of Jewish values as you lead in any part of life . . . treating Jewishness as a tool kit to lead more effectively, more meaningfully, more compellingly, whether you do that on the floor of the New York Stock Exchange, at Catholic Charities of America, your local day school, the board of UJC, or anything else. . . .
>
> It would be interesting to see if the places that are being studied [in this research] and the Jewish leaders [who] are being talked to actually represent

where Jews are, or where those conducting the study would like them to be. To talk about a credible study of Jewish leadership and not be at YPO is insane.

SK: *What is YPO?*

Young Presidents Organization. Probably the most prestigious network for emerging corporate leadership under the age of fifty in America. . . .

We have Jews leading everywhere and we have young Jews leading everywhere. What we don't necessarily have is Jews accessing Jewish wisdom to inform the practice of leadership. And [if] we ask about that, [then] this work then moves from being an exercise in ethnic wagon-circling to really accessing thousands of years of a tradition to see if it has *any value to add* when Jews go out in the world to practice leadership in whatever area they may be.

Drawing an explicit distinction between *Jewish leadership* ("Jews, by genetic or ethnic or conversionary experience, exercising leadership in Jewish organizations") and *leading Jewishly* (Jews and non-Jews using the Jewish wisdom tradition "to maximize their own personal contribution . . . to the performance of the group that they are committed to or performing within"), Hirschfield's CLAL seeks to alter rabbis' understandings of their role in society:

America loves the clergy, it really does. And so rabbis, whether they always know it or not, have a special relationship . . . with the American public by virtue of being rabbis. And if they could worry less about how many people are sitting in the pews on any given Shabbes, and more about the special mandate they have as the holders of wisdom that many people with no interest in ever going to the synagogue would still like access to, and that Americans deeply respect if it's framed in a useful . . . way, then they have a role to play that's larger than synagogue recruitment or getting people to "do like the rabbi."

Rabbis have a role, I believe, as American spiritual leaders and teachers of Jewish wisdom . . . and I think helping them to know that and to build the skill set to do that . . . are all critical, and [are] all part of our Rabbis Without Borders initiative.[51]

One might read the universalizing thrust in the work of Hirschfield's and copresident Irwin Kula's CLAL as a response to the successes of the more inwardly focused peoplehood agenda advanced by the organization under Greenberg in the 1970s and 1980s. A similar effort to reorient American Jews and the American Jewish rabbinate away from the survivalist priorities of the late twentieth century can be seen in the work of the Institute for Jewish Spirituality (IJS), established by Rabbi Rachel Cowan after she left the Cummings Foundation. As she describes it:

> Our initial analysis of the situation was that the spiritual life of the American Jewish community was quite dead. . . . There was tremendous interest in continuity and a survival agenda, an identity agenda, an Israel agenda, a memorialization agenda. . . . But there wasn't really an attention to this very flat center of organized Jewish life, which was . . . a very antiquated religious dialogue.

IJS has sought to advance the ideal of a more spiritually sensitized, rooted, and enriched American Judaism. Its conception of rabbinic leadership, and how it should be cultivated, derives from its understanding of where it hopes to lead American Jewry. Envisioning rabbis as first and foremost *spiritual* leaders, IJS's Rabbinic Leadership Program "helps rabbis find structure, support and guidance for their own spiritual growth and, upon this foundation, helps them develop as spiritual guides and teachers for others."[52] The program is rooted in a two-stage model of social change (influence leaders so that they can similarly influence others) and in an understanding of the obstacles that have prevented this change from occurring naturally. In Cowan's words, "[The rabbis] were coming like dry sponges, people who had been squeezed dry by the pressures of the job, whose own relationship with God had suffered enormously, who were needing prayer while not being able to pray, who were not feeling authentic in their work. . . ."

What emerges in IJS's Rabbinic Leadership Program is a model of leadership development tailored to serve particular goals and to respond to a particular definition of the problem that leaders need to address (namely, the problem of a spiritually impoverished American Judaism). Hence, in sharp contrast to most of the other JLCIs under consideration here, the methods of leadership training in IJS's program for rabbis include silent meditation, text study of classic Hasidic thought, intense prayer experience, "and also yoga . . . [in order] to say, 'Judaism doesn't only live in the head.' . . . For most rabbis, their whole training had been completely head-oriented. And this is not saying the head doesn't matter, but the head isn't the only relevant organ in spiritual life."

In the debates over what constitutes a legitimate use of the words "leadership" and "leadership development," there is often a universalizing tendency— a push toward identifying a common definition of leadership that implies a generalizable methodology of leadership development that can be transferred across domains. Such an approach would probably not settle upon yoga and meditation as core methodologies of leadership training. But the logic of these methods for IJS, given its diagnosis of the problem and the specific changes it seeks to advance, should be plain. What we see, then, is evidence of a grounded, field-specific, and goal-specific approach to leadership development, which exists in parallel with the more generalizing, field-independent approach also present in the JLCI arena. Most programs navigate between these two poles, and it is this navigation that leads the JLCI enterprise to simultaneously display such commonality and diversity of practice.

In the examples just presented, I have located specific social change missions within individual JLCIs. Yet this paints too narrow a portrait and misses the broader significance in the interaction between the programs and the efforts to shape Jewish life. Here again, the JLCI field's grounding in independent foundations is key. Because foundations can combine an explicit mission-focus with a pool of funding that exists to be given away, they are able to pursue their missions not only through single grants, but through multiple ones as well. They are well positioned to engage in field building, by using their grant making to seed a network of programs working in different ways to realize common goals.

Especially notable for developing leadership programs as part of a strategic approach to field building is the Nathan Cummings Foundation. Under rabbis Rachel Cowan (1990–2003) and Jennie Rosenn (2004–present), the foundation's Jewish Life and Values Program has made a series of JLCI investments that have linked together concerns for social justice, diversity, and empowerment of a young generation. The three themes were united in Joshua Venture, for example, which Cummings cofounded. There, empowerment was emphasized, even as the projects selected for the initiative tended to have a progressive social agenda and an emphasis on expanding the boundaries of Jewish community (e.g., Klein's Keshet advocating for GLBTs, Yavildah McCoy's Ayecha advocating for Jews of color, and Meredith Polsky's Matan advocating for special needs children). In contrast, social justice was at the foreground of the Selah program, founded by Cummings in partnership with Jewish Funds for Justice (JFJ) and the Rockwood Leadership Institute. Since its creation in 2004, Selah has provided leadership training to eight cohorts of Jewish professionals—more than two hundred individuals—working in organizations such as the American Jewish World Service, AVODAH: The Jewish Service Corps, Gay Men's Health Crisis, the New York Civil Liberties Union, Service Employees International Union, and UNICEF. Consultant Shifra Bronznick, who worked with Cummings and JFJ on the development of Selah and who in 2008 was lead author of *Visioning Justice*, a Cummings-sponsored study of the Jewish social justice field,[53] credits Cowan with focusing the foundation on the link between leadership development and field building:

If you look at Rachel's work, a lot of it was about creating alternative path-ways before there were names for this, almost cradle to grave: Jewish spiritual-ity, Jewish healing, Jewish social justice. She really was the original funder and sometimes co-conceptualizer of some of these kinds of initiatives. And at some point, as she was exiting her role at the Cummings Foundation, I think she started thinking about, "What is it going to take to sustain this?"

They had made this attempt at something called Amos, of bringing organi-zational leaders together. . . . But she was really struggling with how we're going to build this field. And obviously leadership was a piece of the issue.

In *Visioning Justice*, the preface is provided by Cowan's successor, Jennie Rosenn, and Cummings' president Lance Lindblom, who articulate in proud terms the foundation's strategy of treating leadership development as a core element of field building:

> Since its inception, the Jewish Life and Values Program of the Nathan Cum-mings Foundation has sought to strengthen American Jewish life and create a more just world through advancing Jewish social justice.
>
> Our work has taken many forms—from seeding new initiatives to help-ing established organizations increase their impact; from identifying and sup-porting emerging leaders to developing communities of practice. As a catalyst in developing the field of Jewish social justice, the Nathan Cummings Founda-tion has sought to be both prescient and responsive.[54]

Other foundations have undertaken JLCI-driven field-building work in other arenas. ACBP's Grand Street, *Slingshot* guide, Slingshot Fund, and 21/64 (the last of which consults on multigenerational and next-generation philanthropy) can be seen as efforts in building a field of innovation in Jew-ish philanthropy. Even the JLCI field itself can be understood, at least in part, as a product of the Wexner Foundation's efforts dating back to the 1980s to place the issue of leadership on the Jewish communal agenda. The foundation is explicit in defining its work in these field-building terms. As its president, Larry Moses, notes, this includes its work via the three fellowship programs but extends beyond it as well:

> Les and Abigail [Wexner] spearheaded, and our foundation has been a pri-mary support for, the Center for Public Leadership at Harvard. And in a sense, just as the Wexner Foundation has been an attempt to persuade the larger Jew-ish community that leadership matters and that it deserves to be taken seri-ously and that it's a good investment, I think the Center for Public Leadership at Harvard . . . is Les' attempt to persuade the academy of the same thing: that leadership is a serious body of research and applied knowledge that is criti-cally important in human affairs.

JLCIs as a Field of Knowledge Creation

The Wexner Foundation's relationship with Harvard's Center for Public Leadership provides a ready conduit for integrating the knowledge produced at the center into the practice of the foundation's fellowship programs. Other foundations straddling Jewish and non-Jewish worlds also find themselves similarly positioned as information brokers. The Cummings Foundation and its grantee, Jewish Funds for Justice, built on their connections with Rockwood to bring the latter organization's expertise to the shaping of Selah. Yet information flows in two directions. JLCIs are themselves producers of knowledge that can be exported beyond the confines of the Jewish nonprofit sector. For example, drawing on expertise gained through 21/64 and Grand Street, ACBP consults and provides programming on next generation philanthropy for organizations like the Council of Foundations and the Association of Small Foundations.

Or Mars' assertion about the Wexner Graduate Fellowship Program, which he directs, can be seen as true of the JLCI field as a whole: "A lot of what we do is defining what leadership is." This process of definition entails appropriating and adapting ideas from "outside" sources. One can easily compile a "leadership library" of key texts that inform the efforts of JLCI program directors. These are often drawn from the business best-seller lists, and include titles like Jim Collins' *Good to Great*; Daniel Goleman, Richard Boyatzis, and Annie McKee's *Primal Leadership*; Ronald Heifetz's *Leadership without Easy Answers*; Marty Linsky and Ronald Heifetz's *Leadership on the Line*; Roger Schwarz's *The Skilled Facilitator*; and Douglas Stone, Bruce Patton, and Sheila Heen's *Difficult Conversations*. Other models are drawn from communities of practice. Approaches such as "critical friends," drawn from the education world, and "one-to-ones," drawn from community organizing, bear within them their communities' distinctive perspectives on what leadership is and how it can be exercised.

JLCIs are also sites of experimentation and creativity, in which program professionals evolve their own definitions of leadership and models of leadership development. CLI's Yoni Gordis and Beth Glick describe how, in the course of designing a program for the first cohort of their Kivun Intensive, they "stumbled upon" a metaphor and approach that would come to define CLI's thinking about leadership:

> BG: We think really hard about how to get people in a room and bring out what they can offer each other. . . .
> YG: One of the ways that we looked at it, through a program that Beth designed—the Kivun Intensive—was to imagine the human body. We looked at five body

parts, each of them representing an aspect of the individual: Head equals knowledge. Heart equals values. Hand equals skills. Belly equals intuition, potentially a little bit of laughter too. And feet equals experience. Our goal at our gathering is to affect people on all five of those levels. . . . Leadership involves acting from all five of those places, and if we miss out on one of them, it's not as effective.

SK: *How'd you arrive at the body metaphor?*

YG: It came from here [CLI]. We didn't import it. . . .

BG: I think it may have come out of conversations about, at the end of this five-month intensive program, how do we want these individuals walking out and being in the world differently from when they started? . . . We wanted them coming out of this program feeling much bigger and more powerful and more influential. . . . And so some of this "body" stuff came out of looking at all the different aspects of them as individuals and their potential for really embodying that leadership. . . .

So, we designed a personal assessment that touched on these different elements of the body. And the entire retreat really had the body as a theme. . . .

YG: I remember a moment where we came up with it. . . . I copied from the Internet a body outline and we drew on it. . . .

The more we've tried it out in that program, we realized that what we stumbled upon, in the thinking around the Kivun Intensive, actually [serves as] an organizational representation of who we [as CLI] are and how we think about leadership.

SK [with a smile]: *"Embodying leadership?"*

YG [with a smile]: "Leadership incarnate." [laughter]

CLI's story is representative. Most of the program professionals I spoke with described processes of organizational learning in which programmatic decisions initially made for pragmatic reasons or with only an inchoate understanding of their rationales were later refined into well-articulated philosophies guiding practice. The near-ubiquitous JLCI practice of cohort learning evolved in a similar manner in many organizations. For example, Larry Moses and Wexner Foundation Vice President Elka Abrahamson in separate interviews, each spoke of the evolution of the Wexner Foundation's thinking about cohorts:

LM: This notion of cohort learning for leaders, I don't think this is something we understood in theory before we started these programs. I think it's something that we understood in practice. And I think a lot of our best insights in terms of the developing of these programs were insights that came to us in doing, even though all three of the programs were thought out so carefully.

EA: We really came to see the cohort as so essential to leadership development. Key! If self-awareness is central to leadership development, which I'm pretty clear it is, then having a place where you could hold up a mirror to yourself with other voices is required. . . . We've overtly discussed the cohort as an intentional learning group. . . . How are you [the fellow] going to use [the cohort] and leverage it?

One area in which JLCIs have, perforce, been creators rather than importers and adaptors of knowledge involves Jewish leadership learning. The place of studying Jewish text, culture, and history in leadership curricula is a problematic issue. Some practitioners draw a distinction between leadership learning and Jewish learning. Others see the two as integrally linked. We thus are returned to our earlier question about whether leadership is understood in terms of generalizable capacities to be mobilized in a variety of domains or in terms that are highly context- and goal-dependent. The most forceful articulations of the centrality of Jewish learning to Jewish leadership development stake their claims on the argument that mission, vision, and values are imperative for the exercise of leadership. Rae Janvey, alumna and former director of the Wexner Heritage Program and subsequently a consultant to JLCIs like the Berrie Fellowship and The Conversation, puts it in these terms: "Leaders need inspiration, motivation, which comes from Jewish learning. So, Shaul, with all due respect to leadership knowledge, leadership education, nonprofit management, without the inspiration and the motivation, which comes from Jewish learning, we ain't going anywhere."

UpStart Bay Area's director, Toby Rubin, also a Wexner Heritage alumna, hired a Jewish educator to join her staff, out of a belief that Jewish literacy is crucial to Jewish innovation: "If, at the end of the day, the person didn't have access to their tradition, to play with it and mess with it, then what are they offering?"

When drawing on Jewish sources to inform practice, individual programs each have particular emphases. For example, PresenTense builds on models that its cofounders, Aharon Horwitz and Ariel Beery, drew from the Betar and Hashomer Hatzair Zionist youth movements in which they had been longtime student leaders. Beyond this, one can also see in the JLCIs, collectively, a developing community of practice that is creating its own distinctive vocabulary. The leadership principle of *tzimtzum*, for instance, adapted from kabbalistic tradition, is commonly invoked to assert that leadership at times involves holding back in order to create space for others to act.

In the leadership lexicon of Ronald Heifetz, the tradition in which I myself as a Wexner Graduate alumnus am steeped, the JLCI field is an *adaptive* project, not a *technical* one. It is not presenting Jewish organizations with fixed definitions of what leadership is, nor is it simply applying readymade templates of leadership development. Rather, the field is engaging in a dynamic attempt to evolve understandings of what leadership means, and to create practices that can foster it thoughtfully, responsively, and responsibly. Because the enterprise is an always unfinished, ever-evolving process of definition and redefinition, the conversation that unfolds is very much a part of the process itself.

Research such as the present study is part of the conversation as well. From the field's inception, it has played a constitutive role. Researchers—whether as academics from schools of leadership or management, as students of contemporary Jewish life, as program evaluators, as program officers, or even (especially) as longtime colleagues and friends of foundation professionals—have shaped the thinking that informs the work of programs in the JLCI field. They have done this not only through their scholarship but also by moving back and forth into different roles within the network of programs—serving as consultants, evaluators, members of program selection committees, program faculty, and sometimes even as program officers.

With regard to the contributions of written scholarship, I have already pointed to the example of Sarna's historical piece, *The Great Awakening*, which informed Bennett and Levin's thinking about the creation of Reboot.[55] Research, including program evaluation, has also introduced terminology into the field, such as "the bloomed and the groomed," which was popularized by a study of the Wexner Graduate Fellowship conducted in the mid-1990s by Sarna, Charles Liebman, and two authors of chapters in the present volume (Fishman and Cohen).[56] Research has also helped to define fields simply by naming them—such as Avedon and Landres' piece on the innovation ecosystem.

Professionals working with JLCIs understand the power of research to define and legitimize a field. Speaking of how isolated instances of grassroots activity burgeon into broader phenomena, Or Mars, of Wexner, points to an oft-cited start-up, the independent minyan (prayer community) Hadar:

> There [are] ideas from the street. . . . People say, "Oh, we better learn some ideas from Hadar." But then, all of a sudden, [the sociologist] Steve Cohen [of this volume] writes about Hadar and it becomes academic. . . . There's a role academics [play] in creating a certain sense of movement and legitimacy. I mean, when Steve starts getting very interested in independent minyanim and writes about it, then, all of a sudden, there's more sense of a movement about it.

Roger Bennett and Shifra Bronznick take this recognition a step further. In separate interviews, each spoke about research as a *strategy*:

> RB: The other strategy we've employed is to study the hell out of this field, in a way to legitimize it.
>
> SB: We're about to come out with this survey [on work-life policies in Jewish organizations]. Why do I have a survey? So people have something to start a conversation in their own institution about how to make change.

The innovation ecosystem study conducted by Joshua Avedon and Shawn Landres (the latter of whom served as a consultant on the research project that produced this volume) was frequently mentioned by my interviewees. Many had picked up the term "ecosystem" and were using it to speak of the JLCI field. Nina Bruder, of Bikkurim, argues that "the study that Shawn did . . . [is] solidifying, and anchoring, and naming the sector, and also putting numbers and data behind it. And it's showing. I think it'll gain legitimacy." Landres himself, like Bronznick, shows a penetrating awareness of the power of research to shape a field:

> Purely by doing the study . . . we actually created a conversation. We didn't just make a contribution to it, we actually set the terms. And if you go into the blogs and you look at the debate, suddenly people had something to react to. But we really did frame it, and even when people were annoyed with certain findings, or struggling with certain emphases . . . it was within the hermeneutical frame that we created.

Research on the JLCI field does not stand outside the field but actually helps constitute it. The chapters in this volume, including this chapter, should be understood in this light, and recognized as part of the phenomenon that they study—shaped by it, and if they are read, shaping it. This is not only because the research that led to this book was sponsored by a foundation involved in the JLCI field but because we, the authors, are ourselves enmeshed in the field. Whatever language we use here to speak about issues of youth, leadership, and change is not and cannot be neutral language. We are helping to create the phenomenon that we are studying through the choices that we as researchers are making. What is the field? What are its boundaries? What language should we use to speak of it? Are we speaking about "leaders" or "leadership?" "Leadership" or "innovation?" A "field" or an "ecosystem?" Should youth, or age, be a relevant category? If so, what counts as young? Is youth a matter of biological age or social age? Do we want to divide organizations and leaders into dichotomous types? If so, on which side of the divide should we place each specific case? What terms should we use to label the camps? Mainstream vs. emergent? Establishment vs. innovators? *Alte kackers* (old farts) vs. *Yinge pishers* (young pissers)?[57]

In the research project that resulted in this volume, the researchers have individually and collectively confronted all these questions. We have argued over how best to answer them, sometimes agreeing and sometimes not. If the answers offered here present themselves with an aura of facticity, then that is a problem of our genre. Neatly bound books can, by their nature, mislead, presenting a false sense of closure when in fact the questions remain wide open.

Returns on Investment

The rooting of JLCIs in independent foundations has had the effect of prompting quite a bit of investment in the people selected to participate in these programs. This has implications not only for the participants but for the programs themselves.

JLCIs have been able to provide their participants with a powerful set of material and nonmaterial resources to enhance their capacity for exercising leadership and for effecting change. Among the advantages conferred by the programs are the following:

Recognition, affirmation, and legitimation, which, in turn, can generate feelings of empowerment and also open doors that might otherwise have been closed.

Material support in the form of cash, stipends, tuition support, office space, access to alumni grant funds, etc.

Skills training in a variety of areas, such as fundraising and running meetings.

Capacity development for individuals, as distinct from skills training (e.g., developing awareness of self and surroundings on multiple levels).

Shared vocabulary for reflection on skills and capacities.

Emotional support through retreats, safe spaces, and friendship networks.

A *social support network,* including mentoring, coaching, and advising.

A *power network* that can be utilized for partnering, sharing information, opening doors, etc.

Shifra Bronznick traces the implications of this investment in people beyond the impact on individual participants. Consulting for the Cummings Foundation during its work developing Selah, Bronznick studied models used by other leadership development programs. She examined what happens after people graduate from the programs:

SB: I went around to a lot of different places to try to learn about what people were doing in terms of cohorts. And, of course, I had a real revelation when I really looked at the Wexner program. . . . What I realized is that because the Wexner program . . . had made such a big upfront investment in the people it trained, that it made sense for them to keep them together for ongoing leadership development. It's almost like they were protecting their originally frontloaded financial [investment]. . . . "If I spent $100,000 on people's educations, then it makes sense for me to invest in their continuing development."

SK: *Sunk costs.*

SB: Right. I don't think that they necessarily said it that way, but all of a sudden a light bulb went off in my head and I saw it that way.

A trend across the JLCI field in recent years has been a strategic rethinking of alumni engagement. A number of programs have dispensed with the term "alumni" altogether; participants are now understood simply as being in a different phase of the program. In some instances, programs have hired professionals specifically dedicated to an alumni relations portfolio. Some programs, such as the Dorot Fellowship and ROI, have established alumni networks and special funding pools that alumni can access for financial support of their projects.

Heightened attention to alumni relations certainly benefits program participants. Yet the cultivation of alumni networks also redounds to the advantage of the sponsoring foundations themselves. JLCI networks not only link program participants with one another, they also link the foundation into this network of individuals who are advancing toward ever greater positions of influence in a range of diverse organizations. Alumni become key resources for foundations, offering back to their patrons various skills that they have acquired, serving formally and informally as consultants on a range of issues, and serving as conduits of information. Foundations, through their alumni networks, can keep their fingers on the pulse of the organized Jewish community, and can also mobilize their networks to advance foundation goals.

Although the manifest purpose of the JLCI programs is to empower and enhance the leadership potential of individual participants, their latent function is to empower and enhance the leadership potential of the very foundations that sponsor the programs. The effect is to accelerate a shift in the national-level power structure of the organized American Jewish community, away from the federation/denomination-centered model of the twentieth century and toward a decentralized foundation-driven model for the twenty-first.

Transinstitutionality and Macroeconomic Shifts

A common denominator running through the JLCI field is the emphasis on building networks across traditional lines of demarcation. The STAR Schusterman Rabbinic Fellowship engages students across denominational divides. In addition to being transdenominational, the Wexner Graduate Fellowship is transsectoral, joining rabbinic and cantorial students with students of Jewish education, nonprofit management, and academic Jewish studies. PLP bridged the volunteer-professional divide. Bikkurim and Joshua Venture Group incubate programs that transcend existing institutional structures by operating outside of them. ROI's global network crosses boundaries of nationality and language.

The intellectual roots of this effort to open up the Jewish organizational world can be traced to the "We Are One" ethos of the federation system as well as to the critiques leveled by the havurah movement and other voices of 1970s Jewish counterculture. Yet this ideational lineage alone does not explain how and why the transinstitutional thrust has become near-universal in the JLCI field. Ideas must be able to take root. Many aspects of the counterculture did not outlast their particular moment, and in many ways the federation ethos has waned. In this instance, we will be better served by structural explanations that focus, narrowly, on the funding mechanisms and institutional base that sustain the JLCI field itself and, broadly, on macroeconomic trends.

From the field's inception, the vast majority of JLCIs have been creations of independent foundations that are not formally accountable to any single denomination, training institution, or set of communal organizations. The financial and structural independence of the foundations enables and even encourages them to think about Jewish communal interventions in transinstitutional terms.

For two decades, young Jewish leaders have been socialized in foundation-based programs whose models and ethos have been explicitly pluralistic and transinstitutional. When the foundations behind this system have asked researchers to assess the culture of young Jewish activists, researchers have typically found young leaders who are less likely to identify with denominational labels or with the institutions whose confines they are being encouraged to transcend. This should come as no surprise. The foundations have, in fact, been key agents instilling this culture of pluralism. Yet communal discourse often mystifies this culture of boundary-crossing by imagining that it emerges from some uncharted terrain of youth psychology, rather than from the socializing institutions in which it is steeped.

The JLCI field should not be seen as the sole structural grounding of this ethos of pluralism, however. The rise of both the field and the ethos are part and parcel of broader macro-economic shifts that have been reshaping organizations and work since the 1970s. These shifts, variously described as the death of the organization man, the rise of the creative class, the emergence of a risk society, and the rise of flexible accumulation, involve a transition to a post-industrial economy whose rapid transformations force organizations to be increasingly nimble in order to remain competitive.[58] The erosion of centralized giving and allocations via federations and the concomitant privatization of philanthropy via independent foundations are parts of this broader trend. So too is the shift in Jewish communal professional training programs from social work and communal service to non-profit management.

We see similar shifts toward greater flexibility at the individual level as well, within the workforce. In this regard, we can interpret the rise of JLCIs as a consciously adaptive response to the changing needs of an American labor market. Among the key shifts in American work in the latter part of the twentieth century has been the decline of long-term commitments between employers and employees. Because professionals can no longer expect to spend their lives working in one organization, they must develop transferable skills that can enable them to sculpt successful careers across a number of different workplaces.[59] In this environment, transinstitutional programs for continuing professional education become at least as important as university- or seminary-based degree-granting programs.

Whether viewed from the perspective of the organization or the worker, the economic moment can be seen as pressing organizations and individuals alike to remain flexible and avoid ossification within rigidly bounded structures. That such a situation would give rise to a culture of pluralism and boundary-crossing should not be unexpected. Yet such a culture does not simply "emerge." It is created. Among the forces creating this culture in the American Jewish organizational world are foundations and the transinstitutional leadership programs they have built.

From Common Endeavor to Diverse Encounters:
The New Peoplehood

The transinstitutional thrust has helped American Jews develop a new way of thinking about the question of how Jews, ideally, should relate to one another. The rise of this new model needs to be understood both as a reaction against and as an elaboration of the guiding model that informed Jewish collective action vis-à-vis other Jews in the post-1967 era of American Jewish politics. This older model, commonly referred to as "peoplehood," centered on intertwined notions of kinship, memory, unity, mutual responsibility, and survival.[60] On the domestic front, this integrative model emerged in efforts to memorialize the Holocaust. On the international front, it was constituted through advocacy for Israel and heavily ritualized political action to free oppressed Jews in the Soviet Union and elsewhere. But with the success and routinization of the memorializing efforts, the liberation of the oppressed Jewish communities, and the factionalization of American Jewish pro-Israel politics into right, left and center camps after the demise of one-party Mapai rule in Israel, mass mobilization around the peoplehood model of Jewish collective action waned.[61]

Even as the decline of the post-1967 peoplehood paradigm was being lamented,[62] new practices were emerging to ground a novel articulation of the preferred way for Jews to relate to one another. From sources as disparate as the Jewish feminist movement; the klezmer revival; the neodiasporist thrust in Jewish studies;[63] and the efforts of the federation system, Chabad, and foundations like Lauder to revitalize Jewish life in postcommunist Europe, a common emphasis emerged on the value of affirming and engaging with the vast diversity of the Jewish experience.

The emphasis on "Jewish diversity" represents an important departure from the primacy of "Jewish unity" in the politics of the 1960s and 1970s. In many ways, the change finds its roots in the broader shift from a more centralized to a more multipolar polity. Although I have characterized this shift primarily in terms of the rise of nonfederated philanthropy in the American Jewish community, it is actually much broader and includes the pluralization of Israeli democracy that attended Likud's 1977 ascent to power for the first time, the reassertion of Jewish denominationalism in the United States,[64] and the rise of an independent locus of Jewish intellectual production in secular universities, among other things.

The leadership development programs have played a part in this matrix.[65] The overwhelming majority of the fellowships are structured around cohort learning, with cohorts carefully selected to maximize their internal Jewish diversity. Central to the fellowship experience in these programs is a process of community building in which Jews of different religious and political stripes learn to work together, not by erasing their differences but rather by celebrating, wrestling with, and occasionally transcending these differences. The key behavioral practice—not public, vocal political action, but private, intimate interaction with others in the cohort—anchors and realizes a way of thinking about Jewish collectivity that comprehends a whole through the encounter with many diverse parts.

The shift from proclaiming unity to encountering diversity represents, from one perspective, a sea change in the way that American Jewish institutions are creating practices through which Jews imagine and engage one another. From another perspective, the new emphasis on diversity can be seen as a reconfiguration of the "We Are One" ethos that many donors and foundation professionals brought with them from the federation world. The continuities are evident in the words of Rabbi Hayim Herring, former director of the STAR rabbinic fellowships and onetime executive in the Minneapolis Jewish Federation. Speaking of the STAR programs, he says:

> We work a lot on collaboration. And we try to expand the notion of success to include everybody's success in the community. And that the community as a whole, when all the parts are working, is better for each individual part. . . . At the second retreat, where people trust one another, there's some very rich conversations about, "What do we each like about our [denominational] movement? What do we not like about it?" And lo and behold, [the rabbis] discover that what they don't like about their movements, they share quite a bit. . . . And at the same time, when they hear what they're each proud of, that is one of those powerful moments as well, where people begin to see that holistically, everybody has a contribution to make. [Those are] big, powerful . . . mind-set changes that will pay off in the future.

And yet the discontinuities with the peoplehood politics of the 1970s are crucial. The leadership fellowships have not simply devised new means to achieve old goals. By helping shift practice from large demonstrations to intimate conversations, the fellowship programs have helped enshrine new paradigms prescribing how Jews should ideally relate to one another. Am Yisrael's common endeavors have given way to Klal Yisrael's diverse encounters.

Owning the Future

On one hand, the decentralization of Jewish philanthropy via the rise of family foundations as independent power bases alongside the federation system has been a generative force that has institutionalized an apparently sustainable field of community-wide leadership development. Moreover, the foundations' lack of formal accountability to other Jewish institutions has enabled and even encouraged them to structure their leadership development and change initiatives in ways that foster boundary crossing, discourage denominationalism and sectoralism, and advance innovations that threaten entrenched patterns of institutional action. On the other hand, the foundations' lack of formal accountability introduces new forms of systemic risk to which the centralized system of federated philanthropy had not been subject. Speaking to this issue, UJA–Federation of New York executive director John Ruskay asks whether a foundation-driven philanthropic system will itself be sustainable over the long term, especially insofar as the decisions over funding and over the initiation and cessation of operations rest with donors and boards alone: "The major foundations that were with us around 1999 are still here for the most part. There aren't a whole lot more," he says. "I regret that many of them are in spend-down mode, and they will be gone in five to ten years."[66]

It seems reasonable to hypothesize that the present system, in which autonomous foundations and communally governed federations operate sometimes in partnership and sometimes in tension, mitigates problems associated with both excessive centralization and excessive decentralization. But lacking systematic research on the problematics of federation-foundation relations, we simply do not know whether this is so.

Whatever such research might reveal, it is already clear that the move from the pre-1980s federation-centered polity to today's foundation-driven multipolar model has changed the position of the federations vis-à-vis leadership and change efforts.[67] With little expectation that such efforts should be centrally coordinated at the national level (à la the Institute for Jewish Life), and with foundations having clearly taken the lead in the field, the stakes have been changed for the federation system. JFNA maintains its support of Bikkurim and its own executive recruitment program (FEREP), and some large city federations, such as New York's and Toronto's, are making substantial investments in Jewish social entrepreneurial start-ups. Yet few would argue that the future of Jewish communal innovation and leadership development rests primarily on the role that federations will or will not play. So long as the JLCI field finds its primary institutional grounding in private foundations, its future will be tied primarily to the dynamics within the foundation world.

Against this backdrop, federation interventions in the foundation-driven JLCI field may be best understood not in terms of what they accomplish for the JLCI grantees but of what they accomplish for federations themselves. Amidst a decades-long redistribution of power away from the federation system, a lack of involvement in cultivating change leaders could signal the irrelevance of federations to the shaping of the Jewish future. Investments in innovation such as JFNA's stake in Bikkurim, the UJA–Federation of New York's support for the Six Points Fellowship for Jewish artists, and the Jewish Federation of Greater Los Angeles' Jewish Venture Philanthropy Fund can be seen as strategic moves by federations to adapt, assert relevance, and position themselves in a symbolic economy in which innovation is valued.

This discussion points to an important reality about the distribution of power in the Jewish nonprofit sector. Material and symbolic power are not distributed in identical ways. Nor is there only a single form of symbolic power. Federations retain the ability to provide grant recipients with material support and with a stamp of approval that legitimizes recipients as partners in a common Jewish enterprise.

What most federations do not possess, but their venture grant recipients do, is the symbolic power that comes with being able to claim the Jewish future *and to have these claims recognized*. The reasons why this power is wielded by grant recipients and not by federation grantors is straightforward enough. There is nothing in the relationship between the federation system and the social entrepreneurs that departs significantly from the standard theory of competition for symbolic and material power laid out by Bourdieu a generation ago. It is a classic instance of a network establishing itself as an avant-garde by defining a symbolic power that stands in opposition to material power.[68]

Recognizing the network dimension is crucial, because it enables us to see that the symbolic power does not inhere in any objective traits of the individual actors but rather in the system of relationships among them. That is, one does not need new ideas to acquire the label "innovator." Nor does having new ideas automatically earn one the label.[69] Instead, the symbolic power is acquired by deploying the language of innovation in a way that is recognized as legitimate by others whose similar claims are reciprocally recognized. This *reciprocity of recognition*, which Kadushin has termed "collegial certification," is key.[70]

An example may help to clarify. Consider a hypothetical three-organization network that includes Jumpstart, PresenTense, and the Jewish Federations of North America. Imagine that Jumpstart and PresenTense recognize each other as "innovators" but do not so recognize JFNA. The first two organizations have thus consolidated in their hands symbolic control of the term "innovation." JFNA can affirm Jumpstart and PresenTense's control by recognizing these organizations as innovators (perhaps by directing venture philanthropy their way). It cannot, however, exercise veto power over their control of the language because JFNA is not itself recognized by PresenTense and Jumpstart as a legitimate claimant to power over the use of the term. Note that the power to control the term does not rest with either Jumpstart or PresenTense individually. It comes into existence only through the social act of their mutual recognition.

The potency of this symbolic power to claim the Jewish future should not be underestimated. The national federation system's loss of this power, which it once commanded, has accompanied and accelerated its loss of agenda-setting power, at first, in small ways, to the counterculture activists and then later, in much larger ways, to the foundations. Forging investment-based partnerships with those who now wear the mantle of innovation would seem to be a sine qua non for federations to begin to effect a reversal of fortune.

One should expect, however, that those with whom the federations would partner will more willingly accept the funding than share the accolades. Self-interest alone offers reason for them not to cede their avant-garde status by recognizing the federations among their ranks. For one thing, this status is constructed oppositionally. There can be no avant-garde without an "establishment" to define itself against.[71] Moreover, those most vested in the claim to avant-garde status seek to monopolize this symbolic power precisely because they do not command financial power.[72] As compared with the material-rich federations, the claim to the future is some of the only leverage that resource-poor individuals and organizations have.

But what of the foundations? Where do they fit into the power struggles of this symbolic economy? It is not a coincidence that foundations have managed to escape placement within the binary mapping that separates the alleged establishment/mainstream/*alte kackers* from the so-called innovator/alternative/*yinge pishers*. They are the only actors in the system that simultaneously command high degrees of both material and symbolic power. The former aligns them with federations and distinguishes them from their JLCI grantees. The latter does the reverse.[73]

Yet the invisibility of the foundations in the *alte kacker/yinge pisher* map should not be explained away as simply an empirical reflection of their unique position straddling the two sides. The effort to reduce a complex system to an us/them, future/past, powerful/weak, central/marginal dichotomy is a *strategy* used by players in their struggle for symbolic power. In this struggle, none of the actors has an interest in trapping the foundations on one side or the other of the *alte kacker/yinge pisher* divide. For the JLCI awardees, reserving the "establishment" label for the weakened federations rather than for the more powerful foundations enables these recipients to engage in symbolic politics while avoiding an oppositional orientation to their benefactors. For the federations, their loss of power to the foundations gives them strong disincentives to frame the foundations either as "innovators" or as the "establishment," for each in a different way would affirm foundation ascendance over federations. For the foundations, their command of both symbolic and material power already maximizes their room for maneuver. Mapping themselves onto one side or the other would serve only to constrain. With nothing to gain from the contest, they can comfortably absent themselves from it. It is this power to float above the fray that enables the foundations to position themselves neither as *alte kackers* nor *yinge pishers*, but as *balabosim*, or "masters of the house."[74]

Conclusion

The past decade has seen a flurry of interest in the notion that an emerging generation of young Jewish adults will innovate models of Jewish living that meet the needs of the time. In the Jewish communal conversation around this notion, the categories of youth, leadership, and change have been so often grouped together that it seems as if any one of them immediately implies the other two. Yet this way of speaking is a historically specific creation of research-informed programmatic initiatives of foundations, foundation-sponsored scholarship of researchers, and self-representations of those who are at once recipients of foundation largess and objects of scholars' research.[75]

Characteristic of the Jewish communal discourse about young leadership is that it has involved foundations and researchers talking *about* youth. The asymmetry is stark. The former (foundations and researchers), unexamined, act as subjects. The latter (youth), exposed, are made objects to be studied, analyzed, programmed for, invested in, and adulated. And yet the holistic and unfolding enterprise that is "young Jewish leadership" is a system in which the foundations and researchers are integral actors. If we ignore them, if we render them invisible by not turning the lens of research back onto them to consider the system in its entirety, we will inevitably misconstrue the dynamics of generation, leadership, and innovation at work in the current American Jewish historical moment.

In this chapter, I have sought to render the invisible visible. In the process, I have offered evidence suggesting that—contrary to the assumptions of the "young Jewish leadership" field itself—the largest, most significant, and most far-reaching innovation of the past three decades has been associated neither with youth nor with the enhancement of individual talents and capabilities. Rather, it has involved the creation of a new institutional mechanism for helping define and accomplish the work of the American Jewish community. This new mechanism is, of course, the private philanthropic foundation. Its genesis can be traced (in addition to its roots in U.S. tax code) to an intergenerational partnership between largely preboomer philanthropists and baby boomer and Generation X Jewish communal professionals.

The creation of the Jewish foundation sector has been and remains a potent agent of communal change. It has revolutionized the American Jewish polity from one built around centralized and communally governed philanthropy into one built around multiple, independent power centers with few, if any, formal bonds of accountability toward one another. In exchanging the checks and balances of the federation system for the flexibility and speed of the independently operating private organization, the foundations have seized the agenda-setting power once wielded by the federations. Whether we are speaking of the growth of day schools, the prioritization of Israel-experience travel, or any number of other major communal changes since the 1980s, we can see the investment priorities of private foundations re-shaping the character of American Jewish life. This is true of the present case as well. We can fairly say that the foundation sector has built a field of young leadership development, enshrined in it the counterculture's ethos of pluralism, created structural forces that undermine tendencies toward denominationalism and isolation in separate silos, and, in the process, defined an entire American Jewish conversation about youth.

No doubt, there are problems with this conversation. Foremost among them, the celebration of youth and of novelty distracts attention from the alternative model for thinking about generation and innovation that foundations themselves embody. Bringing together professionals and laypeople who represent four generations, the foundations have established a model of innovation that transcends the rhetorical dichotomies of young versus old, lay versus professional, and entrepreneurial versus establishment. The reality that they embody is far more complex, far more rich, and far more generative than can be recognized from the communal conversation that they have helped create.

In spite of its shortcomings, the conversation that the foundations have sparked teaches us something both profound and unexpected. If we consider the personal capacities that are agreed upon to be central to the efforts to cultivate leadership and innovation—vision, risk, change, and effectiveness—we can see that these capacities are equally viable as descriptors of the organizational strengths of independent foundations. The foundation world has created a model of personal leadership in its own image.

APPENDIX: LIST OF INTERVIEWS

Elka Abrahamson, Columbus, OH, August 17, 2009
Ariel Beery, Jerusalem, Israel, May 1, 2009
Catherine Bell, by telephone, July 13, 2009
Roger Bennett, New York, NY, June 10, 2009
Shifra Bronznick, New York, NY, August 7, 2009
Nina Bruder, New York, NY, June 9, 2009
Cindy Chazan, New York, NY, August 6, 2009
Maurice Corson, by telephone, November 10, 2009
Rachel Cowan, New York, NY, June 12, 2009
Shai Davis, Jerusalem, Israel, May 1, 2009
Gail Dorph, by telephone, September 2, 2009
Shimon Felix, by telephone, September 1, 2009
Ellen Flax, New York, NY, June 9, 2009
Beth Glick, Vancouver, BC, August 12, 2009

Sharna Goldseker, New York, NY, June 10, 2009
Yonatan Gordis, Vancouver, BC, August 12, 2009
Irving Greenberg, by telephone, November 2, 2009
Andrea Hendler, New York, NY, June 9, 2009
Hayim Herring, Minneapolis, MN, July 27, 2009
Bradley Hirschfield, New York, NY, June 11, 2009
Bethamie Horowitz, New York, NY, August 6, 2009
Aharon Horwitz, Jerusalem, Israel, May 1, 2009
Steve Jacobson, Providence, RI, June 5, 2009
Rae Janvey, by telephone, September 9, 2009
Shawn Landres, by telephone, August 19, 2009
Robyn Lieberman, by telephone, September 1, 2009
Or Mars, Columbus, OH, August 17, 2009
Aliza Mazor, by telephone, September 15, 2009
Lisa Farber Miller, by telephone, August 4, 2009
Larry Moses, Columbus, OH, August 17, 2009
Toby Rubin, by telephone, November 10, 2010
Steven Shaw, by telephone, November 10, 2009
Amanda Silver, New York, NY, June 12, 2009
Karla Van Praag, by telephone, July 13, 2009
Rhoda Weisman, by telephone, November 12, 2009
Two anonymous interviews, June 9, 2009, and October 1, 2009

NOTES

My thanks go to all those interviewed for this chapter; to the research team, its consultants, and the AVI CHAI Foundation; to Tali Schwartz Berkovitch, Eileen Ruchman, David Abusch-Magder and Ruth Abusch-Magder, Linda Willingham, Pam Kelner, Andrew Ely and Rachel Kanter, Danny and Rebecca Deutsch, and Jeff and Michelle Feig.

1. Eli Valley, "Social Entrepreneurs Lost in Space," *Forward*, March 27, 2009.

2. The name "ROI" suggests the dual meaning of "return on investment" in English, and in Hebrew, *ro'eh*, shepherd, a classic position of leadership.

3. Interviewees and their organizations are listed in the appendix. Interviews were conducted in Israel, the United States, and Canada between May 2009 and November 2010, and were recorded, transcribed, and then coded and analyzed using ATLAS.ti, a software package for qualitative data analysis.

4. The term is from Daniel J. Elazar, *Community and Polity: The Organizational Dynamics of American Jewry* (Philadelphia: Jewish Publication Society of America, 1995).

5. Jack Wertheimer, *A People Divided: Judaism in Contemporary America* (New York: Basic Books, 1993).

6. For example, on the challenges of mobilizing the federation system toward greater investment in Israel experience programs, see Shaul Kelner, *Tours That Bind: Diaspora, Pilgrimage and Israeli Birthright Tourism* (New York: New York University Press, 2010), 39–44.

7. Gary Rosenblatt, "The Life and Death of a Dream," *Baltimore Jewish Times*, November 7, 1980.

8. Unless otherwise noted, all quotations are from interviews conducted for this chapter.

9. Protestors demanded greater CJF investment in Jewish education. On Shaw's organizing role, see Rosenblatt, "The Life and Death of a Dream"; Gershon Yakobson, "Revolt Fun Yiddisher Yugent Kegn Dem Philantropishen 'Establishment,'" *Der Tag Morgen Journal*, November 24, 1969; Gershon Yakobson, "Vegn Mentshen, Zachn, Un Gesheenishen," *Der Tag Morgen Journal*, December 1, 1969.

10. Rosenblatt, "The Life and Death of a Dream," 54.

11. Ellenson later became president of Hebrew Union College; Eisen, chancellor of the Jewish Theological Seminary of America; Lipstadt, a world-renowned expert on Holocaust denial and an Emory University professor with a named chair.

12. Of the conference, held in Pawling, New York, Greenberg says, "We told [the invitees] we had picked them as people capable of communal teaching and leadership. They had the chance—the talent—the mission of shaping and leading the community and not to be satisfied to just be academics" (personal correspondence, Greenberg to Kelner, April 8, 2010).

13. The 1990 National Jewish Population Survey reported that more than half of all Jews marrying in the five years prior to the study married someone who was not Jewish. The finding sparked fears among American Jewish leaders that the community was withering through assimilation. Steven M. Cohen, "Why Intermarriage May Not Threaten Jewish Continuity," *Moment*, December 1994; Barry A. Kosmin et al., *Highlights of the C.J.F. 1990 National Jewish Population Survey* (New York: Council of Jewish Federations, 1991).

14. Steinhardt, a hedge fund manager who retired from Wall Street in 1995 with a fortune estimated at more than $300 million, established the foundation and hired Greenberg in 1993 to serve as its first executive director. See Michael Massing, "Should Jews Be Parochial?" *American Prospect*, November 6, 2000.

15. Rosenblatt, "The Life and Death of a Dream," 42.

16. Ibid., 42–48.

17. Ibid., 50–52; Council of Jewish Federations and Welfare Funds, *Venture in Creativity: A Report on the Institute for Jewish Life* (New York: Council of Jewish Federations and Welfare Funds, 1977), appendix I, i–iv.

18. Arnold Gurin, cited in Rosenblatt, "The Life and Death of a Dream," 51.

19. Gary Rosenblatt, "Beyond UJA: Alternative Philanthropy," *Baltimore Jewish Times*, September 14, 1979, 40.

20. In conjunction with the Jewish Museum and the 92nd Street Y, Radius sponsored dialogues in which the likes of Harold Bloom, Peter Berger, Cynthia Ozick, Adin Steinsaltz, Arthur Green, Ruth Wisse, Eugene Borowitz, Paula Hyman, and John Murray Cuddihy would grapple with existential questions of religion, postmodernity, Judaism, and the soul. The first Radius program was held in 1977. The Institute was formally established in the following year.

21. Andrea Jolles, "The Matchmaker," *Present Tense*, Autumn 1983, 40.

22. Gary Rosenblatt and William Novak, "Why a New Generation of Jews Looks to This Man as Their Mentor," *Baltimore Jewish Times*, February 26, 1982, 58.

23. Radius Institute, "Developing Your Organization's Effectiveness and Appeal: Technical Assistance Workshops 1985–86," flyer, personal papers of Steven Shaw; Yonatan

Gordis, "On the Value and Values of Jewish Social Entrepreneurship," *Journal of Jewish Communal Service* 84, no. 1/2 (2009); Rosenblatt and Novak, "Why a New Generation of Jews Looks to This Man," 55.

24. Jolles, "The Matchmaker," 39.

25. Gary Rosenblatt, "The Fellowship," *Baltimore Jewish Times*, February 26, 1982, 50.

26. The Radius Fellowship, typed membership list (undated). Personal papers of Steve Shaw.

27. Rosenblatt, "The Fellowship," 50–51.

28. According to Elizabeth Boris, "More than 16,200 new foundations were formed between 1980 and 1995, which is over 40% of the total number of active grantmaking foundations." Elizabeth T. Boris, "The Nonprofit Sector in the 1990s," in *Philanthropy and the Nonprofit Sector in a Changing America*, eds. Charles T. Clotfelter and Thomas Ehrlich (Bloomington and Indianapolis: Indiana University Press, 1999), 19–20.

29. On the role of foundations in Jewish communal agenda-setting, see Shaul Kelner, "Who Is Being Taught? Early Childhood Education's Adult-Centered Approach," in *Family Matters: Jewish Education in an Age of Choice*, ed. Jack Wertheimer (Hanover: Brandeis University Press, 2007), and Kelner, *Tours That Bind*.

30. The subsequent creation of the Jewish Funders Network can be read as evidence that a consciousness of being a field took root within the foundations themselves.

31. "On the Radius Institute," mission statement on organizational letterhead (undated). Personal papers of Steve Shaw.

32. Steve Shaw to Lee and Rona Javitch, September 7, 1984, with enclosures. Personal papers of Steve Shaw.

33. Shaw to Javitch, "Consultation of Jews and Inherited Wealth," June 1, 1982, conference program and attendee list on organizational letterhead. Personal papers of Steve Shaw.

34. Jolles, "The Matchmaker." Gary Rosenblatt, "Mainstreaming Alternative Ideas," *Jewish Week*, May 13–19, 1994; Rosenblatt and Novak, "Why a New Generation of Jews Looks to This Man."

35. David Harvey, *A Brief History of Neoliberalism* (Oxford and New York: Oxford University Press, 2005). For an overview of these socioeconomic transformations, see the PBS documentary by Daniel Yergin and Joseph Stanislaw, *Commanding Heights: The Battle for the World Economy* (WGBH, 2002).

36. Joshua Avedon and Shawn Landres, *The Innovation Ecosystem: Emergence of a New Jewish Landscape* (Los Angeles and New York: Jumpstart, the Natan Fund, and the Samuel Bronfman Foundation, 2009).

37. The program was announced in 1981 and ran its first cohort in 1982–1983. Ernest Stock, "Multi-Country Agencies in Jewish Education," in *Jewish Education Worldwide: Cross-Cultural Perspectives*, eds. H. Himmelfarb and Sergio DellaPergola (Lanham: Institute of Contemporary Jewry in conjunction with the University Press of America, 1989), 564.

38. Dana Raucher, "Training Tomorrow's Leaders," *Contact: The Journal of the Jewish Life Network/Steinhardt Foundation*, Summer 2003.

39. Jonathan Cohen, "In Memory of Prof. Seymour Fox," *Kol Hamercaz: A Newsletter of the Melton Centre for Jewish Education*, August 2006; Commission on Jewish Education in North America, *A Time to Act* (Lanham: University Press of America, 1991);

Annette Hochstein, *The Israeli Experience: Senior Personnel for Jewish Education* (Jerusalem: Jewish Agency for Israel, 1988); Charles Hoffman, "1989 Jewish Agency Comptroller's Report: Boardroom Machinations," *Jerusalem Post*, June 27, 1989; Barry W. Holtz, "Azkarah—in Memorium: Seymour Fox" (paper presented at the CAJE 32 Conference Program, St. Louis, 2007); Shaul Kelner et al., *Recruiting and Retaining a Professional Work Force for the Jewish Community: A Review of Existing Research* (Waltham: Cohen Center for Modern Jewish Studies and Fisher-Bernstein Institute for Leadership Development in Jewish Philanthropy, 2004), 18. The Commission on Jewish Education in North America was convened by the Mandel Associated Foundations, the JCC Association, and JESNA in collaboration with the CJF.

40. For a review and critique of the "personnel crisis" trope, see Kelner et al., *Recruiting and Retaining a Professional Work Force for the Jewish Community*.

41. On the dot-com aesthetic, see Richard Lloyd, *Neo-Bohemia: Art and Commerce in the Post-Industrial City* (New York: Routledge, 2006).

42. Although coined in the 1970s, the phrase "social entrepreneurship" did not enter common American usage until much more recently, and remains a concept whose meaning is contested. Outside the Jewish nonprofit sector, the term connotes the use of a market-based financial mission to serve social ends. This valence is less true within the Jewish sector. See Yonatan Gordis, "On the Value and Values of Jewish Social Entrepreneurship"; Matt Grimes, "Strategic Sensemaking within Funding Relationships: The Effects of Performance Measurement on Organizational Identity in the Social Sector," *Entrepreneurship Theory and Practice* 34, no. 4 (2010).

43. Some caveats: as the 1980s-era fellowships evolved, some expanded their definitions of leadership to encompass social entrepreneurs, artists, and others for whom leadership is not necessarily exercised from within extant communal institutions. Moreover, certain individuals have received support from both the leadership fellowships and change incubators. Finally, even after the innovation-oriented initiatives of the 2000s emerged, new programs were still being created in the older tradition.

44. Founded in 1987, Echoing Green is a social venture fund based in New York.

45. See the alumni page on the Joshua Venture Group website: www.joshuaventuregroup.org.

46. Kelner, *Tours That Bind*; Leonard Saxe and Barry Chazan, *Ten Days of Birthright Israel: A Journey in Young Adult Identity* (Waltham: Brandeis University Press, 2008).

47. Jonathan D. Sarna, *A Great Awakening: The Transformation That Shaped Twentieth Century American Judaism and Its Implications for Today* (New York: Council for Initiatives in Jewish Education, 1995).

48. Visit the Reboot website at www.rebooters.net to read about these cultural products.

49. Another good example of such a foray is the December 2009 "Consultation on Jewish Innovation and Social Entrepreneurship," convened jointly by Jumpstart, JFNA, and JESNA's Lippman-Kanfer Institute, and cosponsored by ACBP and the UJA–Federation of Greater Toronto.

50. *Hechsher*, literally, refers to the official rabbinic certification that food is kosher.

51. Rabbis Without Borders "seeks to position rabbis as American religious leaders and spiritual innovators who contribute Jewish wisdom to the American spiritual landscape." Its inaugural 2009–2010 cohort includes twenty-two rabbis and sixteen rabbinic

students from across the denominations. See www.clal.org and www.rabbiswithoutborders .org.

52. See the page for rabbis on the Institute for Jewish Spirituality website: http://www .ijs-online.org.

53. Shifra Bronznick and Didi Goldenhar, *Visioning Justice and the American Jewish Community* (New York: Nathan Cummings Foundation, 2008).

54. Ibid., 4.

55. Sarna, *A Great Awakening*.

56. Steven M. Cohen et al., *Expectations, Education and Experience of Jewish Professional Leaders: Report of the Wexner Foundation Research Project on Contemporary Jewish Professional Leadership* (Waltham: Cohen Center for Modern Jewish Studies and Argov Center for the Study of Israel and the Jewish People, 1995).

57. The *alte kacker/yinge pisher* terminology was suggested by Steven M. Cohen in personal conversation. Of all the dichotomizing terms in use, I consider it best because it calls attention to the moral judgment that all ostensibly neutral terms disingenuously deny that they are making. The terms' satiric nature also conveys clearly the notion that the binary opposition between two camps is not an actual description but, rather, a rhetorical trope.

58. Ulrich Beck, *Risk Society: Towards a New Modernity* (London: Sage, 1992); Amanda Bennett, *The Death of the Organization Man* (New York: William Morrow & Company, 1990); Richard Florida, *The Rise of the Creative Class* (New York: Basic Books, 2002); David Harvey, *The Condition of Postmodernity* (Malden and Oxford: Blackwell, 1990).

59. Daniel B. Cornfield, Karen E. Campbell, and Holly J. McCammon, eds., *Working in Restructured Workplaces: Challenges and New Directions for the Sociology of Work* (Thousand Oaks: Sage, 2001).

60. Jonathan S. Woocher, *Sacred Survival: The Civil Religion of American Jews* (Bloomington: Indiana University Press, 1986).

61. On the concept of peoplehood as being historically contingent and anchored in specific practices, see Shaul Kelner, "Ritualized Protest and Redemptive Politics: Cultural Consequences of the American Mobilization to Free Soviet Jewry," *Jewish Social Studies* 14, no. 3 (2008).

62. Steven M. Cohen and Arnold M. Eisen, *The Jew Within: Self, Family and Community in America* (Bloomington: Indiana University Press, 2000); Jonathan Woocher, "'Sacred Survival' Revisited: American Jewish Civil Religion in the New Millennium," in *The Cambridge Companion to American Judaism*, ed. Dana Evan Kaplan (New York: Cambridge University Press, 2005). See also Steven M. Cohen, *Religious Stability and Ethnic Decline: Emerging Patterns of Jewish Identity in the United States* (New York: Florence G. Heller Jewish Community Centers Research Center, 1998); Samuel G. Freedman, *Jew vs. Jew: The Struggle for the Soul of American Jewry* (New York: Simon & Schuster, 2000); Jack Wertheimer, *A People Divided*.

63. Representative texts include Caryn Aviv and David Shneer, *New Jews: The End of the Jewish Diaspora* (New York: New York University Press, 2005); David Biale, ed., *Cultures of the Jews: A New History* (New York: Schocken, 2002); Sander L. Gilman, *Jewish Frontiers: Essays on Bodies, Histories, and Identities* (New York: Palgrave Macmillan, 2003).

64. Freedman, *Jew vs. Jew*; Wertheimer, *A People Divided*.

65. Here, I am speaking only of the JLCI field's leadership development stream, not of its change incubation stream.

66. Jack Ukeles, "Talking with John Ruskay: Looking Forward," *Journal of Jewish Communal Service* 85, no. 1 (2010): 8.

67. This section applies more to the federation's relationship to the innovation stream than to the leadership development stream, and more to the national system and large cities than to smaller communities where federations continue to serve as hubs of relatively centralized philanthropic polities.

68. Pierre Bourdieu, *The Field of Cultural Production: Essays on Art and Literature* (New York: Columbia University Press, 1993).

69. This has been a lament of federation professionals: "We are innovating too. Why doesn't anyone acknowledge that?" But it misses the point. The labels are not indicators of an actor's actual traits but rather relational terms indicating an actor's position in a network.

70. Charles Kadushin, *The American Intellectual Elite*, republication of the 1974 edition with a new introduction (Somerset: Transaction, 2005), xii.

71. Interestingly, local federations that have managed to participate successfully in the network of avant-garde collegial certification, such as Boston's Combined Jewish Philanthropies, have done so in part by positioning themselves as *nonrepresentative* of federation culture.

72. Bourdieu, *The Field of Cultural Production*.

73. The foundations' symbolic alignment with their JLCI grantees involves them in the dynamic of collegial certification that consolidates the two groups' power over the language of innovation. Indeed, this is a major part of what the foundations offer through their JLCI programs. Beyond the material support they provide, foundations, by virtue of their symbolic power, confer prestige.

74. And it is the power to stand outside the fray and comment on everyone else that enables the researchers to position themselves as *talmid chochems*, "wise students" or "smart alecks" (and, likewise, to be dismissed as *luftmenschen*, "ivory tower thinkers.") Symbolic politics are at play here too.

75. Readers should not misinterpret this as a claim that researchers are "in the pocket" of foundations, or that foundations are misled or manipulated by researchers or grantees. I am arguing that each party to the conversation has informed the thinking of the other two. Through this social dynamic, they have converged on a common understanding.

Conclusion

T HE CHAPTERS in this volume have introduced readers to a broad
range of leaders and programs for the population of Jews between
ages twenty-two and forty. Through the accumulation of rich and
revealing quotations, we hear firsthand from these leaders how they think
about Jewish questions and relate to Jewish collective enterprises. Quantitative data further flesh out the picture by granting readers access to the responses of nearly five thousand individuals to survey instruments. Through
textured analyses, the contributors to this study, then, strive to make sense
of an evolving story.

But what, at heart, is that story? First and foremost, it is about a new
generation of Jews who are choosing to invest of themselves as leaders of
programs benefiting the Jewish people, in general, and specifically their Jewish peers. Contrary to oft-expressed worries about a dearth of interest
among younger people in Jewish life, this study has identified, interviewed,
and surveyed thousands of Jews in their twenties and thirties with strong
Jewish commitments. In the process, it has uncovered important areas of
continuity and discontinuity.

To begin with the former, these young leaders have not arisen in a vacuum: many, though not all, were groomed, rather than having bloomed. In
highly disproportionate numbers, they have been exposed to various forms
of Jewish education. Large majorities have attended Jewish summer camps,
spent significant time studying or volunteering in Israel, and been active in
Jewish campus life. The percentage who attended Jewish day schools is far
greater than the norm for non-Orthodox Jews. A significant number, moreover, have participated in leadership training programs run by foundations,
long-established organizations, or start-up ventures such as the PresenTense
institutes. All this confirms the correctness of a remark by Nina Bruder, director of the federation-sponsored Bikkurim program, an incubator of new

ideas and initiatives, who observes, "The outsiders are really insiders." Most of the young leaders studied in this project are products of the American Jewish community, even if they have put their own spin on some of the core values they imbibed. They continue to engage in the same conversation, but are not necessarily replicating the institutional structures in which that conversation initially took place or arriving at the same conclusions as their elders.

The discontinuities are most apparent in the views expressed by leaders in the nonestablishment sector. Some important actors in this arena are receptive to criticism of Israeli policies and some take quite radical stances on the matter. More broadly, nonestablishment leaders tend to favor social justice causes with a universal mission over narrower Jewish ones. Nonestablishment leaders also exhibit less interest than their establishment peers in "protective" issues such as the defense against antisemitism, resisting intermarriage, and supporting social service programs to alleviate the distress of needy Jewish populations. Nonetheless, nonestablishment leaders continue to care about the Jewish people, identify strongly with its culture and history, and express pride in being Jewish. Thus, a fair reading of the mood of nonestablishment leaders must note the important areas of continuity, as well as the discontinuities.

Nonestablishment leaders are also in conversation with Jewish peers who relate positively to establishment organizations and support their causes. Our study provides ample evidence of continuing dialogue among young Jewish leaders connected to all kinds of organizations. Establishment and nonestablishment leaders, and also their followers, move easily from one setting to the other and share experiences. The outlook of these leaders, too, is fluid rather than fixed.

A second lens through which this work may be read is *community*. At its most basic level, this study highlights the creation of a network of new programs and initiatives by younger Jewish leaders. These efforts sometimes are at odds with establishment counterparts but often complement them. It is not so much that a countercommunity is forming, although that is true in a few places, but that a far more diverse community has emerged. Efforts at addressing diversity and creating niche marketing are reaching Jews who in the past had felt disenfranchised. The interaction of these various initiatives with the existing organizations, the preferences of young Jews for one type of collective program as opposed to others, and new platforms for social communication are altering the very nature of community on the American Jewish scene.

These developments, in turn, may be read through yet a third lens, the *historical*. What is it about the current moment that sets it apart from earlier eras? Patterns within American society overall have created new conditions that shape younger Jews. In a post-centralized world in which no single organization or government sets the terms of engagement, American Jewish life not surprisingly also lacks strong central institutions. Indeed, the proliferation of initiatives and attention to diversity we have observed among younger Jews is no less true of their age peers in the broader American society. The tendency of younger Jews to relate to local programs and distance themselves from national organizations also results from a decentered world. Still a second noteworthy historical development has been the embrace of gender equality as both an ideal and a lived reality. Indeed, among younger leaders, women are in the majority. Given changes in America's educational and volunteering patterns, the activism of Jewish women in leadership positions is hardly surprising, even if noteworthy. Third, the emphasis young leaders place upon meaning is also much in tune with contemporary concerns. With so many competing claims on their time, younger people are acutely sensitive to the need for programs to compete for their attention by offering high-quality experiences, rather than relying upon feelings of obligation to draw participants. And fourth, the emergence of new social media with their powerful and rapid means of organizing, announcing, mobilizing, and recruiting is also very much a twenty-first-century phenomenon that shapes the thinking and behavior of young Jewish leaders.

To these lenses we may add one more—*policy*: What are the implications of this study for Jewish communal life, Jewish leaders of all ages, and especially younger Jews? Readers will draw their own conclusions, but here are some that seem especially ripe for reflection.

It seems reasonable to assume that we are watching the American Jewish communal structure change before our eyes. Some organizations are withering and disappearing, others are thriving, and new ones are emerging. These shifts are not caused solely by the actions or inaction of younger Jews, but their preferences are having an impact. The communal system is changing, and all players will have to be mindful that the system we have known since the end of World War II is rapidly reconfiguring. How can the larger network of Jewish communal institutions prepare for these changes?

Not only is the map of organized Jewish life changing but small organizations and programs geared to every conceivable niche population are multiplying, resulting in a community that increasingly lacks a center. Fragmentation and localism are the order of the day. One nonestablishment leader imagines organized Jewish life of the future as looking "like a forest, but a forest of bonsai trees, not a forest of redwoods. . . . There will be many small trees that are all separate entities serving separate populations with very small ecosystems that support them." This formulation overstates, though it is revealing in its minimizing of the national organizations. It is not at all clear that large institutions will disappear and that only localism will prevail. Yet if such an outcome is fated, how will the vast conglomeration of organizations, institutions, programs, and initiatives hold together? And how do we bridge the divide between those who prefer local, face-to-face associations over large organizations, on the one hand, and those who regard national organizations working with one another as essential to the effective pursuit of Jewish interests and advocacy? These questions point to the need for sustained thinking about Jewish communal life in the emerging new world.

Particularly within the nonestablishment sector, we see evidence of a growing emphasis on Jewish learning and literacy and a desire to nurture religious and spiritual growth. Much in this agenda is healthy and serves as an important corrective to misplaced priorities in the past. Key institutions such as the national organizations, denominations, and foundations should consider how to foster these trends as a means to strengthen American Jewish life.

To be sure, some establishment institutions may take umbrage at the approaches of nonestablishment leaders to Israel. After five decades of relatively strong consensus on Israel, we are witnessing far greater dissensus. As they assess the significance of these changes, organizations and foundations with a protective orientation would do well to attend to the language of discourse about Israel and then determine whether disagreements are actually based in ideology or sensibility. Criticism of Israeli politics, particularly when it emanates from Jews, is not necessarily identical to hostility to Israeli society. In the nonestablishment sector, where we find the sharpest critics of Israeli policies, large numbers of leaders have studied in Israel, are fluent in Hebrew, and maintain personal relationships with Israelis. Though she notes the strong diasporist pride of the cultural leaders she has interviewed, Sylvia Barack Fishman also underscores just how much creative American Jews draw upon Israeli culture in their literary, musical, and artistic work. It remains to be seen whether Jewish organizations can find ways to foster conversations about Israel that bridge the differences, even as they allow for disagreement.

Similarly, challenges arise in regard to peoplehood issues. A substantial population of young leaders retains a protective posture on matters of anti-semitism, support for Israel, ensuring Jewish communal services to the Jewish needy, and connection with Jews abroad. And significant numbers of younger leaders are inclined to offer service to non-Jewish populations. Perhaps it is time to test whether a larger conversation can be launched to define particularistic Jewish missions. What might such missions entail? And how might they be synchronized with the desire of many younger Jews to offer service to nonsectarian causes?

Given the range of views about the proper Jewish agenda and how to implement it, how can we best foster serious conversations among all players, including older and younger leaders, establishment and nonestablishment ones? Too often, communal conversation has tended either to spotlight younger leaders who share their dissenting views as outsiders or older leaders who fret about the missteps of the next generation. The more useful way to approach the emerging communal reality is to break down some of the barriers. Our team project intentionally included three researchers from the baby boomer generation and three under forty-one, so that we could speak— and argue—across generational lines. Facilitating such conversation is not only tactically advantageous; it also acknowledges the diversity of views within generations and sectors of Jewish involvement. We will need honest brokers to mediate among the diverse groups and interests.

A number of the large Jewish foundations have assumed a role in training young Jewish leaders. The essay by Shaul Kelner examines how influential their leadership programs have been. Implicitly, many of these programs tend to favor nonestablishment over establishment types. If foundations seek to serve as honest brokers and evenhanded agents of change rather than as advocates for one type of Jewish leader, they need to reconsider their relationship to establishment leaders. Who, after all, will see to the stability and sustainability of organized Jewish life, if not the established organizations? Moreover, given the diversity of the Jewish population, why not invest in young establishment leaders along with those in the nonestablishment sector?

Establishment organizations will have to rethink their governance structures to make room for younger Jewish leaders. These younger leaders find ample opportunities outside the Jewish community and also in the nonestablishment sector to rise rapidly to positions of influence. Establishment organizations tend to place younger people on a slower track, testing them and socializing them into the organizational culture before elevating them to positions of influence. This frustrates many creative young people who have taken the initiative in other settings and do not want to "wait their turn." One can acknowledge the virtues of mentoring and grooming as the preferred way in establishment organizations, while also recognizing that time is not working in favor of these organizations.

For their part, younger Jewish leaders might reexamine their views of the establishment. For all its weaknesses, it played a major role in educating them. Were it not for the substantial investments of older leaders in Jewish education, and in the expansion of formal and informal settings for such education, Jews now in their twenties and thirties would not have acquired the Judaic skills and expertise that serve them so well. Younger leaders also might reconsider the accomplishments of the national organizations that so many of them disdain. The federation system, the Jewish community relations sphere, the old-line social service agencies, and conventional synagogues all have contributed to a rich and self-confident American Jewish culture. Unquestionably, they all have their shortcomings and are in need of reform. Younger leaders who have been the beneficiaries of these institutions might think about how to revamp rather than wash their hands of them.

The ways young leaders think about the relationship between Jews and non-Jews, their desire to include the latter in programs, and their openness to intermarried Jews suggest a major shift in how Jews think about the boundaries of Jewish life. Indeed, the very notion that boundaries ought to exist may further erode. This trend is likely to deepen the chasm separating the Orthodox from all other types of Jews. For those who care about that divide, serious thought will have to be devoted to bridging those worlds.

As new and successful organizations grow, primarily led by young people, what funding structures will be available when start-up grants are completed and federations and foundations lack the resources to offer help? Perhaps, it is time to create a new mechanism to ensure an ongoing funding relationship between the start-ups and potential supporters, either locally or nationally.

The Internet serves as an extraordinary platform for the dissemination of Jewish ideas and a recruiting vehicle for Jewish causes. Studying patterns of usage, Ari Y. Kelman has found that on the local level, users prefer a single central portal to gain access to local programs and news. Communal leaders should consider developing local hubs in places where such portals do not exist. By contrast, no single portal will work on the national and international levels, where users expect far more options to navigate. The still larger question is how to leverage the Internet to broaden connections among Jews.

We have already posed the question of whether younger leaders can be placed on a faster track to exercise influence within the established organizations. But there is also a second question: Can these organizations led by younger Jews alter their way of doing business so that the means of communication—"flat" ways of organizing and the absence of hierarchies that characterize the start-up sector—can penetrate the cultures of the establishment organizations? Is there a way to bring the creativity and entrepreneurship of young Jewish leaders into the structures of the mainstream organizations? Established organizations will also have to consider whether they are prepared to support young leaders who care about the groups' core concerns but want to go about furthering those causes in new ways.

A well-rounded Jewish education is increasingly becoming a prerequisite for assuming Jewish leadership positions—not yet for all, but for most leaders. We may speculate on the consequences of this new reality. Perhaps the improved and multipronged forms of Jewish education to which younger Jewish leaders have been exposed are driving their inclination to foster high-caliber educational and cultural programming for their peers. Their standards tend to be higher than those of their elders. The positive side of this development is a rising bar of expectations, which can only benefit American Jewish religious and cultural life. The negative side is that a large gap may be opening between well-educated Jewish leaders and the rank-and-file among their age peers, who may have comparatively little Jewish education to speak of. As many of these younger leaders recognize, closing this educational gap is an urgent goal.

The proliferation of small organizations and initiatives is making it possible to address the diversity of the younger Jewish population far better than in the past. But this positive development, in turn, poses a question: What holds the multiplicity of organizations, programs, and initiatives together? Are there common concerns unifying American Jews? The coming challenge will be to find overarching causes and commonalities to bridge the fragmenting population of American Jews. For that, we will need a generation of leaders who have the commitment and abilities to strengthen Jewish collective action on a national and international scale.

As noted in Steven Cohen's survey research, whereas 91 percent of the older establishment leaders identify with a denomination, only about half that number (45 percent) of the younger nonestablishment leaders affiliate with any religious movement. For the older establishment leaders, denominational allegiance is a prevalent, if not necessary, form of social identification. For the younger nonestablishment leaders, it is an option but clearly not compelling. None of this should surprise us. Research on the allegiances of younger Christians indicates great fluidity and transient identification with the mainstream Protestant movements. Similar patterns of change are at work on the Jewish scene. Judging from the dramatic shifts in allegiance among younger leaders, especially in the nonestablishment category, we may observe that American Judaism is undergoing a significant reconfiguration of denominational identification.

Finally, let us not forget that Jewish leaders of all ages and outlooks share a fundamental commitment to strengthening Jewish life. All are trying to improve programs in order to attract more Jews in their twenties and thirties to participate. And all agree that only a minority of the potential market of younger Jews has been reached. The talents of all Jewish leaders will be required to draw the majority of younger Jews into active Jewish engagement. If nothing else, this is a common cause to which all Jewish leaders can subscribe, even if their solutions differ.

The larger question, as we conclude this study, is how to assess the relative significance of the three sectors in which younger leaders operate—the establishment, the nonestablishment, and those involved in a mix of the two. My own mapping essay and Sarah Bunin Benor's case study of younger Jews in Los Angeles document the extent of social crossover between these groupings. Rather than finding fixed and impervious boundaries separating the establishment from the nonestablishment sectors, we noted how easily individuals move between the two. Yet with all this movement, the question still remains: which set of ideas and values is capturing the imagination of young Jewish leaders? Establishment leaders tend to be far more concerned about protective issues—antisemitism, the security of Israel, Jewish continuity, Jewish communal services, and intermarriage. Nonestablishment types are far more interested in what they regard as progressive causes, such as the environment, social justice for all, aid for the downtrodden, and pro-peace approaches in the Middle East, as well as creating opportunities for expressive encounters at cultural events, religious services, and study sessions. Establishment leaders, for their part, are also far more positively inclined to the structures and approaches of mainstream organizations, while the latter seek alternatives, focus mainly on local rather than national or international Jewish concerns, and strive for a far more open, pluralistic, and flexible set of Jewish options than are currently offered by the established organizations.

The strength of the nonestablishment sector is rooted in its being in sync with large swaths of the American Jewish population, especially the non-affiliated sector. It has been given enormous support and encouragement by well-endowed foundations that have nurtured nonestablishment leaders and promoted their perspectives in the process. The nonestablishment sector is associated with innovation and start-ups, thereby symbolizing the new and original, even if many of its forms feel generic within the current youth culture. And to a great extent, the nonestablishment sector dominates the youth cultural scene, which lends it great reach and authority.

The establishment sector of young Jewish leaders is not lacking in its own resources. A substantial amount of its energy derives from recent immigrants or children of immigrants for whom protective themes resonate, along with Orthodox Jews and *baalei teshuva* (newly Orthodox Jews), who collectively constitute a growing proportion of the engaged American Jewish population. The establishment sector also benefits from money and connections. On balance, those who gravitate to roles as lay leaders in the establishment organizations are professionals and successful businesspeople who enjoy the networking and mentoring offered by these organizations. The established organizations seem to benefit from sociodemographic trends as well: as younger Jewish leaders grow older, form families, and climb the socioeconomic ladder, some tend to move toward the establishment's causes and institutions. Finally, younger leaders in the establishment sector have already brought some of the newer techniques of communication and more flexible ways of decision making into the structures of mainstream organizations, thereby rendering those agencies more competitive.

The jury is still out. Members of the research team envision different scenarios for the future, with some seeing the nonestablishment leaders as the trendsetters who are reshaping the culture for their peers and others imagining a future in which nonestablishment and establishment agencies will coexist, where the movement of ideas and personnel will cross-fertilize both sectors, and where convergence, rather than schism, will prevail. However one comes out on this question, the research team's lively internal debates ought to be replicated in many sectors of the American Jewish community, for the eventual resolution of these questions will have profound implications for the future direction of Jewish communal life in the United States.

Acknowledgments

The research team acknowledges with appreciation the support of the AVI CHAI Foundation at every step of our work. Arthur Fried and Mem Bernstein have been engaged with this project from its inception, offering wise counsel and asking tough questions, because they recognized the project's potential for uncovering rich data on emerging trends in the American Jewish community. Yossi Prager, AVI CHAI's executive director for North American operations, and Deena Fuchs, the foundation's communications director, have served as valuable sounding boards and insightful advisors, giving generously of their time and advice. The research team benefited from ongoing interactions with three consultants, Professor Riv-Ellen Prell, Shawn Landres, and Dr. Jack Ukeles. Their responses to our work have sharpened our thinking, exposed us to outsiders' perspectives, and increased our confidence that our individual and collective findings are important. Tali Berkovitch played a significant role in making contact with a broad range of young Jewish leaders and helping to disseminate our online survey instrument. We offer thanks to the ever-efficient and helpful Ezra Kopelowitz and Debbie Perla, the heads of Research Success, who managed our survey.

Appendix

The Research Design

The research team set out to learn the ways Jewish leaders in their twenties and thirties think about Jewish issues, organize programs for their peers, and are formed. Initially, the greatest challenge we faced was associated with the absence of basic information about the universe we were studying. As no national population study of American Jews has been conducted over the past decade, we lacked up-to-date information on the total numbers of Jews in this age group and the proportions who involve themselves in any form of Jewish activity. There is also no comprehensive directory of programs, initiatives, and organizations addressed to this age population.

Although we amassed lists of programs and organizations reaching Jews in their postcollege decades, other gaps in knowledge have not been filled. We still lack reliable information about the universe of Jews in their twenties and thirties overall, and those involved in Jewish activities. This project, therefore, makes no claims about either the proportionate weight of younger Jews who participate in Jewish programs or the relative numbers of Jews and Jewish leaders in their twenties and thirties who participate in the programs of establishment organizations versus nonestablishment ones.

Through the efforts of Tali Berkovitch, a graduate student in Jewish education at New York University, the team was able to compile several long lists: of organizations in which young Jews engage; of gatekeeper organizations that have direct links to and email addresses of the leaders of these organizations; and of names of people in different parts of the country and in different types of organizations who seem to be playing a leadership role.

During the half year before the project fielded a survey, all six members of the research team spoke at length with Jewish leaders. Collectively, over the course of the project, team members interviewed at least 250 young Jewish leaders of all kinds in different parts of the country. We interviewed rabbis of all denominations who work with Jews in their twenties and thirties; cultural figures who are producing books, music, recordings, films, and art for this population; founders of social justice organizations, communes, blogs, Internet sites, and independent minyanim; and significant numbers of young leaders active in mainstream Jewish organizations as volunteers and as founders of affinity groups for immigrant populations and others with particular traits and common interests. Some team members also attended events run by and for Jews in their twenties and thirties in order to observe the leaders in action.

We then supplemented these types of data with sociological literature on trends within the general American population in this age group and also on the changing ways in which Americans are organizing themselves communally. To offer context, we drew upon historical literature on changing demography and youth cultures. And to capture regional variations, we were attentive to differences between the scene in the large coastal cities and the so-called heartland, as well as urban versus suburban differences.

Based upon initial interviews and questions that we generated at our various team meetings, the six members of the research group collectively developed a survey instrument. This was circulated to our many lists and contacts, with the request that the recipients spread the instrument to their acquaintances. In time, we also fielded a version of the same survey to the membership lists of five different types of organizations, which yielded more responses from leaders and followers alike. Quantitative data were also gathered about which Jewish Internet sites are most often visited and serve as key connectors to other sites.

By drawing upon different kinds of data—interviews, field observation, survey responses, and sociological and historical literature—we were able to cross-check our findings and inferences. Working as a team, we met every few months for two-day sessions at which we critiqued one another's work and strove to understand the larger implications of our individual research projects. We also benefited from the perspectives of three outside consultants.

Index

and Keshet, 31–32; and new programs, 33; and younger nonestablishment leaders, 58–59
boundary crossings: artistic, 162–64; younger Jewish leaders and, 181
boundary fluidity, in JLCI, 265
Boyatzis, Richard, 300
bridging, 131–33, 202, 307–8
Brit Tzedek v'Shalom, 155n17
Bronfman Philanthropies. *See* Andrea and Charles Bronfman Philanthropies
Bronfman Youth Fellowships in Israel, 263, 278
Bronstein, Rabbi Daniel, 40n15
Bronznick, Shifra, 122–23, 298–99, 304–6
Brooklyn Jews program, 5
Brous, Rabbi Sharon, 176, 178–79, 181
Bruder, Nina, 292–93, 304, 322–23
Bukharians, 25
bureaucracy, establishment organizations and, 127
Burson, Clare, 197–99; *Silver and Ash*, 198–99
business models, of communal organizations, 17

car, choice of, in Los Angeles, 120
Carter, President Jimmy, 271
case studies, for online Jewish life, 245–51
Cashmore, Pete, 258n17
Center for Leadership Initiatives, 293–94
Center for Learning and Leadership, 267–72, 278, 280, 295
Chabad, 7
Chabad Houses, 16, 29
Chabon, Michael, 204; *The Yiddish Policemen's Union*, 163, 170–73
Chai Life Series, 14
Chandler, Rabbi Sarah, 165–66, 184
change-cultivation programs, 263
charitable giving: patterns of, 70–72, 72 (table 2.19), 148; younger Jewish leaders and, 136–38
Charles and Lynn Schusterman Foundation, 293
Chevra, 30

Chicago, 35; and Club 1948, 23; and Kfar, 14–15
childbearing, delayed, 187–89, 203
Chulent, 43n65
church hopping/shopping, 185
"church-state" separation, in American Jewish community, 266, 270
"church within a church" model, Christian, 48
cities: as locus for independent minyanim, 14–15; as setting for American Jewish fiction, 163. *See also names of cities*
City College of New York, 267–69
Cleveland Federation, 35, 44n76; and "concierge" position, 35; Young Leadership Division, 11, 35
clicking through, 230
closed network, use of term, 224
Club 1948, Shabbat on the Beach, 23
clustering patterns, of Jewish websites, 234–35, 252
coalescence, 163
Coalition for Alternatives in Jewish Education, 274–75
Cohen, Stephen P., 276
Cohen, Steven M., 1, 31, 135, 148–49
cohousing movement, 15–16
Collaborative, The, 23
collectives, offering Jewish programming, 15–17
collegial certification, 312, 321n73
Collins, Jim, 300
Combined Jewish Philanthropies, 8
comedy, 9
commandedness, 167
Commission for Jewish Education in North America, 280
community, American Jewish: "church-state" separation in, 266, 270; current social change in, 80–82; and Internet, 216; and Israeli immigrants, 28; Los Angeles and, 119; new forms of, viii; redistribution of power in, 266; and Russian Jewish immigrants, 27; and support for nonestablishment efforts, 205; younger Jewish adult engagement

nonestablishment phenomena, growth of, 47–48, 80–82

nongovernmental organizations, growth of, 81–82

non-Jews, and influence of new Jewish music, 199–201

Norich, Sam, 276

Nussbaum, Rabbi Rachel, 17

occupation, younger Jewish leaders and, 141–49

one-to-ones, 300

online group blogs and magazines, 226–27

online Jewish life, 48, 214–53

online news outlets, 226–27

Open Space gatherings, 288

oral history interviews, for study of JLCI, 265

organizational life, Jewish: distinct spheres of, 128–33; seen as exploitative, 2

organizations, Jewish: glut of, 150, 166; and Internet, 216–17; ongoing importance of, 219; online presence of, 232; social justice, 166; websites, 226, 236–37. *See also* establishment organizations; nonestablishment organizations

organized Jewish community: current social change in, 80–82; high valuation of, and establishment/nonestablishment leadership, 69–70, 71 (table 2.18); inclusion in, 125–26; and online life, 214–53; use of term, 47, 122–23

Orthodox Archipelago, 235–36, 239

Orthodox feminism, 182–84

Orthodox Forum, 189–90

Orthodox Judaism: and approaches to Jewish peoplehood, 140–41; and blogs/blogging, 241–42; as category, 176; and delayed marriage, 189–90; as denominational identity, 59–61, 60 (table 2.9), 61 (table 2.10); and family focus, 40n12; and GLBT outreach, 31; and immigrant Jews, 28; and independent minyanim, 177–78; and Jewish

liberalism, 77; outreach programs, 29–31; refugees from, 43n65; and Russian Jewish immigrants, 26; websites for/about, 226, 234, 236. *See also* creative traditionalists

Orthodox leaders, as study participants, xii

Oseary, Guy, 194

Ostrower, Francie, 147

outdoor activities, 33–34, 180

overlapping participation, in establishment/nonestablishment groups, 130–31

page views, Internet, 221

parenthood, deferred, 5

parochialism, rejection of, 167

participation, overlapping, in establishment/nonestablishment groups, 130–31

particularism, Jewish, rejection of, 174

partnering, among Jewish organizations, 13; federation-foundation, 292–93

partnership minyanim, 178, 183. *See also* minyanim, independent

Patton, Bruce, 300

Pazit.org, 170

peoplehood, Jewish, 308–9; new views, 308–10; younger Jewish leaders and, 135–41, 168–75, 202

Perlman, Yitzhak, 192

Pew Internet and American Life Project, 219, 257n7

Philadelphia, 8; and Chevra, 30; and The Collaborative, 23; Conservative population, 46; Federation, 23

philanthropy, American Jewish, 4; alternative, 274, 276, 278, 308; centralized, 266–67, 278; and generational priorities, 276, 289, 300; nonestablishment organizaitons and, 21–24; Russian Jewish immigrants and, 26. *See also* charitable giving; federations, Jewish; foundations; leadership and change initiatives, Jewish; *names of organizations*